Slaves of Fortune

Slaves of Fortune

Sudanese Soldiers
& the River War
1896–1898

RONALD M. LAMOTHE

JAMES CURREY

James Currey
is an imprint of Boydell & Brewer Ltd
PO Box 9
Woodbridge, Suffolk IP12 3DF, UK
www.boydell.co.uk

and of

Boydell & Brewer Inc.
668 Mt Hope Avenue
Rochester, NY 14620, USA
www.boydellandbrewer.com

Copyright © Ronald M. Lamothe 2011

1 2 3 4 5 14 13 12 11

All Rights Reserved. Except as permitted under current legislation
no part of this work may be photocopied, stored in a retrieval system,
published, performed in public, adapted, broadcast,
transmitted, recorded or reproduced in any form or by any means,
without the prior permission of the copyright owner.

The right of Ronald M. Lamothe to be identified as
the author of this work has been asserted in accordance with
sections 77 and 78 of the Copyright, Designs and Patents Act 1988

British Library Cataloguing in Publication Data
Lamothe, Ronald M.
  Slaves of fortune : Sudanese soldiers and the River War,
1896–1898.
  1. Slave soldiers--Sudan--History--19th century.
  2. Sudan--History--1881-1899. 3. Great Britain--
  Colonies--Africa. 4. Egypt. Jaysh--Military life.
  I. Title
  355.3'3'08625'09624-dc23

ISBN 978-1-84701-042-1 James Currey (Cloth)

The publisher has no responsibility for the continued existence or accuracy of URLs for external or
third-party internet websites referred to in this book, and does not guarantee that any content on such
websites is, or will remain, accurate or appropriate.

Papers used by Boydell & Brewer are natural, recycled products
made from wood grown in sustainable forests.

Typeset in 10.5/11.5 Monotype Ehrhardt
by Avocet Typeset, Chilton, Aylesbury, Bucks
Printed in Great Britain by CPI Group (UK) Ltd, Croydon CR0 4YY

To Karen

Contents

List of Illustrations, Figures & Maps	ix
Acknowledgements	xi
Glossary	xiii
Egyptian Army Ranks & Turkish Honorifics	xv
Transliteration Note & List of Abbreviations	xvii

Introduction
'Ali Jifun's Fashoda Homecoming   1

1
"Backbone of the Egyptian Army"   11

2
"Servants of His Highness the Khedive"   44

3
"Flavour of Domesticity"   72

4
"Brotherhood that Binds the Brave"   121

5
"Tea with the Khalifa"   155

Contents

Epilogue
Mutiny at Omdurman   189

Bibliography   205
Index   215

List of Illustrations, Figures & Maps

Illustrations

1.1	"Types of Sudanese soldiers – the raw material"	13
1.2	"Types of Sudanese soldiers – the finished article"	13
1.3	'Abdallah 'Adlan c. 1933	22
1.4	Officers of the XIIth Sudanese Battalion, c. 1888	29
2.1	Portrait of a Nuba officer, IXth Sudanese Battalion	52
2.2	IXth Sudanese at Wau displaying regimental flags	53
2.3	"The fight for the Khalifa's standard"	61
3.1	Sudanese Soldiers wearing full kit	77
3.2	"Sambo's Wife"	79
3.3	The departure of the XIth Sudanese from Aswan	80
3.4	NCOs of the No. 7 Company, XIIth Sudanese	97
3.5	The Nile Expedition: camp life at Wadi Halfa	104
3.6	"Dancing the 'Dillluka' on Dongola Day"	106
3.7	*Tombura zar* spirit-possession healing ritual	107
4.1	Shilluk war dance with long shields and spears	124
4.2	"Types of Sudanese soldiers"	124
4.3	"Egyptian Army types in the Soudan"	126
4.4	"The Dark Side of Campaigning in the Soudan"	128
4.5	"The 9th Soudanese welcoming the Camerons"	135
4.6	"Six of the 10th Lincolns and Six of the 10th Soudanese"	137
4.7	"Brothers in arms": mutual congratulations after Atbara	144
4.8	Mahmud and soldiers of the Xth Sudanese	146
4.9	"After the Battle of Atbara" painting by Godfrey Giles	146
4.10	Cameron Highlanders storming the *zariba* at Atbara	149
5.1	"Omdurman: The First Battle at 6:30 a.m."	156
5.2	"Soudanese troops waiting Dervish attack"	167
5.3	"General Macdonald's Brigade repelling an attack"	174
5.4	"Macdonald's Brigade resisting main Dervish attack"	174
6.1	Banner outside SPLM headquarters at Khartoum Hilton in 2005	202

Figures

4.1	Diagram of Anglo-Egyptian advance on Mahmud's *zariba*	142
5.1	Plan of the Battle of Firket	158
5.2	Diagram of the Egyptian Army attack on Abu Hamed	160
5.3	Battle of Omdurman: Phase One	163
5.4	Battle of Omdurman: Phase Two	164
5.5	Diagram of the change of front by Macdonald's brigade	165

Maps

1.1	Sudanese soldiers, recruitment areas & ethnic groups	10
1.2	Egyptian Army, Turkiyya garrisons	18
1.3	Egyptian Army battlefields, 1883–1899	35

Acknowledgements

Historians are lucky. They get to spend hours on end living secret lives of the mind, traveling to distant times and places in vicarious splendor. In my case there have been several years now in which a part of me was most certainly living in the nineteenth-century Sudan – at Egyptian Army barracks and River War battlefields, among Turco-Circassian pashas and British beys, alongside Mahdist *ansar* and Sudanese slave soldiers. And for this, my vivid and extended mental sojourn on the Nile of "Sirdar and Khalifa," of 'Abdallah 'Adlan and 'Ali Jifun, there are many people to thank.

To begin, I am indebted to the many archivists and librarians in the United States, United Kingdom, Egypt, and Sudan who assisted me during my research for this book, in particular those at the Mugar Library at Boston University, the Sudan Archive at the University of Durham, the National Army Museum in Chelsea, the National Archives at Kew, the Royal Anthropological Institute in London, the British Library Newspaper Reading Room in Colindale, the Bodleian Library at Oxford, the Rare Books and Special Collections Library at the American University in Cairo, and the National Records Office in Khartoum. Of special note among these individuals is the inimitable Jane Hogan, Keeper of the Sudan Archive at the University of Durham.

As I made my way up the Nile from Cairo to Khartoum, there were also numerous Egyptians and Sudanese who helped me in various capacities, some of whom I owe special thanks: Kheirallah Ahmed el Faki, the kind octogenarian in Abu Hamed who led me to the grave site of Sidney and Fitzclarence, where "unnamed, unnumbered in the sand, their dead black troopers sleep" per Sir Rennell Rodd's poem; Muhammad, the Ja'ali taxi driver who took me over the piste from Atbara to Nakheila, the site of Mahmud's *zariba*; and lest I forget the Sudanese intelligence officer in Omdurman, the one person – following a misunderstanding at the Karari battlefield (now a military training base) that resulted in my detainment – I was able to convince that I was simply an overzealous historian and not an American spy.

Of course, this type of rookie mistake would never have been made by my role models, scholars of Sudanese history such as Richard Hill, Peter Malcolm Holt, Richard Gray, Robert Collins, Martin Daly, Jay Spaulding, Rex Sean O'Fahey, Janet Ewald, Ahmad Sikainga, and last, but by no means least, Douglas Johnson. Indeed, to Douglas Johnson I owe a personal debt of thanks. For starters, it was his 1989 *Ethnohistory* article on military slavery in Northeast Africa that first confirmed to me – after I stumbled upon it one day on JSTOR – that my work on Sudanese soldiers was both worthwhile and needed. He was also generous enough, when I had the pleasure of visiting him in Oxford, to share with me a list he had personally compiled of biographical data on Sudanese soldiers. And over the past year he has continued to give of his time and expertise, sending me pages and pages of detailed, insightful feedback and editorial advice, not to mention book references, geographical information, proper transliterations, and what have you.

Other mentors, scholars, colleagues, friends, and family members who have provided like inspiration, encouragement, and constructive criticism, as well as various other forms of support and asssistance – and to whom I am incredibly thankful – include: James McCann, John Thornton, Cathal Nolan, Andrew Bacevich, David Killingray, Joye Bowman, Jean Hay, James Pritchett, Diana Wylie, Parker Shipton, Charles Dellheim, Wendy James, Heather Sharkey, Cherry Leonardi, Michael Reimer, Steve Howard, Tara Thielhelm, Juliet Latham, Nariman Abdel Rahman, Laura Mann, David Levering Lewis, Melissa Graboyes, Brian Casady, Andrea Mosterman, Masse Ndiaye, Alfredo Burlando, Joe Pearce, Barbara Pearce, Gaby Zarazua, and Kristina Freier. And of course I would be remiss if I did not also thank my mother and father, Barbara and Ron Lamothe, who both somehow sold me on the cliché that I could accomplish anything I set my mind to if I worked at it hard enough. My father, a history teacher himself, revered the discipline, and historians in particular, and so I suppose it is not surprising that I was drawn to the field myself, and never bore of it.

Lastly, I want to thank my two daughters, Madeleine and Parker, for putting up with my research trip abroad, not to mention all the time I spent over the past few years writing rather than being a dad. And most of all, I would like to thank my wife Karen. Without exception, she has supported each and every bliss or beat of a different drummer that I have ever followed, including this one. It was her sacrifices that made this book possible, and to whom it is dedicated.

Glossary

'abd	slave; plural *'abid*
amir	commander; plural *amara*
ansar	companions, helpers; followers of the Mahdi
bashi-bazouq	irregular soldiers
bazinqir	slave soldiers from merchant armies
Daftardar	keeper of the register of lands
dura	sorghum
fellahin	Egyptian peasant farmers; singular *fellah*
ghaffir	watchman
ghazwa	slave raid; plural *ghazawat*
hakim	physician, doctor
jallaba	northern Sudanese traders and merchants
jebel	hill, mountain
jibba	patched smock worn by the followers of the Mahdi
jihadiyya	Sudanese slave soldiers in Turco-Egyptian and Mahdist armies
Khalifa	successor; 'Abdallahi was the Khalifa, successor of the Mahdi
khalwa	Koranic school
Khedive	title of the Turkish viceroys in Egypt from 1867–1914
khor	dry riverbed
Mahdi	an expected messenger for the restoration of the *umma* and the expected end of the world; title assumed by Muhammad Ahmad
Mahdiyya	period of Mahdist rule in the Sudan from 1885–1898
Mek	minor king
malakiyya	the "civilian" area of a government town, where discharged soldiers often settled
ma'mur	junior civil administrative official in charge of a sub-district or *ma'muriyya*; post held by Egyptians and Sudanese
marisa	local beer made out of sorghum
mudir	provincial governor
mulazimin	the Khalifa's bodyguard
nizam al-jadid	The New Regulations
Redif	Turkish for Reserves
reth	king of the Shilluk
shaykh	religious leader and/or local political authority
tukl	hut
Turkiyya	era of Turco-Egyptian rule in the Sudan from 1820–1885
'ulama	Islamic legal scholars

Glossary

umma	the greater Muslim community
wali	ruler, governor-general
wadi	streambed
zariba	armed camp, often fortified by a thorn fence; plural *zara'ib*

Egyptian Army Ranks for Officers, Warrant Officers, Non-Commissioned Officers & Men

(with corresponding English equivalents)

sirdar	commander-in-chief
ferik	lieutenant general
liwa	major general
miralai	colonel
kaimakam	lieutenant-colonel
bimbashi	major; plural *bimbashia*
saghkolaghasi	adjutant-major; plural *saghkolaghasia*
yuzbashi	captain; plural *yuzbashia*
mulazim awal	lieutenant; plural *mulazimim awal*
mulazim tani	second lieutenant; plural *mulazimin tani*
solkolaghasi	warrant officer; plural *solkolaghasia*
bashshawish	company sergeant-major; plural *bash shawishia*
bulukamin	quartermaster-sergeant; plural *bulukat omana*
shawish	sergeant; plural *shawishia*
ombashi	corporal; plural *ombashia*
nafar	private; plural *anfar*

Turkish Honorifics

Pasha	distinction conferred upon military commanders of high rank and provincial governors by Ottoman sultans and khedives of Egypt; in the Egyptian Army the title was carried by officers at the rank of *sirdar*, *ferik*, and *liwa*
Bey	originally signified the son of a king or sultan; by the 1890s it was a civil and military title of courtesy more generally given to, among others, Egyptian Army officers at the rank of *miralai* and *kaimakam*
Effendi	honorific bestowed upon Egyptian Army *bimbashia*, *saghkolaghasia*, *yuzbashia*, *mulazimim awal*, and *mulazimin tani*; usually applied to educated persons literate in Turkish or Arabic

Agha honorary title applied to illiterate or near-illiterate officers and senior non-commissioned officers, as well as uneducated civil officials

Transliteration Note

Arabic terms, titles, and proper names have been transliterated using no diacritical marks other than ' to indicate the letter *'ayn*. Other Arabic words, place names in particular, assume their more conventional English forms in most cases (Khartoum, for example, rather than al-Khartoum, exceptions such as Bahr al-Ghazal notwithstanding). And still other personal names, locations, and titles – directly quoted or more commonly occurring – have been left unchanged from their original sources, often leading to multiple spellings of the same word (Aswan, Assuan, Assouan, for example). In effect, and for better or worse, transliterational flexibility has thus won out over consistency in form.

Abbreviations

BL	British Library
CAIRINT	Cairo Intelligence File, NRO classification
CE	Common Era
FO	Foreign Office, NA classification
IRE	Intelligence Report, Egypt
NA	The National Archives of the United Kingdom
NAM	National Army Museum
NCO	non-commissioned officer
NRO	National Records Office, Khartoum
PRO	Public Record Office, NA classification
P.T.	piastre
SAD	Sudan Archive, Durham
SIR	Sudan Intelligence Report
WO	War Office, NA classification

Introduction

'Ali Jifun's Fashoda Homecoming

Fashoda will be different from what I remember it in the days of Meg Niadok Wad Yor, and I can scarcely hope to see my country again myself. But, such as I am, I shall serve the Government as long as my horse will carry me, and if I live to see No. 2 Company of the 12th Soudanese behave as I hope and know they will when the great day comes at Omdurman, then I shall be ready to go, and Ali Gifoon will not perhaps have lived for nothing.

'Ali Jifun, "Memoirs of a Soudanese Soldier"
The Cornhill Magazine, October 1896[1]

'Ali Jifun was coming home. Some forty years since he had last seen *fōte chol*, "the country of the Shilluks," he watched as the fort at Fashoda came slowly into view, the Nile flowing past him on its way north to Khartoum, and to Egypt.[2] Captured as a young man by Baggara slave dealers and enrolled into the Egyptian Army, 'Ali Jifun had fought in countless battles over the years throughout Northeast Africa, and once even as far abroad as Mexico. And now here he was on the morning of 19 September 1898, this old Shilluk soldier returning to his place of birth, not yoked as a slave, but as an adjutant-major in a conquering army. Indeed, at *saghkolaghasi* he was the highest-ranking Sudanese soldier in the whole Egyptian Army at the time.[3] Doubly ironic was the fact that he and his fellow Sudanese soldiers were steaming up the Nile to reclaim Fashoda in the name of Abbas II, the Khedive of Egypt, whose great-grand uncle's taxes were the indirect cause of his enrollment four decades earlier. Of course, the Frenchman Jean-Baptiste Marchand had something to say about Anglo-Egyptian claims to the region that September day, but that is a tale – an "Incident" – well told in the history books. The story of 'Ali Jifun's Fashoda homecoming, on the other hand, and more broadly, that of all Sudanese soldiers who fought in the "River War," was forgotten by history, a Nile narrative never told.

River War redux: Sudanese soldiers & "the enormous condescension of posterity"

Though the "downfall of the Dervishes" has been chronicled numerous times since "Kitchener of Khartoum" reconquered the Sudan at the close of the nineteenth century – from Winston Churchill's classic *The River War* (1899) to Dominic Green's more recent account *Three Empires on the Nile* (2007) – little has been written about the Africans who participated in this campaign. Ignoring, or misrepresenting, the role played by Sudanese and Egyptian soldiers, imperial and military historians have time and again, for example, recounted the Battle of Omdurman by describing the ill-fated "charge of the 21st Lancers" in vivid detail, or focusing on the battle solely in terms of it being "the most signal triumph ever gained by the arms of science over barbarians."[4] In so doing, one gets the false impression that the River War was largely won by British Army regiments and the Maxim gun rather than Sudanese infantry battalions – that, along with Egyptian troops, made up some two-thirds of the Anglo-Egyptian army at Omdurman, and were of a strategic and tactical importance to the Nile Campaign far exceeding that of the British troops involved.

The River War's historiography is especially striking in that so much of what eyewitnesses documented was overlooked or discarded by future historians. Unless one was inclined to revisit archival manuscripts or dust off old campaign tomes published in the 1890s, it would appear that the Nile Campaign was waged largely by pith-helmeted "Tommies"; that women played no role in these events whatsoever; that Sudanese soldiers were unskilled and undisciplined, and thus unreliable in combat; and that there was little if any interracial camaraderie between Sudanese soldiers and their British brethren, nor any fraternization by the former with Mahdist troops and civilians. In effect, Sudanese soldiers come off as no more than military automatons cum battalion numbers – nameless, faceless, rank-and-file, imperial pawns, seemingly assimilated, perhaps oppressed and exploited, but somewhat liminal figures, possessing neither identity nor agency, neither culture nor history. Such depictions, or lack thereof, ultimately give the impression that Sudanese soldiers were ahistorical ciphers, and of little if any relevance to either "the Egyptian Question" or the broader Scramble for Africa.

Moreover, even if one were to dig through the archives or dust off those long-ignored contemporary sources, new and oftentimes related – since rehashed and repeated – errors and omissions would emerge, engendered by historical context and ignorance of the facts: the belief that Sudanese infantry battalions, formed during the reorganization of the Egyptian Army in the mid-1880s, was something of a new phenomenon; the notion that these units consisted of freshly recruited "volunteers" rather than longtime slave soldiers; the conceit that these so-called "raw" recruits could only have been turned into "finished" soldiers thanks to the unique leadership capacities of the British officer; and finally, the widely held assumption that Sudanese soldiers were a geographically and ethnically homogeneous lot, made up almost exclusively of "martial races" from the Upper Nile, the Shilluk and Dinka in particular.

Introduction

As it turns out, the opposite is true for each one of these depictions, regardless of historiographical or archival origin. Sudanese soldiers – some of whom were in fact officers and non-commissioned officers – played a decisive combat role in every battle of the River War, and subsequently bore the brunt of Anglo-Egyptian casualties. Moreover, they occupied many essential non-combat roles during the Nile Campaign, serving as interpreters, spies, recruiters, policemen, and ethnic liaisons. Women, specifically the wives and camp followers of Sudanese soldiers, functioned in numerous social, economic, and military roles, contributing greatly to the success of the campaign. Far from unreliable, most sources indicate that Sudanese soldiers – many of them with decades of combat experience in the region – demonstrated tremendous stamina, skill, discipline, and courage in the heat of battle, and often outperformed their British and Egyptian comrades.

Relations between Sudanese and British soldiers, rather than being non-existent or exclusively racist, were marked by both respect and disdain. In fact, there was often great camaraderie, competition, and mutual admiration between Sudanese and British troops – both in camp and in combat, but especially following military victories or shared hardships. Sudanese troops regularly fraternized with Mahdist prisoners of war and deserters, not to mention the local populace. Not only were most of their enemies fellow Muslims, and thus among the *umma*, but many of them had served in the "old Egyptian Army" and/or were from their same ethnic group, same village, and occasionally, even the same family. These ethnic and kinship ties, subsequently, led to the immediate and successful recruitment of ex-Mahdists into Sudanese battalions, and also positively affected the "hearts and minds" of the region as Kitchener's army made its way deeper into the Sudan.

Far from being a new phenomenon in 1884, Sudanese soldiers had been serving in Egyptian armies since the time of the pharaohs, and had made up the crack regiments in the armies of Turco-Egyptian *walis* and *khedives* for much of the nineteenth century, from Muhammad 'Ali's reign through that of his great grandson, Tawfiq Pasha. Moreover, the Sudanese soldiers that enlisted into the "new Egyptian Army" in the 1880s and 1890s, despite euphemisms about them being "volunteers" or "long service men," embodied an indigenous, long-standing institution of military slavery in the Nile Valley, one that Britain merely inherited and then adapted according to its imperial needs. And indeed there is little to suggest that British commanders truly held that these men were fully emancipated, or that Sudanese soldiers saw themselves as anything other than slaves; and the same goes for how most civilians in Egypt and the Sudan saw them at the time.

And yet to be a "slave soldier" in Northeast Africa during the nineteenth century, as it turns out, was a rather ambiguous and evolving condition. Put simply, it was less about one's legal status as "slave" than it was about one's military and social status as "soldier." Most evidence indicates that these men were more often proud than ashamed of being "slave soldiers," and thus self-manumitted in many respects. In any case, Sudanese soldiers were not the "raw material" that British military reformers of the Egyptian Army believed them to be. Nor were they homogeneous in makeup, representing only the most warlike of

"Equatorial tribesmen." Rather, these "pioneer" Sudanese battalions sprang from a deep pool of battle-tested, veteran soldiers, and their ethnic and regional origins were quite diverse. Many of these soldiers, or their soldier-fathers, did originate from the Upper Nile and Equatoria, but many others came from the Nuba Mountains of southern Kordofan, from Dar-Funj, or from villages along the Blue Nile. And some of them hailed from even more distant locations, from areas that are today part of Chad and Uganda.

Slaves of Fortune is thus intended to be a historiographical restoration of sorts, an Africanist's attempt to reinterpret and rectify Churchill's "River War" by bringing Sudanese soldiers back into the picture. In reviving these men from the historical obscurity they have so long occupied, this book aims to demonstrate not only how imperial forces transformed the lives of Sudanese slave soldiers such as Shilluk *saghkolaghasi* 'Ali Jifun, but also how these same lives simultaneously shaped imperial destinies, and both African and European history in the process. Some might refer to this restoration project as "history from below," aka social history, for its concern with Sudanese soldier identity and social condition. Others might call it "new military history" for its emphasis on the daily lives of these soldiers rather than the operational details of battles in which they fought. Still others would say that it includes elements of "new imperial history," considering its examination of both British martial race ideology and Ornamentalism. And a few would even make the point that it contains bits and pieces of good old-fashioned military history, as one chapter in particular has much to say about ammunition returns and fighting tactics. Scattershot as it may appear, this rather eclectic, agnostic approach is entirely intentional. Purposely eschewing the sometimes dogmatic tendencies of area studies, and in the belief that no branch of history, geographical area, or topic of inquiry should be considered mutually exclusive or academically devalued, this book employs whatever means are necessary to achieve its primary narrative and analytical goals as African history: one, to come closer to depicting it, to employ Ranke's phrase, *wie es eigentlich gewesen* [how it actually happened]; and two, in so doing contribute to the ongoing deconstruction of the false binary, once prevalent, of resistor/collaborator, transcending it with historical complexity and context.

Unfortunately – the African historian's lament – the primary sources for such an endeavor remain largely European. That said, these sources are plentiful, and when read against the grain are quite revealing. In addition to the published and unpublished official sources found in The National Archives of the United Kingdom and the Sudan Archive at the University of Durham, there are the firsthand accounts of the Nile Campaign written by British officers in the Egyptian Army, regular British Army soldiers, and civilian eyewitnesses. These private sources can be found at Durham as well as in the archives at the National Army Museum in London, the holdings at both of these locations also containing numerous unpublished photographs of late nineteenth and early twentieth-century Sudanese soldiers. Lastly, there are the published primary sources – books and articles, and their accompanying photographs and illustrations – produced by River War participants and observers, be they soldiers, war correspondents, campaign photographers, or special artists, the rarest of which can be found at the British Library and within its newspaper collections at Colindale.

There are also significant unpublished primary sources to be found in Africa. First and foremost, there are relevant documents to be found in Egypt and the Sudan, most notably those housed at the National Records Office in Khartoum. And indeed among the many intelligence and administrative reports, letters, and dispatches to be discovered in the NRO – most notably those within the Cairo Intelligence [CAIRINT] files – there is a fair amount of material on Sudanese soldiers in the Egyptian Army. But even these sources, one finds, were written chiefly by British military and intelligence officers, as well as colonial administrators, serving in Egypt and the Sudan during the Mahdiyya and Anglo-Egyptian Condominium period. As for whether and to what extent there are pertinent documents in Cairo at the Egyptian national archives, Dar al-Wathaiq al-Qawmiyya, or among the Arabic sources at the NRO, it is unclear. In any case, it remains unknown to this author, whose attempts in Cairo and Khartoum to access these materials were unsuccessful, for reasons both bureaucratic and linguistic.

Albeit few and far between, there are a handful of "memoirs" and "life stories" of long-serving Sudanese soldiers who fought in the River War that were published in magazines and journals. Perhaps the most fascinating of these is 'Ali Jifun's "Memoirs of a Soudanese Soldier," published in *The Cornhill Magazine* in 1896. It is one of the rarest of the rare – a detailed, autobiographical account of life as a Sudanese slave soldier, given by a sixty-year-old Shilluk officer who had served some forty years in the Egyptian Army. A close second to 'Ali Jifun's memoir in terms of its historical value as an authentic African voice is "The Life-Story of Yuzbashi 'Abdullah Adlan," another remarkable and rare autobiographical account of a long-serving Sudanese soldier, recorded in 1933 and eventually published in *Sudan Notes and Records* in 1961. One might also include in this category the incredible two-volume *The Memoirs of Babikr Bedri*, whose author – although serving in the Khalifa's army rather that of the Egyptian Khedive, and thus not a "Sudanese" soldier per its nineteenth-century meaning – provides a number of anecdotes that are quite revealing in terms of the social status of Sudanese soldiers.

Be that as it may, these sources are by their very nature problematic. All of these documents, even the "memoirs" of Sudanese soldiers like 'Ali Jifun and 'Abdallah 'Adlan, were ultimately penned by outsiders who saw Africans as their racial inferiors, and who had little knowledge of Sudanese viewpoints. Nonetheless, at least these sources include details on the conditions of service and daily lives of Sudanese soldiers, not to mention some account of their contributions during the Nile Campaign, which is more than can be said for most secondary sources published since.[5] Indeed, one of the unfortunate consequences of the historiographical ascendancy of *The River War* is that Churchill's "account of the reconquest," despite being over a century old, still casts a long shadow over all that is written – and all that is remembered – about these events even today. As a result, it seems that the greater body of contemporary histories and firsthand accounts of the Nile Campaign, published in the 1890s, have been overshadowed and largely ignored. The upshot is that one continues to find essentially rehashed versions of Churchill's omissive narrative filling the bookstore shelves.

This is unfortunate, for there is much to be taken from these other accounts, especially those written by "old Sudanics" such as Bennet Burleigh of the *Daily Telegraph*, or more experienced, knowledgeable journalists the likes of Ernest Bennett of the *Westminster Gazette*, G. W. Steevens of the *Daily Mail*, E. F. Knight of *The Times*, and A. Hilliard Atteridge of the *Daily Chronicle*, not to mention army officers such Henry Alford and W. Dennistoun Sword (*The Egyptian Soudan: Its Loss and Recovery*, published 1898) or Harry Lionel Pritchard (who in 1899 anonymously penned *Sudan Campaign, 1896–1899*). Though their writings are often tainted by Victorian attitudes to race and Anglo-paternalism, these authors – longer in the tooth and often more careful observers than the young Winston Churchill, who arrived in the Sudan only weeks prior to the Nile Campaign's conclusion – had a keener eye for what was happening in front of them. Unlike *The River War*, these other contemporary accounts contained numerous details on daily life within Sudanese infantry battalions, and on a few rare occasions even quoted or paraphrased actual Sudanese soldiers. Unwittingly perhaps, it was these eyewitness accounts, and these anecdotes, that have helped make it possible to rescue Sudanese soldiers from what historian E. P. Thompson once called "the enormous condescension of posterity."[6]

The chapters that follow this introduction are laid out in a semi-chronological yet largely thematic fashion. CHAPTER ONE, "Backbone of the Egyptian Army," provides a background history of Sudanese soldiers, from ancient times to the launch of the Nile Campaign in 1896. Focusing on the Egyptian Army's use of Sudanese troops during the Turkiyya, and following the army's reorganization by the British in 1883, this chapter covers the reasons behind Sudanese recruitment; the means by which these men were enslaved and enrolled; the military organization and deployment of Sudanese units; the ethnic backgrounds and enlistment status of these soldiers; as well as the military roles and combat record of Sudanese battalions prior to the River War. One of the central arguments of this chapter is that the transition from "old" to "new" Egyptian Army in the 1880s, even despite British reforms, represented continuity more than it did change for Sudanese soldiers. CHAPTER TWO, "Servants of His Highness the Khedive," opens at the Battle of Firket in June 1896, which serves as a springboard to examine Sudanese soldier identity and social condition. In so doing it delves into the unique nature of military slavery, explains why manumission status was less important for Sudanese slave soldiers than patronage, and discusses how there often existed real possibilities for social and economic stability, even advancement, for these men. This chapter also attempts to shed light on how Sudanese soldiers self-identified, and explores the complex and often conflicted, sometimes paradoxical, nature of their position as Khedival soldiers serving in the Sudan. CHAPTER THREE, "Flavour of Domesticity," examines daily life within Sudanese battalions, and breaks down the conditions of service for Sudanese soldiers into the following subcategories: pay, rations, clothing, and arms; camp followers; health and disease; military advancement; discipline; daily life; and retirement. Although these men were well fed, well clothed, well sheltered, and well paid, not to mention well armed, it shows that life in a Sudanese infantry battalion was more of a mixed bag than the above generalizations suggest. The chapter ends with the August 1897 Battle of Abu Hamed, and the conditions of burial for Sudanese soldiers killed in action. CHAPTER FOUR, "Brotherhood that Binds the Brave," explores the unique character and scope of interactions between Sudanese soldiers and their British military brethren, focusing especially on interracial camaraderie and competition. It reveals that these relationships were not monolithic, and were engendered as much by Ornamentalism's "constructed affinities" as they were by Orientalism's notions of "otherness." The chapter ends with a case study of the April 1898 Battle of the Atbara, in which the above phenomena are vividly represented. CHAPTER FIVE, "Tea with the Khalifa," highlights not only the decisive military role played by Sudanese troops throughout the Nile Campaign, but also the many non-combat roles these men occupied during the same years. In addition, this chapter both debunks Churchill's misleading portrayal of Sudanese soldiers at the Battle of Omdurman, and explores the essential role they played in facilitating good relations between the British and indigenous populations of the Upper Nile – and at the direct expense of the French – during the Fashoda crisis. The book's epilogue provides a brief narrative of the 1900 mutiny at the Omdurman barracks, and in the process discusses its multiple causes, various outcomes, and broader implications.

In conclusion, and critical to this historiographical exhumation, *Slaves of Fortune* proposes to show that Sudanese soldiers were not imperial automatons, nor were they ahistorical ciphers. Although subject to violence, natal alienation, and other forms of "generalized dishonor," per Orlando Patterson's slavery paradigm, these men somehow endured, and in effect transcended their social deaths by making meaningful lives out of what fate handed them. Indeed, they were much more than simply identity-less, powerless, collaborator-lackeys, "martial races" cum tools of empire, and largely inconsequential to African and European history. Rather, they were flesh-and-blood historical actors with complex allegiances and identities, both as individuals and as "Sudanese soldiers" more broadly. And within those six Sudanese infantry battalions that fought in the River War – listed as they always were, rather coldly, in Roman numerals IX through XIV – there were thousands of unique biographies, each life marked by its own loves and loyalties, friendships and rivalries, conflicting emotions and human frailties, sometimes manifesting themselves in acts of malice and score-settling, at other times in remarkable and unexpected acts of grace and human kindness.

Contrary to conventional wisdom, as soldiers in the Khedive's army these men possessed a sense of collective strength and martial pride, and the agency that came with it. Sudanese soldiers sometimes mutinied, and were not above transferring their allegiance to another patron should circumstance dictate. Again, social death had engendered social rebirth, their new lives as Egyptian Army soldiers providing them with opportunities for domestic comfort and economic security, even advancement, as well as new forms of honor and power. Not only could these men rise through the ranks, but in certain matters they were afforded privileges not given to other Anglo-Egyptian troops, such as higher pay than Egyptian conscripts, and the ability to have family lives while serving.

On the battlefield Sudanese soldiers often acted independently, favoring their own fighting tactics over those dictated by their officers, occasionally reaping the scorn of the latter, but also demonstrating their firm belief – and reality in some cases – that they knew better than the British how to defeat the Mahdists. And so, in a sense, they were at once both colonial pawns and agents of their own destiny, reshaping the history of the Sudan just as the history of the Sudan had reshaped their lives. It must not be forgotten, as well, that the mere existence, and understood potential, of Sudanese soldiers – whose possession was seen by some colonial propagandists as part of a zero sum game between England and its rivals – itself influenced the "official mind" of the Victorians, and thus affected the Egyptian Question and ultimately the Scramble for Africa, tied as they were to the "Cape to Cairo" dreams of British imperialists.

Of course, as a military category, "Sudanese soldier" was a construction, born of empire and racism, and imposed by outsiders. And yet it was a martial label that became self-fulfilling of a kind. Proud, skilled, experienced, and reliable soldiers, bonded by fortune and fraternity, their Muslim faith, and allegiance to Khedive and commander, it was Sudanese soldiers themselves that made the category stick. And it was they, moreover, who gave it layers of depth and social meaning, and left as its legacy a "Sudanese," sometimes termed "Nubi," identity and culture that would spread, metamorphose, and continue to express itself into the twentieth century and beyond, both in the Sudan and throughout East Africa – from the King's African Rifles to the Sudan Defence Force, from the White Flag League to the Sudan People's Liberation Movement.

Notes

[1] Percy Machell, "Memoirs of a Soudanese Soldier (Ali Effendi Gifoon)," *The Cornhill Magazine*, October 1896, 492. "Ali Gifoon" is an Egyptian form of the Arabic to English transliteration.

[2] In the Shilluk language, *fōte* means "native country" or "home," and *chol* is the plural of *Ochōlo*, "a Shilluk man." The common designation "Shilluk" was given to them "by the Arabs" according the German missionary and linguist Diedrich Westermann. Diedrich Westermann, *The Shilluk People: Their Language and Folklore* (Philadelphia: The Board of Foreign Missions of the United Presbyterian Church of N.A., 1912), xx.

[3] Herein and henceforth the use of the term "Sudanese" [*Sudani*] refers to its nineteenth-century connotation, meaning "Blacks" from the central and southern Sudan; today's northern Sudanese were referred to by their ethnic group names, or collectively as "Arabs." As well, by the time of the River War, "Sudanese" had become its own military category in the region – a means to differentiate black African riflemen from all other soldiers in the Egyptian and Mahdist armies (e.g., the Egyptian Army's "IXth Sudanese").

[4] Winston S. Churchill, *The River War: The Reconquest of the Sudan*, 4th ed. (London: New English Library Ltd., 1973), 289. The original version of the book, entitled *The River War: An Historical Account of the Reconquest of the Soudan*, was published in two volumes by Longmans, Green, and Company in 1899, and has been out of print since its abridgement to a single volume in 1902. However, a new edition of the original, unabridged version, edited by Churchill scholar James W. Muller, is forthcoming from St. Augustine's Press. It remains to be seen to what extent this long-awaited critical edition will conform or run counter to the above-mentioned historiography and/or address some of Churchill's blind spots when it came to the role of Sudanese soldiers in the campaign.

[5] See, for example, Philip Warner, *Dervish: The Rise and Fall of an African Empire* (London: Macdonald and Jane's, 1973); Philip Ziegler, *Omdurman* (New York: Alfred A. Knopf, 1974); Michael Barthorp, *War on the Nile: Britain, Egypt and the Sudan, 1882–1898* (Dorset, United Kingdom: Blandford Press, 1984); Henry Keown-Boyd, *A Good Dusting: A Centenary Review of the Sudan Campaigns, 1883–1899* (London: Leo Cooper, 1986); Robin Neillands, *The Dervish Wars: Gordon and Kitchener in the Sudan*,

1880–1898 (London: John Murray, 1996); Edward M. Spiers, ed., *Sudan: The Reconquest Reappraised* (London: Frank Cass Publishers, 1998); Michael Asher, *Khartoum: The Ultimate Imperial Adventure* (London: Penguin Books Ltd., 2005); Dominic Green, *Three Empires on the Nile: The Victorian Jihad, 1869–1899* (New York: Free Press, 2007).

6   E. P. Thompson, *The Making of the English Working Class* (London: Victor Gollancz, 1963), 12.

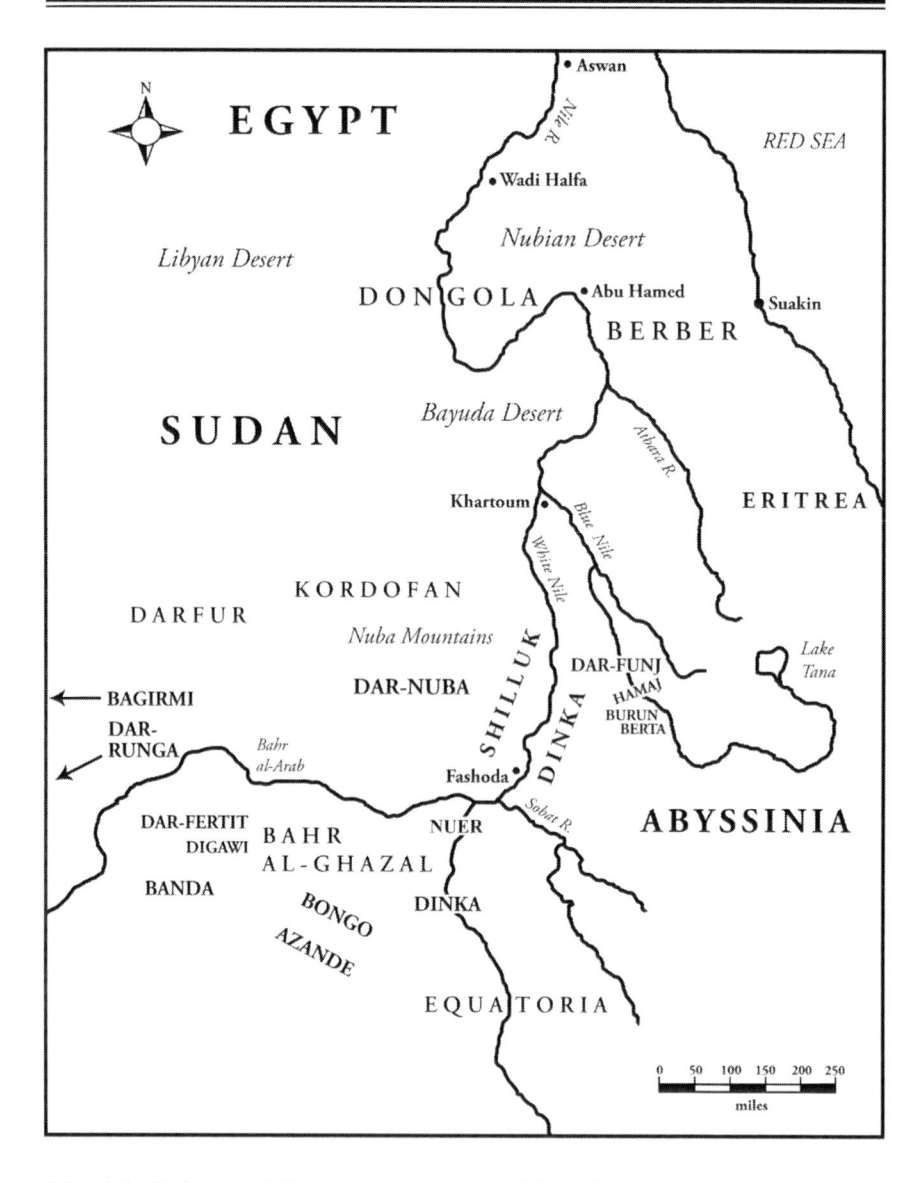

Map 1.1 *Sudanese soldiers, recruitment areas & ethnic groups*

1
"Backbone of the Egyptian Army"

It must be just as obvious to you as it is to me – speaking as an enthusiast regarding the future and with the practical experience of the fighting qualities of Black (Sudanese) troops – one can foresee an enormous acquisition of fighting strength by any Major Power whose influence is paramount in the Sudan – just as we utilise our Indian Troops to fight outside of India, so will the power holding the Sudan be capable of raising a large army of some of the best fighting material in the world, for use outside the Sudan – of course this is looking a long way ahead, but it is a point that should not be lost sight of, in considering the ultimate fate of the Sudan and it would be a pity to let others into the Sudan, when the game is practically in our own hands.

F. R. Wingate to J. J. Leverson
5 January 1890[1]

Whereas historians have tended to ignore, or understate, the contributions of Sudanese soldiers, Francis Reginald Wingate never did. He understood better than most the important military role they served in the Nile Valley, and could potentially occupy throughout the British Empire. The Upper Nile's hydro-strategic importance to Britain in terms of Egypt and the Suez Canal notwithstanding, for Wingate and the War Office that "wretched stuff" of Sudan's Bahr al-Ghazal, as Lord Salisbury once referred to the region, also possessed those "martial races" that might prove useful in protecting British interests in Africa and elsewhere, and conversely, might otherwise be employed by rival Powers were "the ultimate fate of the Sudan" to be otherwise.[2] Regardless, the idea of Sudanese soldiers in an Egyptian army – be they mercenaries, slaves, or per British circumlocution, "volunteers" – was not a new one, nor was it a case of "raw material" being turned into "finished article" as purported by imperial propagandists. There was nothing raw about these recruits, nor was there anything new about their martial reputation or status as military slaves. For although the new Egyptian Army's "pioneer" Sudanese battalion – the IXth –

was established in 1884, it was by no means the first of its kind. Most of these soldiers were veterans of many a campaign, often possessing far more combat experience than the British officers who commanded them.

Sudanese soldiers & the "old Egyptian army"

To say that Sudanese soldiers serving in an Egyptian army was not a new phenomenon in 1884 is rather an understatement. Indeed, they had been recruited into Egyptian military service from the time of the pharaohs, as early as the Sixth Dynasty of the Old Kingdom.[3] And although, in the case of these Nubian soldiers, their status as slaves or mercenaries is debatable, one sees in ancient Egypt the earliest precursor to modern Sudanese military slavery, and a practice manifested for largely the same reasons.[4] Over the millennia, the use of Sudanese slave soldiers in Egypt would continue. Toward the end of the ninth century, for example, some 40,000 "Blacks" served in the standing army of Egyptian governor Ahmad ibn Tulun; and the Fatimids (969–1171 CE) imported Nubians and other Sudanese slave soldiers into Egypt in such great numbers that they came to dominate the army during the final years of Fatimid rule.[5] Over time, however, Egypt's use of slave soldiers would not be limited to those of Sudanese origin, nor would all slave soldiers of Sudanese origin serve only in Egypt. Mamluk slave soldiers, most notably, originally from Central Asia and the Caucasus, swelled the military ranks of Egypt for over six hundred years (1169–1798 CE); and Sudanese slave soldiers could be also found in the Sudan itself during the eighteenth century, in the royal armies of Sennar, Taqali, and Darfur.[6]

Be that as it may, it was in the 1820–1821 invasion of the Sudan by Muhammad 'Ali – the Macedonian-born Turkish viceroy and "founder of modern Egypt" – that one finds the most direct and relevant linkages to Sudanese battalions raised for the Nile campaigns of the 1880s and 1890s. Following his "massacre of the Mamluks" in 1811, Muhammad 'Ali sought to both solidify his power and lay the groundwork for his imperial aspirations with the creation of a modern army per *nizam al-jadid* [The New Regulations]. Himself a military man, upon his arrival to Egypt in 1801 he had seen firsthand Napoleon's *Armée d'Orient*, and had also fought alongside British troops. These disciplined and well-trained armies no doubt impressed him, and served as models for his *nizam al-jadid*. Of equal influence were recent Ottoman military reforms – the new structure and tactics of Sultan Selim's *nizam-i cedid* [New Order]. Moreover, Muhammad 'Ali had witnessed French military instructors successfully train Copts, Maghribi, and Mamluks along European lines, the latter case in both the French Army and for Khusrav Pasha, his predecessor as Ottoman viceroy. Model at hand, it then became simply a matter of finding the soldiers.[7]

Muhammad 'Ali's decision to create an army of Sudanese slave soldiers was neither his first choice, nor in the end his final answer to the problem of recruitment. His decision was based on several factors, not least of which was the

1.1 *"Types of Sudanese soldiers – the raw material"*
(Count Gleichen, *The Anglo-Egyptian Sudan*, 1905)

1.2 *"Types of Sudanese soldiers – the finished article"*
(Count Gleichen, *The Anglo-Egyptian Sudan*, 1905)

vulnerable condition of the Sudan at the time, especially in the case of the Funj kingdom of Sennar. Regardless, his initial attempt at military reform in 1815 involved Albanian soldiers, not Sudanese. In August of that year he tried to impose a new rigor and discipline on his existing Albanian troops – the core of his army now that the Mamluks were disbanded. The experiment failed miserably. Once rumors got out among them that the Pasha intended "to train them according to *al-nizam al-jadid*, copying the positions of the French," and even worse, "wanted them to put on tight clothes and to change their appearance," the Albanian soldiers conspired to assassinate him. The plot was foiled, but street riots and looting in Cairo ensued. In the end, Muhammad 'Ali gave up the idea altogether, and chose to rid himself of these unruly troops by sending them off to fight Wahhabis in the deserts of Arabia.[8]

The idea of conscripting Egyptian *fellahin* was initially passed over as well. Muhammad 'Ali believed them too economically valuable to Egypt as agricultural laborers, and thus did not want to separate them from their villages. And it was only later, when Sudanese recruitment went awry, that this option was employed on more than an ad hoc basis. Exactly where and when the plan to use Sudanese slaves originated is unknown, but following the Albanian debacle, the idea of raising an army of more docile and obedient soldiers from outside Egypt – with no allegiances other than to him – must have appealed to Muhammad 'Ali. As well, there were indeed precedents for conscripting black Africans into military service, both in Islamic tradition, as in the case of the Fatimids, and more recently, by the Pasha's own predecessor and rival, Khusrav Pasha. A few years earlier, Khusrav had formed a regiment of Sudanese slaves to serve as his personal guard, trained in French tactics by 24 deserters from Napoleon's army. Moreover, the plan of raising an army of Sudanese soldiers had a built-in advantage to it, both practical and economic, for Muhammad 'Ali could use these same forces to more easily govern and more cheaply garrison the very territories in the Sudan that he conquered.[9]

In any case, the primary aim of Muhammad 'Ali's 1820–1821 invasion of the Sudan – more than gold and taxes, control of Red Sea trade, or the pursuit of remnant Mamluk *amara* – was the acquisition of black slaves for military conscription.[10] A pre-reform army of 4,000 soldiers under the Pasha's third son Isma'il left Cairo in July 1820. Made up of various "Turks" and Maghribis, Bedouin and Ababda tribesmen, not to mention three *'ulama*, an American artillery officer, a French archaeologist, and two English "amateurs of antiquities," this force fought its way south along the Nile, eventually reaching the Blue Nile Valley and the kingdom of Sennar in June 1821. A second army under Muhammad 'Ali's son-in-law, the *Daftardar*, followed soon thereafter, heading into central Kordofan toward the sultanate of Darfur.[11]

The initial *ghazawat* south of Sennar resulted in only about a thousand individuals, and those in the Nuba Mountains around double that number, the combined figure far short of the 20,000 that Muhammad 'Ali had hoped to capture in these raids. But in 1822 and 1823 the number of slaves coming from south of the Nuba Mountains increased by ten and twenty-fold, and it is estimated that some 20–40,000 were captured during this two-year period. The consequent problem for the *Daftardar*, and ultimately the Pasha's plans for an all-Sudanese army, was the attrition rate for these slaves on the way north to Egypt. The vast majority never made it to the training camps in Aswan; although a typical "season" of *ghazawat* might yield three to five thousand slaves, the total number of fit recruits arriving in Egypt was much lower, typically in the hundreds.[12]

Those slaves arriving to Aswan and deemed fit for service were vaccinated and clothed in calico vests, and soon thereafter issued rations, uniforms, rifles and bayonets. Most being from non-Muslim groups, they were also promptly converted to Islam by Egyptian *shaykhs* per order of the Pasha. Muhammad Bey Lazughlu, the viceroy's deputy, oversaw the military school at Aswan, but the training itself was initially conducted by French, Italian, and Spanish veterans of the Napoleonic wars, and later, by an official French military mission.[13] And although the military designations and commands remained in Turkish, the essential rank structure and code of discipline was based on the French model.[14]

Originally, its planners intended that the new army would be divided into six regiments of 4,000 men, each regiment [*alay*] made up of five battalions [*orta*], each battalion consisting of 800 men. This was only on paper, however, and when they later decided to reduce the number of battalions to four, with 816 men per battalion, the total number of soldiers per regiment was lowered to 3,264. And yet, even these numbers proved difficult to attain, as many Sudanese trainees died in the camps or on the march to Cairo, suffering from fever, dysentery, and acute homesickness. Indeed, these losses were so great that in December 1823 the Pasha even considered importing doctors from the United States with experience treating diseases common to slaves in the American South. For Muhammad 'Ali, the upshot was that "the black army of his dreams" was becoming just that, more dream than reality. And out of the 20,000 Sudanese enslaved between 1820 and 1824 only some 3,000 were still alive in 1824. This figure was far surpassed by the actual number of soldiers sent to capture these slaves in the first place, thus undermining the central point of the invasion. Ultimately, this problem of diminishing returns was solved by conscripting Egyptian *fellahin*, first on an ad hoc basis in Upper Egypt in 1822, and then, two years later, on a massive scale throughout Egypt; by 1824 some 30,000 *fellahin* were receiving military training, and before long made up the majority of Muhammad 'Ali's *nizam al-jadid* army.[15]

Nonetheless, Sudanese regiments formed during these years quickly gained a reputation as some of the best fighting material in the Egyptian Army. These troops were highly valued – and widely employed – by Muhammad 'Ali and his successors, who continued to recruit Sudanese soldiers in large numbers, primarily in the Nuba Mountains of southern Kordofan and along the Blue Nile, and later, further south in the Bahr al-Ghazal region. In the early days of the Turkiyya, and through the 1840s, this involved government organized *ghazawat* conducted by the army or nomadic subjects such as the Baggara.[16] Sometimes these slave raids were led by the provincial governor, and occasionally even by the Governor-General of the Sudan, as was the case in 1843 when Ahmad Pasha led a large expeditionary force up the White Nile and into Dar-Funj.[17] Other times, smaller scale *ghazawat* took place, often springing from Turco-Egyptian taxes – tribute that could be paid in kind, in the form of slaves – imposed in newly conquered territories. These slave raids could result in numbers ranging from a few hundred to several thousand, depending on the scale of the *ghazwa*.[18]

During the middle years of the Turkiyya this slave trade increasingly fell into the hands of private, mostly European, merchants known as "Khartoumers," and armed Arab traders, the trade mushrooming once slaves replaced ivory as the main commodity coming out of southern Sudan. What emerged was the *zariba* system, in which interlocking, often competing, private armies and slave encampments, expanding further south along the Nile and its tributaries, dominated the Sudanese slave trade and provided the majority of recruits for the Egyptian Army. These private armies were composed of slave soldiers commonly known as *bazinqir* – locally enlisted and thus knowledgeable of the countryside. In any case, enlistment figures continued to benefit from the fact that slaves could be provided in lieu of taxes.[19]

In fact, this is how 'Ali Jifun, the aforementioned Shilluk *saghkolaghasi* from Fashoda, ended up a slave soldier. According to his memoir, he was captured following a Shilluk cattle raid against the Baggara:

> We had accomplished some twenty-four hours of the return journey, and were marching our spoil through the dense grass and undergrowth which lay between us and the Nile, when the Baggara, who had assembled and followed us, attacked in overwhelming force. We fought desperately, but were completely outnumbered. I was first wounded on my ear, then on my knee and fell helpless to the ground.
>
> My brother Guma, seeing my condition, came to my assistance, but was killed while endeavouring to protect me from the Baggara spears. In this way I fell into the hands of the great slave-dealers of the Soudan, and left my native country.
>
> Day after day I was urged along, wounded as I was, my head in a sheber, or wooden yoke, the other end of which was fastened to the hump of an ox. Whenever I lagged or showed signs of falling I was severely beaten with korbashes, and when we halted for the night I was bound in such a manner as to render sleep impossible…
>
> …During the remainder of this journey, which lay through Beled Obo, Fungur, through the country of Kennan, and on past Gebel Dair, I was always bound to an ox by day, and secured hand, foot, and neck by night, until at last we reached the zeribas on the outskirts of El Obeid. That afternoon Bokhari bargained long with another Arab for a Dongolowi horse which he greatly coveted, and in part-payment for which he wished to sell me. The horse was examined, and I was sounded with equal care by my possible purchaser. The bargain, however, apparently fell through, for next morning I was handed over as a part of the Baggara tax to Government, and thus entered upon my military career. I understood that I was handed over to the Government as part of the Baggara's annual tax (tulbeh el murdan) which they paid in cattle or in slaves, which they captured from time to time.[20]

There were also some instances where sons of tribal leaders and local rulers ended up in Sudanese battalions. In 1858, for example, according to "The Life-Story of Yuzbashi 'Abdullah Adlan," Sa'id Pasha, while visiting Khartoum, "demanded that children from the families of three big sheiks should be sent in to join the army – one from among the sons of the Sultan of Darfur, one from Ibrahim Sabun the Dinka Chief of Kawa and the third from my father's household."[21] Though only eight at the time, 'Abdallah 'Adlan was pledged to the *wali* for later enrollment into the Egyptian Army, a commitment that ultimately led to a 68-year career in the military.

Sources of slave recruits in the Sudan decreased following the appointment of Samuel Baker as Governor-General of Equatoria in 1869. Khedive Isma'il provided the British explorer-cum-administrator with 1,200 Egyptian and Sudanese troops, and instructed him, among other agenda for the province, that he was to suppress the slave trade.[22] Through the 1870s, others were to follow in Baker's footsteps, men such as Charles Gordon and Romolo Gessi, but the continued demand for Sudanese soldiers only manifested new and more creative means of recruitment. One of these stemmed from the suppression itself, where slaves confiscated from arrested traders would then be directly enrolled into the army. Others included conscripting convicts and prisoners of war; subcontracting private slavers; and conducting, under the auspices of a local *mudir* or central authorities, more "discreet *ghazwa*" and "quiet raiding."[23]

The case of Sudanese soldier Faraj Sadik is reflective of this era. According to his "life history," published in 1951 by former Darfur Province Commandant of Police A. C. Hope, he was born about 1863 at Shakka on the Bahr el Arab, southern Darfur, and found his way into the Egyptian Army circa 1873 following an attack made against the Bideiria by his ethnic group, the Shatawi. When Hassan Pasha Duessa, representing the Egyptian government, "came to restore order," he settled the conflict, according to Faraj Sadik, "by sending us back to our homes as we had been the aggressors, and forcibly enrolling some of the boys into the Army." The ten-year-old Faraj was taken to El Obeid, where he "was made to learn to blow a bugle" and spent the next five years. He was then transferred to Khartoum, where he served for six months, before being sent on to Kassala. In Kassala, he joined the "4th Coy of the Kassala Infantry Battalion," but was again transferred after only four months to Massawa, where he remained for the next several years.[24]

In any case, the enlistment of Sudanese slaves into the Egyptian Army continued unabated for the entire Turkiyya. And for good reason from the Khedive's perspective, as Sudanese slave soldiers, known collectively as *jihadiyya*, were of such great value to him – both in terms of garrisoning the Sudan and southern Egypt, and as crack expeditionary forces for use in Africa and abroad. Most Turkish and Egyptian soldiers loathed serving in the Sudan, and often succumbed to tropical diseases when stationed there. And so beginning in the 1830s, Egypt's security and defense burden in the Sudan increasingly fell on Sudanese slave soldiers. At one time or another there were army garrisons in the Egyptian Sudan manned primarily by *jihadiyya* regiments in Khartoum, Suakin, Tokar, Sinkat, Kassala, El Obeid, Sennar, Fadasi, Fazoghli, Wadi Halfa, Berber, Dongola, Taufikia, Fashoda, Lado, Gondokoro, Rejaf, Amadi, Rumbek, Wau, Deim Zubayr/Sulayman, Bara, and El Fasher. In addition, these same troops served in numerous capacities within Egypt proper and in its territorial possessions throughout the region, from guarding the Citadel in Cairo to fortifying the Red Sea enclave at Massawa.[25]

It was from these various locations that *jihadiyya* regiments, and more often individual companies of Sudanese slave soldiers, engaged in myriad odd skirmishes and minor forays over the years, all in the name of the Khedive of Egypt. They also functioned in these territories as tax collectors and slave raiders, and in the final years of the Turkiyya, provided military support for the anti-slavery efforts and territorial expansion undertaken by Samuel Baker, Charles Gordon, and Emin Pasha. And as Mahdism swept the region in the early 1880s, they were

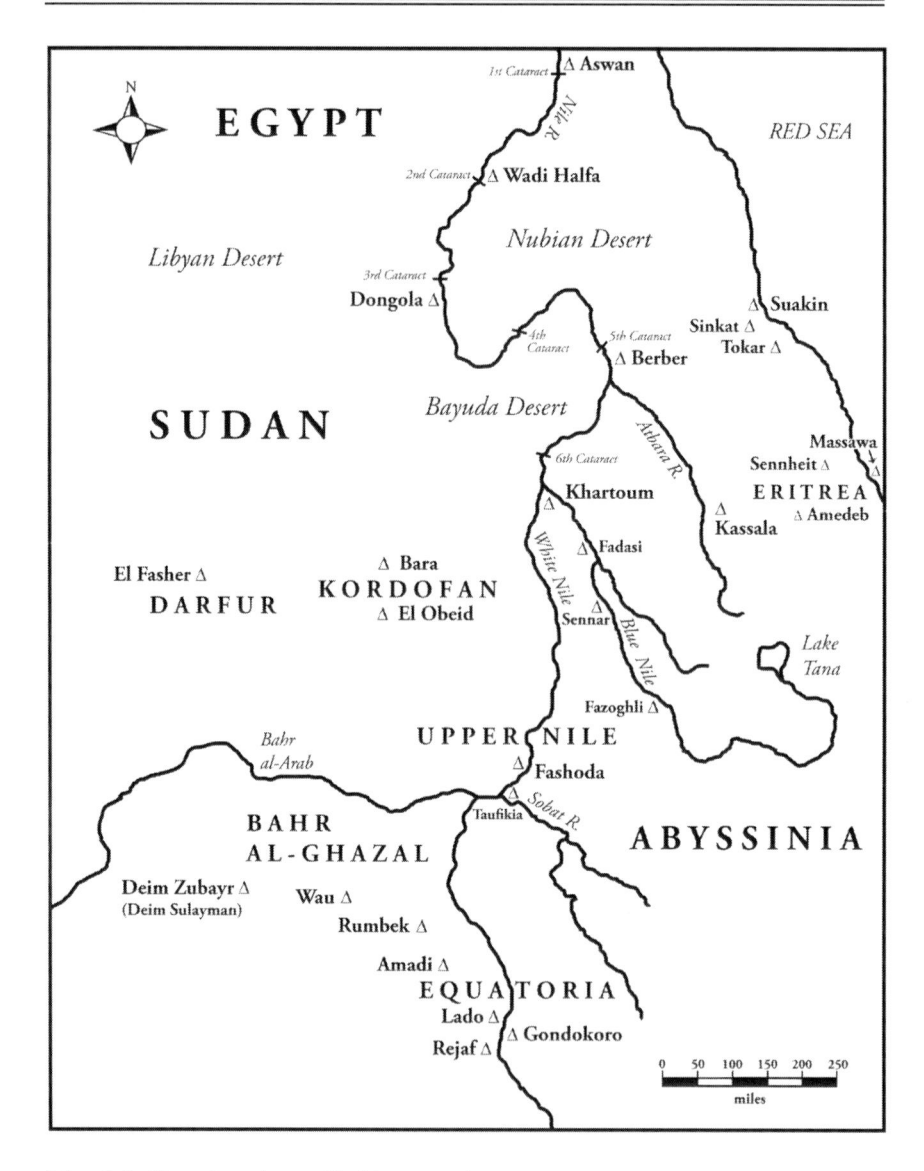

Map 1.2 *Egyptian Army, Turkiyya garrisons*

also among the forces sent to confront the Mahdi's *ansar*, and later, that staged Egypt's evacuation of the Sudan in 1884–1885. In fact, General Gordon's chief-of-staff during the siege of Khartoum was a Sudanese soldier named Faraj Muhammad al-Zaini.[26]

The deployment of Sudanese slave soldiers, however, was not limited to locations in Northeast Africa. Right from the start, these troops were used as expeditionary forces. The first instance was in 1823, when some of the first Sudanese trainees – captured during the 1820–1821 invasion – were among the six battalions sent to put down a rebellion in Greece, then a province of Ottoman Turkey. Two Sudanese regiments were also sent to Arabia in 1835 to fight rebellious Wahhabites in the Hijaz. And between 1831 and 1840 Sudanese soldiers served the interests of Muhammad 'Ali in Syria as well, taking part in two civil wars. There is even evidence that they fought for the Ottomans against the Russians in the Crimean War.[27]

One of the most interesting uses of these troops, however, was in Mexico from 1863–1867, when Muhammad Sa'id Pasha lent 446 Sudanese soldiers to French Emperor Napoleon III for use in Maximilian's army. Such were the contributions of this "Black Corps d'Elite" in Mexico that on their return journey to Egypt they stopped in Paris, where they were decorated in the courtyard of the Tuileries Palace with French Campaign Medals and some of them with the Cross of the Legion of Honor.[28] And during the final decade of the Turkiyya, Sudanese soldiers also participated in two failed Egyptian invasions of Abyssinia [Ethiopia] against the forces of King Yohannes IV, four companies defeated at Gundet in 1875, and one regiment at Gura in 1876.[29]

Sudanese soldiers 'Ali Jifun & 'Abdallah 'Adlan

To give a better picture of how Sudanese soldiers functioned in the "old Egyptian Army," it is worth looking at the biographies of two such soldiers: 'Ali Jifun and 'Abdallah 'Adlan. By sheer breadth of experience and duration they are both remarkable military careers. And indeed, this appears to have been the very reason why these two life stories were first recorded for posterity by their British authors. And yet, considering both the tumultuous nature of nineteenth-century Sudanese history, and the fact that slave soldiers were "enlisted for life," as the euphemism went, these two military résumés were perhaps less the exception than the norm. They also vividly show how the so-called "raw material" from which the Sudanese battalions of the "new Egyptian Army" were formed in the 1880s was the furthest thing from "raw," as many of the men had decades of military experience in the region already behind them.

Take the career of 'Ali Jifun.[30] Following his enrollment into the Fifth Regiment (No. 2 company of the Second Battalion) of the Egyptian Army, he spent the early 1860s stationed at El Obeid in the Kordofan region of the Sudan. 'Ali Jifun first saw action in an expedition launched against the rebellious "Takallas," sent with the object of arresting Makk Nasir wad Abakr, the local Taqali leader who had refused to pay the government tax. After a confused and bloody mountainside battle in which three-quarters of his fellow soldiers were killed or injured, he joined a second, much larger force, from all parts of the Sudan and led by the Governor-General, to avenge the defeat. Makk Nasir surrendered without a fight, but 'Ali Jifun's battalion ended up accompanying the Governor-General on another mission, the relief of Massawa, a Turkish garrison hundreds of miles away on an island in the Red Sea. His battalion, joined by three others and some artillery and *bashi-bazouq*, routed the forces of Ahmad Arei – a local notable leading the Massawa revolt – at Arkiko, and reoccupied the garrison at Massawa.

Following the relief of Massawa, 'Ali Jifun and his battalion were sent back, by long march via Kassala, to El Obeid. Six months later he was on the move again, part of a force sent to Jebel-el-Tow, the mountain headquarters of "the Nuba chief," who had refused to pay the government tax. They advanced upon the Nubas, ultimately came to terms with them, and returned again to El Obeid. Soon thereafter, 'Ali's battalion was sent to put down a revolt among the Baggara, on request by the Fungur Shaykh. This accomplished, he returned to El Obeid, and was soon ordered to Egypt, where he eventually served two years in the cavalry at Alexandria after sojourns in Cairo, Keneh, Alexandria, Mariot, Alexandria again, and Chibin el Kom, where he spent three months as a mule transport driver. He then spent over a year as part of an artillery battery, in the Egyptian garrison at Fom el Bahr.

Come 1863 'Ali Jifun was ordered again to Alexandria, where he boarded the French steamer *Seine* bound for Mexico, embarking on a four-year military adventure in the name of the Napoleon III. Based in Vera Cruz, he and his fellow Sudanese soldiers functioned in various roles and engaged in numerous military forays over the next several years: escorting trains; serving as mail carriers or in cavalry patrols; besieging rebel strongholds in Tlacotalpan and on the island of Koneklia; marching against these same forces in Coquite, Cosomoloapan, and Puebla. And it was here in Mexico that 'Ali Jifun and his "Black Corps d'Elite" further solidified the reputation of Sudanese soldiers as some of the best mercenary fighters in the world; as one of their French commanders, Marshal Foret, said of them: "Ce ne sont pas des soldats, ce sont des lions" [these are not soldiers, these are lions].

In 1867 'Ali Jifun returned to Egypt, to Alexandria via Toulon and Paris, and then on to Toora, near Cairo, where he was re-embodied into the Egyptian Army's Second Regiment. He spent the next four years stationed at Massawa, the former Turkish garrison that was now controlled by Egypt. According to his memoir, about a year of this was spent at Arafale, where his company collected salt taxes. Over the next fifteen years, based along the Abyssinian frontier, mostly at Amedeb, 'Ali participated in countless military skirmishes and tax enforcement forays: versus the Baseh [Kunama] of Jebel Samero; the Segelogedad; the Baseh of Jebel Afile, near Senheit; Shaykh Hammad at Analeh, near Geera; the Samereh near Alummo; the Shaykh 'Ali Wad Shata of Moghreb; the Gadein between Kassala and Amedeb; and the inhabitants of Jebels Amassa, Dumbelaz, and Onduruk. In another expedition, his company, along with five others, was sent by the Governor of Kassala to reduce a fortified position atop Jebel Gogeh, from where a deserting *ombashi* from 'Ali Jifun's battalion had led the local Barea and Baseh on raids of the neighboring Gadein, Sebderat, Beni Amer, and Shukrieh. His firsthand description of the ensuing conflict provides a rare and vivid picture of one of these engagements:

> Soon we found we could get no higher [on the mountain], as there was only one path up to the top, and that was very narrow and filled with obstacles. The women in the fort were all screaming at us by this time, and shouting to our commander that he had better take his soldiers away, for if we came any further we should all be killed. Seeing that it was impossible for the battalion to go on, I went to the commandant and said we must either go back or send a selected party on while the rest remained in support. He said the latter

course would be useless; but I saw it was our only chance, so called to Gilo Ayed, who is at present the oldest bugler in the 12th Battalion, and who was my bugler that day, to take my horse and give me his rifle and bayonet. Then, taking another bugler and twelve picked men with me, I climbed round the reverse side of the hill, and then we crawled up unobserved until we could see straight into their position. Taking a steady aim, we fired and dropped four of them, at the same time sounding the bugle for the rest of the battalion to come along. Two more were killed, and then the Baseh made for me and my party. We fired as fast as we could and withdrew slowly, until luckily the remainder of my company, which had followed me without orders, came up and kept them off until the battalion succeeded in reaching the top. The rebels mostly took refuge in their caves, and we were some fifteen days clearing them out. The onbashi himself succeeded in making his escape, but all who fell into our hands were killed. One of our men, a big, strong Soudanese named Someet, acted as executioner, and as the rebels were driven out of their hiding-places they were taken to him to be beheaded. Their heads were finally arranged in rows in a conspicuous position upon the hilltop, and, having collected all their property, we returned to Amedeb.[31]

With the rise of Mahdism in the early 1880s, 'Ali Jifun was caught up in the besiegement of eastern Sudan by forces under Osman Digna. Sent to reinforce and defend Kassala in November 1883, he and his company attempted to drive off the fuqara and darawish – Arabs fighting under Osman Digna's deputy Mustafa Hadel. This and further attempts over the next year and a half were ultimately to no avail, and 'Ali found himself in the summer of 1885, along with the rest of the Kassala garrison, with nothing to eat, as the siege entered its final stages. A truce between the local *mudir* and the darawish was reached, whereupon he and many of his fellow Sudanese soldiers took "advantage of this opportunity to escape," and fled to Massawa. Arriving in Egypt later that fall, already a twenty-five-year veteran, 'Ali Jifun was posted to the recently formed Xth Sudanese Battalion of the new Egyptian Army.

'Abdallah 'Adlan's military career prior to 1885 was equally remarkable.[32] Promised to Sa'id Pasha in 1858 at age eight, 'Abdallah spent the next two years at a local *khalwa*, followed by three years at the government school in Kassala. Around 1863 he was enrolled into the Egyptian Army and was sent to Cairo, where he entered the army music school. He spent nine years at the school, and then, as a Cyprian cornet player in a regimental band, was sent to eastern Sudan, to Massawa, Senheit, Amedeb, Kassala, and back, attached to forces under Munsinger Pasha, a Swiss military adventurer set on expanding the Khedive's domains in the Horn hinterlands. He even put his instrument in storage in 1875 to fight under Munsinger in his ill-fated campaign to seize the rock-salt mines of the Haramat Mountains; its end came in the middle of the night, when 'Abdallah's *zariba* was ambushed by Somali tribesmen, and Munsinger was killed.

After serving the next four years at Senheit in the First Battalion, he was sent back to Egypt for another year of instruction in order to lead a regimental band consisting entirely of Sudanese soldiers. He spent the next five years between Kassala, Amedeb, and Senheit, serving with his regimental band, but also, on occasion, patrolling for taxes among the local populace. Sometimes these tax-collecting forays escalated into armed conflicts, and 'Abdallah was involved in several of these battles – in his "life-story" he mentioned one with "a certain Maria tribe (Hamra and Zerga) living between Asmara and Senheit," and

1.3 *'Abdallah 'Adlan c. 1933*
(Bredin, "The Life-Story of
Yuzbashi 'Abdullah Adlan")

another against "the Kushtan tribe which lived in the direction of Adowa." In the latter case, his Second Battalion was among the 36,000 soldiers under Prince Hassan (Khedive Isma'il's son) that fought in a bloody three-day battle with Abyssinians at a place called Medin:

> The Abyssinians attacked us in our zariba in great numbers. They galloped forward on mules and then sprang off and tore away the thorn bushes and poured in amongst us. But we held our ground and by the evening the corpses were piled high in front of the zariba. On the third day of the battle our battalion commander ordered us to leave the zariba and advance. We did so and were fighting hand to hand with the enemy when the rest of the army, fearing that we might be driven back and the Abyssinians follow us into the zariba, opened a heavy fire on friend and foe alike and killed many of our men. During the fighting I received two sword cuts and a bullet in the thigh. The Abyssinians used firearms which they discharged with lighted matches and many of their bullets were made of stone and ebony. At the end of three days fighting neither side had gained any advantage and the two commanders agreed to break off hostilities.[33]

Upon recovering from his wounds, 'Abdallah 'Adlan returned to Senheit and went on tour with his regimental band. Like 'Ali Jifun, he and his battalion were sent to defend Kassala in the wake of local revolts associated with the rise of Mahdism in the Sudan. Not long thereafter, he joined a military escort charged with delivering a consignment of arms to General Gordon in Khartoum, who had been sent there to command the Egyptian evacuation of the Sudan. He soon found himself caught up in the Mahdist siege of Khartoum, and three months after his arrival, on 26 January 1885, he and his fellow soldiers were overwhelmed by Muhammad Ahmad's *ansar* in a final assault on the city. 'Abdallah survived the battle by throwing himself "down among the dead and wounded while the Dervishes poured over us into the town." Stripped of his Egyptian Army uniform, he was given "Dervish clothes" and put into a new Mahdist column being sent to attack his former garrison at Kassala. The garrison held out for two days, but on the third day was defeated by the Mahdists, despite the reluctance of 'Abdallah and his fellow Sudanese soldiers to participate in the attack: "We who had been soldiers of the Khedive did not like to fight against our former comrades and so we hung back, taking no part in the battle."

Now back in Kassala, he was allowed to live with his family in his former home, but told to keep himself "in readiness to serve the Mahdi." The call up came a few months later, and he and his former battalion were placed under the command of Osman Digna, who was leading an attack on the port of Suakin. Miraculously, in the course of preparations for the attack, 'Abdallah and his contingent of ex-Egyptian Army soldiers were left alone by Osman Digna during a war council – at the same time as heavy rains created a large *wadi* further separating them – and effected a midnight escape. Two days flight brought them to the shores of the Red Sea, where they set up a defensive *zariba* – having heard that Osman Digna sent an armed pursuit party. What happened next is best described in 'Abdallah 'Adlan's own words:

> We made a zariba round each battalion with our families inside and were preparing to defend ourselves to the last when we saw a British gunboat steaming past. One of our officers, a yuzbashi named Selim Eff. Kirkir had been a signaler and knew some English and flashed a message to the ship using a looking-glass as a heliograph, saying that we were Turkish soldiers deserting from the Mahdi's army. By this time the Dervish horse had come into view and were rapidly approaching our zariba. The captain of the gunboat then told us to abandon our zariba so as to leave the field of fire clear for his guns. We did so and moved along the shore and as the Dervishes entered our zariba the gunboat opened fire on them. Many were killed and the remainder retired. The captain of the ship then sent a signal to say that he wished to see our commanding officers. It must be remembered that we were all dressed in Dervish jibbas and he clearly wished to make sure that our story was true. Five of our officers were taken on board over a ladder between the ship and a reef and when they returned they divided us up into detachments and listed us. In the meantime the gunboat had got a message through to Suakin telling them to send transports for us and next day an Egyptian man-of-war arrived to take us off.[34]

Two weeks later, in May of 1885, he and his battalion set sail for Suez, and then went by train to Cairo, where they were housed in the Egyptian Army barracks at Abbassia. Later that year he was discharged, but like 'Ali Jifun, was soon posted to one of the re-formed Sudanese battalions in the new Egyptian Army, in 'Abdallah 'Adlan's case as a band instructor with the XIIIth Battalion in Aswan.

Sudanese soldiers & the "new Egyptian Army"

Despite imperial rhetoric of the time and its historiographical echo – and notwithstanding some of the actual military reforms instituted by Lord Dufferin and Sir Evelyn Wood – the transition from the "old" to "new" Egyptian Army in the 1880s represented more continuity than change for Sudanese soldiers. Though nominally "volunteers," their enlistment status and conditions of service remained somewhat ambiguous, and rather akin to military slavery. These troops were now under British commanding officers rather than Frenchmen, Turco-Egyptians, or Americans, but their ultimate patron was the same – the Khedive of Egypt. And although British military reformers in Egypt touted their transformation of "The Fellah as Soldier" from a "bye-word [sic] for cowardice" into the picture of "steadiness and gallantry," it was widely recognized among these same reformers that Sudanese infantry battalions were "the backbone" of the Egyptian Army, and the critical piece in maintaining Egyptian defense and security interests in the Nile Valley south of Aswan – a role they had served since the time of Muhammad 'Ali.[35]

Be that as it may, the Khedive's army did undergo a rebirth in the 1880s, necessitated by Britain's 1882 occupation of Egypt and the army's formal disbandment. "*L'Armeé Egyptienne est dissoute*," decreed Khedive Tawfiq on 19 September 1882, doing with the pen what Wolseley's British and Indian forces had already accomplished at Tel el-Kebir six days earlier. And so it was that battlefield defeat and geopolitics conspired to mark a new chapter in the history of the Egyptian Army, but indeed it was a long time in coming. Following decades marked by corruption, low morale, disorganization, and one military debacle after another, the Egyptian Army was in a deplorable state when Sir Evelyn Wood became the *sirdar* and commenced its reorganization in 1883. Twenty years earlier, upon his ascension to *wali* of Egypt, Isma'il Pasha had himself attempted to rebuild the Egyptian Army into the military power it was prior to Sa'id Pasha's reign (1855–1863), and likewise, with territorial ambitions more akin to his grandfather Muhammad than his uncle Sa'id. However, as was the case for many of Isma'il's grand plans that went bankrupt, he overextended himself. In the end, he did further damage to the power and prestige of the once most formidable army in the Middle East, a failure ultimately contributing to his own abdication in 1879.

Of course, Khedive Isma'il's imperial appetite was not wholly to blame for the military failures of 1875–1876, when his forces were defeated at Gundet and Gura by the Abyssinians; in fact, one could argue that it was underlying flaws within the Egyptian Army itself at the time that precluded any chance of victory. Despite a concerted investment in modern military equipment and foreign mercenaries – most notably, fifty American Civil War veterans – the Egyptian Army during Isma'il's reign had numerous, deep-rooted problems, not only in its conscription and training methods, but in its organization and command structure as well. However, the most festering of problems was that of low morale among of the *fellahin* rank and file, a product of the increasingly abysmal conditions under which these soldiers served: bad food, bad pay, poor medical attention, inadequate housing, shoddy uniforms, and harsh punishments, all the while not knowing when if ever one's service with the colours would come to an end.[36]

Khedive Tawfiq's new *sirdar*, Sir Evelyn Wood, and British commissioner Lord Dufferin were determined to fix these aforementioned problems when the two men took on the task of rebuilding the Egyptian Army in 1883. The first step in its reorganization was the selection of Wood's staff, some two dozen British officers from the Queen's Army, now given provisional appointment in Egypt. Below them were the cadres of the battalions, Egyptian officers and non-commissioned officers chosen from "the remains of the old army," included among them a number of Turkish soldiers of good reputation. At the outset, the *sirdar* and his staff decided that the new Egyptian Army was to be a *fellahin* army, made up of two brigades with four battalions in each, as well as a cavalry regiment and four artillery batteries. British officers would command the first brigade, Egyptian officers the second. The initial size of the army was set at 6,000 men, the recruits to be provided by the fourteen provincial governors of Egypt in proportion to their population. Although F. R. Wingate was later to claim that these first *fellahin* conscripts "were of a finer stature and greater suitability than those obtained since," an initial tally of privates, including water carriers, taken by Wood on 28 January 1883 indicated that they were still 3,219 men short of the proposed establishment for these lower ranks. By the end of March, upon the army's first recorded review before the Khedive, the numbers had increased slightly, and the total strength of the army, including officers and men, now stood at 3,500. But this was well short of the figure of 6,000 that Lord Dufferin had originally proposed, and even that number was set in consideration of the army being used solely for "the defence of Egypt proper," and "irrespective of events in Sudan."[37]

By the end of 1883, however, the rebuilding of the Egyptian Army could no longer be conducted irrespective of events in Sudan. Compelled by the spread of Mahdism, as well as renewed doubts about *fellahin* soldiers in the field, its reformers reconsidered the size, makeup, and eventual deployment of this new Egyptian Army. The first blow came on 5 November 1883, when a riff-raff army of 6,000 men under Hicks Pasha – assembled from Arabi's defeated soldiers and 3,000 untrained rejects that had been passed over as physically inadequate earlier that year by Sir Evelyn Wood – was annihilated by Mahdist forces in Kordofan at a place called Shaykan. The battle took a quarter of an hour and only three hundred of Hicks Pasha's men lived to tell about it.[38] This was followed by the 4 February 1884 loss at El Teb, when Egyptian infantry battalions under Baker Pasha, part of a force of 3,700 sent to relieve the besieged garrison at Tokar, threw down their arms and fled the field when attacked by a Mahdist force less than a thousand strong; more than half of Baker Pasha's troops were killed or captured.[39]

Of course, neither Hicks nor Baker was fighting with the *fellahin* battalions raised and trained for the new Egyptian Army. Rather, these were the dregs of the old, disbanded army, who fought under Arabi at Tel el-Kebir, or were time-expired conscripts or enlistment rejects. Indeed, in the case of former Arabi troops on the Hicks Pasha expedition, they had to be brought from Egypt to the Sudan in chains to prevent desertion.[40] Nonetheless, these military debacles in the Sudan, in the words of Wingate, "convinced even the most sanguine that it would be dangerous to trust entirely to Egyptian troops in the field…and tended to confirm the statements of those who prophesized disaster."[41]

In the wake of these two defeats, and in response to the increasing military threat posed to Egypt by the armies of the Mahdi, Sir Evelyn Wood and his staff decided in early 1884 to both increase the size of the Egyptian Army and to augment its forces by raising non-Egyptian battalions. Just as Muhammad 'Ali had done almost seventy years earlier, the first, ill-fated attempt focused on raising a new Turkish brigade, made up of Albanian soldiers recruited by Zohrab Bey. And like history repeating itself, it was not long before a mutiny among the nucleus of its first battalion led to its disbandment, and Wood scuttled plans for a Turkish brigade. It was at this point decided to "experiment" by raising a Sudanese, or "Black," battalion from among the remnants of a battalion then at Suakin, made up of Sudanese soldiers from the first battalion of an Egyptian Army regiment stationed at Massawa in the early 1880s; joining them were Sudanese soldiers from other Red Sea littoral garrisons as well, refugees from Berber, Sennar, and Kassala. This "pioneer" Sudanese battalion, designated the IXth, was raised on 1 May 1884 at the Red Barracks in Abbassia, Cairo. Six British officers were appointed to the battalion, with Major Henry Hallam Parr its commanding officer, and Captain Archibald Hunter second in command.[42]

Although the 1 May 1884 date has made its way neatly into the official records and history books without qualification, it turned out to be a false start, and it would be several months before the IXth Battalion was truly formed. Even before they arrived in Cairo for re-enlistment, Sudanese troops had been in a mutinous state – the disgruntled soldiers having been mulcted of their pay and rations for years while serving in the old Egyptian Army. In fact, when Major Parr arrived in Suakin in early 1884 "to instil [sic] some discipline into the troops," he found they "had given vent to their displeasure by slashing the Adjutant Major over the head with a sword bayonet." Nonetheless, of the 1,500 Sudanese men who arrived at the Abbassia barracks in Cairo that spring, some 800 were deemed fit and put into the IXth's four companies.[43]

Not all of the mutinous spirit among these Sudanese troops had been weeded out, however, nor was the "extreme keenness" of their British officers well received by the veteran soldiers, many of whom were "of advanced age, and had not previously been used to work [sic] very hard at drill." According to the battalion's chronicler, these men had little interest in returning to the Sudan in relief of Gordon, and "after many years of fighting and sojourning...were distinctly for a quiet time in Egypt." Things came to a head when they were ordered to surrender their Remington rifles in exchange for Martini-Henrys. When the men refused to give them up, it was secretly arranged that a regiment of British cavalry and a Royal Horse artillery battery, backed by an infantry battalion, would seize the rifles following the customary "Pile Arms" and "Break Off" order during Parade. Before this could be executed, however, Sir Evelyn Wood decided to inspect the troops for himself, and address them regarding their mutinous conduct.[44]

The upshot of this meeting between the *sirdar* and his new Sudanese battalion was that the entire IXth was disbanded. The soldiers were given free discharges, but also given the opportunity to join a re-raised IXth as "volunteers," the conditions of pay being 2½ Egyptian piastres per diem, and "something extra for the married men." Of the discharged battalion, only some one hundred soldiers, mostly Shilluk and Dinka that "had held aloof from the mutiny," volunteered to serve with the new IXth – now led by Archibald Hunter – in July 1884. Paradoxically, during the re-formation of this "volunteer" IXth Battalion that summer, in order to fill the rolls of its two original companies Hunter was "empowered to press gang any black in the country."[45]

In spite of these initial difficulties, there were several good reasons why British commanders would turn to Sudanese soldiers when looking to expand the size of the Egyptian Army in 1884. First, in the minds of British commanders, the addition of Sudanese troops – with their martial reputation and experience in the region – would bolster the Egyptian Army where it needed it most: fighting spirit and reliability in combat. In the wake of Tel el-Kebir, Shaykan, and El Teb, doubts about the fighting abilities of Egyptian *fellahin* troops were at an all-time high, and it was believed that black, all-Sudanese battalions might add a "picturesque" and "dashing element" to the new Egyptian Army, and be just the kind of "men whom a commander would most readily pit against the reckless courage of the dervishes."[46] British commanders and soldiers had witnessed the fighting pluck of Sudanese soldiers firsthand at Tel el-Kebir in September 1882; the consensus among them was that whereas the Egyptian troops had made a rather "poor showing," the Sudanese "were the only Khedivial soldiers who made anything of a stubborn stand," and "held on long after the main body of Arabi's force had abandoned their intention of driving the British into the Suez Canal or the sea."[47]

Second, from a practical standpoint in 1883–1884, large units of Sudanese soldiers already existed, remnants of the disbanded Egyptian Army stationed at besieged garrisons throughout eastern Sudan. Thus there was a ready-made pool of recruits – already on the ground, already loyal to the Khedive – from which British commanders could choose. In theory, it was simply a matter of transporting them from the outlying Egyptian provinces to Cairo for re-enlistment, retraining, and eventual redeployment. A third and not unrelated reason why British commanders turned to Sudanese troops in 1884 was because as lifelong soldiers, and widely regarded as the best fighting material in the region, they had come to represent a military gain or loss in a zero-sum game taking place between the Egyptian Army and Mahdist forces. Every disbanded Sudanese slave soldier that was not re-enrolled into the Egyptian Army was thus a potential recruit for the Mahdists; in fact, there were several thousand *Sudani* already in Muhammad Ahmad's army by 1884, slave soldiers and deserters, as well as prisoners of war, from defeated Egyptian Army regiments. Known collectively as *jihadiyya*, these professional black soldiers were highly valued by the Mahdi, particularly for their military training, and it was they who were issued the majority of captured enemy firearms.[48] Indeed, the Mahdi's successor, the Khalifa 'Abdallahi, believed them to be so valuable that he later issued a decree prohibiting any "black" over the age of seven from leaving the country.[49]

Newly raised Sudanese battalions thus served the Egyptian Army's immediate need for increased numbers and at the same time diminished the ultimate military potential of its enemy. Moreover, as indicated by the Wingate to Leverson letter excerpt that opened this chapter, there was also the growing realization that these "martial races" from the Sudan might prove invaluable in the Scramble for Africa, and at the expense of imperial rivals. Echoing Wingate's thoughts, with the reconquest of Sudan still four years away, was Alfred Milner, then Under-Secretary for Finance in Egypt:

> Immediately to the north of Uganda, and thence onward to the southern limit of the Khalifa's dominions, is a country as rich in first-rate fighting material as any in the world. Tribes of the same character as those who in the Sudanese battalions form the backbone of the Egyptian army, or who, under the name "Gehadia," are so formidable an element in the Khalifa's military strength, will be within the reach and at the disposal of any civilized Power, which has once firmly established itself on the Nyanza Lakes.[50]

And so it was that the IXth Battalion of the new Egyptian Army, the so-called pioneer Sudanese battalion, indeed the legacy of Sudanese slave soldier units dating back six decades – if not four millennia – came to be in the summer of 1884. And over the next four years, the IXth was joined by four additional Sudanese battalions: the Xth, on 2 January 1886 (to which 'Ali Jifun was first assigned); the XIIIth on 21 June 1886 (to which 'Abdallah 'Adlan was first assigned); the XIth in January 1887 (created from the Sudanese reserve upon reorganization of the Egyptian police, largely made up of the same mutinous men who had chosen not to re-enlist during the first attempt to raise the IXth back in 1884); and, finally, the XIIth on 13 November 1888 (to which both 'Ali Jifun and 'Abdallah 'Adlan were transferred).[51]

Whereas British-commanded *fellahin* battalions numbered 668 men under three British officers, and were organized into four companies, Sudanese battalions – seen as lacking in *sang froid* and in need of "greater control" – were broken into six companies and led by four rather than three British officers per battalion, raising the total strength to 759.[52] During this time period, however, as new Sudanese battalions were being formed and soldiers reassigned, this number varied considerably; for example, British officer Betram Reverly Mitford wrote that when he joined the Sudanese IXth in September 1886 it "was very strong, some 1,000 all ranks, as we took on all likely men and passed them on in batches to Assuan, where Smith-Dorrien was forming the new XIIIth."[53] In any case, by the early 1890s, with the addition of these five new battalions, the number of Sudanese soldiers in the Egyptian Army had grown to represent some thirty percent of its total forces.[54]

Again, these first new Sudanese battalions were made up of former slave soldiers from the disbanded and besieged Egyptian Army, many from Khartoum, and even more from the other evacuated garrisons throughout the Sudan. B. R. Mitford later recalled, for example, that the first two companies in his battalion "had most of the men from the relieved garrisons, and of the men that came down from Khartoum in Nushi Pasha's steamers."[55] Following this initial absorption in the mid-1880s, however, the recruitment of Sudanese for service in these "black battalions" became much more difficult. This was due primarily to the state of the Sudan at the time, and the decreasing numbers of Sudanese slaves arriving into Egypt. Ironically, the Khalifa's own recruitment needs – the same needs that led him to prohibit "blacks" from leaving the country – worked in combination with the success of Anglo-Egyptian efforts in suppressing the slave trade, and led the new *sirdar*, Francis Grenfell, to write in an 1890 War Office minute paper that "the number of Equatorial tribesmen arriving from the

1.4 *Officers of the XIIth Sudanese Battalion, possibly at Qasr al-Nil barracks, Cairo, Egypt, between 1888 and 1890 (the officer in the middle row, second from the left, is likely 'Ali Jifun)*
(Photographer: G. Lekegian, reproduced by permission of Durham University Library)

Sudan, who are the main source from whom recruits for the Sudanese Battns of the Egyptian Army are drawn, is abnormally small."[56] So diminished were the numbers of Sudanese recruits that in the same paper Grenfell suggested Sudanese soldiers should no longer be provided for service to other foreign powers, probably referring to Hermann von Wissmann's employment of them during the 1888–1889 Bushiri uprising in German East Africa:

> Under the circumstances and in view of the recent authorisation to a Foreign Power to obtain some Sudanese recruits, and in regard to the fact that the recruiting authorities in the Provinces are experiencing considerable difficulties in raising even the small number of men required for this foreign service, I have thought the present a fitting occasion to submit to Your Excellency the advisability of bringing the matter to the notice of the representatives of the various Powers with a view to their being informed that the meager supply of Sudanese recruits is insufficient to meet the demands of the Egyptian army, + that being the case…in future it will not be possible to comply with their demands for Sudanese recruits required for service beyond the Khedivial Dominions.[57]

Be that as it may, new Sudanese recruits continued to be enlisted into the Egyptian Army throughout the 1880s and early 1890s, albeit in smaller numbers. Many of these recruits were either prisoners of war, captured in the 1884 battles of El Teb and Tamai, or deserters from the Khalifa's army, the latter mostly "bazingirs" and ex-Egyptian Army soldiers, making their way to garrisons throughout Egypt and its outlying provinces, and doing so "on pain of death should their destination be discovered."[58] The War Office did everything it could to encourage these flights to Egypt, even circulating notices to this effect among potential recruits in Sudanese towns and villages. As early as 1886, for example, F. R. Wingate had sent 200 copies of the following notice, translated into Arabic, to Leslie Rundle, Officer Commanding of the Upper Egyptian garrison at Wadi Halfa:

> Notice
> This is to let all Sudanese know that His Highness the Khedive graciously permits Sudanese to enter his Army in certain battalions and has commanded that they receive pay, clothing allowances + food at the following rates.
>
> > Each private receives month P.T. 75
> > Each Corporal receives month P.T. 80
> > Each Sergeant receives month P.T. 90
>
> In addition to the above each man is allowed to have his wife with him if the exigencies of the service permit and she receives £E.3-60 per annum....
>
> If any man is disabled on Service + is unable on discharge to earn his living, then he is allowed by H.H. the Khedive a pension equal to ½ his pay to keep him in Comfort as long as he lives....
>
> All Sudanese who desire to come back or to enter the Egyptian Army will be well received at Halfa, Korosko, Assuan, Derawi, Cairo or Suakin.
>
> If any men have served formerly in the old Army they will be given a free pardon.[59]

Interestingly, although Sudanese recruits were in short number at the time, British commanders were picky about their natal origins and ethnic parentage. They favored "Equatorial tribesmen" with two "black" parents over so-called "Egyptian blacks," men with a Sudanese lineage but born and/or raised in Egypt, and in many cases having "only one black parent."[60] This latter category of Sudanese recruit was considered wholly undesirable: "It has been found that this class does not make in any degree so good a soldier as the *soldats que les noirs de race equatoriale*," wrote Grenfell in 1891.[61] According to Wingate, "As a rule these men, after long residences in the country, are considered to make less reliable soldiers than those who come direct from the Sudan."[62] And so with few exceptions, and despite lagging numbers, Sudanese residing in Egypt were not recruited for service in the "black" battalions, even though they were subject to the same laws of conscription as the *fellahin*.

When it came to the ethnic backgrounds of Sudanese soldiers in the new Egyptian Army, one finds that these battalions of "Equatorial tribesmen" were far more heterogeneous than their British officers ever knew, or cared to describe them. Although most sources indicate that these units were made up largely of men from the Upper White Nile, mostly of Shilluk and Dinka origin, there were many other ethnicities and regions of Sudan represented among them. In fact, it was 'Ali Jifun himself who wrote that when he first joined the Egyptian Army in the late 1850s, "I found Soudanese of every kind among my comrades, but no Shilluk."[63] Many of these men had been captured and enrolled during the Turkiyya, and thus originated from a wide range of slave-raiding areas: the Nuba Mountains of southern Kordofan; Dar-Funj; villages along the Blue and White Niles; and later, when the slave trade migrated further south, the Upper Nile and Equatoria provinces, and especially in the Bahr al-Ghazal region.

However, a 1901 anthropometric study of almost two-hundred Sudanese soldiers conducted by the British Association for the Advancement of Science – that in addition to listing their measurements, noted their ethnic background and village or district of origin – showed an even greater ethnic and geographical diversity than this, indicating that these men were "drawn from a very wide region of Africa, extending westwards as far as Bornu and Baia, and southwards to Uganda."[64] It was reported that although the "greater number belonged to Kordofan, to Dar-fur, Dar-nuba, or Dar-fertit, or to the Shilluk or Dinka tribes," one could also find soldiers within these Sudanese battalions that originated from various other ethnic groups and far more distant regions: the Banda, Bongo, Digawi, Niam-Niam [Azande], and Nuer (Upper Nile); the Hamegawi [Hamaj], Burun, and Berta (Blue Nile/Ethiopian border); and the Bagirmi and Dar-runga (Central Sudan, later French Equatorial Africa).[65]

In and of itself, this degree of diversity – unknown and/or ignored by most nineteenth-century British officers, imperial statesmen, and war correspondents – undermines the notion that these men were primarily from two or three "martial races" found along the Upper Nile. Moreover, this diversity is to say nothing of the mixed ethnic background or disparate natal origins of many Sudanese soldiers, and as such one must be careful not to simplify the "dynamic reality" of the Sudan, in the words of one scholar, by perceiving it "as a static mosaic of tribes each immutably living within its own little world."[66] And this was especially true for the next generation of Sudanese soldiers – the sons of soldiers born in Egyptian Army camps during the 1880s and 1890s.

Take, for example, the complicated background of Sudanese soldier 'Ali 'Abd al-Latif, the early Sudanese nationalist who co-founded the White Flag League in 1924. He was born in 1896 (or 1892, or 1894) in Wadi Halfa, the frontier province of Egypt, the son of a Sudanese soldier named 'Abd al-Latif Ahmad. His father, said to have been from the Nuba Mountains, had been a household slave living in al-Khandaq, a center of trade on the west bank of the Nile south of Dongola. Requisitioned to serve in al-Nujumi's *jihadiyya* for the 1889 Mahdist invasion of Egypt, 'Abd al-Latif Ahmad either deserted or was taken prisoner after the Battle of Toski, and ended up enlisted into the Egyptian Army. His mother, al-Sabr, was of Dinka origin, and she had also been a slave living in al-Khandaq prior to marrying 'Abd al-Latif Ahmad. Like so many of the so-called "negroid but detribalized" of his generation, 'Ali 'Abd al-Latif thus came from a mixed ethnic background and was born well outside the southern Sudan.[67]

In any case, some of these same British officers, statesmen, and correspondents, and even subsequent historians, also tended to emphasize that Sudanese battalions were made up of "volunteers," giving the impression that these men were fresh new recruits rather than older, veteran, slave soldiers. By doing so it seems these authors were attempting to distance the "new Egyptian Army" from its prior existence, and in this case its continued reliance on Sudanese soldiers whose manumission status remained ambiguous. To begin with, although pay and rations, as well as living conditions, for both Egyptian and Sudanese battalions improved when the British reorganized the Egyptian Army in the 1880s, there is little evidence that Sudanese soldiers were ever considered truly emancipated men, possessing the same rights and freedoms as British, or even Egyptian, soldiers – not by their British commanding officers, nor perhaps, even the men themselves. In fact, their conditions of enlistment seem to indicate the opposite, and their ascribed legal status – be it "volunteer" or "slave," or as the British would more palatably refer to them, "long service men" – had little to do with their actual social condition and self-conception.

Whereas Egyptian conscripts in 1888 were required to serve six years in the army, five in the police, and four in the reserve, Sudanese soldiers in the new Egyptian Army prior to 1903 were enlisted "for life or until medically unfit for further service."[68] This was not so different from how things had been in the old Egyptian Army prior to its disbandment, when Sudanese soldiers, according to 'Abdallah 'Adlan, "were not allowed to retire but just worked and served until they dropped," and there "was no such thing as leave of absence."[69] There is some indication that efforts were made to institute set terms of enlistment for Sudanese "volunteers," as evidenced by the following contract form dating from the 1880s:

CONTRACT FOR SOUDANESE OF VOLUNTEER BATTALION

Between _____
representing the Egyptian Government, on the one part,
and _____ on the other part.

Engagement

The undersigned engages to serve H.H. The Khedive, in H.H's Army, for a period of four (4) years from this date, under the following conditions:

Conditions of Service

1. He will be subject to Military discipline and will be bound by the Military laws and regulations, in force in the Egyptian Army.

2. He will be liable to serve wherever the Corps in which he may be serving may be ordered.

3. If killed in action £20 will be given to his widow or children as indemnity. A sum, not exceeding £20 will be granted for wounds received in action, or less according to the severity of the wound.[70]

However, to what extent this contract was employed or followed in practice remains unclear. Its term of engagement is contradicted by other documents from the same time period, and also by what was later reported in the *Handbook of the Egyptian Army*. "Enlistment Certificate A, Soudan Battalions," for example, likewise dating from the 1880s and found in the same intelligence file as the above contract form, indicated that service for a Sudanese soldier was "as long as my services may be required."[71] If anything, these contracts may have led to greater confusion among battalion commanders rather than less.

At one point in summer of 1886, for example, Horace Smith-Dorrien, *kaimakam* of the newly raised XIIIth Sudanese Battalion, wrote to the army Adjutant General that "I should be glad to be informed if there is any limit to the time the men of the Battalion under my command are enlisted for."[72] Puzzled by the response he received ("Surely your men sign a similar contract as men of the 9th Battl – in other words server under the same conditions – Men of 9th Battl. Engage for four years"), Smith-Dorrien followed up this letter by stating that "No – they sign no contract whatever – I really don't think one is necessary, but it ought clearly to be laid down that a man may claim discharged after completing 4 years service – and that if the Govt discharge him before, he should receive a certain amount of compensation."[73]

Indeed, it seems that many commanders divested themselves of such pretensions and additional paperwork. W. H. Besant, *kaimakam* of the XIIth Sudanese Battalion, wrote the following to his Brigade Major in 1889: "I cannot see that there is any object in keeping the record of a mans [sic] services who is enlisted for an unlimited period and who is as a rule a volunteer."[74] Referring to the same army service form as Besant, the *kaimakam* of the XIth Sudanese Battalion, H. A. Macdonald, requested the Brigade Major to "please cause me to be officially told that it is not necessary in the case of Soudanese soldiers who are enlisted for life as their service does not count toward discharge nor transfers to Reserves + they receive no good conduct pay or pension."[75]

And yet, it is also interesting, and telling, that enlistment terms and formal contracts seem to have been a non-issue for the actual Sudanese soldiers in question. According to Smith-Dorrien's above memo, although he was seeking guidance on the matter of enlistment terms, he noted that "oddly enough the question has never arisen + no man coming to enlist has wanted to know for what period he was enlisting."[76] Moreover, and also revealing in terms of the way de facto military slavery continued to function under the British, Smith-Dorrien concluded by noting that he was "rather afraid if they had to sign a contract that it might stop men from enlisting."[77] Succinctly capturing this everyday reality for Sudanese soldiers was *Daily Mail* war correspondent G. W. Steevens: "The black is liable to be enlisted wherever he is found, as such, in virtue of his race; and he is enlisted for life."[78]

More striking, however, in terms of how British commanders truly saw these men, are documents indicating that upon enlistment these Sudanese "volunteers" were branded. In a 14 March 1888 letter sent from Aswan to the Adjutant General, Major Donne, *kaimakam* of the Xth Sudanese, suggested the idea: "All [Soudanese] recruits should be Branded or marked in some way."[79] Donne then followed up on it less than a week later: "By branding men with a star, or some such mark on the left arm, will guard against bad characters and discharged soldiers again enlisting; it will also be a valuable aid in apprehending deserters, for in nine cases out of ten Soudanese have neither guarantors, or Mudiriehs."[80] One finds no mention of the practice in public documents, service memoirs, or by war correspondents, but it seems that Donne's suggestion may have been taken up because one sees in "Enlistment Certificate A, Soudan Battalions" the following condition, listed as number four on the certificate: "I have no objection to being branded or marked as a soldier."[81] This British practice, of course, harks back to the branding of Sudanese slave soldiers that took place during the Turkiyya; in the mid-1870s, for example, the Governor-General of Sudan instituted – at first only among recruits from recently conquered Darfur, but later for all Sudanese recruits – a policy where they were branded with the Arabic letter *jim*, which stood for *jihadi* [regular soldier].[82]

Rising action to reconquest

Ambiguous enlistment status notwithstanding, Sudanese soldiers in the new Egyptian Army came to play a central role in Anglo-Egyptian efforts to stem the tide of Mahdism after the fall of Khartoum, and by the early 1890s, in military preparations for the inevitability of "reconquest." The first notable action seen by the pioneer Sudanese battalion, the IXth, was on 30 December 1885, when British and Egyptian troops defeated 6,000 of the Khalifa's invading forces at Ginnis. Although only two companies, some 150 men, of the IXth Battalion were engaged alongside the 79th Cameron Highlanders, according to one British officer they were "certainly a most undefeated lot," and showed "their usual splendid courage and disregard for danger."[83]

Two Sudanese *anfar*, Sa'id Abou and Fadl el Mula, were killed in action at Ginnis, and one Sudanese officer, a *mulazim tani* named Farag Abu Zeid, as well as four non-commissioned officers and men, *ombashi* Gaber Hanna, *anfar* 'Abdallah Ahmad, 'Adallah Adam, and Faragalla Ahmad, were wounded, the latter four of them fatally. Nineteen of the men were later mentioned by the *sirdar* in a 20 January 1886 Army Order for their conduct and bravery in the battle, and in previous operations. In remembrance of the action, "as a token of their esteem and friendship" and a precursor of the kind of camaraderie that existed between British and Sudanese troops during the River War, the Cameron Highlanders presented the IXth with a Colour inscribed "Ginnis" and requested the battalion "to consider itself the 2nd Battalion Cameron Highlanders."[84]

In the spring of 1887 the IXth Sudanese Battalion also formed the main body of an Egyptian *coup de main* at Sarras, another borderland action along the Nile, defeating an advance guard of two hundred Mahdists under Nur el Kanzi some thirty-five miles south of Wadi Halfa.[85] Albeit a smaller engagement, Sarras (28 April 1887) was a notable victory in the mind of British commanders because it was, unlike the action at Ginnis, "fought by Egyptian troops, entirely independent of British or other support."[86] Of the three hundred men of the IXth who participated, thirteen non-commissioned officers and men were killed; and two officers and twenty-two non-commissioned officers and men were wounded. Of particular note, a Sudanese junior officer, *mulazim tani* Muhammad Abu

Map 1.3 *Egyptian Army battlefields, 1883–1899*

Sheila, was decorated with the 5th Class Medjidieh per order of Khedive Tawfiq.[87]

Yet even more indicative than Sarras as to the added value that veteran Sudanese soldiers brought to the new Egyptian Army was what took place near Suakin the following year – first at Handoub on 17 January 1888, and then in the Battle of Gemaizeh on 20 December 1888. Although the attempted capture of Osman Digna at Handoub turned into something of a debacle, it again demonstrated the initiative, knowledge, and savvy of Sudanese soldiers, and further solidified their growing reputation as the best combat troops in the Egyptian

Army. The retreat from Handoub, a mere footnote in most historical accounts, becomes even more relevant herein when considering that the Sudanese soldiers who stormed Osman Digna's base and turned "a catastrophe…into a gallant retreat," did so on the sly.[88]

Colonel Herbert Kitchener, who was Governor of the Red Sea Littoral at the time, and who proposed the attack on Handoub, had been forbidden by Cairo from using Suakin troops under any circumstances for advance movements. Most sources, however, tend to overlook this fact and merely indicate that Kitchener's small force consisted of a cavalry squadron, a camel corps company, some three hundred "friendlies," and a company of the Xth Sudanese Battalion – without ever explaining how he was able to circumvent the above proscription against such deployments. In *Mahdiism and the Egyptian Sudan*, Wingate even covered for Kitchener somewhat by suggesting that the Sudanese "were for the most part recent deserters from the enemy who had belonged to the garrison at Kassala, and were taken on this expedition owing to their local knowledge of the rebel camp."[89] Yet according to the unpublished *Historical Records of the Tenth Sudanese*, it was not just recent Sudanese deserters who fought at Handoub, but a company of the Xth left behind at Suakin for "depot details" following the battalion's departure for Aswan.[90] And in a classic case of being in the right place at the right time, these records also indicate that the veteran Shilluk slave soldier 'Ali Jifun, now *mulazim awal* and in his early-to-mid-fifties, was the company commander that day. His "first fight after joining the new army," 'Ali Jifun nonetheless brought his many years of experience leading men in battle directly to bear when things started to go wrong.[91]

However, this battalion history, as well as the details of Kitchener's retreat from Handoub to Suakin, still does not reveal how 'Ali Jifun and his company were allowed to participate at Handoub in the first place. For this, there is but a single campaign memoir, detailing how "several of the men belonging to the Sudanese regiments of the garrison had brought their arms, and dressed in *gallabeas* [tunics] had mixed themselves with the Arab levies."[92] When Captain T. E. Hickman, second in command, brought this to Colonel Kitchener's attention, Kitchener is said to have replied, "Oh, Give them ammunition and say nothing."[93] And so it seems, if this source is to be believed, that it was upon their own initiative that the soldiers of the Sudanese "depot details" company of the Xth Battalion attached themselves to Kitchener's irregular forces at Handoub. It turned out a good thing for Kitchener that they did, for when his "friendlies" scattered in the face of a Mahdist counterassault, it was the Sudanese soldiers who held firm and effected an orderly retreat back to Suakin, suffering some forty percent casualties in the process.[94] According one British officer, a *bimbashi* named McMurdo, who was present at Handoub:

> It was during the retirement and for the second time that day that the old soldiers of the 10th shewed their sterling steady qualities and it is a recognised fact by us few British officers who were present at the affair, that had it not been for the gallantry and steadiness of the 10th we must have all been scuppered. As it was, the 10th with the rest of the little force, with ammunition practically finished, retreated helping their wounded and carrying their dead for about two hours along the Suakin road with a semi-circle of about 1000 dervishes harassing us. M.A. Ali Eff Gafoon ['Ali Jifun] was badly wounded in the leg just

after the retrograde movement commenced and I remember Shrawish [*sic*] Rehan Said of the Xth – taking command and doing yeoman service collecting ammunition for his men and keeping off the Dervish rushes. There is but little more to record. We reached Suakin about 11.30 a.m. after a very nasty time of it and I can only repeat that it was mainly due to the fighting qualities and steadiness of the old soldiers of the Xth that we were not annihilated and that a catastrophe was turned into a gallant retreat.[95]

'Ali Jifun in his memoirs likewise mentioned McMurdo, his command, and the leg injury he sustained during the fight: "I was in command of the detachment of Soudanese which had been left behind when the 10th Battalion marched across the desert to the Nile, and was wounded in the leg during the engagement. I should not have been able to get back, had it not been for the assistance of Bimbashi McMurdo, who, though wounded himself, took me up with him on his horse until I was out of danger." Later that year 'Ali Jifun was promoted *yuzbashi* and given command of the "No. 2 Company" of the XIIth Battalion.[96]

The Battle of Gemaizeh, though less revealing than Handoub in some respects, was perhaps more significant in that it was here one saw for the first time all four of the new Sudanese battalions in action at once. Indeed, at Gemaizeh they made up a majority of the infantry troops – four of the seven battalions deployed were Sudanese. And it was here also that Sudanese troops occupied the first and second lines of the army's attack formations, a combat precedent that would be followed in the River War. Dislodging the entrenched forces of Osman Digna "in the most gallant manner at the point of the bayonet," and killing some 500 of the enemy in the process, it was a complete rout of the Mahdist forces.[97] Only six Egyptian Army soldiers were killed, including a Sudanese soldier from the Xth Battalion, and forty-four wounded, among them fifteen Sudanese soldiers from the Xth and four from the IXth, one of whom, *nafar* Dein Breil, died from his wounds six weeks later. Among the list of officers, NCOs, and men mentioned in dispatches for admirable behavior at Gemaizeh, one again finds the venerable slave soldier 'Ali Jifun.[98]

It was in the summer of 1889, however, when the Khalifa 'Abdallahi's attempt to invade Egypt met with utter defeat at the Battle of Toski, that the Egyptian Army demonstrated how far it had come since Tel el-Kebir and Tamai. Unaided by British reinforcements (with the exception of a squadron of Hussars), the Egyptian Army killed some 1,200 Mahdist soldiers all told, and took some 4,000 of them as prisoners and deserters, suffering only 22 killed and 137 wounded in the process.[99] And this complete annihilation of the invading army, including the death of its leader 'Abd al-Rahman al-Nujumi, marked the beginning of the end for Mahdist regional hegemony, as well as the genesis of Anglo-Egyptian designs for reconquering the Sudan.[100]

As was the case at Gemaizeh, Sudanese battalions (the IXth, Xth, XIth, and XIIIth) played the key role in all of it, first in the action at Argin on 2 July 1889, and then in the decisive battle at Toski on 3 August 1889. In the case of the IXth Sudanese, among the forces that attacked al-Nujumi's position, the battalion "played a conspicuous role and practically decided the issue" according to its commander.[101] The soldiers of the XIIIth Sudanese, as well, including the aforementioned 'Abdallah 'Adlan, found themselves right in the thick of things at Toski, suffering over forty percent of the casualties of all those engaged – 15 killed and 53 wounded.[102] For their efforts at Argin and Toski, there were numerous promotions, decorations, and gratuities for Sudanese soldiers. And their numbers would soon rise, as many of the 4,000 prisoners and deserters were later enrolled into Sudanese battalions.[103]

Following the defeat of Osman Digna's forces at Tokar on 19 February 1891 – an action where the XIth and XIIth Sudanese battalions, along with the Fourth Egyptian Battalion, put an end to Mahdist pressure on Suakin – there followed a five-year interlude that separated the above-mentioned actions from the larger "River War" to come. During this combat hiatus between Tokar and the launching of the Dongola Campaign in 1896, it is interesting to note how often these Sudanese battalions were on the march, redeployed from one garrison to the next. Take, for example, the movements of the Sudanese IXth Battalion during these years. In the spring of 1891 the IXth was moved from Wadi Halfa to Aswan. In January 1892 it returned to Halfa for maneuvers, but was then sent back to Aswan within ten days following an influenza outbreak. In March of 1893 the battalion was marched across the Nubian Desert to Suakin, where it was stationed until the end of 1894. From Suakin it was sent to Tokar, where it stayed for a year before returning to Suakin toward the end of 1895. In March 1896 the IXth left Suakin for Wadi Halfa – 120 miles across the desert at one stretch, marching from the Red Sea (Kosseir) to the Nile (Qift) in four days – and remained there for two days before heading south to Akasha to join the Sudanese XIth, XIIth, and XIIIth battalions, already assembled for the advance on Dongola.[104]

The advance on Dongola had been ordered following Menelik's stunning victory over the Italians at Adwa on 1 March 1896 – which was to become both the spark and pretext for launching the "reconquest" of the Sudan. Ostensibly, the Anglo-Egyptian invasion of the Sudan was made to divert the attention of the Mahdists from Italian-held Kassala. But the underlying reason for its launch stemmed from French designs on the Upper Nile, and the understanding that it was to be but a first step in retaking the entire Sudan, long seen in military and political circles as inevitable.[105] Be that as it may, the Egyptian Army in March of 1896 was not the same one that fled the battlefield at Tel el-Kebir in 1882, or the same shabby force that Hicks Pasha led in defeat against the Mahdists in 1883. Following a decade of vigorous retooling, and matched by a string of victories along the Nile River and Red Sea Littoral, this new Egyptian Army – an army that now included six Sudanese battalions – was in a state of military strength and readiness that almost assured its success in the River War prior to a shot being fired.

Among those Sudanese soldiers assembled at Akasha that March were both 'Abdallah 'Adlan and 'Ali Jifun. In fact, 'Ali Jifun had anticipated the onset of the Nile Campaign for some time, as evidenced by his final reflection in "Memoirs of a Soudanese Soldier," recorded in late 1895. Looking back on four decades in the Egyptian Army, 'Ali Jifun told Percy Machell "though I am old in years, and have seen the sun go down in many parts of the world at the close of many weary days, yet I thank God that I have lived to hear the 'Advance' sound."[106] And with it, the long-expected reconquest was begun, Sudanese soldiers once again at the front line.

Notes

1. Francis Reginald Wingate to Julian John Leverson, 5 January 1890, Sudan Archive, University of Durham (hereafter cited as SAD), excerpt from fair copy of 252/2/3–10. Wingate was at this time a *kaimakam* in the Egyptian Army, and in charge of its intelligence office.
2. Archibald Hunter, for example, an Egyptian Army officer with long experience commanding Sudanese battalions, at times "engaged in flights of fancy…and dreamt of raising armies among Shilluk and Dinka people that would conquer all Africa," according to one of his biographers, all in order to, in Hunter's own words, "settle the hash of meddling French and Belgians and Germans and Portuguese and Dutch et les autres." Archie Hunter, *Kitchener's Sword-Arm: The Life and Campaigns of General Sir Archibald Hunter* (Staplehurst, United Kingdom: Spellmount Limited, 1996), 61.
3. Ian Shaw, *The Oxford History of Ancient Egypt* (Oxford: Oxford University Press, 2000), 120.
4. "Nubia" and "Nubian" are rather imprecise and fluctuating terms, referring to both geographical and ethnic origins. It may be more useful herein to consider its evolution into a more general term denoting black, enslaveable peoples than it is to try to pinpoint certain ethnic groups or regions on the map. For more on the above-mentioned "earliest precursor" and "same reasons," see William Y. Adams, *Nubia: Corridor to Africa* (Princeton: Princeton University Press, 1977), 137, 168. In line with Säve-Söderbergh, Adams argues that the primary use for Nubian slaves during pharaonic times was "to bolster the ranks of the Egyptian army itself." He also makes clear, supported by Bruce Trigger, that such bolstering fluctuated, depending on the time and place, between "voluntary recruitment" and "forcible enslavement."
5. P. M. Holt and M. W. Daly, *The History of the Sudan: From the Coming of Islam to the Present Day*, 3rd edition (Boulder, CO: Westview Press, 1979), 20; Andrew McGregor, *A Military History of Modern Egypt: From the Ottoman Conquest to the Ramadan War* (Westport, Connecticut: Praeger Security International, 2006), 13.
6. See R. S. O'Fahey and J. L. Spaulding, *Kingdoms of the Sudan* (London: Methuen & Co Ltd, 1974); Jay Spaulding, *The Heroic Age of Sinnar* (Trenton, NJ: The Red Sea Press, 2007); Janet J. Ewald, *Soldiers, Traders, and Slaves: State Formation and Economic Transformation in the Greater Nile Valley, 1700–1885* (Madison, WI: The University of Wisconsin Press, 1990).
7. McGregor, *A Military History of Modern Egypt*, 48–49, 67; Khaled Fahmy, *All the Pasha's Men: Mehmed Ali, His Army, and the Making of Modern Egypt* (Cambridge: Cambridge University Press, 1997), 79–82. As Khaled Fahmy has argued, Muhammad 'Ali's fascination with the French "seems to be overstated" and that at one point in 1822 the Pasha actually turned down a new organizational scheme "because it was blindly copying the structure of Napoleon's army," two weeks later ordering it to be redrafted "along the lines of Sultan Selim's army."
8. Fahmy, *All the Pasha's Men*, 85–86.
9. Richard Hill, *Egypt in the Sudan, 1820–1881* (London: Oxford Univ. Press, 1959), 25; Fahmy, *All the Pasha's Men*, 80, 86; McGregor, *A Military History of Modern Egypt*, 53.
10. For more on Muhammad 'Ali's reasons for the invasion, see Hill, *Egypt in the Sudan*, 7–8; Gérard Prunier, "Military Slavery in the Sudan during the Turkiyya, 1820–1885," *Slavery and Abolition*, April 1992, 129; Fahmy, *All the Pasha's Men*, 86–87.
11. Hill, *Egypt in the Sudan*, 8–13; McGregor, *A Military History of Modern Egypt*, 68–70, 74–75; Holt and Daly, *The History of the Sudan*, 49–53.
12. Robert O. Collins, "The Nilotic Slave Trade: Past and Present," *Slavery and Abolition*, April 1992, 141; Richard Gray, *A History of Southern Sudan, 1839–1889* (Oxford: Oxford University Press, 1961), 5; Hill, *Egypt in the Sudan*, 25; Prunier, "Military Slavery in the Sudan during the Turkiyya," 130–131.
13. Hill, *Egypt in the Sudan*, 25; Gray, *A History of Southern Sudan*, 3; Ahmad Alawad Sikainga, *Slaves into Workers: Emancipation and Labor in Colonial Sudan* (Austin: University of Texas Press, 1996), 16; Richard Hill and Peter Hogg, *A Black Corps d'Elite: An Egyptian Sudanese Conscript Battalion with the French Army in Mexico, 1863–1867, and Its Survivors in Subsequent African History* (East Lansing: Michigan State University Press, 1995), 7; McGregor, *A Military History of Modern Egypt*, 78–79.
14. Hill, *Egypt in the Sudan*, 26, 47. According to Hill, "The old military vocabulary was ransacked for suitable designations": *miralai* [commander]; *kaimakam* [lieutenant-colonel]; *bimbashi* [battalion commander; head of a thousand, "a term of long genealogy in the Ottoman army"]; *saghkolaghasi* [commander of the right wing; adjutant-major, "reflecting the French influence"]; *solkolaghasi* [commander of the left wing; "roughly the equivalent of the sous-adjutant-major"]; *yuzbashi* [company

commander; literally "the head of a hundred"]; *mulazim* [lieutenant]; *mulazim awal* [first lieutenant]; *mulazim tani* [subaltern].

15. Fahmy, *All the Pasha's Men*, 89–93; Prunier, "Military Slavery in the Sudan during the Turkiyya," 131; Sikainga, *Slaves into Workers*, 16; Hill, *Egypt in the Sudan*, 7, 25.
16. Turkiyya [*al-Turkiyya*] refers to the era of Turco-Egyptian rule in the Sudan from 1820–1885. For more on these early slave raids see Prunier, "Military Slavery in the Sudan during the Turkiyya," 134–135; Douglas H. Johnson, "The Structure of a Legacy: Military Slavery in Northeast Africa," *Ethnohistory* 36, No. 1 (Winter 1989): 77.
17. Ahmad Pasha enrolled the male slaves who survived the march back to Khartoum into the Egyptian Army. Collins, "The Nilotic Slave Trade: Past and Present," 141–143.
18. Prunier, "Military Slavery in the Sudan during the Turkiyya," 135; Johnson, "The Structure of a Legacy," 77; see also Richard Hill, *On the Frontiers of Islam: Two Manuscripts Concerning the Sudan under Turco-Egyptian Rule, 1822–1845* (Oxford: Clarendon Press, 1970), 41–42.
19. See Douglas H. Johnson, "Recruitment and Entrapment in Private Slave Armies: The Structure of the Zara'ib in the Southern Sudan," *Slavery and Abolition*, April 1992, 162–173; also see chapter two in Richard Gray's *A History of Southern Sudan, 1839–1889* (1961); Collins, "The Nilotic Slave Trade: Past and Present," 146–148; and Sikainga, *Slaves into Workers*, 12–15.
20. Percy Machell, "Memoirs of a Soudanese Soldier (Ali Effendi Gifoon)," *The Cornhill Magazine*, July 1896, 39–40.
21. G. R. F. Bredin, "The Life-Story of Yuzbashi 'Abdullah Adlan," *Sudan Notes and Records* XLII (1961): 37. 'Abdallah 'Adlan's father was the Sultan 'Adlan Badi of Jabal Bulli in the Fung.
22. Richard Hill, *A Biographical Dictionary of the Anglo-Egyptian Sudan* (London: Oxford University Press, 1951), 69.
23. Prunier, "Military Slavery in the Sudan during the Turkiyya," 135, 137.
24. A. C. Hope, "The Adventurous Life of Faraj Sadik," *Sudan Notes and Records* XXXII (1951): 154.
25. Prunier, "Military Slavery in the Sudan during the Turkiyya," 132–133; John P. Dunn, *Khedive Ismail's Army* (London and New York: Routledge, 2005), 25. It is difficult to know the total number of Sudanese troops serving in the Egyptian Army during the Turkiyya, but based on Gerard Prunier's estimates, it appears that the figure ranged from 5,000–9,000 at any given time. Of course, as he points out, there was often a substantial difference between "paper estimates" and the actual number of soldiers on active duty; for instance, examining an 1865 survey of armed forces in the Sudan he finds that of the 10,644 soldiers of the first four regiments, "that only some 2,600 men, roughly 26 per cent of the total number, were on active military duty."
26. Hill, *A Biographical Dictionary of the Anglo-Egyptian Sudan*, 125.
27. Sikainga, *Slaves into Workers*, 16; Hill, *Egypt in the Sudan*, 47, 86–87n; Dunn, *Khedive Ismail's Army*, 18. In terms of the Crimean War, although Hill rightly points out that "its Sudanese composition in 1853 is uncertain," Dunn has found a source describing "hideous Negroes from Nubia" as among the Egyptian forces arriving at Constantinople.
28. See Richard Hill and Peter Hogg, *A Black Corps d'Elite: An Egyptian Sudanese Conscript Battalion with the French Army in Mexico, 1863–1867*, 7, 116–117. It was believed that Sudanese soldiers, themselves originally from a region in Africa not unlike Mexico's *Tierra Caliente*, would be more resistant than European troops to the tropical diseases found inland of Vera Cruz.
29. Hill, *Egypt in the Sudan*, 120–121. General summaries of the above-mentioned military campaigns can be found in Andrew McGregor's *A Military History of Modern Egypt* (2006), 144–156.
30. The following biographical details and quotations are taken from Percy Machell, "Memoirs of a Soudanese Soldier (Ali Effendi Gifoon)," *The Cornhill Magazine*, n.s. 1 (July–October 1896): 30–40; 175–187; 326–338; 484–492. 'Ali Jifun told Percy Machell that his name "in my own country" was Lwaldeed [Lual Dit]. How he came to take on the name 'Ali Jifun is unknown, but it is used herein to avoid confusion, and as this was the name he used throughout his military career. The term "Effendi" is a Turkish honorific and denoted 'Ali Jifun's place within the hierarchy of Egyptian Army ranks; in general, it applied to educated persons literate in Turkish or Arabic.
31. Machell, "Memoirs of a Soudanese Soldier," *The Cornhill Magazine*, September 1896, 333.
32. The following biographical details and quotations are taken from G. R. F. Bredin, "The Life-Story of Yuzbashi 'Abdullah Adlan," *Sudan Notes and Records* XLII (1961): 37–52.
33. Bredin, "The Life-Story of Yuzbashi 'Abdullah Adlan," 40.
34. Ibid., 43–44.
35. Alfred Milner, *England in Egypt* (London: Edward Arnold, 1892), 174, 170. Alfred Milner, Under-Secretary for Finance in Egypt, devoted an entire chapter in his 1892 book *England in Egypt* on "The Fellah as Soldier."
36. See John P. Dunn's *Khedive Ismail's Army* (2005) for a more detailed analysis of these military failures

and underlying flaws in the Egyptian Army during Khedive Isma'il's reign. Also see chapters 10 and 11 of Andrew McGregor's *A Military History of Modern Egypt* (2006).

[37] F. R. Wingate, *Mahdiism and the Egyptian Sudan: Being an Account of the Rise and Progress of Mahdiism, and of the Subsequent Events in the Sudan to the Present Time* (London: Frank Cass & Co. Ltd., 1891), 206–208, 214–215, 219; *Handbook of the Egyptian Army* (London: Eyre and Spottiswoode, 1912), SAD 114/3, 12; Lieut.-Colonel Count Gleichen, ed., *The Anglo-Egyptian Sudan: A Compendium Prepared by Officers of the Sudan Government* (London: Printed for His Majesty's Stationery Office by Harrison and Sons, 1905), 252.

[38] McGregor, *A Military History of Modern Egypt*, 182; Holt and Daly, *The History of the Sudan*, 92.

[39] Wingate, *Mahdiism and the Egyptian Sudan*, 95–96.

[40] McGregor, *A Military History of Modern Egypt*, 181.

[41] Wingate, *Mahdiism and the Egyptian Sudan*, 219.

[42] Ibid., 220; Alfred Milner, *England in Egypt*, (London: Edward Arnold, 1892; London: Darf Publishers Limited, 8th ed., 1901, repr. 1986), 147. Citations are to the 1986 Darf edition; J. I. Wood-Martin, *IXth Sudanese Regimental Historical Records*, 1913, SAD 110/11/3–5.

[43] Wood-Martin, *IXth Sudanese Regimental Historical Records*, SAD 110/11/3.

[44] Ibid., 5–6.

[45] Ibid., 6–7.

[46] Milner, *England in Egypt*, 147, 149.

[47] Bennet Burleigh, *Khartoum Campaign 1898, or the Re-Conquest of the Soudan* (London: Chapman & Hall, Ltd., 1899), 2.

[48] P. M. Holt, *The Mahdist State in the Sudan, 1881–1898: A Study of Its Origins, Development and Overthrow*, 2nd edition (Oxford: Clarendon Press, 1970), 63, 65, 247; Robert S. Kramer, "Holy City on the Nile: Omdurman, 1885–1898" (Ph.D. dissertation, Northwestern University, 1991), 99.

[49] F. Grenfell to M. Fehmy, 23 November 1891, National Records Office, Khartoum, Sudan (hereafter cited as NRO), Cairo Intelligence File (hereafter cited as CAIRINT), 1/25/127.

[50] Milner, *England in Egypt* (1892 ed.), 202–203.

[51] Wingate, *Mahdiism and the Egyptian Sudan*, 222–225.

[52] Milner, *England in Egypt* (1986 ed.), 148; Wingate, *Mahdiism and the Egyptian Sudan*, 221.

[53] B. R. Mitford, "Extracts from the Diary of a Subaltern on the Nile in the Eighties and Nineties," *Sudan Notes and Records* XVIII, Part II (1935): 174.

[54] According to Milner, the strength of the Egyptian Army on 1 May 1892 was 12,547; it consisted of fourteen infantry battalions (depot battalion included), ten troops of cavalry, three field batteries, one garrison battery, and one camel corps, as well as staff, military police, medical corps, engineers, and transport companies. Milner, *England in Egypt* (1986 ed.), 154–155.

[55] Mitford, "Extracts from the Diary of a Subaltern," 181. "Nushi Pasha's steamers" had been sent from Khartoum by Charles Gordon in September 1884 to meet with the British Relief Expedition.

[56] F. Grenfell to M. Fehmy, 18 November 1890, War Office Minute Paper No. 291, NRO CAIRINT 1/25/127.

[57] Ibid.

[58] Burleigh, *Khartoum Campaign 1898*, 2; F. Grenfell to M. Fehmy, 23 November 1891, NRO CAIRINT 1/25/127.

[59] F. R. Wingate, 3 July 1886, NRO CAIRINT 1/25/127.

[60] F. Grenfell to M. Fehmy, 23 November 1891, NRO CAIRINT 1/25/127.

[61] Ibid.

[62] Wingate, *Mahdiism and the Egyptian Sudan*, 221n. This preference for recruits from the African interior was not unique to the Egyptian Army, and similar ideas prevailed in colonial armies elsewhere in Africa. According to David Killingray: "Ideal recruits, it was believed, were those from the 'bush,' men unsullied by exposure to Europen excesses, as were many coastal or urban Africans; these soldiers offered a *tabula rasa* upon which white officers could impose new patterns of behaviour and loyalty." David Killingray, "The 'Rod of Empire': The Debate over Corporal Punishment in the British African Colonial Forces, 1888–1946," *The Journal of African History*, Vol. 35, No. 2 (1994): 205.

[63] Machell, "Memoirs of a Soudanese Soldier," *The Cornhill Magazine*, August 1896, 175.

[64] "Anthropometric Investigations among the Native Troops of the Egyptian Army. – Interim Report of the Committee," *Report of the Seventy-Second Meeting of the British Association for the Advancement of Science, Belfast, September 1902* (London: John Murray, 1903), 351.

[65] Ibid. One finds a correspondent geographical and ethnic diversity amongst the Sudanese soldiers that followed Captain Lugard into Uganda in 1891, and those later recruited for the "Uganda Rifles" by Captain Thruston in 1894. F. D. Lugard, *The Rise and Fall of Our East African Empire: Early Efforts in Nyasaland and Uganda*, Vol. 2 (Edinburgh and London: William Blackwood and Sons, 1893), 217;

J. A. Meldon, "Notes on the Sudanese in Uganda," *Journal of the Royal African Society*, Vol. 7, No. 26 (1908), 125, 138–139; A. B. Thruston, *African Incidents: Personal Experiences in Egypt and Unyoro* (London: John Murray, 1900), 84–87; Douglas H. Johnson, "Tribe or Nationality? The Sudanese Diaspora and the Kenyan Nubis," *Journal of East African Studies*, Vol. 3, No. 1, March 2009, 116.

66 R. S. O'Fahey, "Fur and Fartit: The History of a Frontier," in *Culture History in the Southern Sudan: Archaeology, Linguistics, and Ethnohistory*, eds John Mack and Peter Robertshaw (Nairobi: British Institute in Eastern Africa, 1982), 75.

67 Yoshiko Kurita, "The Life of 'Ali 'Abd al-Latif," draft (Tokyo, 6 May 1996), 4–6; Elena Vezzadini, "The 1924 Revolution: Hegemony, Resistance, and Nationalism in the Colonial Sudan," (Ph.D. dissertation, University of Bergen, 2007), 216–217; see also Yoshiko Kurita, "The Role of 'Negroid but Detribalized' People in Modern Sudanese History," *Nilo-Ethiopian Studies*, No. 8–9, 2003, 1–11.

68 *Handbook of the Egyptian Army*, SAD 114/3, 55.

69 Bredin, "The Life-Story of Yuzbashi 'Abdullah Adlan," 39.

70 Contract for Soudanese of Volunteer Battalion, *Organization of Sudanese Battalions Egyptian Army, 1888–1889*, NRO CAIRINT 1/25/127.

71 Enlistment Certificate A, Soudan Battalions, *Organization of Sudanese Battalions Egyptian Army, 1888–1889*, NRO CAIRINT 1/25/127. The full certificate read as follows: "1. I agree to serve in His Highnesses Army as long as my services may be required, provided always that I can claim my discharge at any time after ten years service. 2. I understand that my pay will be one piastre a day, and that I receive free clothing and rations. 3. I understand that my pay will be increased to two piastres a day after two years service and to 2½ piastres a day after six years service provided my conduct has always been satisfactory. 4. I have no objection to being branded or marked as a soldier. 5. I understand that I have no claims on the Govt., if I am married, or, if I marry during my service without permission, and that only a certain number of N.C.Os and old soldiers of good conduct are allowed to marry and have their families with them."

72 H. L. Smith-Dorrien to Adjutant General, 28 August 1886, NRO CAIRINT 1/25/127.

73 F. R. Borrow to H. L. Smith-Dorrien, 17 September 1886, NRO CAIRINT 1/25/127; Smith-Dorrien to Adjutant General, 22 September 1886, NRO CAIRINT 1/25/127.

74 W. H. Besant to Brigade Major, 12 November 1889, NRO CAIRINT 1/25/127.

75 H. A. Macdonald to Brigade Major, 4 February 1889, NRO CAIRINT 1/25/127.

76 Smith-Dorrien to Adjutant General, 28 August 1886, NRO CAIRINT 1/25/127.

77 Smith-Dorrien to Adjutant General, 22 September 1886, NRO CAIRINT 1/25/127.

78 G. W. Steevens, *With Kitchener to Khartum* (New York: Dodd, Mead & Company, 1899), 12.

79 D. A. Donne, 14 March 1888, NRO CAIRINT 1/25/127.

80 D. A. Donne, 20 March 1888, NRO CAIRINT 1/25/127.

81 Enlistment Certificate A, Soudan Battalions, *Organization of Sudanese Battalions Egyptian Army, 1888–1889*, NRO CAIRINT 1/25/127.

82 Hill, *Egypt in the Sudan*, 138. It should also be noted that decades prior the British Army itself used branding to "mark certain prisoners (using tattoos 'BC' for bad character or 'D' for desertion)," and defended the practice for similar reasons – to prevent fraudulent re-enlistment and protect the public from criminals. Branding in the British Army was abolished in 1871. Edward M. Spiers, *The Late Victorian Army, 1868–1902* (Manchester and New York: Manchester University Press, 1992), 73.

83 Major Chapman to Lieutenant-Colonel Parr, 2 January 1886, Inclosure 1 from Egypt No. 4 (1887), Presented to the House of Commons by Command of Her Majesty (March 1887), NA FO 633/57.

84 Wood-Martin, *IXth Sudanese Regimental Historical Records*, SAD 110/11/11–14.

85 Wingate, *Mahdiism and the Egyptian Sudan*, 315–318.

86 Ibid., 318–319n.

87 Wood-Martin, *IXth Sudanese Regimental Historical Records*, SAD 110/11/16–17.

88 N. H. Hunter, *Historical Records of the Tenth Sudanese* (1886–1910), National Army Museum (hereafter cited as NAM) 1968-07-330-1, 9.

89 Wingate, *Mahdiism and the Egyptian Sudan*, 353.

90 Hunter, *Historical Records of the Tenth Sudanese*, NAM 1968-07-330-1, 6.

91 Machell, "Memoirs of a Soudanese Soldier," *The Cornhill Magazine*, October 1896, 491.

92 'An Officer,' *Sudan Campaign, 1896–1899* (London: Chapman & Hall, 1899), 7; this anonymous officer was in fact Harry Lionel Pritchard, who served in the Egyptian Army during the Nile Campaign.

93 Ibid.

94 Hunter, *Historical Records of the Tenth Sudanese*, NAM 1968-07-330-1, 9.

95 Ibid. Colonel Kitchener himself received a severe bullet wound in the face at Handoub; later that year he was appointed Adjutant-General of the Egyptian Army.

96 Machell, "Memoirs of a Soudanese Soldier," *The Cornhill Magazine*, October 1896, 491–492.

[97] Wingate, *Mahdiism and the Egyptian Sudan*, 366–367.
[98] Hunter, *Historical Records of the Tenth Sudanese*, NAM 1968-07-330-1, 13; Wood-Martin, *IXth Sudanese Regimental Historical Records*, SAD 110/11/20.
[99] *Staff Diary and Intelligence Report, Frontier Field Force*, No. 194, "Casualty Return of the Action of Toski, 3rd August, 1889," NA WO 106/15, 5.
[100] 'Abd al-Rahman al-Nujumi was the same Mahdist *amir* who had destroyed Hicks Pasha's army in 1883 and overwhelmed Gordon's troops at Khartoum in 1885.
[101] Wood-Martin, *IXth Sudanese Regimental Historical Records*, SAD 110/11/22.
[102] "Casualty Return of the Action of Toski, 3rd August, 1889," NA WO 106/15, 5.
[103] Wood-Martin, *IXth Sudanese Regimental Historical Records*, SAD 110/11/22; Hunter, *Historical Records of the Tenth Sudanese*, NAM 1968-07-330-1, 24.
[104] Wood-Martin, *IXth Sudanese Regimental Historical Records*, SAD 110/11/28–31.
[105] According to Lord Salisbury, British Prime Minister at the time, "The Cabinet decision was inspired especially by a desire to help the Italians at Kassala and prevent the Dervishes winning a conspicuous success which might have far-reaching results. In addition we desired to kill two birds with one stone and to use the same military effort to plant the Egyptian foot farther up the Nile." Salisbury to Cromer, 13 March 1896, The National Archives of the United Kingdom (hereafter cited as NA), FO 633/7/171, 110.
[106] Machell, "Memoirs of a Soudanese Soldier," *The Cornhill Magazine*, October 1896, 492.

2
"Servants of His Highness the Khedive"

At times, too, there are more tragic incidents. Thus after Ferkeh [Firket] a soldier of one of the black battalions told his white officer that he had recognized his own father among the enemy's dead. He did not seem much moved by the discovery, but said in a matter-of-fact way, "He was always a bad man, but then he was my father, so I think I should like to wash his body and bury it." Of course he was at once given leave to perform these last rites for the dead Dervish.

A. Hilliard Atteridge, *Daily Chronicle* correspondent[1]

The first engagement of the River War took place on 7 June 1896 at Firket, a village on the east bank of the Nile one hundred miles south of Wadi Halfa. That morning an army of some 9,000 Egyptian and Sudanese soldiers routed a Mahdist force one-third its size in a matter of two hours. Although it is not considered one of the major battles of the Nile Campaign, the action at Firket reveals something of the unique status and complex identity of the Sudanese slave soldier. Identity, of course, is an elusive concept, and the task of describing a collective identity an even more perilous undertaking, in this case doubly so for the dearth and provenance of sources.[2] Be that as it may, an examination of Sudanese soldier identity – and in the process, his social and historical condition – remains an undertaking worth the pursuit. If nothing else, such an inquiry will begin to shed light not only on who these men were and how they lived their lives, but also the African stage onto which they were ushered by the Scramble, recasting them as historical *dramatis personae* – with true agency and impact, hybrid identities and mutable loyalties – rather than nameless imperial collaborators known only by battalion number.

Sudanese soldiers & military slavery

First and foremost, there is an important caveat to be made regarding the term "slave soldier." Lifelong military service as a form of slavery has little relation to the plantation and domestic forms. Military slavery, akin to these others, does initially involve violence, "natal alienation," and "dishonoring," but in most other ways it is quite different from these more familiar types.[3] Questions surrounding the ongoing legal status of military slaves, for example, especially those related to manumission, are far less important than questions surrounding patronage. Moreover, opportunities for social and economic advancement, and the ability of domestic and agricultural slaves to "negotiate their conditions of servitude," pale by comparison to that of military slaves.[4] It has been argued elsewhere that "much of the confusion surrounding the nature of military slavery derives from the Muslim practice of calling these men slaves regardless of their actual circumstances."[5] Per this so-called "Islamicate" practice, a slave is simply "a person of slave origins," and thus military slave means "a soldier of slave origins." This is quite different from the English meaning of slave, or "true slave," which refers to "a person in a state of legal and actual servility."[6]

The Islamicate meaning of "slave" is certainly more apropos in the case of Sudanese soldiers than are Western definitions. For one, as previously discussed, the question of a Sudanese soldier's official status as being that of "slave" or "volunteer," regardless of British circumlocution, remained ambiguous throughout the nineteenth century. Although there were recorded instances of manumissions and "discharges" of Sudanese slave soldiers taking place – even prior to British reorganization of the Egyptian Army – both on an individual level and by whole regiments, this was by no means the norm, and ultimately had little effect on whether a soldier was considered by himself or others to be a "slave" or "slave soldier." Nor did these changes in status necessarily affect whether or not he was to remain a soldier for life. In fact, there were even cases where free men, as well as formally manumitted slaves, chose to become "slave soldiers," and often in the process "lost something of their free status."[7] Further adding to the confusion there is evidence that although still considered slaves, government-owned slave soldiers were seen as "free men," and a separate category from those slaves belonging to private individuals. There is a mid-nineteenth-century Italian manuscript, for example, that describes how prior to the administration of Ahmad Pasha, slaves "who were enrolled in the army were considered free men and received the honour of burial," whereas "slaves belonging to private persons but also the slaves of the government who had not been accepted for the army were thrown out to satisfy the hunger of wild animals."[8]

In the case of Sudanese slave soldiers perhaps a more useful conception of their manumission status is that of self-manumitted, or in the parlance of one scholar, "ipsimitted," by which it is meant that their true slave status withers away "as a matter of course," as their military role evolves.[9] Ultimately, according to this model, a slave soldier's condition as "true slave" is not a permanent one, and thus manumission becomes for him a matter of "fundamental insignificance."[10] For Sudanese soldiers in the new Egyptian Army this idea of "ipsimission" is well served, for it does seem that questions surrounding their legal status are largely moot, and far less important than their common slave origins, racial background, or evolving military role in the region. And although military officials at the time preferred to call these soldiers "volunteers," what becomes evident through the longer lens of history is that these men – some of them the same individuals, in fact – were part of a long existing, Northeast African institution of military slavery, one that Britain merely co-opted per its imperial agenda. And thus if one is to call Sudanese soldiers in the Egyptian Army during the Turkiyya "slave soldiers," and those fighting in the Khalifa's *jihadiyya* "slave soldiers," then one might just as well call those serving in the new Egyptian Army "slave soldiers" too. Its reorganization and improved conditions of service notwithstanding, in the new Egyptian Army one finds the continuities of this regional institution far greater than any differences in form or nomenclature.

Again, there is little to suggest that British commanders truly held that Sudanese soldiers were fully emancipated or possessed the same rights and freedoms as British or Egyptian troops. Nor did the Sudanese soldiers themselves, as suggested by the aforementioned instance when a British commander of a Sudanese battalion claimed that he had yet to come across a single soldier who ever questioned his enlistment period. This was probably because prior to 1903 Sudanese "volunteer" soldiers in the new Egyptian Army were enlisted "for life or until medically unfit," an unlimited period of service no different in practice from that of the old Egyptian Army.[11] In large part, these men were still treated as they had been for decades, as slave soldiers in service of the Khedive. And as a result, life in these battalions could still be violent, oppressive, and demeaning; the men were often flogged, in some cases branded, and deserters were executed. Thus to be a "slave soldier" in Egypt and the Sudan during the nineteenth century was always less about one's legal status as "slave" than it was about one's military and social status as "soldier."

"Ipsimitted" or otherwise, there is evidence that Sudanese soldiers often took pride in their status as slaves, and did not suffer much embarrassment at being labeled as such. Many of the Sudanese soldiers who fought in Mexico during the 1860s, for example, had or were given names directly associated with slavery, such as Bakhit (Lucky Gift), Marjan/Morgan (Coral), Almas (Diamond), and Baraka (Blessing), and even more clearly in some cases, names containing the actual word for slave (*al-'Abd*).[12] In a similar vein of unabashed self-identification, when Isma'il Aiyub, Governor-General of the Sudan, made it policy in the 1870s to brand slave soldier recruits from recently conquered Darfur with the Arabic letter *jim* (for *jihadi*, or regular soldier), "the men considered the brand so great an honour that Isma'il Aiyub got leave to brand all Sudanese recruits to the regular forces."[13] An examination of the English-Arabic Egyptian Army Lists and official dispatches from the 1890s does not immediately reveal as many slave-associated names. However, this may well have been a product of the gradual, sometimes cross-generational, ipsimission of these men – again the idea that a military slave's state of legal and actual servility, often expressed in a name or title, tends to wither away over time. Nonetheless, it is worth noting that one of the highest-ranking and most decorated Sudanese soldiers in the Nile Campaign was *saghkolaghasi* Murgan [Morgan] Mahmoud, whose name means Coral in Arabic, and indicates his slave origins. In any case, this phenomenon does suggest that when Sudanese soldiers saw themselves as slaves – and if so, in the Islamicate rather than Western sense – they were more often proud than ashamed of it.

Patronage, however, was far more important than manumission status for Sudanese soldiers in the Egyptian Army. In terms of the history of military slavery, this is not unusual. A patron, symbolized by a head of state or military commander, is often the glue that holds together armies of slave soldiers.[14] In exchange for loyalty and military service, this patron – the Khedive of Egypt in the case of Sudanese troops – provides his slave soldiers with food, shelter, and security, and many times, some form of payment. This patron may employ these troops as he wishes, wherever he wishes, and may even dispose or transfer them to another patron, as seen when Muhammad Sa'id Pasha loaned some four hundred and fifty Sudanese soldiers to French Emperor Napoleon III in 1863, or when Hermann von Wissmann of the German East Africa Company obtained six companies of Sudanese soldiers from Khedive Tawfiq during the Bushiri uprising in 1889. Slave soldiers, in turn, will remain loyal to this new patron so long as he provides for them; if and when he fails to do so, they are prone to transfer their allegiance to another patron.[15]

There are numerous individual and collective examples of this kind of loyalty and faithful service among nineteenth-century Sudanese soldiers, as well as these very types of patron transfers. In Captain Percy Machell's introduction to 'Ali Jifun's 1896 "Memoirs of a Soudanese Soldier," for example, he writes that when 'Ali Jifun lectured to recruits he would say: "Never think of yourselves, we are all the servants of His Highness the Khedive. Every order given is issued with a view to the advancement of the interests of the service, and must be instantly and cheerfully obeyed. Hunger, thirst, fatigue, wounds, death, are all necessary incidents in a soldier's life. But 'kul meri' (it is all for the Government), and every bugle-call must be obeyed alike." And in fact 'Ali Jifun's memoir itself concludes with the following line: "Effendimiz chok Yasheh! (May His Highness our Master live forever!) THE END." British propaganda purposes aside, 'Ali Jifun's words reveal both a deep allegiance to his patron, in this case the Egyptian Khedive Abbas II, and a firm commitment to serve and obey him "as long as my horse will carry me," as he put it.[16]

It was the loyalty of Sudanese slave soldiers to their patron, the Khedive, and the inherent benefits gained thereof, that came to play a key role in the reorganization of the Egyptian Army back in the mid-1880s. Following its formal disbandment in 1882, and with Mahdism on the rise, there were remnants of Sudanese regiments scattered throughout the region, in particular along the Red Sea Littoral at besieged and defeated Egyptian Army garrisons. It was in part their allegiance to the Egyptian government and the Khedive that led many of these men (including 'Ali Jifun) to Massawa, and eventually to Cairo for re-enlistment, or in some cases inspired them to hold out against the Mahdists "even when its cause was hopeless," rather than joining those forces or returning to their native villages throughout the Sudan.[17] And in the case of veteran Sudanese soldier 'Abdallah 'Adlan, he and his former Egyptian Army battalion members – conscripted into Mahdist military service under Osman Digna after the fall of Khartoum in January 1885 – even went so far as to effect a midnight escape, whereupon they were rescued, returned to Egypt, and reassigned.[18]

Sudanese soldier Faraj Sadik, as well, found his way back into the Egyptian Army under similar circumstances.[19] According to the life history he reported to

A. C. Hope, following his time stationed at Massawa in the early 1880s "rumours came of the rising of the Mahdi and we were ordered back to Khartoum." Faraj, a bugler, was on one of Abu Saud Pasha's boats sent to confront to Mahdi at Aba Island in 1881, and later served in Hicks Pasha's ill-fated 1883 Kordofan expedition. He and his company, along with one other, fled the battlefield at Shaykan and escaped to the Nuba Hills, later rejoining Egyptian Army troops garrisoned at Bara. Following an eight-month siege, Faraj and some fellow Sudanese soldiers joined a contingent of *bashi-bazouq* that defected to the Mahdi at El Obeid. A month later, however, he and eighteen of his brethren deserted the Mahdi, with intentions of returning to Bara. Along the road to Bara they were "caught by armed Kababish and taken to Kagmar," whence they were sold as slaves to a man named Hassan Abu Kort and taken to southern Egypt. Faraj then worked on an island between Bimban and Kom Ombo "watering Hassan's garden and irrigating his crops" until one night he and his comrades "stole on board" a British steamer on its way to Khartoum to relieve Gordon Pasha. According to his memoir, he then accompanied the relief expedition and its retreat, but was left at Abu Klea when his boat was sunk. Two weeks later, following a Mahdist attack, he and those who survived the battle fled to Korti, and eventually made their way to Ordi, Akasha, and all the way to Halfa. Upon his arrival at Halfa, Faraj Sadik was recruited into the new Egyptian Army, first posted with the Sudanese IXth Battalion, but later assigned to the XIth Battalion as a bugler.

There were also cases from this time period when former or serving Egyptian Army troops – Sudanese soldiers absorbed into Mahdist *jihadiyya* units or those stationed at remote garrisons in the Equatoria Province – expressed their continued allegiance and loyalty to the Khedive via open rebellion or resistance to patron transfers. From 1885–1887, for example, *jihadiyya* rebels at El Obeid staged an uprising against the Mahdist state, and even created "a sort of military republic" in the Nuba Mountains. Central to the mutiny was its declaration of allegiance to the Khedive, the installation of the Khedival flag, the playing of the Khedival salute, and its participants swearing by the Khedive's name.[20] In Equatoria, as well, one of the few provinces in the Egyptian Sudan with areas still outside Mahdist control in the late 1880s, scattered companies of Sudanese soldiers remained loyal to their Egyptian patron, and gave particular allegiance to his emblem, the Khedival flag. And in 1891 some six hundred Sudanese soldiers stationed at Kavalli, southwest of Lake Albert, resisted both the attempt by former provincial governor Emin Pasha to enlist them into German service, and at least initially, Frederick Lugard's plan to transfer them to the Imperial British East African Company (IBEAC). Indeed, the only way that Captain Lugard was in the end able to negotiate the transfer was by representing himself as an ally and agent of the Khedive, and his logical successor as new master and patron.[21]

However, in not all cases did Sudanese slave soldiers remain loyal to their Egyptian patron during those tumultuous and desperate times, when it was becoming clear that the Sudan would be evacuated by Egypt and abandoned to the Mahdists. Many of these soldiers transferred their allegiance, and their military services, to the armies of the Mahdi, Muhammad Ahmad, and later, to his successor, the Khalifa 'Abdallahi. But this fact in and of itself furthers the point as to the centrality of patronage among slave soldiers, and how in most cases this trumps nationalist sentiment and/or prior military allegiance. Besieged, unpaid, unfed, and finding themselves on the losing side, many of these Sudanese soldiers either made the choice to seek a new patron in the Mahdi, or were willing to accept him as one, at least temporarily, in the wake of military defeat and forced enlistment in his *jihadiyya*.

Even prior to the fall of Khartoum, following Governor-General Raouf Pasha's 1880 decision to disband several regiments for economic reasons, there were emancipated Sudanese soldiers who "knew no other trade" and "only needed a master," according to 'Ali Jifun, and who soon found "employment" in the Mahdi's growing army.[22] Over time, and following the Egyptian evacuation, the number of Sudanese soldiers serving as riflemen in the Mahdist *jihadiyya* grew, as did the degree of competition between the two regional patrons over these same men. Ironically, although again making the point in terms of patron allegiance transfers, it was to be many of these same Sudanese soldiers that once again changed sides during the Nile Campaign a decade later, rejoining the Egyptian Army when the tide turned against the Mahdists – either by desertion or following defeat in battle.

One last thing that distinguishes military slavery from other forms is its inherent potential for social and economic stability, even advancement. In the case of Sudanese soldiers in the Egyptian Army during the 1880s and 1890s, not only was there relative security and opportunities for advancement, but there were also privileges afforded them not granted to their Egyptian, and in some cases even British, military brethren. In fact, there were many distinct advantages to being a lifelong soldier in a Sudanese infantry battalion at this time in history, in this part of the world, as the Scramble for Africa continued apace. In general, these men were well provided for in terms of food, clothing, arms, shelter, and recreation. They were paid a steady salary, in fact a higher salary than were Egyptian soldiers, and could also receive both military promotions, and in some cases, pensions. Moreover, they were the only soldiers in the entire Egyptian Army, including British officers, who were allowed to have family lives while serving.[23] Not only were "harimat lines" built to house the wives and children of Sudanese soldiers in most Egyptian Army barracks, but these same women and children often became camp followers during military campaigns, fully sanctioned and sometimes supported by the army.

Like slave populations elsewhere in nineteenth-century Africa, the ascribed status of Sudanese soldiers revealed little about their overall social condition.[24] Yes, these men had originally been alienated from their "ties of birth" and perhaps "dishonored in a generalized way," unwitting victims of the slave trade ravaging the Sudan in the nineteenth century.[25] And one should not understate that original deracination, nor the view from that "slaving frontier" or wider power structures embedded within that slaving system.[26] However, it does seem evident that in their lifelong service in the Egyptian Army they were able to transcend this "social death" by assuming new identities, establishing new social ties, and creating for themselves new forms of honor, and agency; and that this unique and privileged status, in turn, engendered among them an *esprit de corps* and collective self-pride. The antithesis of slavery, as others have argued, is not necessarily freedom but belonging, and such was the case with Sudanese soldiers in the Egyptian Army – for theirs was a story not only of social death, but of social rebirth as well.[27]

The Times correspondent during the River War, E. F. Knight, described the unique status of the Sudanese soldier in late-nineteenth-century Africa, and interestingly enough – albeit imperial propaganda to some extent – made explicit mention of the various opportunities presented to him upon his "retirement" from the Egyptian Army:

> The blacks do not, like the Egyptians, serve for a stated period, but pass the greater portion of their lives in the ranks, and are only discharged when they become too decrepit for service. Their battalion is the only home they know; a large proportion of them are permitted to marry; and wherever a black battalion is stationed, there, too, is the *haremutt* set apart for the soldiers' families....A married soldier draws a daily allowance of one piastre and a half for his wife....The black troops are certainly as well cared for as any soldiery in the world, and when they have to leave their battalions as old men, various posts are found for them or they receive grants of land; there is a little colony of these retired veterans on the left bank of the Nile opposite Wady Halfa, and there is a large settlement of them on the Natron lakes, where their children find employment in the carbonate of soda works.[28]

In a later dispatch, however, Knight, much to his credit, reassessed the treatment of these same ex-soldiers, and provided a much less glowing account. He explained that the majority of former Sudanese soldiers received no pension whatsoever, and that most of them ended up without work, land, or any source of income. Nonetheless, the beginning of the passage further supports the notion that the social condition of Sudanese soldiers, while serving, was quite good in most respects:

> While in the regiment he is in many ways better treated than any soldier in the world; his pay is high, his rations excellent, he draws extra pay for his wife and family, and his life is a decidedly happy one. But when he is turned adrift after his long years of marching and fighting, a worn-out old man, incapable of work...he often drifts into abject poverty....Some of these old soldiers get employment as caretakers, watchmen, and so forth; others obtain grants of land; but I understand that for the vast majority of them no provision whatever is made by the Government. Thus it constantly happens that British officers, when walking in Cairo or other Egyptian towns, are accosted by broken-down old men in rags, who have fought gallantly under them in by-gone years, and who now appeal to their charity....It is to be hoped that the Egyptian Government will shortly see its way to abolishing this scandalous state of things by paying small pensions to those who have served it so well.[29]

There is certainly an argument to be made, as with other slave soldiers throughout history, that for the Sudanese soldier the "combination of cultural dissociation and personal dependence...obliterated the soldier's public personality."[30] Moreover, it could likewise be said that Sudanese soldiers, à la the Mamluks, "were not supposed to think, but to ride horses," and thus "were designed to be not a military elite, but military automata."[31] And no doubt heed should also be taken of the paradoxical nature of the Sudanese slave soldier in that although himself a "product of oppression, he helped to oppress."[32] On balance, however, it seems clear that these men were hardly "military automata," completely devoid of identity, agency, or even independence of thought. Nor were they simply an "instrument of repression" due to their "servile status and alien origin."[33] Indeed, rather than relying on resistor/collaborator and master/slave binaries or focusing on their role as imperial tools of oppression, it may be more useful herein and in the chapters that follow to pursue an alternative model – one that inquires more directly into the complexity and everyday reality of who they were and how they experienced their daily lives, and one that looks more closely at how "Sudanese soldiers" themselves "filled the term with social meaning."[34] In other words, although the Egyptians, and later the British, created the Sudanese soldier as its own military category, it also "took on a life of its own" over time through "daily practices, social markers, rituals, and institutions."[35] Moreover, this corporate identity that came into being – the shared mindset and manner of Sudanese soldiers – was not something entirely determined by their enslavers, recruiters, and/or patrons in Egypt and the Sudan, nor was it monolithic in form or a case of complete assimilation. Rather, it was in part their own creation, was of a hybrid nature, and on an individual basis was fluid in both form and practice. Like their "Chikunda" contemporaries in the Zambesi Valley, it was the Sudanese soldiers themselves that "coped with and creatively adapted to the rugged and often hostile social and physical environment in which they lived," and in so doing "created and reproduced new social and cultural institutions that provided order and meaning to their lives."[36]

Sudanese soldier identity

Before attempting to further unravel the conflicted and complex nature of their loyalties, or flesh out their conditions of service and daily lives, it may be worthwhile to begin speculating in a more general way as to the identity priorities of Sudanese soldiers. First and foremost, and at the risk of stating the obvious, they saw themselves as soldiers. There is little evidence, for example, that ethnicity or religion – though categories of identity that affected their lives – defined them as strongly as did their shared experience as soldiers in the Egyptian Army. Of course, tied in closely with this was their collective identity as "Sudanese" [*Sudani*], which at the time had racial, social, and geographical connotations – referring to "Blacks" from the southern Sudan, and associated with slave status. Further solidifying this "Sudanese" identity was the fact that the term, as alluded to above, had also become its own military category within the Egyptian Army; whereas battalions of Egyptian troops were referred to by number only (e.g., the 8th Battalion), all Sudanese battalions contained the "Sudanese" descriptive in their names (e.g., the XIIIth Sudanese). Moreover, it was not uncommon for a Sudanese soldier to actually have "Sudani" in his name (e.g., 'Ali el Sudani), and the identity tag shows up on Egyptian Army Lists as much as any other ethnic reference. In addition, and not unrelated, one is hard pressed to find incidents of ethnic segregation or inter-ethnic tension, for example, within Sudanese battalions, say, Shilluk soldiers living or messing separately from, or having conflicts with, Dinka soldiers while serving in the ranks. While

2.1 *Portrait of a Nuba officer, IXth Sudanese Battalion, Khartoum (possibly), taken between 1900 and 1902*
(Photographer: R. Turstig, reproduced by permission of Durham University Library)

there were no doubt cases where soldiers formed friendships within battalions, or companies, based on ethnic background or kinship ties, as well as instances where inter-ethnic relations were marked by rivalry and/or derision, in general this appears to have been subsumed by their common lot as Sudanese soldiers.[37]

Of course, it is important to note that this "supra-tribal" category of identity was invented by outsiders, and imposed on these soldiers. And yet, with its increasing use by the Turco-Egyptians, and later, its adoption by the British – aided by a common religion in Islam, and uniform patron in the Khedive – over time this constructed designation began to wither away some of the ethnic affiliations that may previously have defined and/or divided these men, and the label took on a life of its own.[38] Embraced by these soldiers, "Sudanese" thus became not only a military classification, but an enduring identity and social status as well, both in the Sudan and throughout the region. In fact, one sees this quite clearly in the case of diasporic Sudanese soldiers used in the conquest and pacification of East Africa, whether it be those recruited by Captain Lugard to further British interests in Uganda, Sudanese "askaris" serving in the Schutztruppe in German East Africa, or those enlisted in the King's African Rifles in Kenya. No mere amalgamation of mercenaries, these men and their descendants maintained a distinctly Sudanese soldier culture and identity – speaking Ki-Nubi, practicing Islam, and following social customs brought with them from the Sudan. And the continued affiliation of these Sudanese, or "Nubis," with the military, along with the social status that often came with it, persisted well into the twentieth century.[39]

2.2 IXth Sudanese at Wau displaying regimental flags c. 1912
(From a photo album of Major E. D. Bally, in the possession of Douglas H. Johnson)

In any case, for nineteenth-century Sudanese soldiers, it is clear that with this overriding "Sudanese" identity also came a great deal of pride and confidence in one's own fighting abilities, and in one's battalion. B. R. Mitford, for example, in his diary extracts wrote how "the IXth became very smart and proud of themselves as being distinct from the brigade."[40] This martial swagger, combined with the unique – and in some cases privileged – status held by Sudanese soldiers, engendered in them both an individual loyalty to the army, and on the battalion level a collective *esprit de corps* that formed the basis for reasonably contented lives serving in the military. Evidence to this effect can be found not only in contemporary accounts of the River War, but also in the many soldier portraits and posed battalion photographs from this time period.

One of the more revealing of these descriptions comes from H. L. Pritchard, in which he recalls an "amusing incident" that took place in the days following the 1897 Battle of Abu Hamed. Colonel H. A. Macdonald, commanding officer of the Sudanese brigade, who had "soundly rated the men who began the independent firing without orders," was awakened one night by a Sudanese soldier and told: "My battalion is very sorry that you are angry with them for firing without orders at Abu Hamed, but we know best what to do, we have been fighting since we were boys, we know the Dervishes, and we know the best way to turn them out of a place, so just you leave things to us, and we'll pull you through." The memoir goes on to say that the soldier "then turned about, and was outside the courtyard before Colonel MacDonald recovered from his surprise and exploded."[41]

Even British officers sometimes conceded that they had much to learn from the Sudanese soldiers under their command. General Hunter, reminiscing about the early years of the IXth Sudanese Battalion, once wrote: "They taught the

Egyptian Army to fight. We British officers, were in truth their pupils in many ways and not their instructors except in discipline."[42] One further example of such tutelage occurred in 1889 prior to the Battle of Argin, when according to B. R. Mitford: "I had two 3-barrelled Nordenfelds, and on my making a position for them at one corner [of the Omda's house], which had a good field of fire, I was checked by an old Shilluk for doing so, as he said that the dervish would be sure to make for the corner of the fort, and then the machine-guns would jam: whereas three or four men would be ever so much safer, and then there were their bayonets. There was a lot in what he said."[43] Again, these anecdotes speak not only to the pride and self-esteem of Sudanese soldiers, but also to their long military experience in the region.

Of course, confidence in their own fighting abilities – not to mention their patronal allegiance and shared identity – may also have stemmed from what has been referred to as a "martial race syndrome."[44] In effect, some of these so-called martial traits and abilities among Sudanese soldiers, and the belief in their existence, were a product of long-term Egyptian and British recruitment policies and "the combination of marginality and dependency" faced by these men upon enlistment, and later, while serving in the ranks: "Once brought into armies both their ethnic and martial distinctiveness are encouraged and exaggerated, giving them a 'vehicle for gaining respect, legitimacy and protection in the larger social order of which they are now, albeit reluctantly, a part.' Thus it was that the peoples of the slave frontier of the Sudan, with their different languages and cultures, became part of a 'martial race' which was identified and maintained as such by a succession of different (and even competing) states."[45]

One sees the possible manifestations of this kind of "martial race syndrome" among Sudanese soldiers time and again in campaign accounts. The following excerpt is rather typical: "The blacks of the Sudanese...have the true soldierly spirit, take a pride in their honourable profession, and are keenly jealous of the reputation of their particular battalions."[46] Likewise, and in respect to the all important "courage under fire," there are the following words, revealing on multiple levels, ascribed to Sudanese soldiers by River War correspondent G. W. Steevens: "For 'we,' they say, 'are like the English; we are not afraid.'"[47] Such "soldierly spirit" and aspired to fearlessness seems to have indeed served Sudanese troops as a "vehicle for respect" and "legitimacy," and during the Nile Campaign it formed the basis for a marked degree of mutual respect and martial kinship between British and Sudanese soldiers.

The above notwithstanding, it would be a mistake to characterize Sudanese soldiers simply as contented, assimilated, and loyal troops, without further examining some of the complexities inherent in this identity given the circumstances in 1896. For Sudanese soldiers making their way up the Nile and back into the Sudan that spring and summer, it must have been the oddest of homecomings, a time of conflicting emotions and challenged identities, an imperial encounter deeply layered in questions of empire, religion, race, and ethnicity. First of all, these men were soldiers in the Egyptian Army, their patron being the Khedive of Egypt, who himself, it must be remembered, remained under Turkish suzerainty. This made them, albeit indirectly, agents of both Egypt and the Ottoman imperialism. Second, having converted to Islam upon their enrollment, they were Muslims, marching side by side with other Egyptian and Sudanese Muslims, yet were serving under and alongside white Anglo-Christian officers and soldiers, and fighting against fellow Muslims in the Mahdists. Moreover, some of these enemy combatants (specifically, those in the Khalifa's *jihadiyya*) were "Sudanese," and from their own ethnic groups and home villages, sometimes even from their own families. Still others among the Khalifa's army were "Arabs" from the very ethnic groups that had originally captured, sold, and enslaved them, and who saw *Sudani* as their racial inferiors. Third, here they were, many of them back in the Sudan for the first time in several years, in some instances, in towns and villages – and among friends and family – they had perhaps not seen since becoming Egyptian Army soldiers, and whose inhabitants perceived them in some cases as liberators, in other cases as invaders.

Of all the improbable "homecomings" one sees during the River War, there is perhaps none more incredible than that of 'Ali Jifun. To recap, he was born at Fashoda around 1836, was captured by the Baggara at about age twenty-three, and then handed over as a slave to the governor of Kordofan Province. Around 1859 he was enrolled into the Egyptian Army, and spent the next four decades serving in Sudanese infantry battalions. During this time he fought in countless battles throughout Northeast Africa, and even spent four years in Mexico as part of the Sudanese contingent sent to assist the French Army from 1863–1867. In September of 1898, 'Ali Jifun returned to his place of birth for the first time in some forty years, now a *saghkolaghasi* and member of Kitchener's armed flotilla on the day of the Fashoda Incident. What his initial perceptions of Fashoda were – this once familiar place, these once familiar Shilluk – one can only imagine, but the scene that took place, and the reaction of the Shilluk to 'Ali Jifun and he to them, was described by others who were there, including the keen observer Bennet Burleigh of the *Daily Telegraph*:

> [T]he natives watched the proceedings with great interest. In fact, as many of the soldiers of the 11th and 13th Soudanese battalions were Shilluks, there had been numerous greetings and interchanges of courtesy between them. The worthy old Lieutenant Ali Gaffoon, a Shilluk, who had been in his youth a sheikh and soldier, and who had fought in Mexico for Maximilian, and since entered the Khedive's service, soon had crowds of his countrymen and countrywomen flocking to see him....
>
> The fraternisation of the Soudanese soldiers and the Shilluks became thorough. An informal reception of the natives, sheikhs, and headmen, some of whom were attended by their wives, was held by the Sirdar ashore and afterwards on board the "Dal." It was observed that, although hundreds of natives were seen, they were only brought forward in batches of less than a dozen to be presented. Besides, a considerable interval always elapsed before the arrival of the succeeding groups. Ali Gaffoon and his countrymen-comrades in the ranks, with pardonable tribal pride, were adverse to bringing their relatives and friends forward until the natives put on some clothes. For that purpose they had borrowed or got together about a dozen Arab dresses of kinds, wherewith to cover the bodies and limbs of the unsophisticated Shilluks....When the Sirdar ascertained the true cause of the delay, time pressing, he intimated he would waive for the nonce their putting on of ceremonial attire. "Let them all come as they are," and they did. They evinced the liveliest interest and pleasure in all they saw and heard in camp and aboard ship.[48]

Although 'Ali Jifun was warmly received by the Shilluk at Fashoda, in so many ways he was an entirely different person than he had been forty years earlier. He had been socially reborn as a slave soldier and Muslim, with deep-rooted loyalties to the Khedive of Egypt and to his battalion. He had spent decades assimilating to the military culture of the Egyptian Army, and had over these many years formed completely new social and familial ties. In short, he had a new identity. And his new identity priorities – his company, the XIIth Sudanese, the Egyptian Army, Islam – trumped the bonds of ethnicity and/or kinship. The reception described by Burleigh demonstrates this fact, for among other things, 'Ali Jifun, and it seems many of his fellow Shilluk soldiers, had adopted Muslim ideas about the inappropriateness of nudity. And perhaps he now saw his own people and customs in a rather different light than he had prior to his years of military service.[49] In fact, one British officer who was at Fashoda that day, Captain Andrew Murray of the Cameron Highlanders, even noted in his diary that he doubted the Shilluk soldiers "cared much to be back in their native country."[50] And so perhaps it should come as no surprise that 'Ali Jifun, though at the time in his early sixties and with the River War concluded, soon returned north to his battalion's base camp at Berber, where it is said he died from an infection only a few months later.[51]

And yet there is no true way of knowing – and more challenging yet, reconstructing – the ambiguities of thought and emotion present in the minds of Sudanese soldiers during the Nile Campaign. Unfortunately, of the few Sudanese perspectives that do exist, surprisingly little is revealed as to how they actually felt or thought about what they were experiencing. Nonetheless, there are some clues as to how these men negotiated the sociocultural challenges and contradictions inherent in their task as reconquerors of the Sudan. First and foremost, one finds that Sudanese soldiers did what soldiers are trained to do, that is, follow commands and engage the enemy, regardless of outside circumstances or individual concerns. As a rule, Sudanese soldiers were extremely reliable in this regard, and did not concern themselves with geopolitics, pan-Islam, and/or racial and ethnic solidarity.

By all accounts, they followed orders and fought, and fought bravely, engaging the enemy – regardless of who was fighting on the other side – with the same kind of blind obedience and zeal that had earned them a reputation as the "backbone of the Egyptian army." As 'Abdallah 'Adlan was to say of his conduct at the Battle of Firket, when he and his battalion came up against a Habbani *amir* who happened to be one of his mother's relatives, "I was a soldier in the service of the Khedive and had to fire like all the rest."[52] 'Ali Jifun, although referring to his service in Mexico in the 1860s, likewise recalled in his memoirs, "Soldiers ordered on service do not generally trouble their minds much about who their enemy is to be or why there is to be war, and we were no exception to the general rule."[53] And this appears to have been the case even when the Sudanese soldier in question had just recently switched sides. The following two excerpts from published campaign accounts are fairly typical in their description of this latter phenomenon:

> These black riflemen, though, ready to fight well under any master, care nothing for Mahdism, and were quite ready now…to enlist at once in the black battalions of the Khedive whom they had been fighting five minutes before, and in whose ranks they had so many of their own relations and friends. The Sudanese black loves fighting for its own sake, and fights against his own brothers without harbouring the least ill-will, and without

feeling the slightest compunction. He is yet one of the kindliest creatures in the world when not engaged in battle, and he makes the best mercenary soldier in the world.[54]

Another strange feature to European minds about these black ex-dervishes was, that once they had donned the Egyptian uniform, they were remarkably faithful to their new leaders. Desertions were rare, and there was never any hesitation upon their part to prove to the Mahdists that they had learned much, and were far better soldiers than their late dervish comrades and relatives. In battle they never hesitated to use lead or steel against brothers or fathers.[55]

Be that as it may, these descriptions, presumably shaped by Victorian attitudes to race, are simply interpretations, and no doubt underestimating the emotional and intellectual capacity of the so-called "Sudanese black." Fighting against your former military brethren and witnessing the gruesome battlefield deaths of old friends and acquaintances, some of whom were from your own village or ethnic group, in some cases relatives and family members, could not have been easy, regardless of how much time had passed and/or one's professional bearing as a loyal and obedient soldier. Some evidence as to the emotional ambivalence and anguish that Sudanese soldiers must have felt in these instances does emerge from the sources, as evidenced by this chapter's lead quotation. Indeed, that very incident, where a Sudanese soldier came upon his own father among the enemy dead after the Battle of Firket, was noted by another contemporary observer, E. F. Knight of *The Times*: "Similar strange meetings occurred over the whole field. A man of the 9th battalion found his father lying dead among the enemy."[56]

The ambivalent nature of the loves and loyalties of Sudanese soldiers was also manifest in other kinds of scenes that took place in the wake of battle. The same black soldiers who during combat "never hesitated to use lead or steel against brothers or fathers," as reported above by Burleigh, also "invariably sought to save the lives of all their own people."[57] Perfectly capturing the push and pull of these conflicted loyalties and emotions are the following two incidents described by E. F. Knight following the Battle of Firket:

> I witnessed a curious incident. No sooner did one of these prisoners appear above the bank, holding a woman by the hand, than one of our Sudanese soldiers gave a loud cry of joy, and would have rushed out of the ranks had he not been forced back into his place by an officer. He had recognized a near relation whom he had not seen for years....Again, when the men of the 10th battalion were attacking the enemy's riverside position, they were set to clear a hut held by a number of desperate men, who fired on them from the loopholes with considerable effect. At last nearly all the defenders were killed and the few survivors surrendered and came out, among them a big black who, no doubt, up to that moment had been doing his best to kill as many of our men as possible; but as soon as he appeared a soldier laughingly ran forward and put his arms about his neck; then several others, recognizing in him an old friend whom they had not seen for years, welcomed him, their faces beaming with pleasure, and there was a general embracing all around.[58]

Above and beyond these battlefield reunions with enemy relatives and old friends, one also finds several instances of more general fraternizing between Sudanese soldiers and Mahdist prisoners of war:

> One result of this presence of ex-Mahdists in the Soudanese battalions is that, once the fight is over, the black soldiers, who have been foremost in the slaughter, are the readiest

to fraternise with and perform little acts of kindness for the prisoners. Many a drink from a water-bottle, many a cigarette, did the captured Dervishes receive as they passed by the ranks of a Soudanese battalion, and with these courtesies came endless inquiries about friends on both sides.[59]

Unfortunately, it was not revealed whether this kind treatment accorded ex-Mahdists was a product of the Islamic concept of *umma*, or whether it differed greatly according to the race and ethnic group of the prisoner. One wonders, for example, if Sudanese soldiers, say from Dar-Nuba, would have provided cigarettes to the Baggara Mahdists, regardless of their shared faith, considering the latter's prominent role in the Kordofan slave trade. In fact, according to war correspondent E. F. Knight, "They hate the Baggara, for very good reasons, and were they not carefully kept in hand would give the men of that tribe no quarter, and would kill the wounded outright, regarding them, and rightly so, as noxious reptiles."[60] And so one might guess that these instances of fraternization and "little acts of kindness" were in part facilitated by the Muslim notion of *umma*, yet mainly took place between soldiers of like races and ethnicities.

In any case, these same *Sudani* prisoners of war – who themselves, in some cases, had been in the old Egyptian Army prior to the rise of Mahdism, and who must have themselves felt somewhat conflicted – were swiftly incorporated into the Sudanese battalions they had just met in battle. These new recruits, in turn, became recruiters and ambassadors themselves. The effect was well recognized by officers in the Egyptian Army:

> Ahmed Bey urged with reason that to advance, as he suggested, on Abu Hamed with black troops would have a very good effect. For then the black soldiers of the Khalifa, who have never been Mahdists at heart and are now very disaffected, seeing the men of the Sudanese battalion, men of their own blood, many of them their relations and friends, entering the country, would refuse to fight them, and would seize the first opportunity to desert to us. The Mahdi, and the Khalifa after him, always fully appreciated the fighting value of these gallant Sudanese blacks, and knew well that they formed the backbone of the Egyptian army.[61]

The positive effects of Sudanese soldiers being part of the conquering Anglo-Egyptian army were not limited to the recruitment of ex-Mahdists. Although there were many inhabitants of the northern Sudan who stood to gain something by the overthrow of the Khalifa and his Baggara ascendancy, and one must be mindful of contemporary sources and their political purposes, there is anecdotal evidence that much of the civilian population – especially in Nubia and among the Ja'aliyyin – welcomed Kitchener's forces with open arms, and were particularly enthusiastic at the sight of Sudanese battalions. Many, like *The Times* correspondent E. F. Knight, cast the populace as "delighted" and "rejoicing":

> The inhabitants were evidently delighted to see the invaders, for they knew that once the Egyptian army was between them and their Dervish oppressors they had nothing more to fear. The men clapped their hands and shouted, the women uttered the shrill lu-luing which is with these people the song of rejoicing, and even the little naked children piped their welcome to us. The people showed complete confidence in the troops, whose conduct is indeed admirable. Fondness of children is a striking trait of the Egyptian character, and both fellahin and blacks are exceedingly kind to them. Thus, while on this march, the good-

natured soldiers were filling up the hands of the little children with the biscuits they themselves could ill spare. The marching to the front of this fine force, in such high spirits, confident of victory, was a sight to be remembered.[62]

The above references to the Baggara, as well as that of the "disaffected" black soldiers of the Khalifa, beg further investigation, for one sees within them the possibility that an additional motive was at play in the minds of Sudanese soldiers – vengeance. For one, many among the enemy were from the same ethnic groups, and in some cases were the very same individuals, who had been responsible for their original enslavement. And though Sudanese soldiers may have come to embrace their new lives in the Egyptian Army, this does not mean that they no longer harbored animosity toward their original captors and subsequent enslavers – the same men who led the *ghazawat* into their homelands, killing and enslaving their relatives and family members, and even in some instances the very same men who had yoked them, marched them north, and sold them in one way or another into the ranks of the Egyptian Army. In fact, Charles Neufeld, the German merchant who spent twelve years a "prisoner of the Khaleefa," made this very point in defense of Sudanese soldiers that did not spare wounded Mahdists after the Battle of Omdurman:

> There was not a man in the Black Battalions who had not, by the old Law of Moses, the laws of his country in which he was then fighting, the law of the Prophet, and the religious law, irrespective of the law handed down from the remotest ages, more right to take a life on that day than any judge in a civilized country has to sentence to death a man who has personally done him no wrong. Every man there was entitled to a life in retaliation for the murder of a father, the rape of a mother, wife, daughter, or sister, the mutilation of a brother or son, and his own bondage.[63]

Thus one can understand, on a certain level, how in the minds of Sudanese soldiers there may have been some old scores to settle. And the same can be said of the aforementioned "disaffected" black Mahdist soldiers, many of whom had themselves been captured by the Mahdists and enlisted into the Khalifa's army. It is arguable that the overall conditions of service for Sudanese soldiers in the *jihadiyya* were not on par with that of their brethren in the new Egyptian Army. Kept in relative isolation at the al-Kara garrison to the south of Omdurman proper, the *jihadiyya* occupied the lowest position in the Mahdist socio-economic hierarchy, and were regularly used as slave laborers in service of the state – cutting wood, collecting straw, hauling bricks, constructing fortresses, and working at the dockyard.[64] As well, and especially while on campaign, the *jihadiyya* were often discontented with their irregular pay and meatless rations.[65] And so there may indeed have been good cause for them to be disaffected, and perhaps good reason for them to want some payback when the tide began to turn against the Mahdists. Lastly, many of these Sudanese soldiers in the Egyptian Army, in addition to having the original grudge of enslavement, had more recent scores to settle, and vengeance on their minds stemming from fights between them and the Mahdists in the years leading up to the River War.

'Ali Jifun, the old Shilluk veteran, hints at this when he writes in early 1896 that "I know when we meet our old enemies again we shall mow them down as a reaper cuts his barley at harvest time."[66] Likewise, among the songs of Sudanese soldiers that were transcribed in the 1920s by D. Hay Thorburn were two that dated from the nineteenth century. The first, "from Dervish times," was translated into English as follows: "To-day, this day of days, we are all gathered together in one place, strong young warriors, and maidens; soak the men in blood, drive away the backs of the enemy."[67] The second, "dating from the time of the Nile Expedition," was a marching song that went: "Birds, birds of war. (*Chorus*) When the steamer comes. Birds, birds, eat. (*Chorus*) When the steamer comes. Vultures, eat. (*Chorus*) When the steamer comes."[68]

Even British soldiers who fought alongside Sudanese troops were aware of the additional motivation their black comrades had in fighting the Mahdists, as evidenced by the following letter excerpt from a Seaforth Highlander named Tom Christian: "Each brigade slept in a square – one British, one Egyptian, two Soudanese. The latter are splendid-looking men, 5 ft 10 in to 6 ft high, and quite anxious to fight the Dervishes, who have carried off their relations into slavery."[69] However, by far the strongest anecdotal evidence that vengeance was part of the story comes from the memoirs of Babikr Bedri, who was in Omdurman in the days immediately following the final defeat of the Mahdists in September 1898:

> That night a soldier who had been a slave of Ibrahim Bey al-Ya'qubabi's came to the door of his house and called him by name. When Ibrahim came out to him he thought he had come to guard him and his family, so he welcomed him and was about to shake his hand; but the soldier shot him dead, and watched him wallowing in his blood. Then his family and the neighbors came out and found the soldier, who had been known to them since childhood, trampling with his boots on the stomach of the corpse; and all went in again and hid themselves, fearing death; and the soldier went off.
>
> Another incident I saw myself. I and some of my relations who were my guests had left my house to visit Muhammad walad Abbashar, who had been in the Karari battle. As we reached the south-eastern corner of the market we saw a Negro soldier leading a slave-girl by the hand, coming out of the market by the gallows, (east of where the post office is now). Then we saw Ibrahim Tamim the merchant from Aswan (who seemed to be the slave girl's master) running after them; and when he had caught them up he seized hold of the girl's hand, to take her back with him. The soldier at once loaded his rifle and shot him, and he leapt up in the air and fell to the ground – we saw it from less than 200 metres away. Then the soldier took the girl's hand again, and they went away laughing loudly. When we asked about it we learnt that the slave-girl had been Ibrahim Tamim's concubine, and that the soldier was her brother, and that both had been born in his house.[70]

This aspect of the River War did not go unobserved by British soldiers and correspondents, and it appears to have been more than anecdotal in nature. Lieutenant Angus McNeill of the Seaforth Highlanders, for example, wrote in his journal that following the Battle of Omdurman: "The Soudanese troops and Jaalin friendlies committed the most fearsome atrocities all night and murdered, pillaged etc. over the whole of the town. Many hundreds of Baggara were killed and I fear a lot of peaceful Jaalins."[71] And although in large part a propaganda piece depicting both the symbolic end of Mahdism and the devoted, albeit "fanatical," nature of the *ansar*, there was an illustration printed in the British newspaper *The Graphic* entitled "The Fight for the Khalifa's Standard" that also suggested a certain degree of cold revenge and retribution – not simply reconquest for the sake of reconquest – as an underlying motive on the part of Sudanese soldiers who fought against the Mahdists at the Battle of Omdurman.[72]

2.3 "The Battle of Omdurman: the fight for the Khalifa's standard"
(J. Gulich from materials supplied by Frank Rhodes, *The Graphic*, 24 September 1898)

This campaign denouement, as symbolic and seemingly unlikely as it may appear on pages of a British newspaper, actually took place and was documented by countless eyewitnesses. In fact, there are descriptions of similar scenes taking place all over the battlefield, and this very same incident was again depicted two weeks later in another British newspaper, *Black & White*, and entitled "Last Stand of the Khalifa's Standard-Bearer."[73] Interestingly, in this second illustration, though in silhouette and of dubious targeting, it appears that the Sudanese soldiers inflicting the symbolic *coup de grace* to Mahdism – and, at least theoretically, slavery in the Sudan – are shooting at the black flag guardian from behind, "in the back," so to speak.

Of course, British commanders and statesmen, not to mention correspondents, may have had ulterior motives for highlighting, indeed propagating, enmity between Sudanese and Mahdist troops. Certainly, by casting black "ex-slaves" in the Egyptian Army as an avenging force, it would appeal to anti-slavery advocates in Egypt and Britain, who had been actively trying to end the slave trade in Sudan for decades. And yet, above and beyond its symbolic appeal for the anti-slavery movement, such divisions may have been accentuated for reasons related to persistent British fears of pan-Islamic sentiment in Egypt and the Sudan. By emphasizing the military role that Muslims, be they Sudanese or Egyptian, were playing in the campaign against the Mahdists, the British may have been trying to respond to pan-Islamic propaganda brewing in Egypt at the time, and in so doing mitigate the kind of Muslim "fanaticism" they feared might someday undermine their control of the country. Evidence to this effect can be found in a 12 April 1898 letter from Lord Cromer, de facto ruler of Egypt at the time, to the British Prime Minister, Lord Salisbury, following Kitchener's "Good Friday" victory at the Battle of Atbara:

> I think it may interest Your Lordship to know that, although the news of the recent victory in the Soudan has been received with real satisfaction by almost all classes in Egypt, whether European or Native, these sentiments are by no means shared by the ultra-Mahomedan coterie which exists in some of the towns in Egypt, notably in Cairo. The representatives of this small party ignore the fact that the Dervishes confound Turks, Egyptians and Christians in one common feeling of enmity, as well as the further fact that Mahomedan troops – notably the black regiments of the Egyptian army – took a distinguished part in the recent action. They only look to one point, and that is that an army composed partly of Christians and partly of Moslem troops officered by Christians has defeated an entirely Moslem force. This they regard as a disaster to Islam....
>
> However this may be, it is, I venture to think, as well to take note of the sentiments which the recent victory has evoked amongst the Pan-Islamic party in Egypt....In dealing with all Egyptian questions it is as well, therefore, to remember that in this, as in all Moslem countries, there is a good deal of fanaticism latent, which occasion may evoke and which, were it allowed to get the upper hand, even temporarily, would speedily wreck the civilising work of the last few years.[74]

This fear of pan-Islamic, anti-British sentiment in Egypt and Sudan did not disappear following the Nile Campaign. In fact, it was such a concern that it greatly influenced both administrative policy and military deployments in the Anglo-Egyptian Sudan for years to come. As part of an effort to keep any and all Muslim or "pseudo-Mahdist" influences out of southern Sudan during the Condominium years, for example, over time the British reorganized Sudanese battalions into "territorial units," made up of locally recruited, non-Muslim troops.[75] By "getting rid of the Moslemizing influence in the shape of Egyptian Officers and fanatical Sudanese N.C.O's, and very gradually dropping the Moslem conditions which prevail in all Sudanese Battalions," British officials also hoped to limit the spread of Egyptian nationalism within the ranks, and remove the conflict of loyalty Sudanese soldiers had to the King of Egypt.[76] Moreover, such measures were intended to mitigate the growing perception among southern Sudanese that their British overlords were no different from those of the Turkiyya and Mahdiyya periods.[77] This creation of "territorial units" as a means to impede the spread of Islam in the southern provinces of the Anglo-Egyptian Sudan, of course, was only one part of what some have considered a "Southern Policy," in which *jallaba* were excluded from the southern provinces, Christian missionaries were allowed to proselytize and teach English to southern Sudanese, and where the learning of Arabic and "Arab" dress was discouraged in Western Bahr al-Ghazal.[78]

Whether and to what extent Sudanese soldiers may have seen themselves as avengers, or liberators, or dare one suggest, makers of a new Sudan – it is impossible to know with any certainty from the available sources. Equally scarce are any clues as to how these soldiers may have perceived the ongoing geopolitical and imperial tumult that was late nineteenth-century Sudan, or how pan-Islamic and/or anti-British sentiments (or anti-"Turk" sentiments, for that matter, which for inhabitants of the Sudan meant all light-skinned outsiders) may have affected how they felt about their Mahdist enemies or Egyptian and British overlords. Be that as it may, there is an anecdote in 'Ali Jifun's memoirs that seems to indicate there was a sense among Sudanese soldiers something greater was at stake, and that the military defeat of the Mahdists was a necessary – if not fated – step that would lead to a more stable, and perhaps even more independent, future for the Sudan and its people. In the form of a prophecy 'Ali Jifun heard from Sayyid Hassan al-Mirghani of Kassala sometime in the 1870s, it provides at least some indication as to how these soldiers may have framed recent Sudanese history, and perhaps justified their role in it.

Albeit translated by a former British officer and published for a Western audience at the outset of the Nile Campaign, the historical prescience of al-Mirghani, grandson of the founder of the Khatmiyya *tariqa* [Sufi religious order], is striking.[79] Even if one were dubious about 'Ali Jifun's ex post facto retelling of the prophecy to Captain Machell, it is quite remarkable that it was published in 1896 yet clearly foresaw the exact location and outcome of the 1898 Battle of Omdurman:

> The burden of the Morghani's prophecies was that evil times were in store for the Soudan. He warned us all 'El marah illi towlid ma takhodhash' (Take not unto thyself a wife who will bear thee children), for a crisis is looming over the near future of the Soudan, when those who wish to support the Dowlah, or Government, must fly, and they will be lucky to escape with their lives *[Egyptian 1884–1885 evacuation of the Sudan]*....
>
> ...The flame of fitna or insurrection would not first appear in the Soudan, but the fire would be kindled in Egypt itself *[Arabi's 1879 revolt and anti-European riots in 1882]*. Then the whole Soudan would rise *[Mahdism of the early 1880s]*, and the people would not be appeased until the land had been deluged in blood and entire tribes had disappeared off the face of the earth. The work of re-conquest and re-establishment of order would fall upon the Ingleez, who, after suppressing the revolt in Egypt, and gradually having arranged the affairs of that country *[1882 Battle of Tel el-Kebir and subsequent British military presence in Egypt]*, would finally occupy the Soudan *[1896–1899 Nile Campaign and subsequent Condominium]*, and would rule the Turk and the Soudanese together for a period of five years....The English regeneration would place the Soudan on a better footing than it had ever been on before...The final struggle for the supremacy in the Soudan would take place on the great plain of Kerrere, to the north of Omdurman; and pointing to the desert outside Kassala, which is strewn with large white stones, he said: 'After this battle has been fought the plain of El Kerrere *[Karari; 1898 Battle of Omdurman]* will be strewn with human skulls as thickly as it is now covered with stones.'[80]

Of course, Sayyid Hassan al-Mirghani's five years turned into fifty-six in the case of the Anglo-Egyptian Sudan. Nonetheless, the prophecy, genuine or not, obviously served 'Ali Jifun, and perhaps other Sudanese soldiers, as a way to make sense of the "evil times" they had lived through, and as a means to psychologically deal with the violence and chaos of events that seemed beyond their control – both those in the past, and those yet to come.

Sudanese soldier Bakhit Mwafi

Of all the incidents and anecdotes emerging from the River War, perhaps none is more layered in the above complexities of identity and history than the reunion of sorts that took place between Bakhit Mwafi and Babikr Bedri in the streets of

Omdurman on 2 September 1898. Bakhit Mwafi was a *bashshawish* in the XIIIth Sudanese Battalion, Babikr Bedri, a merchant of Rubatab extraction. Earlier that day, Babikr Bedri had fought in the Khalifa's army under the Black Flag, and in the wake of defeat had made his way from the Karari battlefield back into Omdurman proper. He was leaving his brother's house when he ran into some soldiers of the XIIIth Sudanese Battalion sitting in al-Hijra Street. Having himself lived in exile in southern Egypt for almost two years following his capture and imprisonment – after participating in al-Nujumi's failed invasion of the country in 1889 – Babikr "knew many of them from my days in Aswan."[81] He inquired with these soldiers about a particular Sudanese *bashshawish* whom he had once met in Aswan in 1890 while out of prison but still in exile – Bakhit Mwafi. One of them led him to Bakhit Mwafi, who upon seeing him:

> ...embraced me and said, "Isn't this wonderful? Two hours ago we were enemies fighting each other; and now we are two friends greeting each other!"
> "Praise be to God for His blessings," I replied.
> He saw my sword, which I was carrying on my shoulder, and said, "Better give me that sword, and I will keep it for you. Perhaps the army will be made free of the city, and a sword like that might get lost." I gave it him.[82]

According to Babikr Bedri, Omdurman was indeed "turned over to the soldiers" for three days of looting. Late on the third day three Sudanese soldiers entered his house "and began to take everything they could find – copper, beads, money, ornaments and animals."[83] However, Bakhit Mwafi happened to be in the neighborhood, and when Babikr ran and told him that he was being looted, Bakhit Mwafi "came round quickly, and we...

> met them at the outer door, loading their loot on a she-ass and on their heads. When they saw us they were taken by surprise and put all the booty down. They let the she-ass go and she ran straight back to her pasture. They began to make excuses for themselves to the Sergeant-Major, who demanded of each man his name, number and regiment. They now displayed a servile humility, very different from the brutal arrogance which they had shown on entering the house. Nevertheless, I began to mediate between them and the Sergeant-Major. But he would have none of it, because they had over-stepped the time limit during which the town was declared open to them, as they very well knew. I continued to press him to let them off. However, he ordered them to put everything back in place and after seeing to this personally, he took them off and I don't know what he did with them. He sent two soldiers from the post to guard us against anyone who might knock.[84]

A couple of weeks later, according to Babikr, his sword was returned to him by Bakhit Mwafi.

If this were the entire story, it would stand on its own as quite an incredible and curious incident. However, when one considers the entire backstory as to how these two men first met, the relationship becomes an even more intriguing and nuanced picture of Sudanese soldier identity and social condition – highlighting the kinds of power, privilege, and agency he often possessed and wielded, as well as raising questions surrounding race, religion, marriage, and family. Moreover, it serves as an important caveat to overstating the vengeance theme already noted.

Back in 1890, while still living in exile but free to move about and work as a tradesman within Egypt, Babikr Bedri was on his way back to al-Ramadi after a trip to Cairo when he heard that his cousin al-Rawda bint Muhammad "had been married off to a Negro soldier" and was living with him in Aswan.[85] Color prejudice and anti-miscegenation sentiment among northern Sudanese meant that such a marriage – between an "Arab" woman like al-Rawda bint Muhammad and a *Sudani* man such as this soldier – was considered a disgrace to Babikr and his family, and regardless of the fact that the soldier was a converted Muslim. And so upon his return to al-Madani, Babikr Bedri, accompanied by a "go-between" named Amina, set off to Aswan "determined to go there and get her away." According to Babikr Bedri, when he got to Aswan his cousin "did come to me and promise quite definitely that she would come with me to al-Ramadi." However, the following day fortunes changed when al-Rawda bint Muhammad invited Babikr to her house for lunch; while she was in the kitchen her husband, whose name was Bakhit Mwafi, came in to her and said "I've told Wodehouse Pasha, and he'll put both Babikr and Amina in prison." Soon a policeman showed up and took Babikr Bedri and his cousin before Wodehouse Pasha. According to his memoirs, the following conversation took place:

> "Is it you who have come for this girl?"
> "Yes," I said. "Both her father and her mother are my first cousins."
> "Is that true?" he asked the girl.
> "Yes," she said, "and he's a friend of my uncle's, too."
> "Will you go with him," asked the pasha, "or will you stop with your husband?"
> "I'll stop with my husband," she replied.
> The pasha laughed, and said to me, "She doesn't want you!"
> "Nor do I want her," I said angrily, and her husband led her away. I went away disappointed, and found a boat to take me to al-Ramadi.

One final and interesting footnote to the story is that when Babikr Bedri got back to al-Ramadi, his chief patron at the time, a rich northern Sudanese expatriate named 'Abdallah Bey Hamza (the same man who had told him before leaving for Aswan that al-Rawda bint Muhammad would not come back), proceeded to call him a fool, and mocked him by saying: "Once the girl has had a taste of the slave's lusty cock, why on earth should she leave it and try yours?" Babikr then responded by saying, "No doubt she was created for the slave's cock, and it for her. What's more, she's young, and was forced to it; so she has her excuses."

First and foremost, this incident and its 1898 postscript well demonstrate the unique status of Sudanese soldiers in the Egyptian Army, as well as some of the contradictions and complexities inherent in the lives and loyalties of these men. To begin, and revisiting some of the definitional questions that opened this chapter, it is worth noting that there is an ambiguity as to the slave status of Bakhit Mwafi, one that supports an "Islamicate" definition that a slave is simply "a person of slave origins," and not, in line with its Western connotation, "a person in a state of legal and actual servility." Although Bahkhit's British commanding officer may have seen him as an "ex-slave," and he was on the books as a "volunteer," it is clear that northern Sudanese such as Babikr Bedri and 'Abdallah Bey Hamza still saw him as a slave, or *abd* in Arabic, and referred to him as such in conversation, which colloquially in the Sudan, it should be noted, was often an indicator of one's race and enslaveable status more than it was one's slave origins. As well, both men resorted to stereotypical notions as to Bahkhit Mwafi's sexual prowess and lascivious nature, all of this despite the fact that he was a respected soldier in the Egyptian Army, was married, and apparently lived in his own house. In addition, his very name, Bakhit, means "Lucky Gift," and indicates quite clearly his slave origins. The fact that he kept this slave name even after he was enlisted, and later promoted *bashshawish*, may also show that Bakhit Mwafi self-identified as a slave. If nothing else, it suggests that he was not ashamed or embarrassed by his ascribed status, as Western conceptions of slavery might expect to be the case.

What is clear is that his ambiguous manumission status had little to do with his social condition. Slave or not, Bakhit Mwafi's position in the Egyptian Army gave him power, prestige, and in this case, the agency and recourse to resolve his dispute with Babikr Bedri by legal means, and with the backing of the local authorities. To what extent she "was forced to it," and regardless of what rights she may or may not have had to leave her husband, the marriage between Bakhit Mwafi and al-Rawda bint Muhammad was seen as legitimate in the eyes of Wodehouse Pasha, as evidenced by his very consideration of the case. Moreover, there is clearly the suggestion that should Babikr Bedri attempt to circumvent Wodehouse's authority, he would be arrested and serve time in prison. Eight years later, when the Anglo-Egyptian army arrived in the city of Omdurman, again it is Bakhit Mwafi who was in the position of power, and whose status, and benevolence, saved Babikr Bedri's house from being looted.

Whether it be on an individual basis, as shown in Bakhit Mwafi's case, or manifested collectively, as occurred periodically in the form of revolts and mutinies within Sudanese battalions, what is clear is that these men were often shapers of their own destinies, and indeed the Sudan's future, rather than simply historical victims or imperial pawns. The other thing the above anecdote demonstrates is the multi-layered character of Sudanese soldier identity, and the contested and complex nature of his loyalties during the Nile Campaign. On the one hand, Babikr Bedri and Bakhit Mwafi are contrary, oppositional figures, and one would expect them to be sworn enemies: Babikr Bedri was a northern Sudanese "Arab" and follower of the Mahdi, a longtime soldier in the Khalifa's army, and the same man who several years earlier attempted to abduct Bakhit Mwafi's wife because he saw this "Negro soldier" as a racially inferior marriage partner for his cousin; Bakhit Mwafi, meanwhile, was a *Sudani* soldier in the invading Egyptian Army, who had no doubt killed in battle many of Babikr Bedri's Mahdist brethren, and who in the eyes of Babikr had disgraced the family when he "forced" himself upon his cousin al-Rawda bint Muhammad (whom Babikr may have intended to marry himself if one is to read into 'Abdallah Bey Hamza's words upon his return from Aswan).

And yet, both men were Muslims, soldiers, and fellow survivors of war, not to mention cousins-in-law, once removed. Interestingly, at least in the mind of Bakhit Mwafi – for whom some resentment toward Babikr Bedri, and perhaps even a desire for payback, might be expected – it was these latter categories (religion, war, and family) that turned them from enemies to friends in the course of two hours following the battle, and outweighed all those things that divided them (supplemented, in part, by Bakhit's adherence to a code of military ethics, or at least, an adherence to the ground rules for looting established by his commanders). For Babikr Bedri in 1890 Aswan this had not been the case, however, as the question of race clearly trumped any notions of family or belief in the Muslim *umma*.

By way of conclusion, and returning to the core identity priorities of Sudanese soldiers, there are the following words of Colonel D. F. Lewis. At the end of his association with the Sudanese IXth after the 1899 Battle of Gedid, Lewis was asked to sum up his experience leading them on campaign. Although reeking of Anglo-paternalism, his description does succinctly capture something of their military allegiance, collective pride, and martial spirit:

> I cannot give you at first hand much of the distinguished service of the old "Tisagis" – the lightest in hand of any Corps I have ever met. I have recorded on a separate sheet a series of notes, but events are long past, but what has not passed is the keen sense of pleasure in looking back to the glorious days when I was with them. Their spring – their sense of duty and fitness – their delightful braced up breeches and high rolled puttees – their daily tender kindliness to myself – I loved them very much and do still. On the occasion of the operations ending at Gedid, we had hard marching and little water. The 9th were once more pre-eminent, in tone, endurance, and dash.
>
> The characteristics of the Battalion as I knew it were:
> 1. An esprit de corps (Self sacrifice readily offered on its altar). There was nothing like it in the Egyptian Army or in few other armies.
> 2. An intense sense of duty, especially on guard.
> 3. A smartness peculiarly their own.
> 4. While men of men, a child like trust in their Bey, and in all their officers – but their whole obedience to the Bey before all the world.[86]

Notes

[1] A. Hilliard Atteridge, *Towards Khartoum: The Story of the Soudan War of 1896* (London: A.D. Innes & Co., 1897), 219.

[2] To make matters worse, the Egyptian Army command discouraged war correspondents from speaking with anyone but British officers, as evidenced by the following 1897–1898 bulletin that all journalists had to acknowledge and sign: "The attention of all newspaper correspondents is called to the fact that attemts [sic] to obtain information from native officers, non-commissioned Officers, & men as well as from Military telegraph clerks and Government employees are not allowed and will involve their informants in serious trouble." Signed correspondent bulletin, "Khartoum Expedition and the Battle of Omdurman," 1898, NRO CAIRINT 1/61/322.

[3] See Orlando Patterson, *Slavery and Social Death: A Comparative Study* (Cambridge, MA: Harvard University Press, 1982), 10–11. Although Patterson acknowledges – in a later chapter of the book and in reference to the slave *ghilman* of the Islamic world – that it "would be absurd to deny that there were indeed great differences [between *ghilman* and other slaves]," he hedges by stating that "in emphasizing the differences, the commentators often go to contradictory extremes" (p. 309), and argues that "while they may have been greatly honored by their doting masters, none of these slaves were in themselves honorable persons" (p. 331).

[4] Allen F. Isaacman and Barbara S. Isaacman, *Slavery and Beyond: The Making of Men and Chikunda Ethnic Identities in the Unstable World of South-Central Africa, 1750–1920* (Portsmouth, NH: Heinemann, 2004), 7.

[5] Daniel Pipes, *Slave Soldiers and Islam: The Genesis of a Military System* (New Haven: Yale University Press, 1981), 15.

[6] Ibid., 16.

[7] Douglas H. Johnson, "Sudanese Military Slavery from the 18th to the 20th Century," in *Slavery and*

Other Forms of Unfree Labour, ed. L. Archer, 142–156 (London: Routledge, 1988), 146. Johnson gives the case of a "free Masalit who joined the Egyptian army and then the Masalit sultan's own *jihadiyya*," and also writes that numerous "free Ja'ali and Danaqla also found themselves in a form of bondage in the armed merchant companies in the Southern Sudan."

[8] Hill, *On the Frontiers of Islam*, 41; also referenced in Hill, *Egypt in the Sudan*, 76n.
[9] Pipes, *Slave Soldiers and Islam*, 18–23.
[10] Ibid., 22.
[11] By comparison, for late-nineteenth-century British Army soldiers, "short service" had already been introduced, which meant that men enlisted for twelve years, spending only between three and seven years with the colours; the rest of their enlistment period was spent in the reserves. However, it is worth noting that in the late eighteenth and early nineteenth century, and during another span in the mid-nineteenth century, British "volunteers" also enlisted for life (from 1783–1806; and from 1829–1847). Byron Farwell, *Mr. Kipling's Army* (New York: W. W. Norton & Company, 1981), 81.
[12] Hill and Hogg, *A Black Corps d'Elite*, 11–12.
[13] Hill, *Egypt in the Sudan*, 138. And indeed the considered "honour" of being a slave was not a new phenomenon in the Sudan, as evidenced by traveler James Bruce's remark a century earlier that in the kingdom of Sennar, with its formidable army of slave soldiers, it was "the only true nobility." The full Bruce excerpt reads as follows: "Upon any appearance of your undervaluing a man at Sennaar, he instantly asks you if you know who he is? If you don't know that he is a slave, in the same idea of aristocratical arrogance, as would be said in England upon an altercation, do you know to whom you are speaking? Do you know that I am a peer? All titles and dignities are undervalued, and precarious, unless they are in the hands of one who is a slave. Slavery in Sennaar is the only true nobility." James Bruce, *Travels to Discover the Source of the Nile, in the Years 1768–1773*, Vol. IV (Edingburgh: Alexander Murray, 1813), 459, as quoted in Wendy James, "The Funj Mystique: Approaches to a Problem of Sudan History," in *Text and Context: The Social Anthropology of Tradition*, ed. Ravindra K. Jain (Philadelphia: Institute for the Study of Human Issues, 1977), 95.
[14] See Johnson, "The Structure of a Legacy," 76; Johnson, "Sudanese Military Slavery from the 18th to the 20th Century," 145–146; Sikainga, *Slaves into Workers*, 32, 58; Pipes, *Slave Soldiers and Islam*, 5–12.
[15] Richard Hill and Peter Hogg liken Sudanese slave soldiers to the *condottiere* of Renaissance Italy: "In brief, you faithfully serve the master or the government who employs, pays, and feeds you, so long as he is capable of doing so. When he is seen to be no longer capable, you transfer, along with your brothers-in-arms, to another master, another government." Hill and Hogg, *A Black Corps d'Elite*, 13.
[16] Machell, "Memoirs of a Soudanese Soldier," *The Cornhill Magazine*, July and October 1896, 31, 492.
[17] Holt, *The Mahdist State in the Sudan*, 16, 141, 180.
[18] Bredin, "The Life-Story of Yuzbashi 'Abdullah Adlan," 43–44.
[19] The following quotes and biographical details pertaining to Faraj Sadik's military career originate from Hope, "The Adventurous Life of Faraj Sadik," 154–158.
[20] Kurita, "The Role of 'Negroid but Detribalized' People in Modern Sudanese History," 3.
[21] Johnson, "Tribe or Nationality? The Sudanese Diaspora and the Kenyan Nubis," 114–115; see also Mark Leopold, "Legacies of Slavery in North-West Uganda: The Story of the 'One-Elevens'," *Africa: Journal of the International African Institute*, Vol. 76, No. 2 (2006), 186; Meldon, "Notes on the Sudanese in Uganda," 123.
[22] Machell, "Memoirs of a Soudanese Soldier," *The Cornhill Magazine*, October 1896, 484–485. Also referenced in Johnson, "Sudanese Military Slavery from the 18th to the 20th Century," 147.
[23] In terms of the British Army, since 1876 the married establishment for rank and file had been reduced on average to four percent; marriages "off the strength" notwithstanding, at the time of the River War it was still predominantly a bachelor army. Myna Trustram, *Women of the Regiment: Marriage and the Victorian Army* (Cambridge: Cambridge University Press, 1984), 48–49.
[24] See Jonathon Glassman, *Feasts and Riot: Revelry, Rebellion, and Popular Consciousness on the Swahili Coast, 1856–1888* (Portsmouth, NH: Heinemann, 1995).
[25] Patterson, *Slavery and Social Death*, 7, 10.
[26] See Wendy James, "Perceptions from an African Slaving Frontier," in *Slavery and Other Forms of Unfree Labour*, ed. Léonie J. Archer (London and New York: Routledge, 1988), 130–141.
[27] See Suzanne Miers and Igor Kopytoff, *Slavery in Africa: Historical and Anthropological Perspectives* (Madison: University of Wisconsin Press, 1977).
[28] E. F. Knight, *Letters from the Sudan* (London: Macmillan and Co., Ltd., 1897), 38–39.
[29] Ibid., 135–136.
[30] Patricia Crone, *Slaves on Horses: The Evolution of the Islamic Polity* (Cambridge: Cambridge University Press, 1980), 79.

31. Ibid.
32. Johnson, "Sudanese Military Slavery from the 18th to the 20th Century," 149.
33. Ahmad Alawad Sikainga, "Military Slavery and the Emergence of a Southern Sudanese Diaspora in the Northern Sudan, 1884–1954," in *White Nile, Black Blood: War, Leadership, and Ethnicity from Khartoum to Kampala*, eds. Jay Spaulding and Stephanie Beswick (Lawrenceville, NJ, and Asmara, Eritrea: The Red Sea Press, Inc., 2000), 24; Crone, *Slaves on Horses*, 74, 79.
34. See Allen F. Isaacman and Barbara S. Isaacman's recent model for studying the Chikunda in *Slavery and Beyond: The Making of Men and Chikunda Ethnic Identities in the Unstable World of South-Central Africa, 1750–1920* (Portsmouth, NH: Heinemann, 2004), 10.
35. Ibid.
36. Ibid., 7.
37. One interesting anecdote that reinforces the point regarding the overall harmonious nature of these relations yet also demonstrates the kind of ethnic ribbing that sometimes took place was reported by B. R. Mitford, a British officer with the Sudanese IXth: "The various tribes got on very well together; one never heard of one lot making a set against another. But they were fond of poking fun at the Nyam Nyams [Azande], and No. 3 Company had a song about 'The Nyam Nyam's wife wears no clothes,' but as the other ladies' walking-out dress was extremely scanty, it was almost a case of pot and kettle." Mitford, "Extracts from the Diary of a Subaltern," 181–182.
38. For more on the origins and distinctions of this *Sudani* "supra-tribal" identity, see G. P. Makris, *Changing Masters: Spirit Possession and Identity Construction among Slave Descendants and Other Subordinates in the Sudan* (Evanston, Illinois: Northwestern University Press, 2000), 23–50.
39. In fact, one still finds sizable "Sudanese" communities in East Africa, most notably the Kenyan "Nubis" of Kibera. For more on the Sudanese diaspora into East Africa and its links to Sudanese military slavery, see Johnson, "Tribe or Nationality? The Sudanese Diaspora and the Kenyan Nubis," 112–131; Leopold, "Legacies of Slavery in North-West Uganda: The Story of the 'One-Elevens'," 180–199; Johnson, "The Structure of a Legacy," 82–84.
40. Mitford, "Extracts from the Diary of a Subaltern," 184.
41. 'An Officer,' *Sudan Campaign*, 137.
42. Wood-Martin, *IXth Sudanese Regimental Historical Records*, SAD 110/11/26.
43. Mitford, "Extracts from the Diary of a Subaltern," 226.
44. Johnson, "Sudanese Military Slavery from the 18th to the 20th Century," 149.
45. Ibid. Johnson's reference to their distinctiveness being a "vehicle for gaining respect, legitimacy and protection in the larger social order of which they are now, albeit reluctantly, a part" is quoted from Cynthia H. Enloe, *Ethnic Soldiers: State Security in Divided Societies* (Athens, GA: The University of Georgia Press, 1980), 27.
46. E. F. Knight, *Letters from the Sudan*, 69.
47. G. W. Steevens, *With Kitchener to Khartum*, 91.
48. Bennet Burleigh, *Khartoum Campaign 1898, or the Re-Conquest of the Soudan* (London: Chapman & Hall, Ltd., 1899), 309–310. This same anecdote was also recorded by British officers H. L. Pritchard and Felix Ready: 'An Officer,' *Sudan Campaign*, 230–231; Felix Ready, diary, 11 October 1898, NAM 1966-09-142.
49. In terms of how the Shilluk "natives" perceived these Shilluk soldiers, there is evidence that they may have felt likewise. Natale Olwak Akolawin reported to Wendy James, for example: "The term *bwonyo* [non-black foreigners, the Arabs and Europeans] is also used to refer pejoratively to those who have assimilated *bwonyo* culture. Those Shilluk who had been taken into slavery or became soldiers in the Turco-Egyptian army and who took up Arab life and culture, and who came back as escapees, or after the fall of Omdurman in 1898, are known as *lui bwonyo* – escapees from *bwonyo*. The Shilluk despise them." James, "The Funj Mystique," 115.
50. Edward M. Spiers, *The Victorian Soldier in Africa* (Manchester, UK: Manchester University Press, 2004), 153.
51. Hill and Hogg, *A Black Corps d'Elite*, 148.
52. Bredin, "The Life-Story of Yuzbashi 'Abdullah Adlan," 47.
53. Machell, "Memoirs of a Soudanese Soldier," *The Cornhill Magazine*, August 1896, 184.
54. Knight, *Letters from the Sudan*, 297.
55. Bennet Burleigh, *Sirdar and Khalifa, or The Re-Conquest of the Soudan, 1898* (London: Chapman & Hall, Ltd., 1898), 213.
56. Knight, *Letters from the Sudan*, 134.
57. Burleigh, *Sirdar and Khalifa*, 213.
58. Knight, *Letters from the Sudan*, 127.
59. Atteridge, *Towards Khartoum*, 219.

60. Knight, *Letters from the Sudan*, 135.
61. Ibid., 77.
62. Ibid., 269–270.
63. Charles Neufeld, *A Prisoner of the Khaleefa: Twelve Years' Captivity at Omdurman* (London: Chapman & Hall, 1899), 285.
64. Kramer, "Holy City on the Nile: Omdurman, 1885–1898," 231–232.
65. Holt, *The Mahdist State in the Sudan*, 198; 'Ismat Hasan Zulfo, *Karari: The Sudanese Account of the Battle of Omdurman* (London: Frederick Warne, 1980), 96–97. Both Holt and Zulfo, however, indicate that the Sudanese soldiers recruited into the Khalifa's elite *mulazimin* forces received more regular pay and rations, and training, than other *jihadiyya*. As well, most of the *jihadiyya* in the *mulazimin* were "slave troops newly obtained from Fashoda and the borders of Mahmud Ahmad's governorate in the west," and thus were of less "dubious loyalty" than Sudanese soldiers formerly in the old Egyptian Army. And so perhaps they may have been less "disaffected" than other *jihadiyya*. Holt, *The Mahdist State in the Sudan*, 207; Zulfo, *Karari*, 95.
66. Machell, "Memoirs of a Soudanese Soldier," *The Cornhill Magazine*, October 1896, 492.
67. D. Hay Thorburn, "Sudanese Soldiers' Songs," *Journal of the Royal African Society* 24, No. 96 (July, 1925): 315.
68. Ibid., 316–317.
69. As quoted in Frank Emery, *Marching Over Africa: Letters from Victorian Soldiers* (London: Hodder and Stoughton, 1986), 163.
70. Babikr Bedri, *The Memoirs of Babikr Bedri*, vol. 1, trans. Yousef Bedri and George Scott (London: Oxford University Press, 1969), 240–241.
71. As quoted in *Omdurman 1898: The Eye-Witnesses Speak*, eds. Peter Harrington and Frederic A. Sharf (London: Greenhill Books, 1998), 146.
72. "Omdurman: The Fight for the Khalifa's Standard," 24 September 1898, *The Graphic*.
73. "The Last Stand of the Khalifa's Standard-Bearer," 1 October 1898, *Black & White*.
74. Cromer to Salisbury, 12 April 1898, NA FO 78/5049.
75. P. M. Holt and M. W. Daly, *A History of the Sudan: From the Coming of Islam to the Present Day*, 5th edition (Harlow, England: Pearson Education Ltd., 2000), 107–108; also see Sikainga, *Slaves into Workers*, 62.
76. Wingate to Crost, 1 March 1911, SAD 300/3/10.
77. Ibid. Wingate, who had succeeded Kitchener as Governor-General of the Sudan in 1899, went on to write that he was "personally convinced that the religious question has a great deal to do with our successful administration in these Southern districts, where the old idea of the Moslem slave-dealer, and that we are more or less the same people under another guise is undoubtedly prevalent." Indeed, a Shilluk *jago* [chief] named Airu told missionaries in 1899: "Master, you speak well. We had here the Turks and they said: Be submissive to us; we will protect you; we will fight your battles for you, we will teach you of God. But they took our cattle, destroyed our villages, and carried our women and children into slavery, and they are gone. Then came the Ansar and they said: Come with us, we have a great army; we will care for you and protect you; we will give you plenty to eat, and a good place to live; we have The Book and we will teach you of God. But they slew our men, and right here where these missionaries built their houses many of our men fell fighting for their women and children. They took away our cattle, destroyed our villages, carried off our women and children, and they too have gone. Now you come and say: We will care for you; we will protect you; we will fight for you; we have The Book; we will teach you. Master, you speak well, but we will see." J. Kelly Giffen, *The Egyptian Sudan* (New York: Fleming H. Revell Company, 1905), 120–121.
78. Holt and Daly, *A History of the Sudan*, 107–108. See also Lilian Passmore Sanderson and Neville Sanderson, *Education, Religion & Politics in Southern Sudan, 1899–1964* (London: Ithaca Press, 1981).
79. Sayyid Hassan al-Mirghani (al-Sayyid al-Hassan Muhammad 'Uthman al-Mirghani II, called al-Sughaiyar to distinguish him from his grandfather) was the son of religious leader al-Sayyid al-Hassan Muhammad 'Uthman al-Mirghani, and grandson of the founder of the Khatmiyya *tariqa*, al-Sayyid Muhammad 'Uthman al-Mirghani I (known as al-Khatim). Sayyid Hassan assumed the leadership of the Khatmiyya *tariqa* upon his father's death in 1869, and was very active in the Kassala area. During the Mahdist revolt in the 1880s, he remained loyal to Egypt and opposed the Mahdi. He died in Cairo in 1886, leaving two sons to succeed him, one of whom – Sayyid 'Ali al-Mirghani – *yuzbashi* 'Ali Jifun also mentioned in his "Memoirs of a Soudanese Soldier." Hill, *A Biographical Dictionary of the Anglo-Egyptian Sudan*, 157, 278–279.
80. Machell, "Memoirs of a Soudanese Soldier," *The Cornhill Magazine*, September 1896, 337–338.
81. Babikr Bedri, *The Memoirs of Babikr Bedri*, Vol.1, 239.
82. Ibid., 240.

[83] Babikr Bedri, *The Memoirs of Babikr Bedri*, Vol. 2, trans. Yusuf Bedri and Peter Hogg (London: Ithaca Press, 1980), 80.
[84] Ibid., 80–81.
[85] The details of this story, and quotes that follow, are taken from Babikr Bedri, *The Memoirs of Babikr Bedri*, Vol. 1, 117–118.
[86] Wood-Martin, *IXth Sudanese Regimental Historical Records*, 1913, SAD 110/11/50–51.

3
"Flavour of Domesticity"

True soldiers' spouses, these women always persisted in following their husbands to war. There was no military transport or supplies provided for them. Yet, though the track was long, and a bare desert, gathering their scant household gear together, mostly a few earthenware cooking-pots, and a goatskin or two filled with grain, wheat, dhurra, and beans, which they carried upon their heads, with their cotton cloths girt round their waists, barefooted, they set out after the army. Those who had babes too young to walk bore them upon their backs or shoulders, the elder children trotting by their moiling mothers' sides. Talk of courage! it was something of a sight to see these poor black women, with their households upon their pates and in their arms, bravely bearing their burdens in order to go campaigning with their husbands and lovers.

Bennet Burleigh, *Daily Telegraph* correspondent[1]

Sudanese soldiers who fought in the River War were well fed, well clothed, and well armed. They were regularly paid, were of relatively good health, and were the only soldiers in Kitchener's Anglo-Egyptian army allowed to have domestic lives. They were frequently given downtime during the campaign for recreational pursuits, religious life, and social gatherings. They even had opportunities for military advancement, and upon their retirement, were sometimes given pensions, civil administration jobs, or cultivable plots of land. Of course, it had not always been this way, especially during the Turkiyya, when military issue was more theoretical than real, when salaries were often many months in arrears, and Sudanese soldiers, according to 'Abdallah 'Adlan, "worked and served until they dropped."[2] And yet it is not so simple a dichotomy as this, for although in most ways the daily lives and conditions of service for Sudanese soldiers in the 1890s were better than they had been in the old Egyptian Army, in certain categories, such as military promotion, their possibilities were more limited. As well, British reorganization had not meant an end to forced marches through the desert, high Sudanese casualty rates, cholera outbreaks in camp, or the harsh, sometimes violent, disciplinary measures that these soldiers often faced. Ultimately, one finds that life in the Khedive's army during this time was much more of a mixed bag for Sudanese soldiers than the above generalizations suggest.

Pay, rations, clothing & arms

Sudanese soldiers who fought in the River War were not paid much compared to their British commanding officers or regular British soldiers attached to the campaign, or even in comparison to indigenous troops found elsewhere in the British Empire. However, their rates of pay were better than those of their Egyptian comrades, and far higher than they had been in the Egyptian Army prior to 1883. During the Turkiyya, Sudanese *anfar* in the Egyptian Army were paid anywhere from fifteen to twenty Egyptian piastres per lunar month (1 English pound = 97½ piastres).[3] According to 'Ali Jifun, when he was first enlisted in the late 1850s his pay was nineteen piastres a month; and in 'Abdallah 'Adlan's life-story it is reported that "regular soldiers were given twenty piastres a month and were paid in coins which got the name 'Abu Teir' as they had French eagles on them."[4]

These pay rates had changed little since the mid-1840s, when regiments paid privates fifteen piastres per month, a figure that itself dated all the way back to Muhammad 'Ali's *nizam al-jadid* of the 1820s. And despite inflation, the twenty piastres per month was to remain the pay rate for *anfar* through the 1860s and 1870s. Whatever the case, these payments were often more theoretical than real, and it was not uncommon for salaries to be months, sometimes even years, in arrears, or never paid at all. Indeed, this was a contributing factor in the July 1865 revolt at the Kassala garrison, when the salaries of Sudanese soldiers in the Fourth Regiment were six months overdue.[5] And one historian of Khedive Isma'il's army has suggested that some "Sudanese troops may not have been paid at all before the 1870s," pointing to explorer Emilius de Cosson's 1877 account in which the Governor of Khartoum bragged that "my men work for food, a few sweet dates and plenty of common tobacco."[6] In fact, it was not uncommon for Sudanese slave soldiers during the Turkiyya to pillage in lieu of payment, or be paid in kind, or be allowed to keep a percentage of the taxes they collected. An anonymous French manuscript from the late 1830s, for example, relates that troops in the Eighth Regiment were "paid in cloth, slaves, and camels, hardly ever in cash." And 'Abdallah 'Adlan, as well, describes how soldiers "who drew no pay during tax collection but lived on their share of the takings" would accompany tax-gatherers and receive one percent of the tax.[7]

With the reorganization of the Egyptian Army in the 1880s, rates of pay for *anfar* in Sudanese battalions were raised considerably. New enlistees were paid one piastre a day, and this per diem was to be increased to two piastres with two years of service, and then two-and-a-half piastres after six years of service; an increase at the three-month mark from one to one-and-a-half piastres was later added, and the length of service requirement for the two-and-a-half piastres was raised to ten years.[8] In any case, by the turn of the century forty-five percent of Sudanese privates were paid at the highest rate, the equivalent of seventy-five piastres per month, or nine Egyptian pounds annually – more than trebling the pay rate for privates in the old Egyptian Army. This was also a much higher rate than was paid at the time to Egyptian conscripts in the same army, two-and-a-half times higher. In addition, married Sudanese soldiers were given another thirty piastres per month as a Family Allowance. Most significantly, these payments were consistently met, were disbursed fortnightly, and were paid in cash.[9]

Sudanese soldiers who were able to rise up the ranks as NCOs and officers were compensated even better: Sudanese *ombashia* were paid at a yearly rate of £E 9.60 (960 piastres or 80 piastres/month); *shawishia* at £E 10.80; *bulukat omana* at £E 11.40; *bash shawishia* at £E 12; *solkolaghasia* at £E 21.60; *mulazimin tani* at £E 84; *mulazimim awal* at £E 96; *yuzbashia* at £E 132; and a *saghko-laghasi*, such as 'Ali Jifun by 1897, at £E 240. Of course, their British commanding officers were paid at a much higher rate, with a *miralai* receiving up to £E 900 annually, for example, some one-hundred times more than a Sudanese private.[10] However, this kind of pay disparity was nothing new, and indeed in the old Egyptian Army the ratio was far worse, running as high as five hundred to one.[11]

Sudanese soldiers in the new Egyptian Army were provided free rations, clothing, and equipment.[12] The scale of daily rations per man was as follows (nine Dirhems equals approximately one ounce):

Bread	250 Dirhems
(or Biscuit)	200 Dirhems
Beans	20 Dirhems
Lentils	20 Dirhems
Rice	20 Dirhems
Butter	6 Dirhems
Meat	35 Dirhems
Salt	5 Dirhems
Fresh Vegetables	45 Dirhems
Onions	5 Dirhems
Soap	5 Dirhems
Coal	45 Dirhems
(or Wood)	150 Dirhems[13]

Although 'Ali Jifun's recollections circa 1895 were that rations during the Turkiyya were "similar to that issued now," other sources suggest that the above 1901 scale was an improvement over those given to soldiers in the old Egyptian Army.[14] If nothing else, they were provided on a more reliable basis than they were prior to the Egyptian Army's reorganization. Prior to 1883, army regulations did dictate daily rations that similarly included bread, beans, rice, and meat, but these prescriptions were seldom met; most of the time rations consisted only of rice and/or *abrek*, sometimes millet porridge for the Sudanese soldiers, and occasionally meat.[15]

'Ali Jifun himself recalled that during this period, "Our usual food on the march consisted of the abrek, or broken native bread, which we carried dry in leather bags, just as the Arabs do to-day, and ate soaked in water. Sometimes our water gave out altogether, and I have often marched for two or three days on nothing but roots and the leaves of trees. When our stomachs felt empty, we tightened our belts and looked forward to better times."[16] When rations were not forthcoming, soldiers had to provide for themselves, often by plundering local villages for food.[17] And indeed the same had been true for generations of Sudanese soldiers, as described in the following 1839 journal entry, written by a Frenchman in Berber: "5 December: 130 soldiers mounted on donkeys left yesterday. Their only ration was a little *durra* bread, very thin and sun-dried, called *abre*. When they are hungry they will make the villages feed them, and the government will say '*ma'laysh*, there's nothing wrong."[18]

Of course, these daily rations, even in the 1880s and 1890s, often varied according to what was locally available in food markets and by circumstances of war. During the Mahdist siege of Khartoum in 1884–1885, for example, 'Abdallah 'Adlan recalled that each soldier "was issued with two and a half bowls of grain every fifteen days and also a little beef."[19] And when the Kassala garrison was under siege during the same time period, 'Ali Jifun and his fellow soldiers resorted to eating their donkeys, gum, and animal hides.[20] During the Nile Campaign in particular, with an army on the march, soldiers' diets depended a great deal on what was available locally along the advance, either in villages along the Nile or at improvised markets set up by camp followers near the army lines. For example, an 1896 illustration caption in *The Graphic* reported: "The advance on the Soudan has caused village markets to spring on all sides of the line of march, for the sale of requisite supplies to the troops. At these fairs vegetables of all kinds, onions especially, are offered for sale, and eggs, Arab bread, green food for the animals, and many other things can be purchased."[21]

In the case of Sudanese soldiers, these rations were usually given directly to their wives, who would then use them to prepare meals at nearby family encampments. Sometimes local women, often *abid*, would also be employed to prepare food for the soldiers.[22] The men ate with each other and/or their families from a communal bowl, sharing such typical Sudanese meals as *kisra* (sorghum pancake), *mulukhiya* (a green leaf vegetable stew), or *tamiya* (*falafal*). Private George Teigh of the Lincolnshire Regiment, for example, noted the following meal in the his journal: "The Niggers on board...here they eat twice a day there [*sic*] food consists of meal made up in the form of a pancake & a drop of oil on top to season it; they also have some kind of vegetables similar to ground peas which they mix up with their paste the [*sic*] eat it with their fingers & seem to consider it a famous feed."[23] In addition to the above-mentioned foods, the wives of Sudanese soldiers would regularly brew *marisa* for their husbands, a mildly alcoholic drink usually made from fermented sorghum. The native bread, in particular, was often remarked on by British soldiers, most of whom found it extremely distasteful: "While here we were treated to the bread given to the Egyptian Army, no other being obtainable. The Egyptian bread being so delicious, that we had to wait until it was dark before we could make a start eating it, as it was so very black in colour and very unpleasant to smell; a great many of us that did chance the eating part of the business were very soon vomiting it up again."[24]

Military clothing, also free issue for Sudanese infantry soldiers, had improved considerably from the days of the old Egyptian Army, when troops were often poorly clothed.[25] In fact, at times during the Turkiyya soldiers had to provide clothing for themselves, as was the case for 'Ali Jifun at Amedeb in the late 1860s: "We collected taxes from the Barea, and out of the goods we took in kind, the women made materials for our clothing. All our rations were supplied locally, and nothing came from Egypt. The uniforms were made up at Kassala; the officers wore red slippers and the men sandals."[26] At other times, when uniforms were issued, they were badly made, and re-supply was a continual problem; Hicks Pasha, for example, once complained that his Sudanese soldiers were dressed "in rags."[27]

Following the Egyptian Army's reorganization in 1883, both the quality and quantity of military clothing increased, and periods of wear were set for each article issued. All Sudanese non-commissioned officers and men received the following items annually: one cholera belt; two pairs of boots; two pairs of drawers and cords; two pairs of khaki frocks; two handkerchiefs; one "immeh" [*imma*, cloth *tarbush* covering] and badges; two pairs of putties; two shirts; two pairs of woolen socks; two complete *tarbushes* [fez-like caps]; and two pairs of khaki trousers. In addition, every other year they were provided one pair of flannel drawers and a woolen jersey, and every fourth year a cloth suit, one great coat, and sashes.[28] Of course, at times the above clothing issue was often more theoretical than real, and varied from battalion to battalion, and over time. This was especially the case in the early years of the new Egyptian Army. B. R. Mitford, a British officer in the Sudanese IXth, for example, recalled that in September 1886 his battalion was "the Cinderella of the Frontier just then; we could not get any clothes."[29] Moreover, according to Mitford:

> There were only 27 pairs of boots in the battalion, and they were kept for the men on guard. When the new guard faced the old guard and the usual compliments had been paid, the latter grounded arms and proceeded to take off their boots, which where handed to the new guard, who put them on while the N.C.O.'s were handing over the odd-ments in the guard-room....The other units in the station had their clothing complete, so our men rather resented not receiving like issue.[30]

By mid-December, however, he was able to report that "we at last received our clothing, boots, etc., and all hands were busy fitting themselves to turn out smart for the Sirdar's inspection."[31]

Sudanese soldiers in the River War were armed with breech-loading Martini-Henry .450 rifles, and had been since late 1885. Prior to that, for a little over a decade during Khedive Isma'il's reign, they had been equipped another breechloader, the Remington, which itself was a great improvement upon the muzzle-loading Minie or *shishkhana* rifles they had previously used.[32] By 1896 Sudanese troops were quite comfortable and adept with the Martini-Henry, many of these soldiers having undergone years of musketry practice with it, to say nothing of their battlefield experience with the rifle. And perhaps this is why they were not re-equipped with Lee-Metfords for the Nile Campaign – the latter a more modern bolt-action, magazine-loaded rifle with almost twice the rate of fire as that of the Martini-Henry, adopted by the British Army in 1888.[33] In any case, other than the fact that "musketry" took place regularly, the sources reveal

3.1 *Sudanese Soldiers on parade wearing full kit, between 1905 and 1911*
(Reproduced by permission of Durham University Library)

little if any detailed information about the training Sudanese soldiers received on how to fire a precision-tooled rifle such as the Martini-Henry. G. W. Steevens, however, does provide the following anecdote, rather interesting because it suggests that more experienced Sudanese soldiers played a role in the training of new recruits:

> After each victory the more desirable of the prisoners and deserters are enlisted, to their great content, in one black battalion or another. Every morning I had seen them on the range at Halfa – the British sergeant-instructor teaching the ex-Dervishes to shoot. When the recruit made a bull – which he did surprisingly often – the white sergeant, standing behind him with a paper, cried, '*Quaiss kitir*' – 'Very good.' When he made a fool of himself, the black sergeant trod on him as he lay flat on his belly: he accepted the praise and reproof with equal satisfaction, as part of his new game of disciplined war.[34]

And as for its care and maintenance, soldiers of the Sudanese IXth "were very good at keeping their rifles in first-rate order, and in looking after their ammunition," according to B. R. Mitford. He added that it was "a bit of a shock at first to see a man with his Martini-Henry all in pieces on his blanket; but one never found that any damage was done."[35]

Finally, each man was given one hundred rounds of Martini-Henry ammunition, carried in two fifty-round bandoliers – one around the waist and one slung over the left shoulder. Interestingly, according to Mitford, the men themselves made these out of ox hides obtained from the meat contractor, and were often "very clever in that work, and turned out quite ornate bandoliers."[36] In any case, the upshot of all of these improvements in clothing and weaponry was that Sudanese soldiers by the 1890s were as a rule well fed, smartly uniformed, and fully equipped – a vast improvement from the days of the old Egyptian

Army, and something that no doubt contributed greatly to troop morale and the overall success of the River War.

Camp followers

Among the most overlooked aspects of the Nile Campaign in terms of its later historiography has been the important role in the campaign played by Sudanese soldiers' wives. Though seldom if ever mentioned in secondary sources, most contemporary accounts of the River War refer to a colony of women that accompanied the Anglo-Egyptian army southward along the Nile. Albeit not officially supported in terms of transport or supplies, these camp followers were nonetheless seen as critical to the functioning of Sudanese troops, and consequently, the overall success of the campaign. Not only did these women provide their husband-soldiers the comforts of home, but they also occupied a number of other important social, economic, and military roles both during and after the campaign.

First and foremost, the character and longevity of these somewhat nebulous spousal relationships varied greatly, as did their prevalence, and they often differed from location to location, and from campaign to campaign. On the one hand, there is enough anecdotal evidence to conclude that in many cases these unions were legal, officially recognized, self-arranged marriages, both encouraged and supported by military commanders, and entered into almost universally by Sudanese troops; moreover, they were formally celebrated with a wedding, might also include a dowry, and were often monogamous. As well, many of these marriages endured regardless of a soldier's reassignment to another garrison or his participation in a military campaign. In fact, when soldiers of the new Egyptian Army's pioneer Sudanese battalion, the IXth, were first sent to the Aswan garrison in 1884, "Harimat Lines for 300 were built, all the men being married."[37] And as early as 1886, Wingate was recruiting new Sudanese soldiers by assuring them that "if the Military necessities prevent the women of a regiment being for a time with it, then the women are taken care of in some safe place where they still receive their allowances and are taken care of until they can rejoin their husbands."[38] According to Captain Gilbert Falkingham Clayton, this was the norm: "Practically every Sudanese soldier is married and the wives are recognised by Government and on the married establishment, which allows for one wife to each man....In every battalion there is an IMAM or priest whose opinion the C.O. asks on questions of matrimony and divorce."[39] Two weeks later Clayton added, "I really think it must be a wedding feast tonight, they are making such a din – I gave two men of the XV Sudanese leave to marry the other day, so I suppose that a joint wedding breakfast is being held tonight."[40]

The depth of marital devotion between Sudanese soldiers and their wives during the River War is evident in both contemporary accounts and official correspondence. Consider, for example, what took place at the Dongola Campaign's launch in 1896 when – running counter to military tradition in the Sudan – most of the wives and families of the Sudanese soldiers were left behind in Aswan and other Egyptian Army garrison towns. The sorrowful scenes of

"Flavour of Domesticity"

'SAMBO'S' WIFE.

3.2 *"Sambo's Wife"*
(Sketch by Angus McNeill in Churchill, *The River War*, vol. I, 1899)

departure that resulted were depicted by many of the newspaper correspondents and special artists following the campaign. According to E. F. Knight of *The Times*: "The train and steamer by which I travelled from the sea to Assuan were crowded with these Sudanese conscripts, whose wives, standing on the railway platforms and river bank, bade them farewell with dismal wailings, impassioned wringing of hands, and what sounded like terrible curses heaped on the heads of those who were tearing their lords away from them."[41] Indeed, the departure of the XIth Sudanese Battalion from Aswan made the front page of *The Daily Graphic*, and was vividly described on page three of the same paper by a local resident:

> March 18th. – Everyone turns out early to see the start, the town being one buzz of excitement, and the little station surrounded by a large crowd to see the troops go off. It is 8:30 a.m. Here they come! with band playing and flags flying, while above all is heard the shrill cries with which women always express either sorrow or joy in the East. There are many last handshakes from the open trucks on which the troops travel to Chellal, many black babies handed round for a last embrace (we are not sure that the men know whose baby it is, they are all so much alike), and then they are off.[42]

A couple of weeks later, a similar scene in Aswan takes place when a sixth and final Sudanese battalion, the XIVth, was raised for the campaign, and it was lucidly described by the same local resident, his racist lens notwithstanding:

3.3 The departure of the XIth Sudanese from Aswan. Top caption: "The girls they left behind them." Bottom caption: "The train load of soldiers leaving the station."
(*The Daily Graphic*, 31 March 1896)

> A new Soudanese regiment is being recruited, and the crowd of female relatives outside the barracks while it is going on is a sight to behold. Their distress at parting with their fathers, husbands, brothers, is manifest, some throwing up their arms to heaven with tragic gestures, while rivers of tears pour down their ugly black faces. Others totally overcome with grief sit in a shapeless bundle on the ground, pouring dust on their heads and filling the air with their heart-rending cries, while some just lean up against the nearest wall and sob piteously.[43]

The affection these women felt for their husbands was not a one-way street, nor does it appear that these marital and familial ties were soon forgotten. Evidence to this effect can be found in British military correspondence in the years that followed. In September of 1897, for example, Rudolf Slatin, assistant director of military intelligence in the Egyptian Army, wrote to Major Fairholme, "A point which should not be disregarded is the fact that the whole Egyptian army ardently longs for the termination of this campaign. Not only the Egyptian soldiers but also the Sudanese battalions which, from consideration of supply and transport, have long been separated from their wives and children, long for rest."[44] Four months later, in January 1898, a War Office memo noted "that as regards *morale*, the whole Egyptian Army has been campaigning for nearly 2 years on end, and not only the men, but the officers too, are getting stale. They are getting tired of the business, and – especially as far as the blacks are concerned – of the separation from their families."[45]

Although in many cases these unions appear to have been marriages in the truest sense, the nature of these relationships varied greatly, ranging from temporary, sometimes multiple, marriages of convenience to conditions that more closely resemble domestic slavery or contractual prostitution. Moreover, there is also evidence that runs counter to the above idea that the marriage establishment for Sudanese soldiers was so universal in practice, or so enthusiastically supported by British commanders. For example, 'Ali Jifun, in his memoir tracing some forty years in the Egyptian Army, never once mentions a wife by name, nor even in passing (the same is the case for 'Abdallah 'Adlan in his life story); and in fact the few things 'Ali Jifun did reveal about spousal relations – regardless of whether it was a product of military indifference or individual choice – seem to undermine the notion that these marriages were anything other than very temporary, and these "wives," quite replaceable: "Soldiers who married had no claims upon the Government for transport of their wives or families when the regiment moved to another district, and it was usual for the incoming battalions to take over the wives of the men they relieved."[46] Further on, upon his recall from El Obeid following the Taqali expedition, he remembered: "No families accompanied us, all wives and children being left to take care of themselves and to seek the protection of other soldiers who would be willing to accept them."[47]

Along these same lines, during the Nile Campaign there was an incident following the Battle of Firket in which a Sudanese woman living in Wadi Halfa was "told by a Soudanese soldier that her husband had left her in his charge." According to the story, the woman "said she knew it was not true as she was aware that they were not friends," but nonetheless "he forced her to live with him." However, it turned out that her first husband had not been killed at Firket, and when this soldier "got back she told him and he, quite cooly [sic], picked up his Martini rifle and shot the other."[48] The behaviors of all three parties in this incident suggest that the woman was a slave wife, chattel whose ownership could be transferred from one soldier to the next. And the reality that in many cases these wives were slaves, even following the Nile Campaign, is evident in a January 1900 letter describing what was taking place as the Sudan was first being reconstituted under Anglo-Egyptian rule, when it was brought to the attention of the *sirdar* that the "former female slaves joined the Black Battalions in such a number that it is said that every man has at least 4 or 5 female followers," with the recommendation that the "female followers to soldiers in the Black Battalions should be limited."[49] Whether these "followers" were acquired as slaves or married these soldiers, or became their concubines, is still unclear, but it may be a moot point.

It is also likely that many of the above-mentioned "former female slaves" were cavorting with the soldiers of Kitchener's army as prostitutes. Among the recommendations made in December of 1898 as to necessary precautions for British troops permanently stationed at Khartoum and Omdurman was for the creation of a cantonment system similar to what had been established in India, with "registration, inspection etc. of prostitutes necessary."[50] There are also sources suggesting that during the River War some of the wives of Sudanese soldiers may have had sexual relations with British soldiers, although the extent and exact nature of these encounters remains unknown. In early 1898, for example, as more and more British troops were making their way to the front to join Egyptian and Sudanese soldiers already deployed, it was determined by Kitchener that out of concern for their health it would be "better for Seaforths to be with the Brigade then [sic] at Assuan where there are 3000 Sudanese ladies of the soldiers here."[51] In another incident two years earlier, James Jay Bleeker Farley recollected that "adjacent to our barracks was a very large mud building full of Soudanese women, wives of the Soudanese troops with the Egyptian army, and one of our men found his way inside; whether the 'devil tempted him, or it was entirely his own idea' or whether it was a case of kidnapping was never made clear, but when rescued by the Regimental picquet he had been stripped stark naked by the women."[52]

Of course, the above-mentioned desire on the part of British military and intelligence officers to limit the number of women attached to Sudanese battalions was nothing new. As early as 1888, only a few years after they had been re-raised, British commanders were already struggling with how to reduce the "Married Establishment" within Sudanese battalions. In the opinion of F. R. Borrow, *kaimakam* of the IXth Sudanese, "All bad crimes originate in the married lines + I am sure crime would be less if the married role was limited to (1) All N.C.Os and (2) from 10 to 20 percent of the best characters amongst the men. It is a noteworthy fact that crime was almost unknown during the time the women were absent from the battalion."[53] The *kaimakam* of the Xth Sudanese Battalion agreed:

> Something should be done to reduce the present Enormous Establishment. Printed conditions should be explained and given to every future recruit. (1) Should not be allowed to marry before he has completed a certain service. (2) Not to enlist married, or if he do [sic]

> Govt will not recognize his family. (3) only men of good character to be allowed to marry. I think the Extra piastre should be continued to those allowed to marry, as it is very necessary. Say married establishment not to exceed 34 per company – including N.C.Os.[54]

This figure suggested by D. A. Donne of the Xth meant only some 140 men per battalion, a married establishment of less than twenty percent.[55] And it appears that Borrow and Donne's recommendations were followed, or at least attempted, as the next year Sudanese battalion Enlistment Certificates included the line: "I understand that I have no claims on the Govt., if I am married, or, if I marry during my service without permission, and that only a certain number of N.C.Os and old soldiers of good conduct are allowed to marry and have their families with them."[56] By the early twentieth century, according to the War Office, the married establishment had been reduced even further, in which only "ten percent of the Black Battalions are given Family Allowance."[57]

Ultimately, what one finds is that these marriages existed over a wide range of possibilities, and a range that varied over time and by location. Even within individual marriages this was the case, as changing circumstances often dictated the exact nature of the spousal union and degree of fidelity – as has been true in marriages everywhere and for time immemorial, and especially in times of war. Add to this the fact that these soldiers were Muslims, and by faith allowed to have more than one wife, and it is not surprising that the Nile Campaign led to new marriages for these men – whether their wives accompanied them as camp followers or not. And these new unions were likewise constituted in a variety of forms and for a variety of reasons. As the *Daily Mail* correspondent G. W. Steevens noted, "As the frontier has ever advanced up-river, the inconstant warrior has formed fresh ties; and now at Halfa, at Dongola, at Berber, the path of victory is milestoned with expectant wives and children."[58] Steevens then went on – albeit via some rather dubious dialogue between two soldiers – to attribute much of this behavior to the acceptance of polygamy among the Sudanese troops:

> It is not so abandoned as it sounds, for the Sudanese are born of polygamy, and it would be unreasonable to expect them not to live in it. Here is a typical case. One day a particularly smart soldier came and desired to speak with his commanding officer.
>
> "I wish to marry, O thou Bey," he said.
> "But aren't you married?"
> "Yes; but my wife is old and has no child, and I desire a child. I wish therefore to marry the sister of Sergeant Mohammed Ali, and he also is willing."
> "Then you want to send away your present wife?"
> "O no, Excellency. My wife cooks very well, and I want her to cook my rations. She also is willing."
>
> So, everybody being willing, the second marriage took place. Mohammed Ali's sister duly bore a son, and the first wife cooked for the whole family, and they all lived happily ever afterwards.[59]

Of course, changing circumstances also sometimes led to divorce, and then remarriage, as was the case for the following Sudanese soldier stationed in the southern Sudan after the River War, as described by Captain Gilbert Clayton:

I asked his reasons [for the divorce] and he said that (1) she was getting old and ugly – he was right! (2) She wouldn't work and make bread and marissa. (3) He was tired of her and wanted to marry someone else. (4) She was a shrew and always nagging. My own senses assured me on point (1). The native officer corroborated on the score of point (2), and as the lady burst into a flood of abuse and recrimination directed at everyone indiscriminately, point (4) seemed to be established. DECREE NISI granted, but man forfeits her dowry, which he had paid to her people (£1.)! All parties satisfied and man marries again next day! Such is the simplicity with which the Gordian Knot is severed in these parts.[60]

This anecdote demonstrates the true difficulty one has in categorizing the ambiguous nature of these marriages. On the one hand, the marriage was considered legal and legitimate in the eyes of the two parties involved, as well as the family of the bride and the British commanding officer; and as such, the soldier has paid his wife's family a dowry, one that he now forfeited upon the divorce. Moreover, much of the soldier's description of his marital problems, not to mention her own recriminations of him and subsequent recompense, bespeaks expectations more akin to the failings of a bilateral love marriage than that of a master-slave relationship. However, on the other hand, the somewhat cavalier way in which the soldier first describes, and then dissolves, the marriage, followed by his remarriage a day later, seems more in line with 'Ali Jifun's characterization of these unions as being anything but temporary, serviceable arrangements. And the fact that one of his main complaints relates to her failure to perform her cooking and brewing duties draws this characterization even further.

Be that as it may, perhaps the two extremes are not so mutually exclusive as they may at first seem, and that many of these marriages operated in both categories at once, and reflected local gender roles and marriage practices, not to mention local political and economic circumstances – influences, cultural and otherwise, that transcend Western definitions. As one popular Sudanese soldiers' fatigue song went:

The leader sings:	The chorus answer:
My wife	is sweet.
Someone else's wife	is sweet.
To the taste	is sweet.
In the house	is sweet.
Smoke-scented	is sweet.
Anointed with oil	is sweet.[61]

And lest one think the decision to maintain or dissolve these marriages lay entirely in the hands of the husband, there is one source – albeit originating from German East Africa – that suggests it was not uncommon for wives of Sudanese askaris to desert their spouses, and remarry other soldiers. According to this account of the Langenburg garrison at the turn of the twentieth century, these "Bibis" sometimes "ran away" from their husbands and were "quickly taken in by another into his hut." Its author goes on to write, "If the Bibi was not happy in the second hut, then perhaps she ran to the third."[62]

Matrimonial ambiguity notwithstanding, it is clear that these women occupied numerous key social and economic – and sometimes even military – functions within the Egyptian Army system, and also played a role in creating its next generation of soldiers, both through reproduction and via ethnic and kinship networks. Moreover, and despite official attempts to limit the number of these marriages and/or keep Sudanese soldiers' wives in southern Egypt during the Nile Campaign, the reality was that many of these women still found a way to accompany their husbands into the Sudan as camp followers:

> Although unrecognized officially, and in consequence not accorded any means of transport, they had contrived to cross the Nile as stowaways, hidden under forage or flour sacks; and they were now trudging slowly along with large bundles on their heads, and in some cases a brace of babies slung over their shoulders. When they arrived at the camp they cooked their husband's food, mended his clothes, and introduced a general flavour of domesticity into the rough camp life. The husbands seemed to be very kind to their wives and children, and the Sudanese portion of the camp was dotted with little family groups, each of them formed under a tree and surrounded by a miniature zeriba. In fact, domestic life has such charms in the eyes of the Sudanese warriors, that they become quite depressed and morose if their women-folk are left behind.[63]

The primary role these women occupied, beyond that of companion and sexual partner, was in providing domestic labor in support of their husbands: cooking their food, making their bread, washing and mending their clothes. When living with their husbands at fortified Egyptian Army garrisons, these activities took place along designated *harimat* lines built specifically for the families of Sudanese soldiers. When on campaign, however, these *tukls* [huts] and family encampments, sometimes in the form of a *zariba*, were far more exposed, and usually located anywhere between a half-mile and two miles away from those of the army. Thick bush and rough ground was preferable, making these camps difficult to penetrate by the enemy.[64]

Within these confines, amid the "thorny mimosa" and "dhoum palms," these women built crude palm-leaf and grass huts or temporary shelters made from brown soldier blankets, where "they washed, ground corn, made bread, cooked food, patched and mended, and waited upon their uxorious soldier lords."[65] They also occasionally brewed sorghum into *marisa* beer for their husbands.[66] Indeed, one of the Sudanese soldiers' songs transcribed and translated in the 1920s went as follows: Oh, women. (*Chorus*: Beer.) Oh, women. (*Chorus*: Beer, women, beer.) Girls of Berti. (*Chorus*: Beer.) Silk-haired Berti. (*Chorus*: Beer, women, beer.) Go to market. (*Chorus*: Beer.) To buy necessary things. (*Chorus*: Beer, women, beer.) Deck your hair. (*Chorus*: Beer.) By the wish of her heart. (*Chorus*: Beer, women, beer.).[67] According to Bennet Burleigh:

> These faithful blacks like to follow their lords to the wars and share their hardships. For better security they pitch their shelters and hovels in thick bush, and take their chances of a dervish raid with the bravest. To-day they were again to be seen with all their poor household goods on their backs – namely, a few earthenware pots, some mats, a goatskin or two filled with grain and what not, trudging behind the troops, and turning into a camp of their own a mile in the rear. Patient and happy creatures, their piccaninnies riding on their hips, as brave as their masters, looking at the soldiers with wonder in their big dark eyes.[68]

One of these Sudanese *zara'ib* was described by Count Gleichen of the Guards Camel Corps, who was attached to an earlier Nile expedition in 1884–

1885: "The interior of the zeriba was a wonderful sight. The whole place was filled with shanties made of poles and matting or ragged carpets, and inside these the blacks reposed, chattering, cleaning their arms, and swearing at their wives, who sat patiently outside cooking dinner. Every available space was occupied with arms, wooden bowls, grinding-stones, carcases [sic] of kids, cooking-pots, spears, corn, and ammunition-boxes....They had not the smallest notions of *meum* and *tumm*; everything was public property, even amongst themselves."[69]

The communal nature of daily life within these encampments was also present during the River War, and there seems to have been a great deal of cooperation and mutual support among the wives of Sudanese soldiers, and between them and their husbands, with special assistance from the group often provided to new mothers and their newborns. According to Burleigh in *Khartoum Campaign*: "I had my attention called more than once to women with almost new-born babies in their arms trudging along to keep up with the army. In such cases the women and men generously did all in their power to lighten the burden of the new mothers. Their household goods were borne upon other already over-loaded backs, and if a donkey was procurable the mother and child were set to ride upon its back."[70] Similarly, he writes in *Sirdar and Khalifa*: "They marched in groups, and helped each other by turns upon the road....The black soldiers did not forget them, but gave of their food to the women; and whenever anything was captured, took the prizes to their wives. In that way, after the fall of Mahmoud, nearly every woman had a load of stores, and many of them got donkeys, taken from the dervish zereba, upon which to transport their babes and baggage back to the Nile."[71]

The cooperative nature of camp life notwithstanding, there is also evidence – albeit from outside the Sudan – suggesting that these wives operated within a hierarchy based on the ranks of their husbands. According to the diary of Magdalene von Prince, the wife of the Iringa garrison commandant Captain von Prince, the wives of Sudanese soldiers stationed in German East Africa fell into something of a pecking order, with the wife of the highest-ranking Sudanese officer always first in line, and often first in physical appearance. Describing the Eid celebration that Magdalene hosted at the end of Ramadan in 1897, for example, she wrote that although all the Sudanese wives wore white and yellow tobes and were served sweets and coffee, the quality of the cloth, as well the physical attractiveness of the women, varied according to rank, and it was only the fine-looking wife of the "Effendi" that accepted a glass of wine.[72]

In any case, the wife of a Sudanese soldier also occupied a more direct economic role in the life of her husband, and family, as she was the one who usually dealt with her husband's army salary and family allowance. According to the *kaimakam* of the IXth Sudanese Battalion, F. R. Borrow, "The majority of men on receiving their month's pay hand it over to some woman in the married lines who contracts to keep them in 'Roosa' for the following month."[73] This practice would continue into the 1890s, and seems to have impressed at least one British correspondent during the Nile Campaign:

> Latitudinarian or eccentric as these negroes may be regarded by Christians in their marital affairs, they never omit to transmit to their wives for the time being, every penny they are

allowed to send them. Indeed, if these Soudanese black soldiers had their wishes acceded to, they would remit the women and children every farthing due them by the paymasters, and all they had acquired by other means, leaving themselves absolutely penniless, such is their uxorious devotion.[74]

In some instances these women played an even more active and entrepreneurial role in the local economy, establishing improvised food markets along the campaign route: "Among the rest who have come on hither are a colony of women and children and natives. They had formed a camp about one mile from ours at Ras-el-Hudi, and opened a kind of market, where dates, tomatoes, and onions, procured by travelling long distances were sold. Most of the women are the wives of the Sudanese soldiers."[75]

In maintaining the overall health and morale of the Sudanese battalions, these women thus came to occupy a significant role in the functioning of the new Egyptian Army, and during the River War in particular. Of course, by the 1880s and 1890s this role was already deeply ingrained in the fabric of Sudanese military tradition, and was recognized as such by both Sudanese and British officers, although sometimes begrudgingly and based on racial stereotypes by the latter: "The blacks *will* marry whether allowed or not and as Soudanese are mercenaries entirely and to allow a liberal marriage establishment means increased inducement to Enlist: The married men make a solid nucleus in a Battn without which I should fear a vast amount of desertion."[76] Following a fire that burned down the *harimat* lines of the XIIIth Sudanese Battalion in 1894, Herbert Kitchener, the ever-parsimonious *sirdar* of the Egyptian Army, wrote to F. R. Wingate:

> Please stamp out any idea that the Govt. is going to house their ladies or pay for them when they burn them down – I do not think it is a good thing to pamper the blacks + I fear that is rather Jackson's failing. £50 is more than any battalion has received + should I think have been ample to assist Battalion funds + the cost to each married man. Of course I quite understand the pressure of Black battalion commanders but this should be resisted. Let the IXth build the huts for the XIIIth ladies but do not give Govt. money or make Govt. responsible in the least.[77]

During the Nile Campaign, when it came to "the question of camp followers," always "a thorny one" for Kitchener, the *sirdar* was far less arbitrary, perhaps realizing the importance of these women to its overall chances of success. His Sudanese officers had declared to him "that their troops cannot march without them," and so although officially unrecognized, more and more the presence of these women was tolerated, and sometimes directly supported.[78] This was especially the case in the last two years of the campaign. "It was not surprising that the *Sirdar* did not object to their presence in the field, and occasionally saw that they were helped with rations when food was not otherwise procurable," wrote correspondent Bennet Burleigh in 1898.[79]

The alternative, of course, could lead to troop desertions, or worse, a revolt. Kitchener was likely well aware of what took place in 1897 in the Uganda protectorate, when disaffected Sudanese troops attached to the J. R. L. Macdonald expedition mutinied in response to Macdonald's refusal to allow all of their wives and children to accompany them.[80] Indeed, this same reason for the Uganda mutiny was mentioned by Nile Campaign correspondent Ernest Bennett: "In fact, domestic life has such charms in the eyes of the Sudanese warriors, that they become quite depressed and morose if their women-folk are left behind. The recent revolt in Uganda seems, without doubt, to have been largely caused by the refusal of Major Macdonald to allow the wives of the soldiers to accompany them – a refusal which, whether it was based on Scotch prejudice or not, most certainly ran counter to the military tradition of the Sudan."[81]

This Sudanese military tradition held strong into the twentieth century. Traveler Yacoub Artin, for example, quoted a Sudanese officer on the subject in 1908:

> Those who are now returning to Khartum have just seen active service against the slave-merchants near the frontier. They are with their wives, and are, therefore, very happy. If, on their arrival at Khartum, they were ordered to go and fight somewhere without their wives, the latter would refuse to be separated; the women would accompany their husbands and treat them to their *zagharites* and *darabukas*. It is for this reason that, whether in war or in time of peace, the black soldiers are always accompanied by their wives, for they are carnivorous creatures with an instinctive love for fighting, and are ready at any time to kill or be killed, on condition that their wives witness their exploits, tend them when wounded, and bury them if they are killed. Their title of greatest glory is that of *Akhu'l-banati* (brother of the girls).[82]

In any case, for Kitchener in 1898, a revolt similar to that which took place in Uganda was to be avoided at all costs, and so camp followers became an accepted part of the military landscape. As it turned out, their sheer presence on campaign had its own additional military benefit – their encampments served as early warning systems against Mahdist attacks. According to one British officer, Charles Repington, at one point during the River War he was asked by brigade commander Hector Macdonald to inspect the outposts; when he reported to Macdonald that he thought them badly positioned, and vulnerable to a surprise attack:

> Mac. grunted, and then asked me to ride out with him. We passed the outpost line, and some way beyond came upon a great body of the women of the Sudanese, who were hiding in the long grass and scrub, and formed a complete outer line of observation. Mac. said that in case of attack all these women would raise such a devil of an outcry that it would be heard for miles, and that he wished no better outposts. We laughed a good deal, and I had to admit that a more effective screen could not well be imagined.[83]

Above and beyond these aforementioned roles, the wives of Sudanese soldiers played a seminal part in reproducing and sustaining Egyptian Army enrollments. Not only did they bear and raise, in so many cases, the next generation of Sudanese soldiers, but there is anecdotal evidence that these women may have facilitated army recruitment via ethnic and kinship networks as well. Take the case of 'Ali 'Abd al-Latif, Sudanese soldier and early nationalist, who himself turned to his maternal "uncle," Rihan 'Abd Allah, when he moved from Dueim to Khartoum at the turn of the twentieth century. Although his father had served in the Egyptian Army, it was 'Ali's Dinka mother, al-Sabr, who truly paved the way for his rise into the "effendiya" class. Indeed, it was thanks to her that he first connected with Rihan 'Abd Allah, an influential Sudanese officer living in Khartoum, and more likely his "uncle" in a broader sense – being a Dinka, and possibly from the same area of the Bahr al-Ghazal as al-Sabr. In any case, Rihan took the young 'Ali into his home, and it was under his auspices that al-Sabr's son first attended *khalwa*, before proceeding to Gordon Memorial College and then Khartoum Military School. Upon his graduation from the Military School in 1913, 'Ali 'Abd al-Latif was awarded the "Sirdar's Medal" for best cadet of the year, and was soon thereafter commissioned *mulazim tani* of the Sudanese XIth Battalion.[84]

Though for over a century they have endured utter historical obscurity, and have received nary a mention in any secondary account of the River War yet published, these women were by no means invisible or insignificant actors at the time these events took place. Rather, they were critical to the functioning of the Egyptian Army, and consequently, the overall success of the Nile Campaign, something contemporary observers noted but was overlooked by later historians. And although these Sudanese soldiers' wives – by reason of place, race, and gender – had few civil rights and led difficult lives, they were not simply passive, voiceless participants, without individual and collective agency, status, or impact. In fact, according to Repington, there was even one occasion during the Nile Campaign when these wives – permission to follow the army having been refused – had "raised Cain, as the saying goes, sent deputations to the general, whoever he might be, and made speeches," and were "supposed even to have made the brick-dust complexion of the Sirdar once show a blush, which must have been difficult."[85] And a couple years later, during the Omdurman mutiny of 1900, these women were again to play a critical and very active, and once more, forgotten role, helping with the negotiations between disgruntled XIth Battalion Sudanese troops and their former commanding officer.[86]

Health & disease

There is relatively little known about the health of Sudanese soldiers. Reasons for this want of information stem from the seeming unavailability of medical records pertaining to the subject, but also due to the dearth of Sudanese perspectives found in the existing documents. It is notable, and curious, for example, that in their memoirs neither 'Ali Jifun nor 'Abdallah 'Adlan revealed much of anything about the state of their health, or that of their battalion, or made any specific reference to health care for soldiers in the Egyptian Army.

Part of this want of medical information may also stem from the fact that many medical conditions were treated, unrecorded, in the *harimat* lines by camp followers, by company *hakims*, or even other Sudanese soldiers, rather than Egyptian Army doctors. Burleigh noted, for example, "Your Soudan soldier makes light of his wounds for a week or so, or until they become too troublesome, preferring to be about among his fellows and do his own doctoring in a rough fashion."[87] British officer B. R. Mitford, in his published diary extracts, recalled similar behavior by one of his Sudanese soldiers following the Battle of Toski:

> Inspecting the guards that evening I noticed a man, who was looking rather queer, had a hole in his jersey near the right breast, with some specks of blood round it. When I asked him what it was, he replied in a matter-of-fact way, 'I was wounded the day before yesterday, but now am quite strong.' I fell him out and had him stripped, and found an enormous hole in his back where the bullet had passed out. He had been shot through the lungs. He had lain quiet at Toski all the day before, but had not felt any pain. He quickly recovered.[88]

Likewise, the one mention 'Abdallah 'Adlan made in his memoir as to medical care in the Egyptian Army was that following a three-day battle with the Abyssinians the doctors "wished to remove the ebony bullet which had lodged in my thigh but I refused to let them do this and it is in my body today. It gives me no pain except that it aches during the wet weather."[89]

Be that as it may, there are official records and other sources from which certain kinds of information about the health of these men can be inferred. And these sources seem to indicate that the health and medical care of Sudanese soldiers in the new Egyptian Army, and during the River War in particular, was better than it had been during the Turkiyya period. And moreover, although they did not seek and/or receive the same level of care as did British soldiers during the Nile Campaign, they may have in fact been healthier. Nonetheless, the sources also reveal that these men (with their supposed "delicate" lungs that predisposed them to "catching cold," according to *England in Egypt* author Alfred Milner) still suffered a number of common ailments and succumbed to a variety of diseases – just as they had in the days of the old Egyptian Army, and despite improvements in medical knowledge and health care.[90] In addition, though Sudanese soldiers may have been better adapted to the local climate than Egyptian and British troops, it did not help them during the cholera epidemic of 1896.

During the earliest years of the Turkiyya, the attrition rate for Sudanese slave recruits was very high. In fact, the majority of them succumbed to fever, dysentery, and acute homesickness before they ever made it to the training camps in Aswan; again, it is estimated that out of the 20,000 Sudanese enslaved from 1820–1824 only some 3,000 were still alive in 1824.[91] And for those that did survive, and who became soldiers in Muhammad 'Ali's *nizam al-jadid* regiments, their long-term prospects for good health and longevity were often not much better. Despite the Pasha's attention to the health and hygiene of his troops, and attempts to modernize the military medical system in Egypt, his army was often plagued by sickness and disease (dysentery, malaria, venereal disease, weals, smallpox, and typhus), especially on campaign or while stationed in the Sudan.[92]

On one campaign in 1835, for example, some 504 soldiers of a newly raised black regiment died on the sea crossing to the Hijaz, with 521 more men left in Berber already sick and bedridden.[93] In another case, an Italian eyewitness living in Khartoum described the typhus outbreak that occurred in December of 1840: "The mortality was great in the country but greater in the army by reason of malnutrition and debility. Two-thirds of the new regiment died as the men were still new at soldiering and unaccustomed to that way of life....Many who fell ill in barracks were carried at once to the hospital but died on the way there."[94] And health conditions were not much better for Egyptian Army soldiers in the generations that followed, whether at outposts in the Sudan, where there was "the near total absence of a medical service" and often sick rates over fifty percent, or while on campaign in the 1863–1867 Mexican adventure.[95]

In the new Egyptian Army, Sudanese soldiers and their family members were given free medical attendance, and during the Nile Campaign each brigade was accompanied a British Senior Medical Officer, who was assisted by a staff of "native medical officers."[96] As the Anglo-Egyptian army moved further south along the Nile, Medical Corps detachments were distributed to every new military station, where field hospitals and casualty wards were set up for sick and injured soldiers. According to W. T. Maud, special artist for the *The Graphic*, who sketched Surgeon-Captain Whiston's field hospital at Merawi in 1897: "Every man reported sick is at once sent to the hospital...and as there are a little over 200 patients in the hospital and a number of out-patients to be inspected every day, Captain Whiston's hands are full of work."[97] Apparently, the most common ailment suffered by River War soldiers that year was malaria, and Sudanese soldiers in particular were also prone to ophthalmia, a severe inflammation of the eye "owing to the bad effect of sand and flies."[98]

The year prior, an Intelligence Report on the 1896 Dongola Campaign listed the following as the most common ailments for the six hundred or so British soldiers participating: simple continued fever (174 cases), dysentery and diarrhea (123 cases), venereal disease (75 cases), enteric fever (41 cases), injuries (37 cases), cholera (24 cases), conjunctivitis (20 cases), rheumatism (11 cases), and hepatitis (1 case).[99] The most prevalent causes of death for British troops on the Dongola expedition, excluding combat, were cholera (21 deaths), enteric fever (20 deaths), dysentery (1 death), pneumonia (1 death), heat apoplexy (1 death), and accidental drowning (3 deaths).[100] Whether and to what extent Sudanese and Egyptian soldiers suffered these same ailments, and whether they did so at similar prevalence rates, is unknown. However, a later Intelligence Report does include some general statistical information on the health of the Egyptian Army, both for the 1896 campaign and the ten years prior. Unfortunately, it does not distinguish between Egyptian and Sudanese soldiers, but groups them together as simply "Egyptian Troops."

In any case, the report indicates that out of an average Egyptian Army strength of 11,147 men between the years 1886 and 1895, the average daily sick rate for Egyptian troops was 3.1 percent (339 average daily sick); that the yearly invalidating rate was 2.7 percent (299 per annum); and that the yearly death rate (excluding cholera but including deaths in action) was 1.5 percent (166 per annum). Interestingly, and despite the above-mentioned reluctance on the part of Sudanese soldiers to seek medical attention, the yearly admissions rate for Egyptian troops during this time period averaged 62.1 percent (6,919 of the 11,147 soldiers); granted, many if not most of these admissions could have been Egyptian soldiers, but considering that five of the thirteen infantry battalions were Sudanese (roughly forty percent), it is likely that at least one or two thousand of these roughly seven thousand yearly "Egyptian" admissions were Sudanese soldiers, if not more during times of combat due to their higher casualty rates.[101]

For the 1896 Dongola Campaign itself, the report indicates that there were 7,760 admissions among Egyptian troops, representing some 67.1 percent of the soldiers, up some five percent from the previous ten-year average. The number of invalids in the 1896 campaign was 364 (3.1 percent), up almost one-half percent from the previous ten-year average. And the number of Dongola Campaign deaths was 408 (3.5 percent), up two percent as compared to the previous ten-year average but essentially no different if the 256 cholera deaths are excluded (1.6 percent versus 1.5 percent). Not surprisingly, when one considers the theater of operations, the average percentage of daily British sick during the campaign was somewhat higher than that of Egyptian and Sudanese soldiers (5.43 percent for British officers and 3.98 percent for British non-commissioned officers and men, versus 3.0 percent for all Egyptian troops). The 1896 admissions and death rates for British troops were also much higher – if one can assume that these were not repeat admissions of the same individuals, almost 98 percent of non-commissioned officers and privates sought care, some thirty percentage points greater than that of "Egyptian" soldiers, and the British death rate more than doubled that of all Egyptian troops (8 percent versus 3.5 percent).[102]

Whether this means that Egyptian troops were in fact "healthier" than British troops is debatable, and what clouds it even further is that again the statistics do not include a breakdown for Egyptian versus Sudanese soldiers. It is quite possible, for example, that the sick rates of Egyptian soldiers were equal to or greater than British soldiers, if the Sudanese represented only a small portion of admissions. Alternatively, if one were to isolate the cholera deaths of Sudanese soldiers, and also include cholera deaths of Sudanese camp followers, the resulting numbers would likely put the Sudanese at the top of the list. And yet, considering that some of the calculated percentages seem to have ignored recent increases in the overall strength of the Egyptian Army (by April of 1896 it had almost doubled in size), it may very well be that these health disparities between British and Egyptian troops are even greater than the above would seem to indicate.

Of all the health problems affecting Sudanese soldiers during the River War, none was so lethal as the cholera epidemic of 1896. Making its way southward up the Nile in June of that year, the disease arrived in Aswan on the 29th, in Wadi Halfa the following day, and by the end of July it had made its way into the Dongola Province, infecting each of the eighteen outposts between Aswan and Suarda. Far more deadly than the Battle of Firket in early June, cholera claimed the lives of some 800 of the first 1,000 cases.[103] In response, troops were immediately moved to camps a mile or so from the Nile River, where the sources of drinking water could be carefully controlled. Quarantines and sanitary regulations were quickly instituted, and strictly enforced, and these measures, combined with the steady rising of the Nile, brought about an end to the epidemic by the middle of August. Nonetheless, the cholera outbreak had taken a deadly toll, especially among the Sudanese soldiers and their families. Among "Egyptian troops" there were 406 cases, of which 260 resulted in death (as compared to twenty-four cases and nineteen deaths for British troops).[104]

The Xth Sudanese Battalion was especially hard hit, as nearly fifty men died from the disease, twenty-five alone between the 18th and 26th of July; this represented some six percent of the battalion, a four percent higher cholera death rate than that of Egyptian troops as a whole.[105] The fact that soldiers of the Xth Battalion often served in fatigue-parties – transporting the dead away from cholera-plagued camps for burial, as well as in the tearing down and burning of infected huts – may have had something to do with this.[106] And for their wives left behind at Halfa, living in the *harimat*, the disease was even more deadly – 197 cases of which 182 were fatal. Regarding the conditions in Halfa, Major Archibald Hunter wrote that the "married women of the black battalion (of course the women stayed behind here + do not go forward till we are securely settled in Dongola) poor things they have died in shoals – All such nonsense as the sanctity of the harem has to give way before the gruesome necessities of a cholera plague and in an enforced inspection of every nook + crannie [*sic*] that I made, I found five corpses, not recent cases."[107] Civilians suffered dearly as well, with 590 total cases and 457 deaths, almost half of them in Aswan. In all, there were 1,218 cases and 919 deaths reported up to the 10th of August. By contrast, combat casualties in the whole Dongola Campaign only amounted to 47 killed and 122 wounded.[108]

The summer of 1896 notwithstanding, it does appear that the health of Sudanese soldiers during the River War was generally good when compared to their Egyptian and British Army brethren, and put alongside previous generations of Sudanese soldiers. Although rather anecdotal, the fact that 'Ali Jifun spent over four decades in the Egyptian Army and lived into his sixties, and that 'Abdallah 'Adlan served even longer and lived well into his eighties, says something about the conditions of service and overall health of Sudanese soldiers in the Egyptian Army. Of course, again these may be exceptional in nature. And yet on the other hand, considering the significant number of "old soldiers" still serving in Sudanese battalions or in retirement during the early decades of the twentieth century, these cases of longevity may be more representative of the whole than they seem at first glance.

Military advancement

One of the unique aspects of military slavery is the potential for social and economic advancement. For Sudanese soldiers in the Egyptian Army this came chiefly via military promotion. Despite their slave origins, Turco-Egyptian chauvinism, and Victorian attitudes to race, the possibility still existed for Sudanese soldiers to be promoted into the commissioned and non-commissioned officer ranks, and during the River War they were well represented as such in all six Sudanese infantry battalions. Be that as it may, these opportunities were also limited, and there appears to have been a glass ceiling of sorts existing for Sudanese soldiers in the 1890s that had not been there for previous generations, and would not be there for the generation of soldiers that followed.

During the earliest years of the Turkiyya, there was no possibility of promotion for Sudanese soldiers in Muhammad 'Ali's *nizam al-jadid* regiments. Initially, all of the officer and non-commissioned officer ranks were occupied by Turco-Egyptians. However, by the end of the 1820s, some Sudanese of long service were promoted from *nafar* to *ombashi* and *shawish*, and one such soldier,

Billal Agha, became the first to receive a commission as *mulazim tani* in 1829 or 1830. Others were to follow in Billal Agha's footsteps in the 1830s and 1840s, most notably Badi Agha, commissioned as *mulazim tani* in 1836, and Khair Agha, commissioned as *mulazim tani* in 1834 or 1835, and further promoted to *mulazim awal* in 1848 or 1849. In addition, 'Ali Khurshid, Muhammad 'Ali's man in Khartoum, saw to it that talented Sudanese youths were soon admitted as cadets into the Cairo Military School for officer training. And so by the 1850s and 1860s, despite a continued preponderance of "Turks," and eventually, the influx of American Civil War veterans and other Westerners, a few long-serving and educated Sudanese soldiers even cracked the higher officer ranks. Adham Bey al-Arifi, for example, served as a *kaimakam* in the Egyptian Army contingent sent by Ottoman Sultan Abdülmecid to fight in the Crimean War. And a little over a decade later, in part due to his role in suppressing the 1865 Kassala mutiny, Adham al-Arifi found himself promoted *liwa* and put in full command of the Khedive's first and second Sudanese regiments.[109]

In most instances, promotion for Sudanese soldiers was based entirely on length of service. Promotion from the ranks based on seniority safeguarded against favoritism, and avoided the social gap often found between officers and men in European armies; however, it also meant that there were few incentives for the more able junior officers, who otherwise might have been given greater responsibility at an earlier age.[110] In any case, by the 1860s and 1870s, as more and more Sudanese soldiers gained seniority, and as Khedive Isma'il further expanded the size of his army, the number of Sudanese officers at the commissioned ranks grew. And among non-commissioned officers in Sudanese regiments, they soon outnumbered the Turco-Egyptians.[111]

In the old Egyptian Army's First Regiment, for example, by 1866 over thirty percent of the commissioned officers were Sudanese (39 out of 124), and a full two-thirds of warrant and non-commissioned officers were Sudanese (306 out of 456).[112] Most notable among this generation of Sudanese officers included: Faraj Azazi, who served in the 1863–1867 Mexican adventure, and was promoted *kaimakam* after almost twenty years in the Egyptian Army; Muhammad Sulaiman, who served in the military for over 30 years, also fought in Mexico, and rose from the ranks all the way to *kaimakam*, "said to have been a cultivated man of high character"; and Muhammad Almas, who entered the Egyptian Army in 1834, commanded the Sudanese battalion in Mexico some thirty years later, and who was later promoted *miralai* and put in charge of the Khedive's 2nd Sudanese infantry regiment.[113]

By the late 1870s and early 1880s unusual circumstances in the Sudan opened the door even wider, as the rise of Mahdism and the regional havoc it wrought led to unique opportunities for high promotion among Sudanese officers left stationed at besieged garrisons along the Red Sea Littoral, in Khartoum, and in the far-flung Equatoria Province – officer ranks that would have been unimaginable for them to attain in the new Egyptian Army. Ironically, at the same time that the Egyptian Army was being rebuilt by British commanders in Cairo, a reorganization that was to scale back previous advancement opportunities and preclude any Sudanese promotions beyond the rank of *yuzbashi*, British commanders in the Sudan such as Charles Gordon were swiftly promoting

Sudanese soldiers into the highest attainable ranks of the army.

One of these men was al-Nur Muhammad. Originally from Sennar, he rose up through the Egyptian Army commissioned ranks, from *mulazim tani* all the way to *miralai*, serving first with Sir Samuel Baker in the early 1870s in Equatoria and Uganda, and then, leading troops against the Mahdists in the Sennar campaign of 1884. That same year Charles Gordon made him governor of Sennar, whence he continued to resist the forces of the Mahdi, losing both legs in battle and taken as a prisoner to Omdurman in 1885. Sixteen years later, Khedive Abbas II, upon his 1901–1902 visit to the Sudan, "decorated him and awarded him a pension."[114] Another of these men was Faraj Allah Raghib, who was promoted *liwa* and put in command of the fort at Omdurman by Charles Gordon during the siege of Khartoum. Following the fort's surrender, the Mahdi appointed Faraj Allah Raghib an *amir*, and in this capacity he later fought against the Abyssinians from 1887–1889. He did not live to see the Anglo-Egyptian reconquest of the Sudan.[115]

Another of this generation was Muhammad Ahmad, a self-educated Sudanese soldier whose father was Turkish, a factor that helped him quickly rise through the officer ranks of the Egyptian Army. Muhammad Ahmad fought in most of the key battles along the Red Sea Littoral in the 1880s and early 1890s – el Teb, Tamai, Hashin, Tofrik, Handoub, Gemaizeh, and Tokar. He was eventually promoted *kaimakam*, and later, given command of the Suakin provincial police force. In 1900 he assisted in the capture of Osman Digna, and in 1911 served with Wingate's Somali campaign. In 1913 he retired from the Egyptian Army at the rank of *miralai*, but was still active in prisoner exchanges in the Yaman during World War I. He died in 1931, considered "one of the finest Sudanese officers of modern times."[116]

And yet of all the Sudanese soldiers whose military careers were affected by the chaotic 1880s, perhaps none is a better case study than that of Faraj Muhammad al-Zaini. Born in the Nuba Hills around 1832, he was "stolen from his parents by slave traders and sold in Egypt." His master arranged his education, a course of study that included both French and Turkish. In 1852 Faraj was enrolled into the Egyptian Army, and like many of his generation, served with the Sudanese battalion sent to Mexico in 1863, and was double promoted from *mulazim awal* to *saghkolaghasi* upon his return to Egypt. The details pertaining to the next several years of his life are a bit sketchy, but it is known that in 1873 he was given command of the Kassala garrison, and held the rank of *miralai*. In November 1875 he and his battalion were to be part of the military expedition led by Søren Adolph Arendrup against the Abyssinians, but on the eve of the battle – and perhaps part of a conspiracy against him led by Egyptian officers – he was charged with a military misdemeanor and sent back to Keren in disgrace. Six years later, while serving second-in-command of a reserve regiment stationed at al-Tura, Faraj again came out on the wrong end of things, court martialed and banished to the Sudan for trying to foment a rebellion among the regiment's junior officers. Following a couple of years stationed in Massawa, he found renewed favor and was made commander of the 1st Sudanese regiment at Khartoum. During the siege of Khartoum in 1884–1885, Charles Gordon first promoted Faraj *liwa* and made him his chief-of-staff, and responsible for the land defense of the city – four miles of ramparts and ditches stretching south and east of Khartoum between the White and Blue Niles. Gordon eventually promoted him *ferik* (one step below *sirdar*) – the highest rank ever attained by a Sudanese slave soldier in the Egyptian Army. Faraj Muhammad al-Zaini was taken prisoner and killed when Khartoum fell to the Mahdists on 25 January 1885.[117]

These types of opportunities for Sudanese soldiers did not exist following Evelyn Wood's reorganization of the Egyptian Army in 1883. All of the highest-ranking officers during this era – from *ferik* to *liwa* to *miralai* – were British; and the battalion commanders – from the *kaimakam* to the *bimbashia* – were always either British or Egyptian, the latter mostly of Turco-Circassian, or Albanian descent.[118] At the outset of the Nile Campaign, for example, British officers commanded twelve of the sixteen infantry battalions, including all six Sudanese battalions and six of the Egyptian battalions; Egyptian officers commanded the remaining four Egyptian battalions.[119] Moreover, among the *bimbashia* of the first sixteen Egyptian Army infantry battalions in 1897, twenty-five of thirty-nine were British, including all eighteen assigned to Sudanese battalions; the remaining *bimbashia* were all Egyptians.[120] By all accounts and with very few exceptions there appears to have been a glass ceiling for Sudanese soldiers at the ranks of *saghkolaghasi* and *yuzbashi*, regardless of their military seniority and experience. Even 'Ali Jifun, a decorated soldier who had spent some forty years in the Egyptian Army, was only promoted *bimbashi* in October of 1898, during the final few months of his life.[121]

Yet there were markers of achievement. Sudanese soldiers dominated the non-commissioned officer ranks of Sudanese battalions during the River War, and were well represented at the commissioned ranks of *yuzbashi*, *mulazim awal*, and *mulazim tani* as well, filling about half of these officer slots in the six Sudanese battalions, Egyptians occupying the rest.[122] And in some of these battalions their prevalence at this higher level – and impact on the success of the Nile Campaign – was even greater. For example, in the XIIIth Sudanese Battalion five of the six companies in 1897 were commanded by Sudanese *yuzbashia*, and quite "fortunately" according to one of its British *bimbashia*, Major Frederick Ivor Maxse, who wrote in a letter home that spring that "a more reliable, stout-hearted, cheery set of old boys you could not wish to have; hard as nails and commanding their men most efficiently."[123] It is to be remembered, as well, that for those few Sudanese soldiers who were able to rise from *nafar* all the way to *yuzbashi*, it meant not only an increase in one's military and social status, but also a substantial increase in pay – a yearly salary almost fifteen times greater, from £E 9 to £E 132 per annum.[124]

'Ali Jifun and 'Abdallah 'Adlan were among the "old boys" of this generation, both serving in the XIIth Sudanese Battalion. But there were many other Sudanese officers who fought in the Nile Campaign also worthy of mention, some of them much younger men than 'Ali Jifun and 'Abdallah 'Adlan, *yuzbashia* in their thirties who led their companies at Firket, and Atbara, and Omdurman. Almas Mursi was one of them, a Dinka from the Bahr al-Ghazal. Born in 1859, Almas Mursi saw his first service in the Egyptian Army in 1873 when still a teenager. He fought in many of the key battles of the 1880s and early 1890s, most

3.4 NCOs of the No. 7 Company, XIIth Sudanese, Omdurman, between 1899 and 1900
(Reproduced by permission of Durham University Library)

notably Gemaizeh (1886), Toski (1889), and Tokar (1891). During the River War he was a *yuzbashi* in the Xth Sudanese Battalion, leading his company from the Dongola Campaign through the Battle of Omdurman.[125] Another was Sa'id 'Abdallah, a Taqalawi who was born in Khartoum in 1864 following Musa Pasha Hamdi's raid on the Nuba Hills. He entered the Egyptian Army and was stationed at Amedeb from 1880–1885. As with 'Ali Jifun and many other Sudanese soldiers who survived the Mahdist sieges of Egyptian garrisons along the eastern frontier, he withdrew to Egypt and joined up with one of the newly raised Sudanese battalions. Like Almas Mursi, Sa'id 'Abdallah fought at Gemaizeh, Toski, and Tokar, and was also promoted *yuzbashi*, XIth Sudanese, and led troops throughout the Nile Campaign.[126]

Beyond the legacy of Turco-Egyptian nepotism and the insidious nature of British racism, one of the things that held back Sudanese soldiers from promotion into the highest military ranks of the Egyptian Army was illiteracy.[127] With very few exceptions, Sudanese soldiers could neither read nor write. There were unique individuals, such as Ramzi Tahir, *saghkolaghasi* in the XIth Sudanese Battalion, whose father worked in the British consular or diplomatic service, and who was said to have "a perfect command of English," a mastery that may have included some degree of literacy.[128] And according to the above-mentioned Major Maxse, there were three native officers in the XIIIth Sudanese Battalion who read English and "liked magazines such as

Harpers, *The Strand*, *Temple Bar*, and anything American."[129] But these were rare cases.

Actually, for potential Sudanese officers, literacy in Arabic may have been equally if not more important than in English. Although the words of command were still mostly given in Turkish, as they had been since the days of Muhammad 'Ali, Arabic was the *lingua franca* of the Egyptian Army, and regularly used in military correspondence. Most sources, however, indicate that even Sudanese officers at the commissioned ranks were "very often illiterate and unfitted educationally to carry on the office work of a company."[130] Most Sudanese soldiers spoke a colloquial form of Cairene Arabic common to Sudan and Lower Egypt, one they would have learned from other soldiers upon their enlistment, or depending on their background and geographical origins, may already have been fluent in to varying degrees. Yet in light of their slave origins and lack of formal education, it is not surprising that very few of these men could actually read or write in any language. And this was a major obstacle for Sudanese soldiers who might otherwise have risen into the higher officer ranks considering their military knowledge and length of service.

To rectify this situation, and provide better training and education for potential Sudanese officers, the British, like 'Ali Khurshid sixty years earlier, began opening up cadet slots at the Cairo Military School for Sudanese – in 1899, following the Nile Campaign, this meant that a quarter of the cadets (25 out of 100) were slated to be Sudanese.[131] In 1905 a second military school was started in Khartoum strictly for Sudanese cadets, many of whom were the sons of old officers and soldiers, with an establishment set at thirty. Cadets spent two or three years in these schools, where they were taught both English and Arabic, the former being the language of instruction in such subjects as arithmetic; algebra; geometry; geography; the history of Egypt and the Sudan; military topography; military law; fortification and tactics.[132]

These expanded educational opportunities paved the way for the next generation of high-ranking Sudanese officers, when the door for promotions beyond the rank of *bimbashi* re-opened for the first time since the days of Gordon Pasha. Ironically, some of these cadets became early Sudanese nationalists and revolutionaries, most notably 'Ali 'Abd al-Latif, who graduated from the Khartoum Military School in 1913.[133] Promoting the somewhat contradictory mottos of "Sudan for the Sudanese" [*al-Sudan li-Sudaniyin*] and "Unity of the Nile Valley" [*wahdat wadi al-Nil*], it was indeed these very officers that helped to set in motion a transformation of the term "Sudanese" from denoting slave origins to that of an inclusive national identity. Some of the higher promotions, of course, would also be received by Nile Campaign soldiers, who, unlike the venerable Shilluk *bimbashi* 'Ali Jifun, were still young enough to benefit when the glass ceiling began to break.

Almas Mursi, for example, the Dinka *yuzbashi* mentioned above, served for another fifteen years following the River War, leading men in the Niam-Niam, Nyima, and south Kordofan patrols, and was eventually promoted *kaimakam* in 1911. He retired in 1915 after forty-three years service in Egyptian Army.[134] Sa'id 'Abdallah, as well, achieved higher ranks following the Nile Campaign – promoted *bimbashi* in 1906, *kaimakam* in 1912, and conferred the honorary rank of *miralai* upon his retirement in 1918.[135] And finally, there was Husain Muhammad Mustafa (1880–1941), who during the Nile Campaign was a *mulazim tani* in 'Ali Jifun and 'Abdallah 'Adlan's XIIth Sudanese Battalion though still a teenager. He served well into the twentieth century, from 1924 as an officer in the Sudan Defence Force, retiring from the military in 1935.[136]

Finally, it should also be mentioned that during the early years of the Anglo-Egyptian Condominium there were opportunities for Sudanese officers, albeit limited, to serve in the civil administration. Most of these officers, some presumably Nile Campaign veterans, were seconded to low-level staff positions in various state and provincial administrative departments. Yet there were a few of them that in the 1910s and 1920s became *ma'murs*, or more commonly, "sub-mamurs," and were put in charge of district security.[137] Of the 138 sub-mamurs in the Anglo-Egyptian Sudan in 1924, according to one source, almost twenty percent were Sudanese officers.[138] 'Ali 'Abd al-Latif, for example, following his time as an officer in the Sudanese XIth and IXth battalions, was appointed *ma'mur* of Shambe District, Bahr al-Ghazal.[139]

Discipline

Sudanese soldiers in the new Egyptian Army were subject to harsh military discipline and often severe, sometimes violent, punishments. In addition to constant drill, these soldiers were regularly given hard labor and sent on extended, forced marches through the desert, sometimes with deadly result. They were routinely flogged, often for minimal offenses, and many were executed. However, in comparison to that which they experienced in the old Egyptian Army, and considering the extreme nature of military punishment found in most European armies at the time, it is important that the point not be overstated. Moreover, there is evidence to suggest that a double standard may have existed when it came to the treatment of Sudanese soldiers. Due to their increasingly significant, and recognized, combat role, combined with the senior status of the many "long service men" in Sudanese battalions, these troops were often afforded leeway and special privileges not given to their Egyptian and British military brethren.

Flogging seems to have been the most common form of punishment for Sudanese soldiers in the Egyptian Army. In fact, in 1888 the *kaimakam* of the Xth Sudanese, D. A. Donne, in addition to urging for "more summary" discipline within Sudanese battalions, even suggested that flogging be done in lieu of fines for certain offenses:

> I think the discipline of a Soudanese Corps might be more summary than it is. By the time a single Court Martial case has been dealt with a vast budget of papers has been collected. I find that a "minor" *Court of Discipline*, with the sol and the four Company Sergt Majors is a most efficacious means of administering justice, and the men fear it. For instance, I tell them, if they find a man guilty, to sentence him to 20 lashes, and up to 14 days Imp. H. L. Fines for Drunkenness are I think very excessive, and act in no way as a deterrent. Blacks do not get drunk like English soldiers – and they very soon recover from the effects of drink. Besides the idea among the men is that their pay so stopped only finds its way into

other officials' hands. I would rather give a man twenty lashes, and I think he would rather have the lashes – It only takes the money from his wife and children which gives me a strong dislike to fining them so excessively. I think 10 piastres should be the limit of fine: anything necessary beyond that should be in lashese or Imp. HL etc. I have found justice and a tight hand to be the best discipline for Soudanese and no race appreciates it more.[140]

Of course, flogging in the Egyptian Army, or any nineteenth-century army for that matter, was nothing new, nor was it restricted to Sudanese troops. For example, although flogging was more or less abolished from the British Army in 1881, it did not disappear completely, and was still an optional form of corporal punishment for soldiers on active service in India as late as 1914.[141] In the old Egyptian Army, when Sudanese soldiers often "were abused by their Egyptian and Turkish officers," flogging was usually done with a four-foot long hippopotamus-hide whip, or *kurbaj*. And according to one account, an Egyptian soldier was once given sixty lashes for a dirty uniform.[142] Egyptian soldiers were not exempt from such punishments in the new Egyptian Army either, and during the Nile Campaign, according to Frederick Gore Anley, flogging of the "Gippy" soldier was used to "great advantage" and was "a form of punishment…used pretty extensively just now, and with very good effect."[143]

Executions of Sudanese soldiers in the new Egyptian Army, as well, were not uncommon in the case of major crimes such as murder. Most often these men were sentenced to death by general court-martial, and either shot or hanged. During the Nile Campaign, however, when by far the most prevalently mentioned reason for execution was desertion, often by recently enlisted prisoners of war, these executions were more summary in nature. Kitchener's Aide-de-Camp, J. K. Watson, for example, jotted in his Lett's Colonial Rough Diary and Almanac on 31 August 1897: "3 deserters caught, 1 killed. 1 wounded." And the next day, the first of September, he wrote simply: "The two surviving deserters were shot at sunrise."[144] A year later, writing in his diary two weeks before the Battle of Omdurman, George Skinner, a sergeant of the Medical Staff Corps, penned: "The news that we first heard on arrival here was that 13 Soudanese soldiers had deserted the previous day with their arms, and that another was caught in the act of deserting and was shot."[145]

The Egyptian Army of the 1890s, however, had no monopoly on military executions, or military discipline for that matter. There were still some eight offenses for which a British soldier could be executed during the Victorian era, even in times of peace, and another twelve in times of war, including "sleeping on his post" and "shamefully casting away his arms in the presence of the enemy." And in the early twentieth century, during World War I, "more than three hundred men were shot or hanged for cowardice, desertion or mutiny."[146] Compared to this standard, the threshold for capital offenses within Sudanese battalions during the Nile Campaign was arguably higher. Moreover, in terms of military discipline, it seems that Sudanese soldiers were cut greater slack, and given more privileges throughout the River War, than were other soldiers in Kitchener's Anglo-Egyptian army. And this double standard – again stemming from the relative seniority and martial reputation of Sudanese soldiers, combined with the belief that their race made them incapable of anything other than a "somewhat rudimentary" conception of military discipline – was to remain in effect once the military campaign was over, and it persisted into the twentieth century.

The greater rates of pay and domestic privileges granted to Sudanese soldiers have already been discussed. However, these were not the only perks they received during the Nile Campaign and beyond. For one, it seems that because manual labor was perceived as being "distasteful" to the Sudanese soldiers, most of it fell directly on the Egyptian troops.[147] Again and again in the documents one sees reference to the fact that *fellahin* conscripts did the vast majority of fatigue work and other manual labor during the River War, and vice versa, that Sudanese soldiers were often exempt from these kinds of jobs. Felix Ready, for example, a *bimbashi* in the 2nd Egyptian Battalion, bemoaning the fact that following the Battle of the Atbara it was Egyptian troops that carried the English wounded, wrote in April of 1898: "The greatest trouble we had was carrying the wounded back to Dahkola which was one of the fatigues which had to be given to the Egyptian troops – the blacks wouldn't be strong enough besides they are never put on fatigues. The stretchers were very rotten and imagine Egyptian carrying English wounded. I really think it was a disgrace to the English troops."[148]

Granted, many of the Sudanese soldiers were more senior and experienced than their Egyptian comrades, and thus far more valuable as fighters than ditch diggers. And indeed, in a way, they had certainly earned this status, many of them having spent decades fighting in the region. However, they were also the beneficiaries of the British tendency to categorize peoples in broad strokes, be they nationalities, ethnic groups, or races; in the Victorian officer's mind, all Egyptians (by which they meant the *fellahin*, Egypt's agricultural workers) were inherently hard-working "laborers," and all Sudanese (by which they meant "blacks" from the southern Sudan) were fearless "warriors" but inherently lazy and undisciplined. During the Nile Campaign, as British commanders delegated work duties and determined battle formations, these were to become self-fulfilling categories – the Egyptians doing the greater share of the manual labor, the Sudanese bearing the greater burden in terms of the actual fighting.

There were other, less significant (though perhaps not to the men themselves), perks and privileges that Sudanese soldiers were accorded during the River War – from water bottles that were "half as large again" as those used by the British soldiers to "undress" made of loose linen that they were regularly allowed to wear for "greater comfort."[149] And on the final approach to Omdurman in August 1898, while the British troops had to sleep "every night in full war paint," by which the author meant "we English have to always sleep in our boots and accoutrements," the Sudanese and Egyptians "simply have out picquets finding sentries under one officer, the remainder turning in like gentlemen."[150] The diaries of British soldiers serving in the Nile Campaign are full of bitter complaints about General Gatacre ("General Backacher") making them go to sleep in their boots.

Special treatment and privileges for Sudanese soldiers continued well after the war, especially in terms of drill. In the 1911 Cairo War Office "Regulations and Instructions for British Officers Serving With the Egyptian Army," for example, it stated regarding parades: "It must be remembered that the Sudanese soldier is enlisted for long service, a fact which is sometimes lost sight of by Officers in a laudable desire to bring their Commands up to a high standard of efficiency in this branch." And it continued as follows: "It will be noticed that the older men drill twice a week only, the remainder, one drill or inspection daily, except recruits whose forenoon drill in hot weather would be Barrack Room instruction. No drills in the afternoon except for Recruits; on Mondays and Thursdays no parades after the early morning one; Friday a Holiday."[151] Finally, in a section entitled *Dealings with Egyptian and Sudanese Officers* it suggested that British officers:

> ...should at all times remember that the senior Egyptian Officers [meaning Egyptian and Sudanese] are older men than they, and are generally possessed of considerable experience and knowledge of the country in which they are serving. Most of them have seen active service in their younger days, and have attained their present position after years of hard and good work. The British Officer must be ever ready, on this account, to exercise infinite tact and patience.[152]

And so although strict military discipline and corporal punishment for Sudanese soldiers was standard operating procedure, being "the backbone of the Egyptian Army" clearly had its privileges.

Daily camp life

Like many a military campaign, the River War involved far more down time for soldiers than that spent marching or fighting. And although the campaign's success was very much a story about the prudent administration and efficient movement of men and material some fifteen hundred miles up the Nile, it still took two and a half years for Kitchener's army to get to Khartoum. And most of this time was spent at military camps in the northern Sudan awaiting the next transport, or the next battle, or the seasonal rise of the Nile. For Sudanese soldiers, these toilsome days in camp, in addition to being times for drill and attack exercises, were periods filled by recreational pursuits, social and religious life, as well as the occasional *daluka* dance. Some of these camp activities were integrated (or semi-integrated) affairs, and brought the Sudanese together with Egyptian and British troops. Others were of a more segregated, or self-selected nature, allowing Sudanese soldiers the cultural space to spend time with each other, whether conducted on a casual basis with family and friends, battalion mates and ethnic brothers, or communed in a more formal way for indigenous and/or syncretic rituals that fell outside orthodox Islam.

According to most sources, the daily routine for soldiers in the Anglo-Egyptian army during the Nile Campaign began with early morning drill. These morning exercises regularly included attack and square formations, as well as musketry. Despite the heat and seeming monotony of it, drill could sometimes be enjoyable for the troops according to correspondent Bennet Burleigh:

> This morning, whilst Gatacre's brigade was attending divine services in camp, the three Khedival brigades were out drilling. A special attack exercise was introduced, to which Egyptians and Soudanese took gaily. They were ordered to charge through their own

zereba. The instructions were to run steadily, and jump into the middle of the brush, and then tramp through. They were warned, above all, to try and keep upon their feet, for if they fell they would be caught in the cruel thorns and torn, besides running the risk of being trampled by comrades charging behind. There were several gallant rushes made over the thick camp zereba. In each instance, led by their British officers, black and Egyptian battalions got through, taking the hedge, with a cheer, in splendid style.[153]

Other than water fatigues, River War soldiers spent much of the rest of the day trying to keep out of the sun, inside their tents or under whatever shade they could find, passing the midday hours in one reposeful way or the other. Later in the afternoon, they would usually get some physical exercise or bathe in the Nile River.[154]

These recreational activities were often integrated, and more than one British soldier's diary makes mention of "Gippies" and "blacks" and "Tommies" all bathing in the Nile, "in the altogether."[155] Sometimes there were football matches that took place among and between these three groups of soldiers. And according to *The Daily Graphic's* Dongola Campaign correspondent, in 1896 the most popular camp games among Sudanese soldiers were rounders and hockey, and that "one of the best matches was that witnessed between the British soldiers of the Maxim Battery and a team from the 13th Soudanese."[156] Occasionally, so-called "gymkhana meetings" were arranged in which Egyptian and Sudanese soldiers engaged in camel races, donkey races, foot races, and tugs-of-war.[157] Finally, it was reported that the "Soudanese Tommies" at Camp Merawi, who "seize hold of any chance of relieving the sameness of the days' routine," even tamed "Nubian gazelles" as pets and that many a Sudanese soldier took them out for runs in the desert on Fridays.[158]

At night it seems that social festivities were of a more segregated nature, as British soldiers often attended "smoking concerts" and camp "sing-songs," whereas Sudanese troops made music of their own – on *daluka* drums, and with wind instruments fashioned from old tin biscuit boxes, the beat of their "tom-toms" accompanied by festive singing and rhythmic dancing within their own encampments.[159] A fairly typical description of these impromptu music sessions was that given by the *Westminster Gazette* correspondent Ernest Bennett, upon reaching "Um Teref" camp in August 1898: "Though it was difficult in twilight to see far ahead of our column, there was no possibility of mistaking the where-abouts of the camp, for the wild music of the Sudanese bands was already in full swing. The first thing these black troops do when they get into camp is to strike up some of their unearthly tunes."[160]

Sometimes these nighttime festivities were of a more formal and elaborate, sometimes contrived, nature – either related to a Muslim holiday, or in celebration of some prior event or recent accomplishment, such as the victory party following the Battle of Atbara, described by Bennet Burleigh:

> In the lines of the Egyptians and Soudanese there were sounds of rejoicing. The fellaheen were chanting in their measured fashion, to the usual accompaniment of much clapping of palms. As for the blacks, they were jubilant and gay. The tom-toms, with ex-bully-beef tins, were craftily beaten, made to pulsate wildly, – a maddening rhythmic iteration. All the while, weird melodies were being sung; so, small wonder that numbers of those simple children of nature took to capering, dancing, and shouting. In the midst of them dervish

3.5 Sketches of camp life at Wadi Halfa. Top caption: "The North Staffordshire men and their Soudanese chums: their favourite midday sport." Bottom caption: "Washing day with the Soudanese recruits."
(*The Daily Graphic*, 12 May 1896)

prisoners, most of them blacks and countrymen of their own, sat and looked smilingly on, almost ready, I fancied, to join in the fun.[161]

"Dancing the 'Dilluka' on Dongola Day" at Merawi was such a festive and memorable scene that it made the cover illustration of the weekly British newspaper *The Graphic* on 23 October 1897. The caption read:

> Our Special Correspondent writes: – "On September 23rd, the first anniversary of the taking of Dongola, Lieut.-Colonel Lewis, commandant of the station, gave permission to the Soudanese soldiers to hold a big *dilluka*, or dance. A series of mud pillars as high as a man had been built, and a good fire was lighted on the top of each, giving an ample and picturesque light. Round every pillar there was a dance, each different from the other. The largest of all was performed by about a hundred men, who were drawn up in a double circle. Each man held a stick in his hand, and when the rough music started the hundred sticks clashed against each other with a not unmusical sound. The dancers themselves moved in a most curious way. Half of them moved from right to left and the other half moved in a contrary direction. As each man passed his fellow moving the opposite way he struck his stick."[162]

Occasionally these religious festivals and *dalukas* were allowed to take place outside the confines of the camp, and sometimes even included local inhabitants and were attended by curious British officers. Such was the case at Berber with the Feast of Bairam in 1898, when "inhabitants, joined by all the native soldiers off duty, met outside the town" for a celebration that lasted well into the night. Generals Kitchener, Hunter, and Gatacre, along with a number of other British officers, came to witness the festivities "in the early part of the evening."[163]

According to *The Graphic*: "The men of each tribe, no matter what regiment they belonged, joined the dance peculiar to their own tribe…In one of the most interesting dances the howling mob danced round and round to the beating of tomtoms, and at regular intervals strike each other's shields with marvelous accuracy all together. Many of the dancers were arrayed in jibbas and armed with shields and spears taken from the defeated Dervishes."[164] This particular description is noteworthy in that it represents an extremely rare instance when any reference was given to Sudanese soldiers retaining, and expressing collectively, their own ethnic identities. One late-nineteenth-century observer, British officer B. R. Mitford, made the point that many Sudanese soldiers knew little about their ethnic backgrounds because they "had been taken from their villages as children, and knew nothing of tribal customs except from hearsay." However, Mitford's diary extracts also provide evidence suggesting that some Sudanese soldiers possessed a greater degree of ethnic knowledge and identity than others, particularly those who "had been initiated into the rites connected with full manhood, before the slave-dealer or the Arab had swooped down and carried them off." And as with the 1898 Feast of Bairam at Berber, religious and/or commemorative festivities seemed to have been the prime vehicle for such forms of ethnic expression according to Mitford: "Some of the headdresses worn at '*dilukas*' were very striking, particularly those of the Shilluk and Fertit tribes. I thought they were purely fancy until Messedaghlia told me that they were copies of what they wore in their own districts in their wild state."[165]

If nothing else, it appears that Sudanese soldiers were given significant

3.6 *"Dancing the 'Dilluka' on Dongola Day"* (Sydney P. Hall, from a sketch by W. T. Maud, *The Graphic*, 23 October 1897)

cultural and social space to practice their religion. Whether it be time allotted for morning and evening prayers, "Holiday" from drill on Fridays, or letup for Islamic festivals associated with Ramadan, British commanders provided their Muslim soldiers with perhaps more religious freedom than one might expect given their Christian backgrounds and pan-Islamic fears.[166] Moreover, there is also evidence, though more rarely found, that other local beliefs and cultural practices were tolerated as well. There is the following quite unique account by *Daily Mail* correspondent G. W. Steevens, for example, describing a pre-battle ritual followed by black soldiers: "They moved off by companies through a narrow alley, and there lay four new-killed goats, the sand lapping their blood. Every officer rode, every man stepped, over the luck token; they would never go out to fight without it."[167]

Yet perhaps an even more revealing, and even rarer, piece of historical evidence linking Sudanese soldiers with indigenous religious beliefs falling outside orthodox Islam is to be found in an October 1897 illustration published by the British weekly *The Graphic*. Entitled "Life in Camp at Merawi: The Devil Dance," the ceremony being depicted here was clearly a *tombura zar* spirit-possession healing ritual.[168] *Zar* is the belief in a certain kind of possessing spirit, as well as the term for the spirits themselves, the mental illness they cause, and the cults associated with this belief found throughout Africa and the Middle East.[169] It has long been thought that *zar*, and the *tombura* form in particular, was first disseminated in North Africa by nineteenth-century Turco-Egyptian

3.7 *"The advance in the Soudan: life in camp at Merawi: the Devil Dance."*
Tombura zar *spirit-possession healing ritual*
(H. M. Paget from a sketch by W. T. Maud, *The Graphic*, 23 October 1897)

armies, via slave soldiers originally from southern Sudan.[170]

To this day many of the recurrent themes and terms associated with *tombura zar* have Egyptian Army derivations: its processions, its ceremonial songs, its hierarchy of officials, and notably, its use of certain titles and words such as *sanjak*, *brigdar*, *meiz*, and *bulbif*. *Sanjak*, for example, is the title for the highest male officiant in the *tombura* cult, deriving from the nineteenth-century Turco-Egyptian term for senior cavalry officers. *Brigdar* derives from the Turkish term *baraq dar*, or "standard bearer," and serves as the title for the assistant to the *sanjak*. *Meiz* means "supper," and is probably derived from the military sense of "mess." And *bulbif* refers to "bully beef," food served at the *meiz*. Above and beyond these lingual associations, anthropologists have discovered that most of the forms, or manifestations, of the *zar* spirit enacted before *tombura* devotees and found within the major spirit modalities of *tombura* represent either ethnic groups from which Sudanese slave soldiers originated or hark back to events of the Turkiyya and Mahdiyya periods.[171] Indeed, according to one anthropologist, these *tombura* spirit modalities are cultural objects, "stereotypes of ethnic, religious, and other categories which are related to the historical memory of the Sudani people."[172]

The first three *tombura* modalities, or *khayts*, represent the Nuba, the Banda (Bahr al-Ghazal), and the Gumuz (Ethiopian frontier), ethnic groups from which many Sudanese slave soldiers either originated or descended. These *khayts* usually embody the supposed violent character, paganism, and/or cannibal nature of these ethnic groups and regions of the Sudan. Within the modality known as *Bashawat* [plural form of *basha*, i.e. *pasha*], to provide another example, one finds spirits representing Mahdist-era Egyptian officers of Sudanese battalions stationed at Suakin. Another of the major modalities, the *Khawajat* [pale-skinned foreigners], is made up of *khayts* manifesting themselves as British colonial officers, replete with ceremonial attire that often includes a pith-helmet, khaki shorts, fly-whisk, pipe, and sunglasses; and within this category there is a spirit named Nimr al-Kinda that some have posited may be the embodiment of Sir Samuel Baker. The *Baburat* modality, to which devotees are now rare, supposedly relates to the "ships" that brought the Anglo-Egyptian army into the Sudan. And in the final category, the Sudanese, one actually finds the renowned Mahdist military leader Osman Digna, who eluded capture by the Egyptian Army for so many years.[173]

Moreover, among the ceremonial *tombura* songs, or *jawabs*, there are many that relate directly to the military experience of nineteenth-century Sudanese soldiers in the Egyptian Army – via references to distinct individuals, locations, and historical events. According to the oral tradition of *tombura* officiants, these songs were composed by *sanjaks* serving in the Egyptian Army and Mahdist *jihadiyya* between the 1860s and 1910s, further evidenced by their structural and thematological similarities to Sudanese soldiers' songs from the turn of the twentieth century.[174] Many of these *jawabs*, for example, seem to reference the 1884–1885 Mahdist siege of Khartoum ("Seven boats full of Christians…We hope the arsenal does not betray us"), whereas others relate to the 1896–1898 Nile Campaign ("The Christian destroyed the *qubba* [Mahdi's tomb]. He is not afraid of God. Bringi turn your weapon.").[175] And the song of Tumburani, the most important *jawab* of the entire *tombura* cult, also refers the the Anglo-Egyptian reconquest of the Sudan:

> Tumburani, o Tumburani there is no God but God.
> Tumburani king of the Sudan
> The soldiers of the Prophet killed a chicken (and)
> Said it was blood money (ransom) for a bull.
> O Bardawil, oh Bardawil, his stomach is big.[176]

This song is performed via the *Khawajat* modality, in the form of a benevolent British colonial officer, and is received by devotees with "much rejoicing." And according to the testimony of recent *tombura* officiants: "Tumburani was the English soldier who invaded the Sudan and took it from the Ansar, the 'soldiers of the Prophet. The battle (of Karari) was terrible and the country was completely destroyed: 'the people were confused. That is why we say that although they wanted to kill a bull, they killed a chicken.' Bardawil was seen as another British officer, but no information was given as to who he was."[177]

In any case, and getting back to the October 1897 illustration published in *The Graphic*, this utterly unique depiction represents one of the best, and so far the earliest found, pieces of documentary evidence connecting Sudanese Egyptian Army soldiers with *tombura zar*.[178] There are a number of things about the drawing and its caption that would lead one to conclude it was depicting a *tombura* healing ritual, and not a "devil dance," as the artist wrongly described it. First, consistent with most *zar* healing rituals, the possessed victims, or patients, were both women, "[t]wo wives of the black soldiery," and were depicted as "kneeling on a piece of matting...enveloped in white muslin." Second, these women were, according to the artist, "in the charge of a third woman, who stood over them." This female figure, occupying the far right side of the frame, was pretty clearly the *umiya* – the woman in *zar* healing rituals who orchestrates the full enactment of the possession, first summoning and then appeasing (not exorcising) the *zar* spirits present in the possessed individuals. What most clearly distinguishes this ceremony as *tombura zar* and not *burei zar* was the presence of a *sanjak*, standing near the *umiya* and strumming his *tombura*, as well as the *nagagir* drummers and flag on the left side of the frame. The *sanjak* is unique to *tombura zar*, as are the *nugagir* depicted here, barrel-shaped, hide-covered drums beaten with sticks rather than by hand, distinguishing them from the *daluka* drum used in *burei zar*. And *bawarig* [banners] such as the one seen here are used exclusively in *tombura zar* ceremonies to mark the *mayanga*, or place of sacrifice, and are not seen at *burei zar* rituals.[179]

Regardless, such spirit-possession rituals and syncretic religious practices seem to have allowed nineteenth-century Sudanese soldiers, like their twentieth-century descendants, to "articulate an alternative, positive self-identity," inverting the notion that as slave soldiers they had no history, no descent, no true religion. *Tombura* may thus have served them as something of an "officialising accommodational strategy" and "Islamic counter-discourse" during the River War, as it did for Sudanese devotees more broadly in subsequent years.[180] For the possessed wives of Sudanese soldiers, *tombura zar* may also have served these women "to articulate certain problems and experiences of everyday life" and performed something of a therapeutic function, indicating social and psychological strains within the *harimat* – stresses and anxieties surrounding marriage, fertility, and infibulation (pharaonic circumcision).[181] And it could even be argued that such cultural expressions of "daily camp life" as described above, especially *tombura zar* ceremonies, represented a "hidden transcript" of sorts for nineteenth-century Sudanese soldiers and their wives, "a critique of power spoken behind the back of the dominant," be these overlords the Turco-Egyptians, the Mahdists, or the British.[182]

Retirement

One final category worth considering is that of the provisions made for Sudanese soldiers upon leaving the ranks. In the old Egyptian Army, according to 'Abdallah 'Adlan, "Soldiers were not allowed to retire but just worked and served until they dropped. When no longer fit for active service, they were put onto light work such as looking after the officers' gardens."[183] Increasingly – first under Khedive Isma'il in 1876, and then again in 1888 and 1899 during the reigns of Tawfiq and Abbas – laws were enacted that provided retired Egyptian Army officers with pensions based on their rank and years of service.[184] As well, over time privates and non-commissioned officers began receiving service gratuities and other "Aids" funds, and eventually pensions, upon retirement or discharge. And in the first two decades following the defeat of the Mahdists, some two thousand ex-soldiers were given plots of land to farm in settlement colonies throughout the Sudan. However, for the vast majority of old, discharged, and retired Sudanese soldiers, little had changed from 'Abdallah 'Adlan's above description of the 1870s – the paper promises of the "Aids" and "Colonisation Schemes" belied a much harsher, often pensionless, sometimes debilitated, reality for most ex-soldiers.

Prior to the introduction of the Egyptian Army Pension Scheme of 1919, only retired officers received pensions, and so there were no provisions made for the ranks below *mulazim tani*.[185] This meant that most old soldiers, when no longer fit for service, had little choice but to find some form of employment – as policemen, prison guards, *ghaffirs* [watchmen], cooks, farm workers, factory employees, woodcutters, as well as other odd jobs.[186] Consider the post-military career of Faraj Sadik, for example, who upon his discharge in 1902 had served in the Egyptian Army for nearly thirty years. Between 1902 and 1914, according to his memoir, he worked as a cook in Khartoum, first for Slatin Pasha, and later, for the Italian mission. In 1914 Faraj Sadik "got a job as a mosquito-killer in the Khartoum sanitary section," a job he held for the next four years. Come 1918 he "went with some camels to Darfur and joined the Police in that Province," and served with them until 1923. He spent most of the next decade working as a gardener in Kuttum, followed by a job in the 1930s – Faraj Sadik now in his seventies – as a *ghaffir* at the Kabkabiya rest house in western Darfur.[187]

Along similar lines, there is the career of *shawish* Faraj Kasim, who had served in the Sudanese Infantry Band for eighteen years beginning in 1891. Correspondence about his pension status in 1946 reveals that although there was a record of a service gratuity of £E 3.5 given to him upon his discharge in 1909 per the Egyptian Army Financial Regulations then in force, he claimed it was never received. Whatever the case, his rank of *shawish* entitled him to no pension at the time, and so he went on to serve in the Fung police force until 1927.[188] Likewise, Abdel Fadil el Jak, who served in the XIIth Sudanese Battalion during the Nile Campaign, was discharged in 1900, and received no pension. Some forty-six years later he was found working in the Dueim Tomato Sauce factory, making £E 1.5 per month, applying for an additional thirty-eight piastres monthly "aid" recently made available for cases such as his by the Financial Secretary in Khartoum.[189]

Those Sudanese ex-soldiers who could not find employment or were physically debilitated in some way, often suffering from war wounds, sometimes found themselves in dire straits. *The Times* Nile Campaign correspondent E. F. Knight described the sorry condition of some of these Sudanese veterans: "Some of these old soldiers get employment as caretakers, watchmen, and so forth; others obtain grants of land; but I understand that for the vast majority of them no provision whatever is made by the Government....It is to be hoped that the Egyptian Government will shortly see its way to abolishing this scandalous state of things by paying small pensions to those who have served it so well."[190] Apparently, and despite attempts to deal with "this scandalous state," things were little improved some eighteen years later when the *sirdar* and Governor-General of the Sudan, F. R. Wingate, wrote the following letter to Colonel Garsia, the Financial Secretary of the Egyptian Army:

> I have just returned form a tour of inspection in Kordofan, Sennar, etc., and at Kosti I inspected about 150 old Sudanese reservists of whom upwards of 50 percent complained that they had received no Aids. I went carefully into practically every case and found that the majority of them were very old men who had borne the burden and heat of the day, many of them covered with wounds, and indeed the very men for whom I had struggled to get the money in the first instance....
>
> For many years it had been looked upon as one of the greatest scandals connected with the Army that old Sudanese, who had fought so gallantly for us both on the frontier and in the eventual re-occupation of the Sudan for something like twenty years, should be kicked out of the Army practically penniless, and many cases of the greatest distress, hardship, and even starvation were brought to my notice. I represented the matter in the strongest manner and asked for a considerable annual grant of money to enable us to rectify this burning scandal, not only in the interests of right and justice, but also because I knew that our atrocious disregard of these old men was having the worst possible effect on our recruiting efforts, and that a feeling of genuine dislike to Government, on the part of the Sudanese, was being engendered throughout the country, owing to our bad treatment of men whose services demanded every possible consideration shown to them.
>
> After an immense amount of wrangling and trouble with the Financial Advisor of that period, it was at last agreed that a sum of £.2500 should be allotted annually, and that in the event of the total amount not being expended in the course of the year, it should be allowed to accumulate as a special fund.
>
> Owing to the organization for the proper distribution of this money being at first somewhat faulty, and it being very difficult to ascertain where a good many of the most deserving of the old discharged Sudanese were living, it transpired that for the first two or three years of its existence the fund was only partially expended and a considerable accumulation resulted. Your predecessor, in conjunction with the Finance Minister, pounced on this accumulation and, to my infinite regret, insisted on its being given up....
>
> The other day, to my horror, the A.G. showed me some correspondence between himself and yourself in which it appeared that another pounce was contemplated. Let me tell you at once that I shall not consent, and I have now most definite proof that there are hundreds of old Sudanese throughout the country who should have had Aids years and years ago, and who are now in great want and distress.[191]

Whether the contemplated second "pounce" took place is not revealed in the documents, but it is clear from this letter and others that despite the various attempts on the part of Wingate and the petitions of ex-soldiers themselves, gratuities and pensions for this generation of Sudanese retirees were seldom disbursed even when they existed on the books.

One initiative for discharged Sudanese veterans of the Nile Campaign that seems to have been more successful, though ultimately abandoned by the late 1920s, was that of the "Colonisation Schemes" of the early twentieth century. Fueled by the Government's desire in the wake of reoccupation to prevent the migration of ex-slaves into towns, to maintain control over discharged soldiers, and to increase agricultural production, select soldiers were allowed to settle with their families at a number of newly established agricultural colonies scattered across the country.[192] Major A. C. Parker made note of its progress in his December 1900 Sudan Intelligence Report:

> During the past month, over 800 men discharged from Sudanese Battalions have been sent at Government expense to the localities elected by them, under the new Colonisation Scheme. The greater portion of them have gone to Kassala, Khartoum, or Sennar Mudiriehs, numbers as follows: Kassala 136; Khartoum 164; Sennar 489. All these men have taken their wives + children and are at the beginning to be assisted by the Gov. with tools, grain, etc.[193]

In fact, similar schemes had been experimented with even prior to the reconquest, both in the Tokar delta and Uganda. The Tokar colony, begun in 1892, had provided ex-soldiers with fertile land on which to cultivate crops and accumulate flocks; it had also served a strategic purpose, establishing a population of loyal inhabitants in an area of the Sudan recently held by the Mahdists. At around the same time in Uganda, settlements of ex-soldiers were set up at Eldama Ravine, at Kibos, and in Bunyoro – to provide food for caravans, supplement garrisons, safeguard lines of communication, and secure new territories.[194]

In any case, Sudanese ex-soldier colonies such as these proliferated following the River War. Most were located in the agricultural districts of the Blue Nile, White Nile, Kassala, and Sennar provinces, but colonies were also set up in the Kordofan, Funj, Nuba Mountains, Upper Nile, and Darfur provinces. By 1922 some twenty-three colonies had been established, with the number of settlers per colony ranging from six (Abu Zabad, Kordofan) to four hundred twenty-five (Kosti, White Nile), some two thousand individuals in total.[195] Early on, as in Tokar and Uganda, many of these colonies served a definite strategic as well as agricultural function, evidenced by their locations along the Blue and White Niles and towards the Ethiopian frontier and the unpacified south – sites where camps of ex-soldiers could be planted to protect communication lines and provide wood for Anglo-Egyptian gunboats and steamers, as well as guard against any neo-Mahdist uprisings. And in fact many of these settlements, under the authority and discipline of senior Sudanese officers, initially took on the appearance of military camps, made up of discharged soldiers all hailing from the same battalion. Indeed, at least two of these colonies were named after specific Sudanese battalions ("Tisagi" = the IXth; "Arbatasher" = the XIVth), and one, after the Cairo barracks where they once lived ("Abbasieh"). Some of these same colonists later benefited from an expanded and popular reserve scheme for old soldiers, for which they were paid a retaining fee, and with an annual call up of only fourteen days light training.[196]

In terms of agricultural production, ex-soldier settlers were given a parcel of land and set up with everything they might need to succeed in farming it – seed loans, grain stores, farm implements, and even initial food rations. And though required to begin repayment on these loans once the first crop was harvested, they were exempt from taxes for the first two or three years. Following this trial period they then became owners of the land, and were required to pay taxes and provide grain to the state. These taxes and grain were collected by salaried, government-appointed colony headmen, many of whom were former Sudanese officers in the Egyptian Army. 'Abdallah 'Adlan mentioned in his life story, for example, that he spent his seventies as the headman of the *Redif* settlement colony at El Obeid.[197]

Albeit not "colonies" in an official sense, settlements of ex-soldiers and their families also grew up around military posts and administrative centers in the Southern Sudan during the early years of the Condominium. These discharged and retired Sudanese soldiers returned to the south, but chose to live in these "nascent urban communities" with each other rather than in rural villages with their ethnic kith and kin. These men often served as policemen, manned wood stations, or found work as traders, tailors, butchers, or mechanics. The principal patron of these ex-soldiers was thus still the government, and before long they and their families came to represent a large percentage of the civilian population in these southern towns, many of them living in what was known as the *malakiyya*, or civilian quarters.[198] One of the more interesting cases of such "retired" Sudanese soldiers was Kong Dungdit, a Gaajak Nuer who had been a slave soldier in both the old Egyptian Army, and after the fall of Khartoum, the Mahdist *jihadiyya*, before being re-enlisted in the Egyptian Army following the Nile Campaign. Kong Dungdit later became a policeman in the Upper Nile Province, then a government interpreter along the Sudanese-Ethiopian border, and eventually served as a native administrator for twenty years – appointed a "traditional chief" of a group of Lou Nuer, a position he held until 1942.[199]

Of course, there were many Sudanese soldiers who fought in the River War that never received pensions, had the chance to become landowners, or retired to ex-soldier colonies and *malakiyyas*. Rather, they died on the field of battle or in a military hospital, buried in unmarked graves. Whereas the casualties of British soldiers in the Nile Campaign always received specific mention in military reports and in the press by name, rank, and serial number, Sudanese killed and wounded were rarely if ever noted in other than broad terms and total numbers, either by battalion or race. In fact, often the battle deaths of Sudanese soldiers were even lumped in together with Egyptian troops as simply "native soldiers killed," with no breakdown whatsoever. And these same "natives" were also usually buried as one, as they were following the 1898 Battle of Atbara, when "fellaheen and Soudanese were buried together in trenches dug outside the zereba," with their British brethren, on the other hand, given a military funeral and "laid to rest in an extemporised graveyard at the edge of the bush, on the northern side of the zareba."[200]

And yet, sometimes even the nameless were to achieve literary immortality, as did the twenty Sudanese soldiers killed at the 1897 Battle of Abu Hamed, made loyal to their fallen British officers even in death in a poem by Sir Rennell Rodd:

> Two white stone crosses side by side
>   Mark where the true blood flowed,
> Where Sidney and Fitzclarence died
>   To win the desert road.
> And ringed about them close at hand
>   In trenches not too deep,
> Unnamed, unnumbered in the sand,
>   Their dead black troopers sleep....
>
> The dark folk tell, as evening dies,
>   A sentry's cry alarms
> The graves from which dead soldiers rise
>   That hear the call to arms;

> And till the new sun's level rays
> Chase night across the sand,
> On guard around their English beys
> The dead battalions stand.[201]

Although a tribute to the heroism and loyalty of Sudanese soldiers, the poem also begins to reveal the kind of dichotomous relationship they had with their British officers – one that was simultaneously based on martial camaraderie and racial chauvinism, and engendered as much by Ornamentalism's "constructed affinities" as it was by Orientalism's notions of "otherness," a Gordian knot of respect and disdain to be cut through in the pages that follow.

Notes

1. Burleigh, *Sirdar and Khalifa*, 167.
2. Bredin, "The Life-Story of Yuzbashi 'Abdullah Adlan," 39.
3. See Dunn, *Khedive Ismail's Army*, 45; Hill and Hogg, *A Black Corps d'Elite*, 8; Sikainga, *Slaves into Workers*, 17; Hill, *On the Frontiers of Islam*, 141; Fahmy, *All the Pasha's Men*, 185; Keown-Boyd, *A Good Dusting*, 97.
4. Machell, "Memoirs of a Soudanese Soldier," *The Cornhill Magazine*, August 1896, 175; Bredin, "The Life-Story of Yuzbashi 'Abdullah Adlan," 38.
5. Dunn, *Khedive Ismail's Army*, 29, 45; Sikainga, *Slaves into Workers*, 17; Hill, *On the Frontiers of Islam*, 141; Fahmy, *All the Pasha's Men*, 91, 182–183; Keown-Boyd, *A Good Dusting*, 97; Hill and Hogg, *A Black Corps d'Elite*, 81–86; Hill, *Egypt in the Sudan*, 112–113.
6. E. A. de Cosson, *The Cradle of the Blue Nile*, Vol. II (London: John Murray, 1877), 233, as quoted in Dunn, *Khedive Ismail's Army*, 45.
7. Hill, *On the Frontiers of Islam*, 141; Dunn, *Khedive Ismail's Army*, 45; Sikainga, *Slaves into Workers*, 17; Bredin, "The Life-Story of Yuzbashi 'Abdullah Adlan," 39.
8. F. R. Wingate, notice draft, 3 July 1886, NRO CAIRINT 1/25/127; Enlistment Certificate A, Soudan Battalions, NRO CAIRINT 1/25/127; *Handbook of the Egyptian Army*, SAD 114/3, 73; Wood-Martin, *IXth Sudanese Regimental Historical Records*, SAD 110/11/5.
9. R. Martin, 19 June 1901, *Notes on the Egyptian Army*, NA WO 106/6306, 1–2, 10; *Handbook of the Egyptian Army*, SAD 114/3, 75. Be that as it may, these rates were still far less than the basic pay of British Army infantry privates, who in 1898 received 1s 3d a day. Thus even a married Sudanese *nafar* with ten years service would still make some forty-five percent less than a British rank-and-file soldier. Spiers, *The Late Victorian Army*, 138.
10. Martin, *Notes on the Egyptian Army*, NA WO 106/6306, 9–10; *Handbook of the Egyptian Army*, SAD 114/3, 72–73. In addition to their annual pay, these officers were also given a "special allowance if serving in the Sudan."
11. Fahmy, *All the Pasha's Men*, 254.
12. Enlistment Certificate A, Soudan Battalions, NRO CAIRINT 1/25/127.
13. Martin, *Notes on the Egyptian Army*, NA WO 106/6306, 1–2.
14. Machell, "Memoirs of a Soudanese Soldier," *The Cornhill Magazine*, August 1896, 175.
15. Fahmy, *All the Pasha's Men*, 185; Dunn, *Khedive Ismail's Army*, 44–45; Sikainga, *Slaves into Workers*, 17; Hill, *On the Frontiers of Islam*, 199.
16. Machell, "Memoirs of a Soudanese Soldier," *The Cornhill Magazine*, August 1896, 179.
17. Sikainga, *Slaves into Workers*, 17.
18. Hill, *On the Frontiers of Islam*, 199.
19. Bredin, "The Life-Story of Yuzbashi 'Abdullah Adlan," 42.
20. Machell, "Memoirs of a Soudanese Soldier," *The Cornhill Magazine*, October 1896, 491.
21. "With the Nile Expedition," 27 June 1896, *The Graphic*.
22. F. M. Gregson, photograph of "Ja'aliyyin women kneading bread during final preparations for the advance on Omdurman, Wad Hamid camp, August 1898," SAD.A27/75. The women in this photo may well have been slaves.
23. George Teigh, journal, 9 September 1898, NAM 1997-04-123-1.
24. George Skinner, diary, 26 February 1898, NAM 1979-09-15-3, 11.

[25] Fahmy, *All the Pasha's Men*, 186–187; Dunn, *Khedive Ismail's Army*, 44; Sikainga, *Slaves into Workers*, 17.
[26] Machell, "Memoirs of a Soudanese Soldier," *The Cornhill Magazine*, September 1896, 331.
[27] Dunn, *Khedive Ismail's Army*, 44.
[28] Martin, *Notes on the Egyptian Army*, NA WO 106/6306, 5. According to Lieutenants Alford and Sword, each battalion's red "tarboush" was "distinguished by a different coloured strip," that of the IXth green, the Xth black, the XIth red, the XIIth yellow, and the XIIIth blue. Alford and Sword, *The Egyptian Soudan*, 116.
[29] Mitford, "Extracts from the Diary of a Subaltern," *Sudan Notes and Records* XVIII, Part II (1935): 175.
[30] Ibid.
[31] Ibid., 180.
[32] Keown-Boyd, *A Good Dusting*, 128; Dunn, *Khedive Ismail's Army*, 36, 65–67; Hill and Hogg, *A Black Corps d'Elite*, 22, 38.
[33] Another possible explanation for sticking with the Martini-Henry – in addition to it having been common practice since the Indian Mutiny to arm "native" troops with the previous generation of rifle as a way to give British garrisons an edge over potential mutineers – was the fear on the part of British commanders that to introduce the Lee-Metford would greatly increase ammunition expenditures for the campaign; this concern was based on the widely held conviction that Sudanese soldiers were ill-disciplined marksmen who "shot wildly" in battle. Keown-Boyd, *A Good Dusting*, 192, 228n.
[34] Steevens, *With Kitchener to Khartum*, 13.
[35] Mitford, *Sudan Notes and Records* XVIII, Part II (1935): 180–181.
[36] Ibid., 175.
[37] Wood-Martin, *IXth Sudanese Regimental Historical Records*, SAD 110/11/8.
[38] F. R. Wingate, notice draft, 3 July 1886, NRO CAIRINT 1/25/127.
[39] Gilbert Falkingham Clayton to his mother, 6 February 1903, SAD 942/7/126.
[40] Gilbert Falkingham Clayton to his mother, 19 February 1903, SAD 942/7/138.
[41] Knight, *Letters from the Sudan*, 2.
[42] "Off to Akasheh," 31 March 1896, *The Daily Graphic*.
[43] "War Scenes at Assuan," 11 April 1896, *The Daily Graphic*.
[44] Slatin Pasha to Major Fairholme, 3 September 1897, NA FO 78/4895.
[45] "The Military Situation in the Egyptian Sudan," 5 January 1898, NA WO 32/6380, 10.
[46] Machell, "Memoirs of a Soudanese Soldier," *The Cornhill Magazine*, August 1896, 175.
[47] Ibid., 183.
[48] James Jay Bleeker Farley, "Some Recollections of the Dongola Expedition," SAD 304/2/13.
[49] Rudolf Slatin to Sirdar, 27 January 1900, SAD 270/1/99–100.
[50] D.G.A.M.D. to Evelyn Wood, 31 December 1898, NA WO 32/5552.
[51] H. H. Kitchener to Evelyn Wood, 12 March 1898, NAM 1968-07-234-1.
[52] Farley, "Some Recollections of the Dongola Expedition," SAD 304/2/5.
[53] F. R. Borrow, confid. letter, 9 March 1888, NRO CAIRINT 1/25/127.
[54] D. A. Donne to F. R. Wingate, 14 March 1888, NRO CAIRINT 1/25/127.
[55] D. A. Donne to Adjutant General, 20 March 1888, NRO CAIRINT 1/25/127.
[56] Enlistment Certificate A, Soudan Battalions, NRO CAIRINT 1/25/127.
[57] R. Martin, *Notes on the Egyptian Army*, NA WO 106/6306, 1.
[58] Steevens, *With Kitchener to Khartum*, 14.
[59] Ibid.
[60] Gilbert Falkingham Clayton to his mother, 6 February 1903, SAD 942/7/126.
[61] Thorburn, "Sudanese Soldiers' Songs," 317.
[62] Elise Kootz-Kretschmer, "Tatu, das geraubte Muvembakind" (Herrnhut: Missionsbuchhandlung, 1927), translated by Katya Skow, July 1988, as quoted in Marcia Wright, *Strategies of Slaves and Women: Life-Stories from East/Central Africa* (New York and London: Lilian Barber Press and James Currey Press, 1993), 186–187.
[63] Ernest N. Bennett, *The Downfall of the Dervishes, or The Avenging of Gordon, Being the Personal Narrative of the Final Soudan Campaign of 1898* (London: Methuen & Co., 1899), 114–115.
[64] Alford and Sword, *The Egyptian Souda* 101, 117; Burleigh, *Khartoum Campaign 1898*, 93, 106.
[65] Ibid. It should be noted that prior to the nineteenth century, women often accompanied European armies on campaign, providing similar domestic comforts and support services – laundering, cooking, mending, and nursing, as well as supplying the men with both food and liquor. Trustram, *Women of the Regiment*, 11–14.
[66] Burleigh, *Sirdar and Khalifa*, 167.
[67] Thorburn, "Sudanese Soldiers' Songs," 319.

[68] Burleigh, *Sirdar and Khalifa*, 197–198.
[69] Count Gleichen, *With the Camel Corps up the Nile* (West Yorkshire, England: EP Publishing Limited, 1975; originally published in 1888), 209–211.
[70] Burleigh, *Khartoum Campaign 1898*, 106.
[71] Burleigh, *Sirdar and Khalifa*, 167.
[72] Magdalene von Prince, *Eine Deutsche Frau im Innern Deutsch-Ostafrika* (Berlin: Mittler, 1903), 78–79, as cited in Wright, *Strategies of Slaves and Women*, 205–206.
[73] F. R. Borrow, 9 March 1888, NRO CAIRINT 1/25/127.
[74] Burleigh, *Sirdar and Khalifa*, 131.
[75] Ibid., 197.
[76] D. A. Donne to Adjutant General, 20 March 1888, NRO CAIRINT 1/25/127.
[77] H. H. Kitchener to F. R. Wingate, 19 June 1894, SAD 257/1/526–527.
[78] H. H. Kitchener to Lord Cromer, 20 June 1896, NA FO 78/4894.
[79] Burleigh, *Khartoum Campaign 1898*, 112.
[80] "Statement by Envoys of Disaffected Soudanese, Janna Bilal being Spokesman," 25 September 1897, Inclosure 1 in No. 17, *Papers Relating To Recent Events in the Uganda Protectorate*, NA WO 32/8417; Mr. Berkely to the Marquess of Salisbury, "Report by Her Majesty's Commissioner in Uganda on the Recent Mutiny of the Soudanese Troops in the Protectorate," 16 May 1898, NA WO 32/8417.
[81] Bennett, *The Downfall of the Dervishes*, 115.
[82] Yacoub Pasha Artin, *England in the Sudan* (London: Macmillan and Co., Ltd., 1911), 111. For more on this military tradition and its twentieth-century legacy, see also David Killingray, "Gender Issues and African Colonial Armies" in *Guardians of Empire: The Armed Forces of the Colonial Powers, c. 1700–1964*, eds. David Killingray and David Omissi (Manchester: Manchester University Press, 1999), 221–248.
[83] Charles À Court Repington, *Vestigia* (London: Constable and Company Ltd., 1919), 163–164.
[84] Kurita, "The Life of 'Ali 'Abd al-Latif," 7–10. The "effendiya" class was made up of civil servants and army officers.
[85] Ibid., 164.
[86] H. C. Jackson, *Behind the Modern Sudan* (London: Macmillan and Co. Ltd., 1955), 189.
[87] Burleigh, *Sirdar and Khalifa*, 253. J. A. Meldon's 1908 "Notes on the Sudanese in Uganda" also mentions how for Sudanese soldiers "it was their custom in those days to doctor themselves, and they had in each company one or more 'Hakims,' who correspond more or less with the witch-doctors of their tribes, but in addition they had and still have the knowledge of many herbs which are useful as medicines." Meldon, "Notes on the Sudanese in Uganda," 126.
[88] B. R. Mitford, "Extracts from the Diary of a Subaltern on the Nile in the Eighties and Nineties," *Sudan Notes and Records* XX (1937): 68–69.
[89] Bredin, "The Life-Story of Yuzbashi 'Abdullah Adlan," 40.
[90] Milner, *England in Egypt* (1892 ed.), 181.
[91] Hill, *Egypt in the Sudan*, 48; Salt, 8 February 1824, FO 78/126, as cited in Fahmy, *All the Pasha's Men*, 92.
[92] Hill, *Egypt in the Sudan*, 48; Dunn, *Khedive Ismail's Army*, 45.
[93] Hill, *Egypt in the Sudan*, 48.
[94] Hill, *On the Frontiers of Islam*, 106.
[95] Dunn, *Khedive Ismail's Army*, 45; for more on the health of Sudanese soldiers during the Mexican adventure see Hill and Hogg, *A Black Corps d'Elite*, 30–33.
[96] R. Martin, 19 June 1901, *Notes on the Egyptian Army*, NA WO 106/6306, 1.
[97] "The Advance in the Soudan: The Field Hospital at Merawi," 6 November 1897, *The Graphic*.
[98] Ibid.
[99] "Death Rate and Sick Returns, Dongola Expeditionary Force, 1896," *Intelligence Report, Egypt* (hereafter cited as *IRE*), No. 50, 28 August–31 December 1896, Appendix G(1), 32.
[100] Ibid.; Atteridge, *Towards Khartoum*, 357.
[101] "Average per cent of Admissions, Deaths, Invaliding and Daily Sick, Dongola Expedition," 28 August–31 December 1896, *IRE* 50, Appendix G(2), 33.
[102] Ibid.; "Death Rate and Sick Returns, Dongola Expeditionary Force, 1896," 28 August–31 December 1896, *IRE* 50, Appendix G(1), 32.
[103] G. Ayoub Balamoan, *Migration Policies in the Anglo-Egyptian Sudan, 1884–1956* (Cambridge, MA: Harvard University Center for Population Studies, 1976), 26.
[104] Ibid.; "Intelligence Report, Egypt," 22 June–18 August, 1896, *IRE* 49, 6, 39 (Appendix S).
[105] Hunter, *Historical Records of the Tenth Sudanese*, NAM 1968-07-330-1, 29.
[106] "Troops Leaving an Infected Cholera Camp," 15 August 1896, *Black & White*.

[107] Archibald Hunter to Lady Gosford, 23 July 1896, Halfa, SAD 1/2, 3; Hunter also wrote in July 1896 that "the black women have gone out over the cholera terribly fast. 27 laid out waiting burial in the morning was no unusual sight." Hunter to "George," n.d., July 1896, SAD 1/2, 10.

[108] "Cholera State, showing numbers of Cases and Deaths, as reported up to 10th August, 1896," 22 June–18 August, 1896, *IRE* 49, 39 (Appendix S); 47 killed, 122 wounded from the N.B. in "Return of Casualties which occurred at the Actions of Hafir and Dongola between 19th September and 23rd September 1896," 28 August–31 December 1896, *IRE* 50, Appendix G(3), 34.

[109] Hill, *Egypt in the Sudan*, 46–47; Hill, *A Biographical Dictionary of the Anglo-Egyptian Sudan*, 27, 67, 80, 198; Hill and Hogg, *A Black Corps d'Elite*, 7–9; Dunn, *Khedive Ismail's Army*, 51–53.

[110] Hill and Hogg raise this point in their study of Sudanese soldiers who fought in Mexico in the 1860s. Hill and Hogg, *A Black Corps d'Elite*, 10–11.

[111] Ibid., 9; Hill, *Egypt in the Sudan*, 108.

[112] Hill and Hogg, *A Black Corps d'Elite*, 9.

[113] Hill, *A Biographical Dictionary of the Anglo-Egyptian Sudan*, 124, 274, 246.

[114] Ibid., 297.

[115] Ibid., 124.

[116] Ibid., 246.

[117] Ibid., 124; see also Hill and Hogg, *A Black Corps d'Elite*, 139–141.

[118] Martin, *Notes on the Egyptian Army*, NA WO 106/6306, 1; McGregor, *A Military History of Modern Egypt*, 194.

[119] Atteridge, *Towards Khartoum*, 340. In addition, all four brigade commanders and all four brigade majors during the Dongola Campaign were British. "Intelligence Report, Egypt," 28 August–31 December 1896, *IRE* 50, 27.

[120] *Army List, 1897* (Cairo: War Office Printing Press, 1897), SAD 111/2, 12–27.

[121] Hill and Hogg, *A Black Corps d'Elite*, 151n66, 165.

[122] *Army List, 1897*, SAD 111/2, 20–25; John Baynes, *Far from a Donkey* (London: Brassey's Ltd., 1995), 47. It is also worth noting that within the *jihadiyya* on the Mahdist side, the *ru'us mi'at* ("captains of hundreds," the equivalent to the *yuzbashia* of the Egyptian Army) were also Sudanese, serving under Ta'aisha commanders. Holt, *The Mahdist State in the Sudan*, 247. In fact, an 1896 Egyptian intelligence report lists the names of these "Rasmiya" within the three *jihadiyya* "Rubs" as follows: Adam Bringi (Sudani), Gohar (Sudani), and Selim (Sudani) in "Rub" No. I; Abder Radi (Sudani), Rizkalla Hamed (Sudani), and Adam En Nai (Sudani) in "Rub" No. II; Abdulla Id (Sudani) and Hasaballa Furawi (Sudani) in "Rub" No. III. "Organization of Dervish and Native Forces in Dongola, with Names of Emirs," 28 August–31 December 1896, *IRE* 50, Appendix F(3), 31.

[123] F. I. Maxse as quoted in Baynes, *Far from a Donkey*, 47.

[124] Martin, *Notes on the Egyptian Army*, NA WO 106/6306, 9–10; *Handbook of the Egyptian Army*, SAD 114/3, 72–73.

[125] Hill, *A Biographical Dictionary of the Anglo-Egyptian Sudan*, 233; Keown-Boyd, *A Good Dusting*, 98; Douglas H. Johnson, "Biographical Data: Sudanese Officers & NCOs" (computer printout given to author by Johnson), 13–14.

[126] Hill, *A Biographical Dictionary of the Anglo-Egyptian Sudan*, 324.

[127] *Handbook of the Egyptian Army*, SAD 114/3, 44; Hill and Hogg, *A Black Corps d'Elite*, 8.

[128] G. E. Matthews to F. R. Wingate, 30 December 1899, Omdurman, SAD 269/12/77 (as quoted in Johnson, "Biographical Data: Sudanese Officers & NCOs," 40).

[129] F. I. Maxse to his father, 4 April 1897, as quoted in Baynes, *Far from a Donkey*, 51.

[130] *Handbook of the Egyptian Army*, SAD 114/3, 44. Major Maxse's above anecdote notwithstanding, he later wrote that Sudanese officers "risen from the ranks…can neither read nor write." F. I. Maxse to his father, 9 April 1897, as quoted in Baynes, *Far from a Donkey*, 47.

[131] Ibid.; Hill, *Egypt in the Sudan*, 46–47; *Handbook of the Egyptian Army*, SAD 114/3, 68.

[132] *Handbook of the Egyptian Army*, SAD 114/3, 68–70.

[133] Kurita, "The Life of 'Ali 'Abd al-Latif," 7–24; Vezzadini, "The 1924 Revolution," 213–223; see also Kurita, "The Role of 'Negroid but Detribalized' People in Modern Sudanese History." In addition to 'Ali 'Abd al-Latif, there was also Zein Abdin 'Abd al-Tam, 'Abd al-Rahman 'Abd al-Radi, Zein al-Abdin Salih, Hassan al-Zein, Muhammad Surur Rustum, Hassan Sharaf, 'Abd al-Wahab Beheri, 'Abd al-Hamid Mirsal, Muhammad 'Abd al-Bakheit, 'Ali al-Banna, Sa'id Shahata, and Sabit 'Abd al-Rahim.

[134] Hill, *A Biographical Dictionary of the Anglo-Egyptian Sudan*, 233; Keown-Boyd, *A Good Dusting*, 98; Johnson, "Biographical Data: Sudanese Officers & NCOs," 13–14.

[135] Hill, *A Biographical Dictionary of the Anglo-Egyptian Sudan*, 324.

[136] Ibid., 170.

[137] Vezzadini, "The 1924 Revolution," 202–203.

[138] Lee Stack, "Memorandum on the Future Status of Sudan," FO 407/198, as cited in Vezzadini, "The 1924 Revolution," 202.
[139] Kurita, "The Life of 'Ali 'Abd al-Latif," 13.
[140] D. A. Donne to F. R. Wingate, 14 March 1888, Assouan, NRO CAIRINT 1/25/127.
[141] Farwell, *Mr. Kipling's Army*, 99. Indeed, Farwell makes the point that when flogging was abolished in 1881, it was replaced by the perhaps equally cruel and unusual punishment known as Field Punishment No. 1, in which a soldier was "tied spread eagle to the wheel of a gun or wagon and exposed without food or water for several hours for up to twenty-one days." Likewise, according to David Killingray, the use of flogging as corporal punishment for African troops in the late nineteenth and early twentieth century was "not particularly unusual," and that "a good deal of regular, and irregular, beating of the rank and file went on in the African Colonial Forces, invariably caning administered by African NCOs, until abolition in 1946." Killingray, "The 'Rod of Empire': The Debate over Corporal Punishment in the British African Colonial Forces, 1888–1946," 201–202.
[142] Sikainga, *Slaves into Workers*, 17; Fahmy, *All the Pasha's Men*, 126–129; Dunn, *Khedive Ismail's Army*, 44.
[143] Frederick Gore Anley to his mother, 2 May 1896, NAM 1984-12-50-34.
[144] J. K. Watson, diary, NAM 1984-12-4-6.
[145] George Skinner, 19 August 1898, diary, NAM 1979-09-15-3, 57. This incident was also recorded by Ronald Forbes Meiklejohn in his journal: "A soudanese is said to have been shot the other day for deserting to the rear." Ronald Forbes Meiklejohn, 19 August 1898, diary, NAM 1974-04-36-2.
[146] Farwell, *Mr. Kipling's Army*, 96, 101.
[147] Bennett, *The Downfall of the Dervishes*, 88. For more on the use of Africans as military labor, see David Killingray, "Labour Exploitation for Military Campaigns in British Colonial Africa, 1870–1945," *Journal of Contemporary History*, Vol. 24, No. 3 (1989): 483–501.
[148] Felix Ready, 18 April 1898, NAM 1966-09-142. The widespread perception that the Egyptian soldier was the "ideal fatigue man" was also referenced in Alford and Sword, *The Egyptian Soudan*, 79.
[149] Alford and Sword, *The Egyptian Soudan*, 139.
[150] E. D. Loch, 24 August 1898, diary, NAM 1986-08-66-1.
[151] *Regulations and Instructions for British Officers Serving with the Egyptian Army* (Cairo: War Office, 1911), 27.
[152] Ibid., 29.
[153] Burleigh, *Sirdar and Khalifa*, 190.
[154] Details on the daily routine of Nile Campaign troops can be found throughout the firsthand accounts of war correspondents and British soldiers. However, one can find a concise summary in Spiers, *The Victorian Soldier in Africa*, 141; and a contemporary description was printed in "At the Front on the Nile," 23 May 1896, *The Graphic*.
[155] Ronald Forbes Meiklejohn quoted in John Meredith, ed., *Omdurman Diaries 1898: Eyewitness Accounts of the Legendary Campaign* (Great Britain: Leo Cooper Ltd., 1998), 67; see also cover illustration, "Washing day with the Soudanese recruits," 12 May 1896, *The Daily Graphic*.
[156] "At the Front on the Nile," 23 May 1896, *The Graphic*; "The Nile Expedition," 18 May 1896, *The Daily Graphic*.
[157] Knight, *Letters from the Sudan*, 220–221.
[158] "Life in Camp at Merawi," 23 October 1897, *The Graphic*.
[159] Spiers, *The Victorian Soldier in Africa*, 141; Bennett, *The Downfall of the Dervishes*, 119–120.
[160] Bennett, *The Downfall of the Dervishes*, 119.
[161] Burleigh, *Sirdar and Khalifa*, 261.
[162] "Dancing the 'Dilluka' on Dongola Day," 23 October 1897, *The Graphic*. In the 1940s and 1950s the urban Northern Sudanese musical genre of *Daluka* was adopted by the Miri of the Nuba Mountains for the bridal dance at wedding ceremonies, and later in the century, for "moonlight dances" associated with adolescent courtship. Gerd Baumann, *National Integration and Local Identity: The Miri of the Nuba Mountains in the Sudan* (Oxford: Clarendon Press, 1987), 49–50, 178–179.
[163] "The Advance in the Soudan: Native Troops Celebrating the Feast of Bairam at Berber," 11 June 1898, *The Graphic*.
[164] Ibid.
[165] Mitford, "Extracts from the Diary of a Subaltern," *Sudan Notes and Records* XVIII, Part II (1935): 182.
[166] And lest one think that every Sudanese soldier in the Egyptian Army was a Muslim convert, there is the unique case of Faraj Sadik. In his memoir, he stated: "When I first went to Aswan with the army I was converted to Christianity at the Italian Mission…by a visiting American Bishop," and that "whenever I was near a Catholic Church I used to attend a Mass." Years later, according to Faraj Sadik: "I took leave from Dongola and because I was a Catholic I went as a servant to a Hungarian doctor, an

ear specialist who was with the Army in Italy. We visited Rome and I saw the Pope, with my master. Afterwards we travelled to many places, amongst others Turin, Milan, Budapest and Vienna. We passed through the Tyrol and then took ship from Trieste to Palestine. As our leave was nearly up we only visited Jerusalem, but we got back to Dongola on time." Hope, "The Adventurous Life of Faraj Sadik," 158.

[167] Steevens, *With Kitchener to Khartum*, 90.
[168] "The Advance in the Soudan: Life in Camp at Merawi: The Devil Dance," 23 October 1897, *The Graphic*.
[169] Susan M. Kenyon, *Five Women of Sennar: Culture and Change in Central Sudan* (Oxford: Clarendon Press, 1991), 184–185.
[170] P. M. Constantinides, "Sickness and the Spirits: A Study of the Zaar Spirit-Possession Cult in the Northern Sudan" (Ph.D. thesis, University of London, 1972), 31–32, 51–59; Kenyon, *Five Women of Sennar*, 189; Makris, *Changing Masters*, 103–117.
[171] See Makris, *Changing Masters*, 149–226; Kenyon, *Five Women of Sennar*, 189, 189n12–13, 191–192.
[172] Makris, *Changing Masters*, 196.
[173] Makris, *Changing Masters*, 193–226; Kenyon, *Five Women of Sennar*, 189–192.
[174] Makris, *Changing Masters*, 227–265.
[175] Ibid., 241–251.
[176] Ibid., 249.
[177] Ibid., 249–250.
[178] Heretofore, the earliest documented connection referred to by *tombura* scholars was that made by B. Z. Seligman, who witnessed two such ceremonies between 1909 and 1911. B. Z. Seligman, "On the Origins of the Egyptian Zar," *Folklore* 25 (1914): 300–323. B. R. Mitford's "Extracts from the Diary of a Subaltern," not published until 1935 but referring to his time in the Egyptian Army during the 1880s and 1890s, describes what appears to be a *burei zar* ceremony.
[179] Kenyon, *Five Women of Sennar*, 185, 185n3, 188, 198, 184–221.
[180] Makris, *Changing Masters*, 3–4, 31.
[181] See Janice Boddy, *Wombs and Alien Spirits: Women, Men, and the Zar Cult in Northern Sudan* (Madison: The University of Wisconsin Press, 1989). Although contemporary sources on the Nile Campaign make no mention of female circumcision, Meldon's "Notes on the Sudanese in Uganda" provides some evidence that it was a common practice within the army: "I have said that the Sudanese women are virtuous up to the time of their marriage; the reason is twofold. Besides the fear of parents' wrath, the girl is subjected to a physical operation in early life, which makes deliberate unchastity difficult. This process is better described in a medical journal. 'Tahar' [*tahur*] or circumcision is performed on male children when about four years old. The operation on the female children is called 'Tahar' also." Meldon, "Notes on the Sudanese in Uganda," 133.
[182] James Scott on "everyday forms of resistance" as quoted in Makris, *Changing Masters*, 3.
[183] Bredin, "The Life-Story of Yuzbashi 'Abdullah Adlan," 39.
[184] The 1876 Pension Law, for example, provided officers of the rank of *saghkolaghasi* or senior (who joined the Army before 23 May 1884) full pay for 35 years of service, two-thirds pay for 30 years, one-half pay for 25 years, one-third pay for 20 years, and one-quarter pay for 15; for those of the rank of *yuzbashi* or junior, full pay came with 32 years of service, two-thirds with 27, one-half with 22, one-third with 17, and one-quarter with 12. In addition, the actual period passed in certain services – during war or at garrisons in the Sudan – counted double. The 1888 Pension Law, later called by Wingate "insufficiently liberal" (the 1876 law having been "too liberal"), scaled back some of the pensions and gratuities of the prior law, especially for long-serving officers earning "Full Pension." For example, officers of the rank of *saghkolaghasi* or senior, with at least 15 years of service, still received one-quarter pay (one-third pay for 20 years), and those of *yuzbashi* or junior one-third (one-half pay for 20 years). Maximum pensions for officers with 45 years of service, however, were reduced from full pay to two-thirds pay for *saghkolaghasi* or senior, and from full to three-quarter pay for *yuzbashi* or junior. "NOTES on the Pension Laws of 1876, 1888, and of the 27th of May, 1899," SAD 272/5/39–41; F. R. Wingate to Lord Cromer, 9 May 1906, Khartoum, SAD 278/5/52.
[185] W. L. Atkinson to W. H. Luce, 6 January 1946, "Petitions by Old Soldiers," NRO Palace 4/8/41.
[186] "Petitions by Old Soldiers," NRO Palace 4/8/41; Johnson, "The Structure of a Legacy," 80.
[187] Hope, "The Adventurous Life of Faraj Sadik," 158.
[188] W. L. Atkinson to W. H. Luce, 6 January 1946, "Petitions by Old Soldiers," NRO Palace 4/8/41.
[189] L. M. Buchanan to Financial Secretary, Khartoum, 11 March 1946, Dueim, "Petitions by Old Soldiers," NRO Palace 4/8/41.
[190] Knight, *Letters from the Sudan*, 136.
[191] F. R. Wingate to Colonel Garsia, 14 October 1914, SAD 192/1/51–54.

[192] See Douglas H. Johnson, "Conquest and Colonisation: Soldier Settlers in the Sudan and Uganda," *Sudan Notes and Records*, NS 4 (2000): 66–70; Sikainga, *Slaves into Workers*, 63–65; Daly, *Empire on the Nile*, 233; Sikainga, "Military Slavery and the Emergence of a Southern Sudanese Diaspora in the Northern Sudan," 28–29.

[193] A. C. Parker, 16 December 1900, *SIR* 76, 2.

[194] Johnson, "Conquest and Colonisation: Soldier Settlers in the Sudan and Uganda," 62–66.

[195] Sikainga, *Slaves into Workers*, 63–65; Sikainga, "Military Slavery and the Emergence of a Southern Sudanese Diaspora in the Northern Sudan," 28–29.

[196] Johnson, "Conquest and Colonisation: Soldier Settlers in the Sudan and Uganda," 67–70.

[197] Sikainga, *Slaves into Workers*, 63–65; Daly, *Empire on the Nile*, 233; Sikainga, "Military Slavery and the Emergence of a Southern Sudanese Diaspora in the Northern Sudan," 28–29; Bredin, "The Life-Story of Yuzbashi 'Abdullah Adlan," 52.

[198] Johnson, "Conquest and Colonisation: Soldier Settlers in the Sudan and Uganda," 71–73; Johnson, "The Structure of a Legacy," 80–82; Sikainga, *Slaves into Workers*, 53–54.

[199] *Sudan Monthly Record*, N.S. 77 (May–June 1935), Southern Records Office (Juba) BD 57.C.1, as cited in Johnson, "Conquest and Colonisation: Soldier Settlers in the Sudan and Uganda," 73–74.

[200] Burleigh, *Sirdar and Khalifa*, 259.

[201] Rennell Rodd poem excerpt from Jackson, *The Fighting Sudanese*, 30–31; this poem, "Abou Hamed," was first published in the British magazine *The Spectator*, and later reappeared in Rennell Rodd's book *Ballads of the Fleet and Other Poems* (London: Edward Arnold, 1901). Interestingly, these verses seem to have been based on local legend, for Winston Churchill, in the first edition of *The River War*, wrote: "The English world has forgotten the event [the Battle of Abu Hamed]. But the Arabs still shun the solitary desert *khor*, and whisper how that, when the nights are dark, the ghosts of the black soldiers march in a ceaseless 'sentry-go' beside the graves of the officers who led them straight, and challenge all who may approach. For more than a year, so prevalent was the belief, it was impossible to persuade servants to live in the adjacent houses." Winston Spencer Churchill, *The River War: An Historical Account of the Reconquest of the Soudan*, vol. 1 (London: Longmans, Green, and Co., 1899), 334–335.

4
"Brotherhood that Binds the Brave"

At the Atbara's margin there was a rare scene of welcome and congratulation when the Soudanese and the British met…the Soudanese, dancing with delight, ran in amongst the British, cheering, waving their rifles aloft, and with their big fists shaking hands with the "Tommies." It was a meeting never to be forgotten I was a spectator of. Mr. Atkins returned their enthusiastic greeting quite as warmly in his own way, hurrahing for the Soudanese and Egyptian troops. Brothers in arms, blacks and whites, their fraternal unity had been cemented by mutual goodwill and close companionship in danger, which must be helpful in any future Soudan campaign. As "Tommy" himself has been overheard since to say, "The bally blacks, after all, can fight a bit, you bet."

Daily Telegraph correspondent Bennet Burleigh[1]

Interactions between Sudanese and British soldiers during the River War existed in something of a paradox. Certainly, one finds plentiful proof of British bigotry in contemporary accounts, the scope and character of which would not surprise any student of Victorian attitudes to race. However, these relationships were also marked by both camaraderie and competition, what correspondent Bennet Burleigh called "a brotherly challenge 'twixt white and black to intrepidity."[2] And while it is true that British soldiers and war correspondents often segregated themselves from Sudanese troops and held them in rather low regard, commonly referring to them as "savages" and "Sambos," there is also evidence that this perception was neither monolithic nor unchanging, particularly following the heat of battle.[3] In fact, most sources indicate that the Sudanese soldier was at the same time both respected and disdained by British soldiers and journalists alike. Much of this respect no doubt arose from the level of courage and fighting "dash" evinced by Sudanese soldiers throughout the Nile Campaign, which was much admired by the British and seemed to confirm their beliefs about "martial races." In any case, the self-fulfilling nature of such discourse – on both ends – engendered "mirror images" between British and

Sudanese troops à la Ornamentalism, "constructed affinities" that transformed their relationships; paved the way for new forms of honor and agency among Sudanese soldiers; and contributed to the ultimate success of the Anglo-Egyptian military reconquest of the Sudan.[4]

Sudanese soldiers & martial race ideology

The idea that the "Sudanese" were inherently martial and thus made good soldiers was not invented by the British. Nor was Britain the only power in the region to employ Sudanese soldiers for reason of their superior fighting abilities. Indeed, the preference for Sudanese soldiers could be traced back decades, if not millennia, in the Nile Valley, and well before the British reorganized the Egyptian Army in the mid-1880s. And they continued to be heavily recruited by the Mahdists throughout the 1880s and 1890s, serving as riflemen in *jihadiyya* units. Moreover, the British belief in "martial races" was not invented in the Sudan, as the idea had already been in use to describe soldiers in the British and Indian armies – from Scottish Highlanders to Nepalese Gurkhas. Be that as it may, the reputation of Sudanese soldiers fell right in line with British martial race ideology, which in turn manifested itself in myriad ways and instances during the River War: how commanders planned and executed the campaign; how British officers, regular soldiers, and war correspondents thought of, interacted with, and described Sudanese soldiers; and indeed how Sudanese soldiers saw themselves, and carried on with British and Egyptian troops both on and off the battlefield.

On the one hand, the martial reputation of Sudanese soldiers was based in reality, and well earned. Rather than being entirely a British construction, it was in fact the product of decades of continued military service in the Egyptian Army, and the combat experience that came with it – a long, self-sustaining dialectic of observed competence and battlefield success. And thus by any objective measure Sudanese soldiers *were* "crack soldiers." Moreover, there is little doubt as to the significant military role that Sudanese battalions played in the Nile Campaign, and an assesement of their performance on the battlefield does nothing if not further distinguish them as skilled fighters. On the other hand, when considering the broader scholarship on martial race theory, and the British model in particular, one sees numerous parallels between the Sudanese case and others worldwide and through history – shared attributes that locate Sudanese soldiers within this discourse more universally.

As observed in reference to other so-called "martial races," whether it be the Gurkhas, Scots, Cossacks, Mongols, or Kurds, groups "commonly labelled as inherently 'martial' have been geographically distinct, usually occupying territories on the regional peripheries of the state…typically remote."[5] The same can be said of Sudanese soldiers in the Egyptian Army. Although over the years they were enslaved and recruited from a number of different areas in central and southern Sudan, from the Nuba Mountains to Equatoria and beyond, these regions were quite "remote" and geographically distinct from the northern Sudan and Egypt. As well, these areas did constitute a state periphery of sorts during the Turkiyya – occupying the farthest reaches of the Egyptian Sudan, Egypt itself something of a frontier province of the Ottoman Empire at the time. Moreover, in the Sudan and Egypt, not only were these areas seen as geographically distinct, the people who lived in these regions were deemed racially distinct, and collectively referred to as "Sudanese," or *Sudani* in Arabic, a racial and geographical category used to differentiate between "Blacks" from central and southern Sudan and "Arabs" from the northern Sudan and Egypt.

The fact that "martial races" through history have often occupied the peripheries of states "also meant that, in many instances, the future 'martial races' had fought quite successfully against absorption into the expanded state," and in the process "won begrudging respect from their encroaching enemies…so impressed with their potential value to the state that they sought to enhance their reliability instead."[6] Again, such was the case with many of the ethnic groups in the Sudan who came to dominate the enlistment rolls of the Egyptian Army. The Dinka and Shilluk, for example, both fiercely resisted absorption into the Egyptian Sudan, and in the process gained a martial reputation. Dating from the 1820s, and indeed mirroring resistance to outsiders on the White Nile that harked back to the sixteenth century, both of these ethnic groups fought the expanding Turco-Egyptian state tooth and nail, earning a reputation with arrows and spears that would eventually put Martini-Henry rifles in their hands.[7]

Another shared attribute of "martial races" found in the Sudanese case, and what has been argued is at the heart of the "Gurkha syndrome," is that the "perfect 'martial race' was an ethnic group that produced men who were both martial *and* loyal," the combination's key ingredient being that of dependency.[8] In other words, because the defeated ethnic group is a minority in the larger state system and has little access to power, it is inherently vulnerable. Thus military service becomes one of the few ways for its members to make a living "in the reordered politico-economic system." And indeed, for these marginalized groups, joining the military turns out to be "a vehicle for gaining respect, legitimacy and protection in the larger social order of which they are now, albeit reluctantly, a part."[9]

Once again, the case of Sudanese soldiers in the Egyptian Army fits this model to a tee, the levels of allegiance and dependency perhaps even heightened by the very nature of military slavery. Experiencing the trauma of enslavement, and the natal alienation that followed, nineteenth-century Sudanese soldiers were extremely vulnerable, and entirely dependent on their new patron, the Khedive of Egypt. This "social death" engendered social rebirth, and with it dependency, leading to the kind of allegiance that has been suggested is a cornerstone in the creation of the ideal "martial race." Likewise, for Sudanese soldiers military service was a rare vehicle for gaining respect, legitimacy, and protection in a reordered Egyptian Sudan, and provided them opportunities for social and economic stability, even advancement, that if anything deepened their loyalty to the Khedive.

The term "Sudanese," as well, used to describe both the "Sudanese" battalion and the individual "Sudanese" soldier, is like the term "Gurkha" in that it is also something of "an ethnic label manufactured by outside military recruiters."[10] Gurkhas originated from "a variety of culturally distinct traditions

4.1 *Shilluk war dance with long shields and spears, Upper Nile Province, c. 1908*
(Postcard, reproduced by permission of Durham University Library)

4.2 *"Types of Sudanese soldiers", Khartoum, taken between 1904 and 1916*
(Postcard, reproduced by permission of Durham University Library)

from within Nepal," and the term was ultimately a British construction "both produced and maintained in the Indian Army and nowhere else."[11] Sikhs, as well, were not the identifiable "martial race" that British officers made them out to be, nor indeed were Highlanders; in fact most "Highlander" regiments in the British Army during the last half of the nineteenth century were made up of poor, urban Lowland Scots, supplemented by English and Irish soldiers.[12] The same was true for "Sudanese" soldiers in the Egyptian Army, who in fact were a quite heterogeneous lot, originating from a diversity of ethnic groups living in southern Kordofan, along the Blue and White Niles, in the Upper Nile and Equatoria provinces, and in the Bahr al-Ghazal. And although the use of the term *Sudani* to describe blacks from these regions has a long history, and did not originate in the new Egyptian Army, the British adopted the label and used it in similar ways as they did with other fictitious "races" like the Gurkhas.

And like the Gurkhas, the Sikhs, and the Highlanders, the notion that the "Sudanese" were a martial race, or were composed of a handful of inherently "martial races," became self-fulfilling to a certain degree. Like these other so-called "martial races," it seems that over time Sudanese soldiers began to see themselves – both individually and collectively – as inherently martial as well, and began to conduct themselves on the battlefield with the courageousness and ferocity that was expected of them. In so doing, and perhaps more than they would have otherwise, they became the "crack soldiers" that everyone believed them to be, everyone now including themselves. And within this reality, of course, came new forms of honor and self-pride, and the kind of opportunities and privileges previously discussed. Thus, again fitting into the broader scholarship on "martial races" in Britain and India, these "constructions profoundly affected the identities of so-called 'martial race' populations...who both embraced and manipulated their own representations as martial heroes."[13]

These shared attributes between Sudanese soldiers and "martial races" found elsewhere in the British Empire were in some ways manifestations of late-Victorian attitudes to race. With the rise of scientific racism, it seems that martial race ideology had a faithful ally, as more and more physical characteristics, and even personality traits, were viewed as measurably attributable to one's specific race. The British thus considered these racial characteristics and traits immutable, and categorized them into complex racial hierarchies. Accordingly, they saw some "races," like the Shilluk, the Dinka, and the "Nubawis," as biologically predisposed to be "warriors," whereas others, such as the Egyptian *fellahin*, they did not: "As soldiers, the blacks are the very reverse of the Egyptians. They are not quick at drill, or fond of it. What they are fond of, and what they shine in, is real battle....They have a natural instinct for combat which training may improve, but which it can never beget. In this respect they are immensely superior to the fellahin."[14]

For example, take the following descriptions that accompanied illustrations drawn by Charles Mills Sheldon and published in the British weekly newspaper *Black & White* in 1896:

> He [Sheldon] forwards a complete series of the strange races forming the Egyptian Army and, having ample leisure at the moment for such investigation, made careful selection

GABER MOHAMED, DINKA

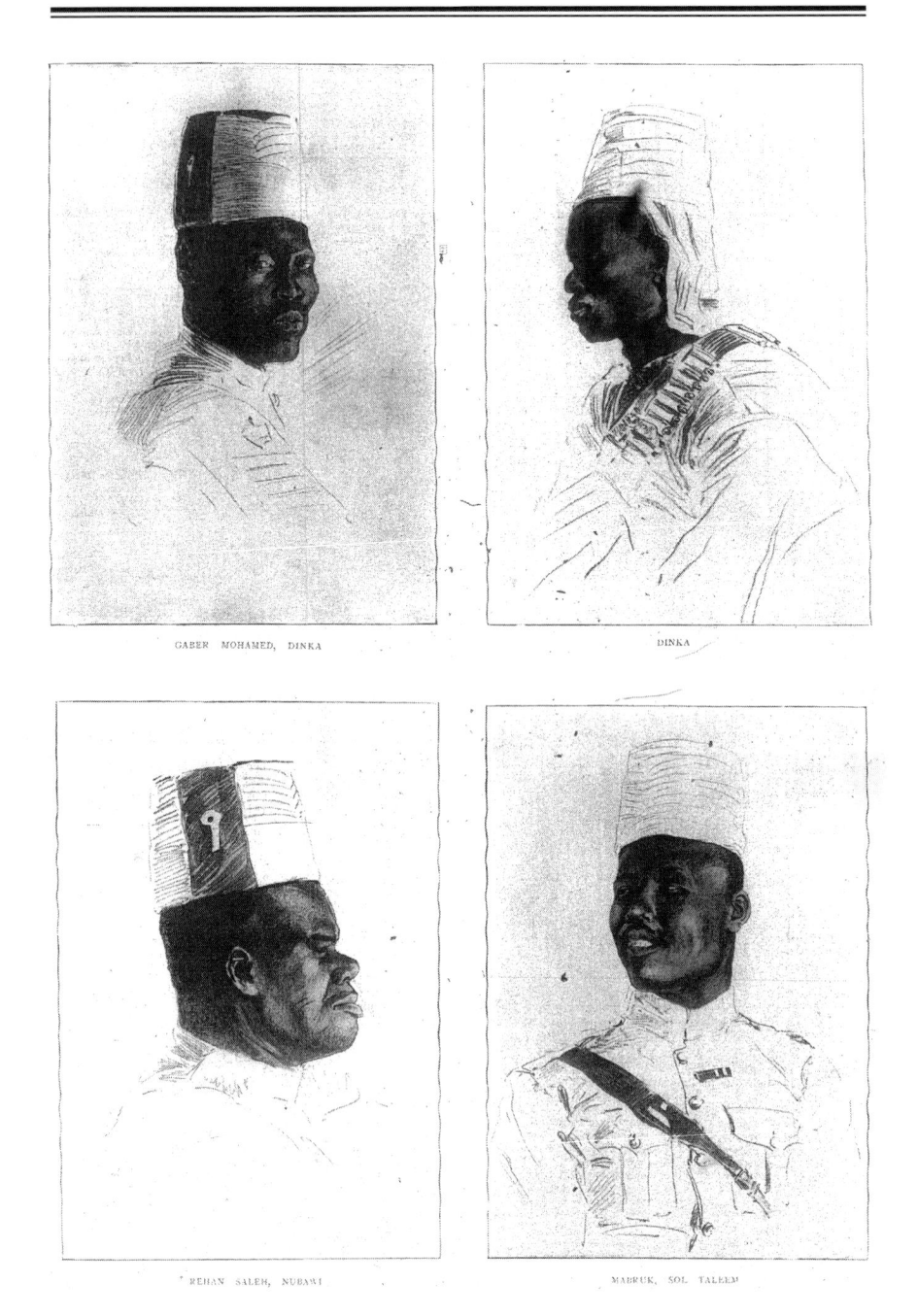

DINKA

REHAN SALEH, NUBAWI

MABRUK, SOL TALEEM

4.3 *"Egyptian Army types in the Soudan"*
(M. Sheldon, *Black & White*, 12 September 1896)

and sketched only typical and characteristic individuals from the ranks of the most celebrated fighting men. That pugnacity is a leading quality of these warriors it is easy enough to believe. The Nubawis and the Dinkas whose portraits appear possess enormous facial strength, and might, by a tyro in physiognomy, be counted upon to render the best possible account of themselves in time of war. Gaber Mohamed, one of the Dinkas, has the most amiable face of the four fighting men which are given on another page. His features are almost purely Ethiopian. As for Sol Taleem, he too affects a genial expression, but it is for the purposes of Mr. Sheldon's picture only, and his customary facial appearance is by no means so genial, as his comrades in the Tenth Soudanese might doubtless testify. But both Gaber Mohamed and Sol Taleem are good-natured children compared to our friend Rehan Saleh. Here is a strong personality if you like, with "Fight!" stamped on every muscle of the grim face and bull-dog nose. Truly, Rehan Saleh of the Nubawi is an ugly customer, and we would rather have him upon our side than against us, a remark applying with equal force to the Dinka in the cartridge belt.[15]

And when it came to Sudanese versus Egyptian soldiers, akin to comparisons between Gurkhas and Bengalis in India, these contrasts were gendered as well. British observers described Sudanese soldiers in language that represented a masculine ideal, and characterized Egyptians as rather cowardly and effeminate: "Scandal says that the native Egyptian officers are already frightened, and say they are going to their death in the Soudan. But the 'yellow bellies,' as they are nicknamed, have no stomach for war, and one black is worth a dozen of them."[16] Indeed, it was the combination of their racial stock and their masculinity that made the "Sudanese," in the minds of British observers, such "dashing" soldiers.

The Sudanese soldier is thus categorically described as "the ideal fighting man" and "full of the military instincts," and the most common quality attributed to him is that of courage under fire.[17] According to war correspondent G. W. Steevens, bravery was esteemed above all else among these Sudanese troops: "A black has been known to kill himself because his wife called him a coward."[18] This sense of masculine honor also comes through, though selectively, in depictions of the Sudanese soldiers as "ferocious" yet "gallant," and not cruel by nature. According to *The Times* correspondent E. F. Knight, "They are not cold-blooded murderers of women and children, and never inflict on wounded or dead foemen the abominable mutilations in which the Baggara delight."[19] Knight later writes that the Sudanese soldier, though he "loves fighting for its own sake…is yet one of the kindliest creatures in the world when not engaged in battle."[20] There is even one instance in which Sudanese exuberance for combat is compared to that of one of the most celebrated "martial races" in European history, the Spartans: "In the lines of the blacks all was excitement and jollity. There was laughing and crowing, tom-toming and singing, as it were the eve of a christening or a wedding party. All the while, too, they were seeing to their arms, and smartening up their personal appearance, after their manner. It was strange to see the sons of Ham exhibiting some of the characteristics of the old Spartans in making ready for battle."[21]

The Egyptian soldier, on the other hand, was drawn in stark contrast to the Sudanese soldier, and depicted as utterly lacking in the above-mentioned qualities that made the Sudanese so reliable and fearsome in combat. "The fellaheen does not possess any of the dash or fighting qualities of the Soudanese," was the

4.4 *"The dark side of campaigning in the Soudan." Top caption: "Despatching wounded Dervishes." Bottom caption: "The reason why."* See n 19, p. 151.
(W. T. Maud, *The Graphic*, 1 October 1898)

conventional wisdom, oft-repeated in print and military dispatches.[22] And whereas the Sudanese soldier was, again, universally seen as "the ideal fighting man," the Egyptian was seen as "the ideal fatigue man."[23] Even their so-called "positive" attributes as soldiers British observers often cast in a somewhat negative light, seeming to reinforce the notion that they were clearly not a "martial race." According to correspondent Bennet Burleigh, for example, "The 'Gippies,' rank and file, as far as 'make-up for a soldier goes,' leave apparently nothing to be wished for. Patient, prompt, obedient, they are full of all the negative qualities requisite for first-class fighting material. Whether they possess the positive qualities – I won't call them virtues – that ensure victory in battle, is quite another affair."[24] Employing very similar language was correspondent E. F. Knight:

> The fellah soldier has wonderful endurance; he can undertake long marches, supports extreme privations with stoical patience, and seems even to enjoy the arduous fatigue duties in which he is now constantly engaged at Wadi Halfa....Cleanly in person, smart in appearance, submissive to authority, quick at learning their drill, sober and cheerful, the fellahin have many of the qualities that go to the making of an excellent soldier; but all who know them would hesitate to say that they possessed any true military instinct. Coming of a peasant race that has been oppressed and enslaved from time immemorial, the fellah is naturally devoid of military enthusiasm; he possesses passive courage, but has never had any relish for a soldier's career, and his highest ambition is to be left alone to live the peaceful life of a cultivator of the soil....They have proved within the last few years that they can fight well; they are cool and steady under fire; but when it comes to meeting a Dervish charge and engaging in hand-to-hand conflict with cold steel they cannot give so good an account of themselves as do the Sudanese who compose the black regiments.[25]

Fitting squarely into British martial race ideology and late-Victorian racial prejudices, of course, was the paternalistic notion that only a so-called "higher race" such as "the Englishman" was capable of leading such "lower races," martial or otherwise, into battle. Just as the British commanders saw the Sudanese foot soldier as the ideal fighting man, and the Egyptian *fellah* as the ideal fatigue man, so too they saw themselves in broad sweeps, albeit ethnocentric ones, as the ideal military officer – taking special pride in the "capacity of Englishmen for the organisation and effective employment of troops recruited from races which, without English assistance, have remained unwarlike."[26]

Alfred Milner, Under-Secretary for Finance in Egypt, in his 1892 assessment of "The Fellah as Soldier" and current state of the Egyptian Army, asked the rhetorical question: "By what magic is it that these men – average British officers for the most part, and no more – have produced such remarkable results? How is it that they have changed the fighting character of a nation in so short a time?"[27] According to F. R. Wingate, a British officer himself, the answer to Milner's question was clear, and "the secret of success," whether in India or Egypt, derived primarily from "the Englishman's power to inspire confidence," and in the case of the Egyptian Army, "to the confidence inspired by its English officers."[28] Thus, in the minds of Victorians, it was the British gentleman officer alone who was capable of turning Shilluk and Dinka "raw material" (and Egyptian *fellahin*, even more so) into a "finished product" ready to take on the Mahdists:

> Our officers, out of what certainly appeared the most unpromising material, have organized a model little army. They have to a high degree displayed that capacity of the British officer, so conspicuous on our Indian frontiers, for bringing out all the good qualities that may exist in native soldiery; they have won the confidence, the respect, and the affection of their men, and have inspired the native officers with some of their own spirit and energy. They have, in short, effected an extraordinary transformation in a long corrupt service – a great work of which Englishmen should be proud, and which, while exciting their jealousy, has gained the admiration of foreign observers.[29]

Tied into this, as well, was the British certainty that they, too, possessed some of the same martial and masculine traits so often attributed to the Sudanese. "I was told about this time that why British officers were successful as company officers with native troops was because they actually went in front and led them; whereas with the Egyptians, the more senior they were, the farther behind, and when affairs were threatening, the first to depart were the seniors in rear, a process which was followed until the men, finding no seniors, officers, or N.C.O.s behind them, followed suit," wrote Horace Smith-Dorrien in his memoirs.[30] In the case of the Xth Sudanese Battalion, for one British officer it was "from commanding officer to recruit a remarkable blend of civilised discipline and primitive manhood, a living example of the virtues of England grafted to the valour of Equatoria."[31]

Remarkable blend as it may have been, a comparison between the Egyptian and Indian Army cases suggests that martial race discourse may have been used in Egypt and the Sudan, as it was in India, to further British strategic and political agenda. In India, according to one scholar, the groups that were "targeted for martial race recruiting in India in the last quarter of the century were, tellingly, also those groups who had remained loyal to the British during the crisis of the 1857 Rebellion."[32] Prior to 1857, it was the high-caste Hindus of northern India that were considered the best soldiers. Following the Indian Rebellion, and in light of their role in fomenting it, these same Hindus were deemed by British officers as racially unfit for military service; whereas groups that had been most loyal to the Raj, such as the Gurkhas and Sikhs, were now considered the most desirable soldiers, and labeled as "martial races" via British construction. In the late nineteenth century, race thus became a "guise in the search for unquestioned loyalty" to the British Empire, and martial race discourse "masked conscious, practical strategies of rule."[33]

Considering the very nature of military slavery, it is certainly arguable that the loyalty of lifelong Sudanese soldiers to their British officers, and their ultimate patron, the Khedive of Egypt, might be more "unquestioned" than that of shorter service Egyptian conscript soldiers. If this was in fact the case, it should come as no surprise that British officers would prefer to lead battalions composed of loyal, battle-tested, veteran Sudanese soldiers over those made up of less committed, often inexperienced, *fellahin* conscripts. Remember, it was the *fellahin* and its new officer class – most notably Colonel Ahmad Arabi – that had led the uprising against the Khedive and European influence in Egypt from 1879 to 1882.

The burgeoning Egyptian nationalist movement, not to mention pan-Islamic sentiment in the region, was a persistent concern for the British in the late nineteenth and early twentieth century. And in this context, maintaining absolute loyalty within the Egyptian Army was seen as an essential element in defending British geopolitical interests in Nile Valley. By having five of the thirteen (later six of fourteen) infantry battalions in the Egyptian Army be Sudanese battalions, perhaps, as in India, the British were hedging their bets against the possibility of further agitation within the ranks, nationalist or otherwise. Moreover, it could be argued that the extensive deployment of loyal Sudanese "martial races" in Lower Egypt and the Sudan ipso facto furthered British imperial interests there as well. Indeed, in 1899, once the "rights of conquest" in the Sudan were decided, it was Britain that held most of the cards, and ultimately determined the future course of the Anglo-Egyptian Condominium.

Whether a conscious guise or not, British officers serving in Egypt, as they did in India, time and again invoked the language of "martial races" to rationalize their personal biases and military agenda. What is telling, however, and exposes the fictitious nature and flexible application of nineteenth-century British martial race ideology, is the inconsistency of the discourse when comparing the Indian and Egyptian Army cases. In India, British commanders in the late nineteenth century claimed it was southern Indians, the dark-skinned sepoys of Madras and Bombay, that were inherently unfit for war due to their "slight" build and "cowardly" nature, and the supposed degenerating effects of their tropical climate.[34] On the other hand, these same commanders argued that northern Indians, "hardier races" such as the lighter-skinned Sikhs and Gurkhas, were "unmistakably superior as soldiers to those of southern India," being of purer "Aryan" descent and not having been exposed to the deleterious tropical environment of the south.[35] As evidenced from the above, in the Egyptian Army case it was quite the opposite. Nineteenth-century British officers serving in the Egyptian Army claimed it was the lighter-skinned, more stout *fellahin* from the less tropical climate of northern Egypt that were for biological and environmental reasons far inferior as "fighting material" when compared to the dark-skinned, slightly built Sudanese of the "equatorial races." The co-existence of these contradictory beliefs again suggests that British martial race ideology was manipulated in the Egyptian Army, as it was in India, according to specific regional circumstances, imperial and strategic interests, as well as the individual whims of military commanders.

Albeit based on military experience rather than racial background, and its self-fulfilling nature notwithstanding, the historical reality that Sudanese soldiers were more dependable than Egyptian soldiers in combat situations weighed heavily on the minds of the British as they prepared for the River War. Even as early as 1890, some six years before the Nile Campaign was launched, a War Office memo on "The Re-Conquest of the Soudan" alerted its readers that "however good the blacks may be they constitute only a part of the army, and just as in a naval squadron the speed of the whole is measured by the speed of the slowest ship, in an army composed of good and indifferent material the fighting value of it, as a whole, is greatly impaired by the inferior quality of a portion."[36]

Likewise, F. R. Wingate, in the draft version of his 1891 book *Mahdiism and the Egyptian Sudan*, wrote that "in the real trial – the fight in the open – dependent entirely on themselves & without that stiffening material in the shape of Blacks; I do not consider that they [*fellahin* troops] have yet been sufficiently tried & moreover it is extremely doubtful – even with most careful training & under the most able leadership – they will ever rank as thoroughly reliable fighting material."[37] This opinion still held firm at the outset of the Nile Campaign in 1896. Lord Cromer, for example, sent the following telegram from Cairo to Prime Minister Salisbury in mid-March: "Mouktar Pasha, whom I saw today, warned me against placing too much reliance on the fellaheen troops. He has confidence in the blacks, but thinks that if we are to go to Dongola we must certainly employ English troops. He is an excellent authority on a point of this sort."[38] And so it appears that even some native Egyptians of high title had grave doubts as to the military worth of *fellahin* battalions, and vice versa, had full confidence in the Sudanese troops.

Once the Dongola campaign got rolling, however, and the Egyptians proved themselves to be far better in combat than their reputation would have predicted, opinions, and to some extent conventional wisdom, began to change. Following the battle at Firket, for example, *Daily Chronicle* correspondent A. Hilliard Atteridge wrote:

> The Soudanese had already made themselves a splendid reputation as fighting men, but in many quarters it had been the fashion to sneer at the fellahin battalions. No one who saw their ideal steadiness in action could doubt for a moment their sterling value. From the officers who led them I heard nothing but praise for their conduct. One who had previously served with the Soudanese said he personally preferred the cool steadiness of the fellahin to the dash of their black comrades. Another, who commanded a battalion said that he was struck by the way in which, after halting under cover of rocks to pour in a final shower of bullets at a range of about 150 yards, on word being given to advance his men all sprang up and left cover without a moment's hesitation.[39]

Of course, these same British officers, once on military campaign, had a vested interest in having their *fellahin* soldiers performing well and positively depicted – both within army ranks and in the press. If nothing else, it may have led to more balanced, objective assessments of them than anything prior, most opinions having been based so predominantly on essentialist notions of Egyptian martial inferiority. And so one finds, for example, Egyptian Army infantry division commander Archibald Hunter writing in the wake of Firket: "I was anxious to give the Egyptian a chance to belie the croakings of their detractors, so I put Taffy Lewis with two Egyptian Battalions, 3rd and 4th, and one Black, the 10th, on the right where the houses were and where there was bound to be a stand. Everybody thought the experiment a trifle risky and was watching the result intently. There was no doubt about it."[40]

Nonetheless, even after they had proven themselves on the battlefield at Firket and throughout the 1896 Dongola campaign, there were still doubters. It seems many British observers, although recognizing improvement, ultimately remained skeptical of *fellahin* martial pluck. Frederick Gore Anley, for example, a British *bimbashi* attached to an Egyptian battalion, wrote with cautious optimism in a letter home following Firket: "They say that this is the first time the Egyptians have ever made bayonet charges. It has been rather a surprise here and everybody now says that the Egyptians did as well as the blacks. Whether they will stick out a real stiff fight remains to be seen."[41] Echoing Anley's sentiments was Lord Cromer in Cairo, who wrote the following to the British Prime Minister in February 1897: "Although the Egyptian troops did well during the recent campaign, the extent to which reliance can be placed in the Egyptian Army is still a matter of some doubt. They have not yet had to withstand a really serious Dervish attack."[42] In the end, it seems that most British observers reconciled their ambivalence about Egyptian troops with the idea that "the two different qualities of the two different races constituting the Egyptian army will be found in combination to supply a thoroughly efficient fighting force."[43]

One must be careful, however, not to take British endorsements of Sudanese soldiers at face value, for imperial constructions sometimes tended to be "mirror images" of British society, what have been called "constructed affinities."[44] These constructed affinities suggest that the British Empire "was at least as much (perhaps more?) about the replication of sameness and similarities originating from home as it was about the insistence on difference and dissimilarities originating from overseas."[45] Thus it should come as no surprise that British observers, particularly gentlemen officers, fostered the notion that Sudanese soldiers embodied many of the character traits so revered by the late-Victorians – such things as courage, valor, daring, resolve, gallantry, bravery, dash, and pluck.

Constructed or otherwise, the perceived martial-masculine affinities between British and Sudanese soldiers underpinned much of the Anglo-Sudanese camaraderie that existed during the Nile Campaign. Some British observers even directly acknowledged this bond between them, men such as H. C. Jackson, who opened his 1954 book *The Fighting Sudanese* with the following couplet from poet Sir Henry John Newbolt's 1898 book *The Island Race*:

> And dearer yet the brotherhood
> That binds the brave of all the earth.[46]

This "brotherhood that binds the brave" was felt on both ends, it appears, as there is anecdotal evidence that Sudanese soldiers fighting in the Nile Campaign constructed their own "mirror images," identifying with their British military brethren in similar ways. Once again, there was the sentiment attributed to them by war correspondent G. W. Steevens: "For 'we,' they say, 'are like the English; we are not afraid.'"[47] And on at least one occasion, as reported by Bennet Burleigh, it seems that the "unsophisticated natives" even turned the tables on the British when it came to martial race discourse:

> As at Berber and other places, many and droll were the critical remarks on the appearance of the troops. The 'kilt' is no longer a puzzle to the native. He has solved its origin and 'raison d'etre' quite satisfactorily to himself. The Highlander he quite understands. "He is like ourselves," they declare. "All these in the petticoats are wild men, fierce men – dervishes if you will, who have sworn to avenge Gordon, and never more appear in trousers until they take Khartoum."[48]

Likewise, in terms of some of the more negative perceptions, be it of Sudanese or Egyptian soldiers, it must be remembered that these observations were made through a subjective, often prejudiced, Western lens. It has been argued elsewhere that "otherness" was an essential element of British imperialism, a phenomenon that served to reinforce notions of Britain's inherent superiority.[49] And depictions of Sudanese soldiers as the exotic, inferior, African "Other" are certainly plethora in the contemporary sources. Take, for example, the following journal entry written by Felix Ready, a British *bimbashi* in the 2nd Egyptian Battalion, describing Sudanese soldiers at the Battle of Atbara: "The blacks who rushed about + looted and shot their rifles up in the air, danced + behaved as the monkey which they really are, they are certainly not men."[50] And so the notion of an interracial brotherhood should not be overstated, remembering that racism was the norm and segregation the status quo.

Ernest N. Bennett of the *Westminster Gazette* noted, for example, "the way, that Egyptian officers, even of high military rank, travel second class with British sergeant-majors and warrant officers."[51] And British soldier Gilbert Falkingham Clayton remarked in an 1898 letter from Halfa, "There is a very cheery mess here, consisting of about eighteen members counting the Egyptian Army fellows (not native officers – they mess separately)."[52] Moreover, although they marched and fought and died together, African and British soldiers were buried apart from each other. Whose choice this was is uncertain, and thus it could well have been a shared, or Muslim, prerogative, with Sudanese and Egyptians likewise desiring separate burial places from the British; unfortunately, contemporary accounts provide no indication as to the policy's origins.

Though seemingly in conflict, these ideas and interpretations were not mutually exclusive. Clearly, most British officers, as well as British regulars and journalists, saw Sudanese soldiers as the exotic and alien "Other," and far inferior to themselves in the hierarchy of "races." And yet, by the same token, many of their depictions do appear to be "in large part about the domestication of the exotic – the comprehending and reordering of the foreign in parallel, analogous, equivalent, resemblant terms."[53] It thus seems evident that these dichotomous attitudes and cross perceptions could coexist within the same individual, and even within a single thought. Consider, as final punctuation on the point, the following lines written by G. W. Steevens (coming right after the above "like the English...not afraid" quote that he credited to this "new kind of black"):

> And is it not good to think, ladies and gentlemen, as you walk in Piccadilly or the Mile End Road, that every one of these niggers honestly believes that to be English and to know fear are two things never heard of together? Utterly fearless themselves, savages brought up to think death in battle the natural lot of man, far preferable to defeat or disgrace, they have lived with English officers and English sergeants, through years of war and pestilence, and never seen any sign that these are not as contemptuous of death as themselves.[54]

Anglo-Sudanese camaraderie & competition

Imperial mindset notwithstanding, most of the sources do indicate that there was a great degree of camaraderie and mutual appreciation between Sudanese and British troops during the Nile Campaign – with very few exceptions, and particularly in the wake of military accomplishment.[55] Bennet Burleigh's

4.5 *"The advance in the Soudan: the 9th Soudanese welcoming the Camerons on their arrival at Berber"* (Frank Dadd from a sketch by R. G. L. Battley, *The Graphic*, 16 April 1898)

dispatches, most notably, contained several such incidences, the following one taking place at Berber in March of 1898:

> As for the Soudanese and Egyptian troops quartered in Berber, they turned out to a man and welcomed the brigade most loyally....Of their own volition they gathered, lined the route, cheered and presented arms as each British battalion marched past....On handshaking, the day that the British and Soudanese soldiers made each other's acquaintance at Berber, there was expended power enough to have run all the looms in Lancashire for twenty-four hours. Great, brawny blacks, Dinkas and Shilluks, grabbed with their huge palms the hands of Camerons, Lincolns, and Warwicks, and wrung them vigorously, spluttering out, meanwhile, laudatory congratulations in English and Arabic. They cheered and whooped, hurrahing loud and long for England's Queen, and then for her soldiers. There was both fervour and pathos in their welcome.[56]

Granted, this description may seem like imperial propaganda, but it is corroborated elsewhere, and represents only one of many documented instances of goodwill between British and Sudanese troops. George Skinner, a sergeant in the Medical Staff Corps, described the very same scene in his diary: "We left Old Berber at 4:30am on Friday 4 3/98 passing through Berber about 6:30am. Here the whole of the Egyptian and Soudanese troops turned out and lined the streets to give us a welcome and a right good one it was (would have done a British garrison praise) the troops went frantic as we marched between them, the Soudanese expecially [sic] showing their joy at the English, by serving us all out with hot coffee they had made ready for our benefit."[57] Lieutenant-Colonel

Ronald Forbes Meiklejohn, of the Royal Warwickshire Regiment, also mentioned the march through Berber in his journal:

> Started at 3a.m. & marched through Berber. We wore red patches on our Khaki helmets & the 11th. Soudanese the same on their "tarbouches." They are to be affiliated with us as a "sister" regiment. All the inhabitants & the Egyptian & Soudanese troops lined the streets cheering & howling as we marched past. We were rather weary some-what tattered & dust-stained. The 11th Soudanese played us through Berber to their regimental march & ours…We have got the nickname of the 11th. Soudanese – "The Fighting Reds."[58]

The affiliation between the Warwickshires and the XIth Sudanese was not a first of its kind. Rather, it followed a precedent set by the IXth Sudanese back in early 1886. Following the 30 December 1885 action at Ginnis, where the 79th Cameron Highlanders fought alongside 150 soldiers of the Sudanese IXth Battalion, the Camerons presented the IXth with a colour "as a token of their esteem and friendship" and the battalion "was requested to consider itself the 2nd Battalion Cameron Highlanders."[59] Twelve years later, following the 8 April 1898 Anglo-Egyptian victory in the Battle of Atbara, the 79th Cameron Highlanders again presented a colour to the IXth Sudanese Battalion.[60] The Xth Sudanese Battalion, as well, became closely affiliated with a British regiment serving in the Nile Campaign, in this case the Royal Lincolnshire Regiment (formerly the 10th Regiment of Foot). Even prior to their arrival in the Sudan, the 10th Lincolnshire Regiment and the Xth Sudanese had exchanged telegrams following the 7 August 1897 Battle of Abu Hamed – the first in congratulation and sympathy on the part of the Lincolns, the second in appreciation and reciprocation to "their brothers-in-arms" from the Sudanese: "We are all convinced that the 10th Regiments British and Sudanese are ready now and always to do their duty as brave soldiers."[61]

This spirit of goodwill between them was to continue throughout the River War, and eventually went beyond official telegrams between officers, down to the soldiers themselves. For example, in March of the following year, when the Royal Lincolnshire Regiment arrived in the village of Darmali, they were greeted by the Xth Sudanese with cheers, cups of tea, and shouts of "You, 10th Inglesey, we 10th Soudanese."[62] Likewise, there is a similar account dating from the same time period in which it was the Lincolns who did the cheering and provided the nourishment: "The Brigade paraded at 4.45am & formed in two lines & three Regiments of the Soudanese passed through the ranks as they went past our fellows cheered them also gave them tea & biscuits."[63] Moreover, there is a remarkable unpublished photograph that was taken at some point during the Nile Campaign in which six men of the 10th Lincolns posed for a group portrait with six men of the Xth Sudanese – the racially integrated nature of the shot no mistake considering its two symmetrical rows of white-black-white-black-white-black soldiers.[64] And in the immediate wake of the Anglo-Egyptian army's victory at Omdurman on 2 September 1898, the Xth Sudanese presented the Lincolns, "who had shown a most friendly spirit toward the battalion," with the captured Khalifa's White Standard as they both marched toward Omdurman, the Xth Sudanese band striking up "The Lincolnshire Poacher" in honor of its brother regiment.[65] A few days later the

4.6 *"Six of the 10th Lincolns and Six of the 10th Soudanese"*
(Photographer: Walter James, courtesy of the National Army Museum, London)

Lincolns reciprocated, presenting the Sudanese Xth with a regimental color.[66]

In terms of relations between Sudanese and Egyptian soldiers during the Nile Campaign, the existing sources reveal very little, but tend to indicate that these associations were characterized by both cordiality and competition. On the one hand, there is anecdotal evidence that they interacted often and got along quite well. War correspondent E. F. Knight of *The Times* wrote, for example: "It was pleasant to observe how the men of different breeds, having little save their religion in common, fraternized; there appeared to be no jealousies among them; while their officers – the Egyptian and the black captains and the Arab sheikhs – were apparently very good friends."[67] On the other hand, F. R. Wingate, although concurring with Knight, suggested in his 1896 "Notes on Army" (subsection on "Relations between Egyptian and Black troops") that this was not always the case: "There is no special camaraderie between the two races each Battalion keeps rather to itself, but since recent fights in which Egyptians & Blacks have fought shoulder to shoulder, there has been more cordiality & friendship between them."[68]

Relations between Sudanese and Egyptian soldiers could also be characterized as competitive, an outcome not surprising considering the segregated nature of infantry battalions in the Egyptian Army. Perhaps the best example of the kind of inter-battalion rivalry that took place during the Nile Campaign again comes from E. F. Knight, as he described how the XIIIth Sudanese, bent on breaking a marching feat put on by the Egyptian 15th, made the 120 miles from Murat to Korosko in 64 hours.[69] This entailed marching some eighteen hours per day – across the desert and during the hot season:

We met our friend Captain Mahmoud Baghat, late commandant of Murat. He told us that the men of his Sudanese company, determined on beating the record march made by their Egyptian comrades, had marched with him from Murat to Korosko in 64 hours – that is, in one hour less than the time occupied on the outward journey by the men of the 15th battalion whom we had accompanied.[70]

Competition between the Sudanese and Egyptians also came in the form of the aforementioned "gymkhana meetings," in which Egyptian Army soldiers squared off against each other in various foot and riding races, and tugs-of-war.

Of course, relations between Sudanese and British troops were also marked by soldierly competition, particularly in the heat of battle or when it came to the claims to victory. In a noteworthy incident following the Battle of Omdurman, for example, it seems that as the Grenadier Guards were leading the way into the city, one of the Sudanese battalions "showed its annoyance at being preceded by firing over the Grenadiers' heads." Apparently, Kitchener himself intervened at this point, "galloping up with a bugler playing the Cease Fire."[71] Nonetheless, in the end it was a Sudanese battalion (the XIIIth) that won the race to the citadel, and the Mahdi's tomb, overtaking the Grenadiers by navigating a maze of side streets.[72] Once at the front of the pack, the battalion's *kaimakam*, Horace Smith-Dorrien, proceeded to order his men to advance in line abreast, and according to his memoirs this "judicious 'Front form companies and quarter-column on the leading company' prevented" the Grenadiers from recapturing the van.[73] And it was not the first time during the campaign that Sudanese and British troops had jockeyed for the lead position. In fact, this sort of competitiveness – often fostered by British officers in the Egyptian Army and directed toward soldiers and fellow officers in the regular British Army – predated the River War by many years. In one notable incident in 1885, following the Battle of Ginnis, Josceline Wodehouse, an Egyptian Army *kaimakam*, began gathering up enemy standards "as fast as ever he could," and "shouting wildly" to another British officer, W. H. Besant, "Don't let the English get the flags!"[74]

Many times, however, these interracial rivalries were of a more recreational nature. As previously mentioned, there were football, rounders, and hockey matches that took place among and between Sudanese and British troops. Again, "one of the best matches was that witnessed between the British soldiers of the Maxim Battery and a team from the 13th Soudanese," according to *The Daily Graphic's* Dongola Campaign correspondent.[75] Interestingly, it seems that relations between British and Egyptian soldiers were not as comradely or competitive as those between the British and Sudanese. One British soldier attached to the Anglo-Egyptian army, for example, remarked that "the Soudanese & our men were always great friends," but noted "one never saw any mingling of the white & Egyptian troops."[76] And indeed this affinity between the British and Sudanese appears to have been the case for some time in the Egyptian Army. Alfred Milner remarked upon the phenomenon in his 1892 book *England in Egypt*:

> A noticeable fact is the sort of natural *camaraderie* which seems rapidly to spring up between the blacks and Englishmen. The former very easily become attached to their British officers, and those officers, on their side, have a curious kind of fondness for the

blacks, which they do not seem to feel in an equal degree for the native Egyptians. This feeling has been known to extend even to the private soldiers of our British regiments, who, on more than one occasion, have readily fraternized with the Sudanese....The curious thing is, that the blacks get on better with the English than they do with the Egyptians, with whom they might naturally be supposed to have so much more in common.[77]

One British officer later explained this "mutual liking by calling attention to the fact that the Soudanese are fond of athletic games and exercise, indulge often in too much liquor, and have other human failings characteristic of Tommy Atkins, and not of the stolid, quiet Egyptian."[78]

This heightened camaraderie may have stemmed from the self-fulfilling nature of martial identity among Sudanese troops and their inherent vulnerability as lifelong soldiers, a function of something akin to the above-mentioned "Gurkha syndrome." Combine this with British "constructed affinities" and the sorts of gendered dyads one finds in late-Victorian martial race ideology, and one might expect that British soldiers would feel more akin to and competitive with the seemingly more loyal, more fearless, and more manly Sudanese soldiers. Nonetheless, there were instances during the Nile Campaign where a spirit of goodwill and competition also existed between British and Egyptian troops. Following the Battle of Atbara, for example, it was noted in a report to the War Office that the "whole of the British wounded were carried by their Egyptian comrades from the Battle Field to the Nile, a distance of 36 miles – a splendid service which will tend to strengthen the good feeling existing between the two forces."[79] And in the Egyptian cavalry, "in the matter of amusements" while on campaign, British and Egyptian officers played polo two afternoons a week.[80]

The fraternal nature of relations between these "brothers in arms" should not be overstated, however, for there existed an obstacle even more daunting than Victorian-era racism or Orientalism: the English and Arabic languages. With very few exceptions, Sudanese soldiers could not speak English, and British Army regulars could not speak Arabic. Whereas British officers in the Egyptian Army studied colloquial Arabic, could speak French, and knew the Turkish words of command, soldiers in the British Infantry Division of the Anglo-Egyptian army – the Warwicks, Lincolns, Camerons, Grenadiers, and others – had no fluency in Arabic whatsoever. Likewise, most Egyptian Army soldiers, particularly Sudanese soldiers who spent their careers in Upper Egypt and the Sudan, knew little if any English.[81]

Moreover, British fluency in Arabic would not necessarily lend itself to clear communication, for many Sudanese soldiers, particularly new recruits, did not even speak Arabic themselves; and the Arabic that was spoken in Sudanese battalions was often a more rustic, colloquial, Sudanese "pidgeon" Arabic quite different from that spoken in Cairo.[82] They may have seen each other as brothers, but they could not speak to each other as brothers truly would – it simply was not possible. Even some of the newly arrived British officers attached to the Egyptian Division, who were in command of Arabic-speaking troops and who tried to learn "Bimbashi Arabic," a Hobson-Jobson version of the language excluding all un-English sounds, had major difficulties with the language, men such as Frederick Gore Anley: "I'm slow at the language which is a dreadful handicap as none of the men and few of the officers speak English."[83] And so although Sudanese and

British soldiers experienced the kind of cross-cultural camaraderie that shared historical circumstance engenders, particularly among soldiers at war, the things that divided them – race, ethnicity, religion, and especially language – precluded the kind of true fraternity that may have existed had these obstacles not been in place.

Be that as it may, one of the things that clearly, and instantly, transcended this linguistic and cultural divide, and appears to have been a great source of Anglo-Sudanese camaraderie, was music, and specifically, the existence of Sudanese battalion bands. Curiously, the only account of these bands found in the archives, and since repeated elsewhere, indicated that they "date from after the Battle of Omdurman," and it went on to suggest they originated from thirty-eight Sudanese boys who "were sent from the front and trained for band work" following the Battle of Firket in 1896.[84] However, it seems obvious from 'Abdallah 'Adlan's biography alone that Sudanese battalion bands predated the Nile Campaign by many years. In his life story, for example, 'Abdallah recalled that the regimental band he was a member of in the early 1880s "consisted entirely of Sudanese: the bandmaster was a Kunjari from Darfur while the others were from all sorts of different tribes – Nuba, Shilluk, Dinka and so on."[85] And this was following his nine years in the Egyptian Army music school in Cairo dating to the mid-1860s, and another year of further music instruction in Egypt prior to being assigned to the above-mentioned all-Sudanese regimental band. Come 1890, six years prior to the Battle of Firket, 'Abdallah 'Adlan was himself in charge of the band stationed at Halfa.[86]

In any case, by the time British infantry soldiers arrived in the Sudan in early 1898, as the River War entered its final stages, Sudanese battalion bands (most notably, the Sudanese XIth's band) had already earned the reputation as "the best in the Egyptian Army." And understandably so, for these full brass and reed all-Sudanese bands could not only play the Khedival marches, but knew "God Save the Queen" as well as the individual British regimental marches such as "The Lincolnshire Poacher" and "Warwickshire Lads." Indeed, they could even play popular Welsh tunes like "Men of Harlech" and the African-American minstrel song "O, Dem Golden Slippers." And at Gordon's memorial service in Khartoum following the Battle of Omdurman, it was the band of the XIth Sudanese Battalion that was chosen to play the solemn march from Handel's "Scipio" as well as Gordon's favorite hymn, "Abide With Me."[87]

This evolution of Western-style military marching bands within the new Egyptian Army, and in particular the emphasis British musical instructors put on the mastery of so many Anglo-Christian tunes, once again gives further credence to the ornamentalist "replication of sameness" argument. Be that as it may, for Lincolns and Camerons, Seaforths and Warwicks, the welcoming nature of these sounds in March of 1898 seems to have ex-ante helped circumvent the kind of racial, religious, linguistic, and other cultural differences that existed between them and the Sudanese, and set the stage for much of the camaraderie and goodwill that was shared by these "brothers in arms" in the months to follow.

The Battle of the Atbara

There is perhaps no better example of how the above phenomena played out during the reconquest of the Sudan than that which took place at the Battle of the Atbara on 8 April 1898. For starters, the Anglo-Egyptian plan of attack, and its heavy reliance on Sudanese rather than Egyptian troops, was a reflection of both British martial race ideology and certain military realities within the Egyptian Army. Likewise, British perceptions of Sudanese troops at Atbara, whether those of soldiers or special correspondents, reveal the same kind of respect and disdain for them, mutually coexisting, that one finds time and again occurring during the River War. Moreover, the assault on Mahmud's *zariba*, the details surrounding his capture, and scene that took place in the immediate wake of victory all vividly illustrate the nature of Anglo-Sudanese competition and camaraderie alluded to above. Finally, the Battle of the Atbara begins to suggest how some of these phenomena may have skewed not only contemporary accounts of the Nile Campaign, but the historical memory of it via late-Victorian misconstructions and selective omissions, and their historiographical echoes.

The battle took place at Nakheila on the Atbara River.[88] It was Good Friday by the Christian calendar, an ideal day to "Avenge Gordon," as British soldiers were implored to do the morning of the battle. The date was also picked by Kitchener for the added element of surprise – being a holy day, it was thought that Mahmud would not expect an attack. Mahmud Ahmad had been dispatched by his uncle, the Khalifa 'Abdallahi, with a force of 16,000 men and camp followers, later supplemented by 3,000 reinforcements under Osman Digna – sent north to engage an Anglo-Egyptian army that by February 1898 was itself 14,000 strong, and concentrating at the juncture of the Nile and Atbara rivers.[89]

Siding with the venerable Mahdist *amir* Osman Digna, in March the Khalifa had ordered Mahmud to leave the Nile and strike eastward across the desert to the Atbara, in an attempt to outflank Kitchener, putting them in a position to retake Berber and destroy the railway at Gineinetti. However, as they approached the Atbara, another dispute arose between Mahmud and Osman Digna, the latter commander advocating that they move their forces even further upriver to Adarama; this would continue to threaten Kitchener's eastern flank and line of communication, and should the *sirdar* pursue them along the low and unnavigable Atbara, he would have no choice but to do so without his flotilla of gunboats. Mahmud, rejecting Osman Digna's plan, and without referring the matter to the Khalifa, chose instead to entrench his army alongside the Atbara at Nakheila, constructing a circular *zariba* of thorns, inside which he built stockades and trench lines, rifle pits, cannon embrasures, and straw huts, the total enclosure some 1,000 yards in diameter.

Kitchener, not to be outmaneuvered, had marched his forces up the Atbara – first to Hudi (March 20), and then to Ras el Hudi (March 21) – in order to intercept Mahmud's army and protect his eastern flank. In the end, after some indecision on Kitchener's part, two reconnaissance missions of Mahmud's *zariba*, and further movement up the Atbara from Ras el Hudi to Abadar (April

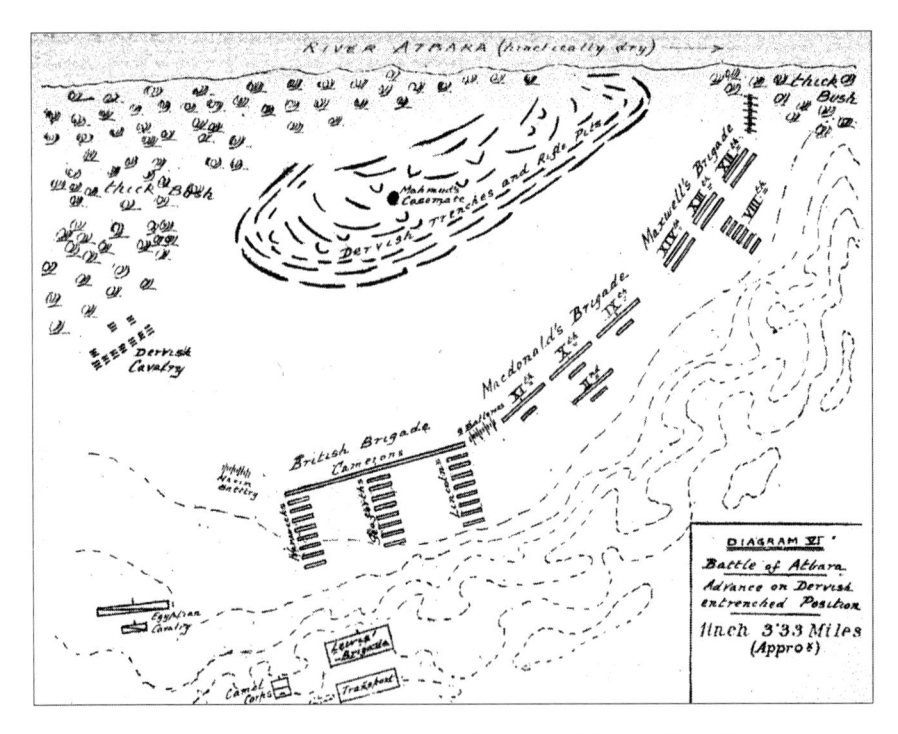

Figure 4.1 *Diagram of Anglo-Egyptian advance on Mahmud's* zariba
(Pritchard, *Sudan Campaign, 1896–1899*, 1899)

4), to Umdabia (April 6), and eventually to Mutrus (April 7), the Anglo-Egyptian attack was set for dawn on April the 8th. The plan of the *sirdar* was simple and straightforward, in both conception and execution – an artillery barrage would be followed by an all out infantry attack on Mahmud's *zariba* from the north, across open ground in a curved formation some 1,500 yards wide.

Considering the martial reputation of Sudanese soldiers, and the grave doubts British commanders had about Egyptian troops when it came to the kind of hand-to-hand combat they might face storming a fortified *zariba*, it was the infantry battalions of the former that were chosen for the task at Nakheila. And although two Egyptian battalions were included in the three brigades that assaulted Mahmud's entrenched forces that morning, a closer look at the attack formation reveals that both of these battalions were positioned in support, and directly behind, three Sudanese battalions in front line. Likewise, the British brigade had one of its own esteemed "martial races," a regiment of Cameron Highlanders, in front line, to the left of these six Sudanese battalions.

Again, the attack formation at Nakheila reflected not only British martial race ideology of the time, but also the key military function that Sudanese soldiers had by then come to occupy in the Nile Campaign. In fact, the strongest troops inside Mahmud's *zariba* were also Sudanese soldiers, *jihadiyya* recruited largely from Darfur and Kordofan. G. W. Steevens described the scene as Kitchener's forces assumed these attack positions that morning at Nakheila:

> The word came, and the men sprang up. The square shifted into the fighting formations: at one impulse, in one superb sweep, near 12,000 men moved forward towards the enemy. All England and all Egypt, and the flower of the black lands beyond, Birmingham and the West Highlands, the half-regenerated children of the earth's earliest civilisation, and grinning savages from the uttermost swamps of Equatoria, muscle and machinery, lord and larrikin, Balliol and the Board School, the Sirdar's brain and the camel's back – all welded into one, the awful war machine went forward into action.[90]

This line moved to within a half mile of Mahmud's *zariba* and halted. There followed an hour and twenty-minute artillery barrage, and then the general "Advance" was sounded at 7:45 a.m.

Fueled by competitive zeal – and the knowledge that attacking a fortified *zariba* at the double would reduce casualties – the Sudanese battalion lines were the first to reach the enclosure.[91] According to one observer they "went through the zariba like paper," and by the estimate of one British officer, Hugh Gregory Fitton, "were inside the trenches 100 yds. in front of the British."[92] Interestingly, even the battalion history of the IXth Sudanese, written as it was by a British commanding officer, was begrudging in its acknowledgement that the Sudanese won the race to Mahmud's *zariba* that morning:

> The "supposed" honour of being first to enter the Zariba has been claimed by most corps engaged. Maxwell's Brigade had the shortest distance to go, next Macdonald's, the British having the furthest. The order was, an advance in "quick time" up to the zeriba, which was obeyed only by the British. Both Sudanese Brigades began to double forward in their excitement. If therefore, either or both Sudanese Brigades arrived at the zariba before the British they did so contrary to orders and can claim no merit for the performance.[93]

The British brigade, meanwhile, marched forward in deep columns rather than extended lines, and "as slow as a funeral," thus suffering more killed and wounded at this stage of the battle than did the Sudanese.[94] It seems, once again, and reminiscent of the Sudanese soldier who told Hector Macdonald eight months earlier "we know best what to do," combat experience and soldierly self-assurance, and the pride and agency that came with it, trumped Western infantry tactics and British military discipline on the field of battle.

Of course, outpacing the British also meant that Sudanese soldiers bore the greater brunt of the initial fighting, and casualties, once inside the enclosure. Case in point was what the Sudanese XIth faced when it was first to arrive at Mahmud's inner stockade, held by some two thousand of his elite guard; the Sudanese company that tried to rush its north-west corner "was all but annihilated," and the XIth lost more men (17 killed, 78 wounded) than any other battalion that fought at the Battle of the Atbara. In the end, it took some twenty-five minutes of intense fighting "with bullet and bayonet" for Sudanese and British troops to clear the *zariba* of Mahmud's army and drive its few survivors to the banks of the Atbara in full retreat.[95]

The leading role in the victory taken by Sudanese soldiers did not go unnoticed by British commanders, war correspondents, and regular soldiers. According to G. W. Steevens, "They attacked fast, but they attacked steadily, and kept their formation to the last moment there was anything to form against." He added that the battle "has definitely placed the blacks – yes, and the once

4.7 Atbara: "Brothers in arms: mutual congratulations after the battle"
(*The Graphic*, 24 September 1898)

contemned Egyptians – in the ranks of the very best troops in the world."[96] George McKenzie Franks, a *bimbashi* in the Egyptian Army, wrote home that of the Sudanese "one can now speak confidently having seen them tried fairly high. They are capital chaps, full of pluck and go, and they did not get out of hand as one has often heard they do."[97] And Kitchener himself wrote to his old friend and the former *sirdar* Evelyn Wood that "after the fight a Tommy was overheard remarking of the blacks 'They be soldiers they be and there is no G__, doubt about it.'"[98]

The "brotherly challenge 'twixt white and black to intrepidity" having been met, at great cost to both, the "Cease Fire" sounded, and the soldiers of both races gathered together in spontaneous celebration of their great victory. According to Bennet Burleigh of the *Daily Telegraph*, "The Soudanese, dancing with delight, ran in amongst the British, cheering, waving their rifles aloft, and with their big fists shaking hands with the 'Tommies.' It was a meeting never to be forgotten I was a spectator of. Mr. Atkins returned their enthusiastic greeting quite as warmly in his own way, hurrahing for the Soudanese and Egyptian troops."[99] As described by Alford and Sword, "The Soudanese danced with delight, and went wildly around shaking hands with every one they came across. As the *sirdar* and his staff rode up, they were met with a perfect roar of cheers, and helmets and tarboushes were waved on the ends of bayonets."[100] Likewise, Steevens wrote of the many handshakes and salutes: "A short shake, then a salute, another shake and another salute, again and again and again…'*Dushman quaïss kitir*,' ran round from grin to grin; 'very good fight, very good fight.'"[101] 'Abdallah 'Adlan's recollections of Atbara suggest a similar sense of collective goodwill and unity of purpose within the Anglo-Egyptian army, in this case on the eve of battle following a speech by Kitchener: "We were greatly encouraged by his words and our hearts were warmed for battle. With one voice the whole army gave a cheer and raised their rifles in the air. We felt that we were unconquerable."[102]

In addition to the aforementioned "honour" of being the first Anglo-Egyptian troops to enter Mahmud's *zariba*, Sudanese soldiers also won the coveted prize of capturing the Mahdist *amir* himself.[103] Soldiers of the Xth Sudanese found him in his *tukl* and hiding under a bed "in the act of getting down into a pit" that he had prepared for just such an eventuality.[104] According to George McKenzie Franks, who happened upon the scene, Mahmud would probably have been killed by these same soldiers, "a pack of savage Blacks" per his description, had he not intervened. However, this account appears suspect when compared to that of Sergeant George Skinner: "As soon as he was seen they rushed down upon him not giving him the least chance of escape or doing himself any injury and dragged him out taking in triumph to the Sirdar."[105]

In any case, this proud moment for the soldiers of the Sudanese Xth was captured by *Black & White* photographer René Bull, and later depicted in a dramatic landscape painting by Godfrey Giles. The photographs are interesting, not only because one of them was later autographed by Mahmud himself, but in light of the fact that the captured Mahdist *amir*, a Taisha Baggara from Darfur, was surrounded by a dozen Sudanese soldiers, some of whom may have once served under him or hailed from Darfur themselves, or were from nearby Kordofan; and it is even more likely that a few of these soldiers had been first enslaved by the Baggara, captured in the Nuba Mountains or along the White Nile. Bennet Burleigh wrote, for example, and seeming to back up Skinner's account rather than that of Franks, "It speaks well for the discipline of the blacks, that though many of them had old and terrible family scores to settle with Mahmoud, once he was got out, he escaped from their hands with nothing worse than their reviling and bitter chaff."[106] And in fact, there is an illustration that was drawn by the special artist for *The Graphic*, W. T. Maud, of Sudanese soldiers later mocking the prisoner Mahmud. Entitled "The Whirligig of Time: Mahmoud, a Prisoner, Mocked by His Old Followers," it included the following caption:

> When Mahmoud was brought a prisoner into camp, he afforded much entertainment to the Soudanese troops. While he sat on his carpet surrounded by his guard, several of the old Soudanese who had served under him in former days came and mocked at him, saying "Ah, Mahmoud, you dog. The time has passed for you to cut my throat."[107]

Certainly, Mahmud was no stranger to the recruitment of Sudanese soldiers, having most recently spent much of 1896–1897 raising troops in Darfur and Kordofan for his *jihadiyya*; many of these soldiers fought to the bitter end defending his *zariba* at Atbara, a number of them manacled by hands and legs inside the trenches to assure they did so.[108] As proud and defiant as Mahmud appears in these photos, head held high and in seeming disregard for his captors, the tables had no doubt been turned on the young Mahdist *amir*.

These images are in some ways a microcosm of much deeper and more complex ironies that marked the lives of Sudanese soldiers, and nineteenth-

4.8 *Captive and captors: the Mahdist* amir *Mahmud and soldiers of the Xth Sudanese, signed by Mahmud*
(Photograph attributed to René Bull, *Black and White War Albums*, Soudan No. 2 –Atbara)

4.9 *"After the Battle of Atbara"* the amir *Mahmud is brought before Kitchener and staff*
(Painting by Godfrey Giles)

century Sudanese history. To begin with, these men, so many of them of slave origins, had gone from being themselves the initial captives and victims, to now, years later, being the final captors and victors – elite forces of an Anglo-Egyptian army set upon destroying the Mahdist state, a polity now dominated by the very people who had first enslaved them, the Baggara. For Sudanese soldiers embarking on the Nile Campaign, it was less the case that they "Avenge Gordon," as it were, than it was a chance to avenge themselves. Of course, the "social death" they suffered via the Baggara, and others, was indeed what had transformed their lives, and identities, and destinies, and led them down the path to where they now found themselves in 1898 – victors at Atbara, captors of Mahmud, and imminent reconquerors of the Sudan.

And yet, there is another layer of irony in that the British, in the form of these crack Sudanese battalions, had paradoxically become, and continued to be, the direct beneficiaries of the slave trade that they themselves had for decades tried to suppress. It goes even deeper, however, both in irony and history, for the extent of Baggara involvement in the very slave trade that the British attempted to suppress originated at least in part from Egyptian taxes that were imposed on them during the Turkiyya, taxes that were often paid in slaves. Many of these slaves, such as 'Ali Jifun, were then enrolled into Sudanese battalions of the Egyptian Army, and were some of the same soldiers that reconquered the Sudan in the name of the Khedive of Egypt, thus completing the imperial circle.

The autographed photo of Mahmud's capture is also interesting in how it differs from the Godfrey Giles painting. In Giles's panorama of the prisoner Mahmud brought before Kitchener, the Sudanese Xth Battalion soldiers are depicted in tight formation around the Mahdist *amir*. They are standing at full attention with dutiful expressions, and are somewhat indistinguishable from the captured Mahmud. It is a solemn and poignant scene, made even more so by the inclusion of the *sirdar* and members of his staff, clearly in full command of the field, and of these men, and not outnumbered by the soldiers of the Sudanese Xth. And thus, in a sense, the Sudanese soldiers depicted in the Giles painting appear to be no more than imperial pawns, doing the ultimate bidding of the British.

In the Bull photograph, on the other hand, these same soldiers, nine of whom are clearly visible, are less uniform in appearance, posture, and expression. Although these men, including Mahmud, are of like race – which is interesting in that these soldiers were "Sudanese," whereas Mahmud was considered an "Arab," something that would be difficult to tell were it not for the *jibba* he is wearing – there seem to be several ethnic groups represented here. Moreover, the soldiers are not at full attention, there is nary a British officer in sight, and the men are looking primarily at the captive Mahdist *amir* rather than the photographer and/or whoever is standing directly across from them. One of the soldiers on the left side of the picture appears to be smiling, and has his Martini-Henry rifle resting on his shoulder. Another, on Mahmud's immediate right, has a furrowed brow, looking rather serious. Ultimately, one has no way of knowing what any of them was actually feeling, or thinking, at the time. Be that as it may, this photograph does depict these men as individuals, not automatons – soldiers whose actions, and agency, had landed them the biggest prize of the day, for which they wanted, and deserved, full credit.

Winston Churchill's *The River War: An Historical Account of the Reconquest of the Soudan*, first published in 1899 and far eclipsing all other accounts of the reconquest both in terms its notoriety and historiographical influence, makes but brief mention of Mahmud's capture. The 23-year-old war correspondent slash cavalry officer cum Nile Campaign historian, who had yet to set foot in the Sudan in April 1898, later wrote merely that "Mahmud himself was captured," and only credits the Sudanese Xth Battalion by inference.[109] Instead, Churchill chose to perpetuate the idea that "the intervention of a British officer alone saved him from the fury of the excited Soudanese."[110] Later editions of *The River War* left out the details of Mahmud's capture entirely, and alluded only to the fact that he was the "most notable prisoner" taken at the Battle of the Atbara, and that "immediately after his capture he was dragged before the Sirdar."[111]

Likewise, only begrudgingly, and only in the first edition of the book, did Churchill reveal that Sudanese soldiers were the first troops to enter the *zariba*; in subsequent versions of the book he avoided the matter altogether, and simply wrote that "at all point the troops broke into the enclosure."[112] Furthermore, he made no mention whatsoever of the scene of jubilation and interracial camaraderie that took place in the wake of the Atbara victory, described in vivid detail by many eyewitnesses and seemingly the stuff of good narrative history. In Churchill's *The River War*, and subsequently, every description of the battle published over the next century, it was as if this scene never happened.

And yet, above and beyond these anecdotal aspects of the battle, perhaps the most glaring omission on the part of Churchill and some of his contemporaries in describing Atbara was the fact that so little reference was made to either the key combat role that Sudanese battalions played or the individual actions of Sudanese soldiers. Whereas the exploits of British troops, the Cameron and Seaforth Highlanders in particular, were given detailed and dramatic form in both words and pictures, those of Sudanese soldiers went largely undescribed. The end result was that British soldiers were painted as Victorian heroes, and Sudanese troops – the majority of soldiers attacking Mahmud's *zariba* that morning – came off as almost ghostlike figures, faceless black ciphers represented solely by battalion numbers. Adding insult to injury, Churchill wrote that during the attack "the firing of the black troops was of the wildest and most reckless description, and although their pluck was undeniable their discipline contrasted unfavourably with the steadiness of the British infantry."[113]

When credit was given to Sudanese battalions for their combat role in the Battle of the Atbara, it often came in the form of praise heaped upon their British commanding officers rather than the men themselves; the above-mentioned quote regarding the Sudanese battalions being "inside the trenches 100 yds in front of the Britsh," for example, was followed by the qualifier "but then the latter had not Hunter to lead them!"[114] Of course, this focus on the heroic deeds and battlefield casualties of white officers and infantry soldiers at Atbara was not only the result of Victorian bigotry and ethnocentrism, it was done to sell newspapers. Nonetheless, it apparently irked some of the British commanders of Sudanese troops, who knew firsthand the more significant role in the battle

4.10 *Cameron Highlanders storming the* zariba *at the Battle of Atbara*
(Painting by Stanley Berkeley)

played by the Egyptian Army, and specifically, battalions IX through XIV. Frederick Ivor Maxse, for example, a British *bimbashi* in the Egyptian Army, complained in a letter home to his father "you probably all feel that the battle of the Atbara was won by white men alone."[115]

Suffice it to say, it was Churchill's often misleading and omissive version of events that held sway in the historical memory of the Nile Campaign, and has made its way into the secondary sources. Take, for example, the following description of what took place at the Battle of the Atbara from the 1972 book *Omdurman*:

> At 7.15 a.m. the troops took up assault positions. Half an hour later the bombardment ceased and at 8 a.m. with bands playing, pipes skirling and shouts of 'Remember Gordon,' Kitchener's infantry swept down upon the enemy. The Camerons led the attack. At the head of the British Brigade they slow marched towards the zariba, stopping from time to time to let off devastating volleys, then marching on again with the calmness and regularity of a parade-ground exercise. Within half an hour it was all over, the dervish zariba had been overrun, Mahmud was a prisoner, Osman Digna had fled once more. Three thousand dervishes were dead and many hundreds captured against a total casualty list for the Sirdar's army of less than 600. But many brave men whom the army could ill spare had perished, and the Highland regiments in particular had suffered sadly with three officers and eighteen men killed and six officers and sixty-six men wounded.[116]

Omdurman is not alone, however, in choosing to pass over the battlefield exploits of Sudanese soldiers in the Battle of the Atbara. Indeed, one would be hard-pressed to find a single history of these events written over the past century that is not guilty of the same general neglect.[117]

Unfortunately, the one aspect of the Sudanese soldier's story that seems not to have eluded this general neglect is a River War legacy rooted firmly in nineteenth-century British racial prejudices. For over a century now, most historians of the Nile Campaign have been simply rehashing the same paternalistic discourse of the late-Victorians, accepting, and perpetuating, the idea that Sudanese soldiers were "excitable, highly strung" and "less amenable to discipline," thus making them "difficult to train."[118] No discussion of their long military experience in the Egyptian Army. No exploration of the various roles, military and otherwise, they occupied during the campaign. No critical examination of their combat record, daily lives, or conditions of service. No stories of Anglo–Sudanese camaraderie or competition. Overlooking all of the above, these writers have instead chosen to regurgitate the very descriptions of these men that warrant the greatest scrutiny, often parroting the racist language found in contemporary accounts without considering their source or factual basis: Was it true that Sudanese soldiers were lacking in discipline? That they shot wildly in battle? Or that they owed their success to the British officers who commanded them? The historical record begs a fuller postmortem.

Notes

1. Burleigh, *Sirdar and Khalifa*, 244.
2. Ibid., 233. Burleigh was referring to the Anglo-Egyptian army's attack on Mahmud's *zariba* at the Batttle of the Atbara (8 April 1898): "A braver sight was not to be seen in a lifetime. An advance was begun as if in review order, but was lifted out of that staccato performance by a tremendous shout, which resounded from right to left of our lines – a brotherly challenge 'twixt white and black to intrepidity. We were in for it now! Steadily went the line of Camerons – General Gatacre, his Staff, and Colonel Money in front. More impulsive, the limber-limbed Soudanese and Egyptian battalions swung ahead of us on the right, and were already firing their rifles."
3. Regarding the use of the racial slur "Sambo" to refer to Sudanese troops, it can be found both in the letters and journals of British soldiers and in published accounts of war correspondents and British officers. H. L. Smith-Dorrien, *kaimakam* of the Sudanese XIIIth, for example, wrote in his published memoirs that "Sambo" was "the name given to our Sudanese troops." Smith-Dorrien, *Memories of Forty-Eight Years' Service* (London: John Murray, 1925), 105. Lieutenants Alford and Sword wrote that "the average Sambo, on enlistment, had not the faintest idea of how to count," which also speaks to the above-mentioned "low regard" many observers had for their intellectual capacities. Alford and Sword, *The Egyptian Soudan: Its Loss and Recovery*, 79.
4. See David Cannadine, *Ornamentalism: How the British Saw Their Empire* (London: Oxford University Press, 2001), xix.
5. Cynthia H. Enloe, *Ethnic Soldiers: State Security in Divided Societies* (Athens, GA: The University of Georgia Press, 1980), 26.
6. Ibid., 26–27.
7. Holt and Daly, *A History of the Sudan: From the Coming of Islam to the Present Day*, 5th edition, 55; Hill, *Egypt in the Sudan*, 63–64.
8. Enloe, *Ethnic Soldiers*, 27.
9. Ibid.
10. Ibid., 39.
11. Heather Streets, *Martial Races: The Military, Race and Masculinity in British Imperial Culture, 1857–1914* (Manchester and New York: Manchester University Press, 2004), 9.
12. Ibid., 9–10.
13. Ibid., 2.
14. Milner, *England in Egypt*, 148 (1901 edition).
15. "From the Soudan," 12 September 1896, *Black & White*; see also "Some Egyptian Army types," *Black & White*, 17 October 1896.
16. "Off to Akasheh," 31 March 1896, *The Daily Graphic*.
17. Alford and Sword, *The Egyptian Soudan*, 79; Knight, *Letters from the Sudan*, 37.

[18] Steevens, *With Kitchener to Khartum*, 90.
[19] Knight, *Letters from the Sudan*, 135. There was an alternative view, and controversy, regarding the treatment of "wounded Dervishes" by Sudanese (and in some cases British) troops during the Nile Campaign, and one that played itself out in the British newspapers. According to most accounts, and especially those relating to Omdurman, Sudanese soldiers committed numerous atrocities in the immediate wake of battle, most notably the killing of wounded enemy combatants. Ernest Bennett, for example, reported that following the Battle of Omdurman, "Our native battalions were soon busily engaged in killing the wounded. The Sudanese undertook this task with evident relish, and never spared a single Dervish along their path." Bennett, however, went on to write: "The barbarous usage of killing the wounded has become traditional in Sudanese warfare, and in some cases it must be looked upon as a painful necessity. The wounded Dervishes – as I saw with my own eyes, and on one occasion nearly felt with my own body – sometimes raised themselves and fired one last round at our advancing line." Bennett, *The Downfall of the Dervishes*, 182–183. See also E. N. Bennett, "After Omdurman," *The Contemporary Review*, 75, 1899, 18–33. Along these lines, Lieutenants Alford and Sword seemed to indicate that the killing of wounded Mahdists following Omdurman, and the inherent dangers associated with it, was a task left entirely to the Sudanese soldiers, and was at least tacitly endorsed by British commanders: "These fanatics had to be despatched, by an advance party of Soudanese, before the Sirdar's army could advance with any degree of safety across the thickly strewn battlefield." Alford and Sword, *The Egyptian Soudan*, 269. Likewise, Winston Churchill wrote "that there was a very general impression that the fewer the prisoners, the greater would be the satisfaction of the commander." Churchill, *The River War* (1899 edition), vol. 2, 195–196, as quoted in Spiers, *Sudan: The Reconquest Reappraised*, 122.
[20] Ibid., 297.
[21] Burleigh, *Sirdar and Khalifa*, 211.
[22] "The Campaign in Egypt," 18 April 1896, *The Graphic*.
[23] Alford and Sword, *The Egyptian Soudan*, 79.
[24] Burleigh, *Sirdar and Khalifa*, 30–31.
[25] Knight, *Letters from the Sudan*, 36–37.
[26] Wingate, *Mahdiism and the Egyptian Sudan*, 203.
[27] Milner, *England in Egypt*, 139.
[28] Wingate, *Mahdiism and the Egyptian Sudan*, 204–205.
[29] Knight, *Letters from the Sudan*, 32–33.
[30] Smith-Dorrien, *Memories of Forty-Eight Years' Service*, (London, John Murray, 1925), 48–49.
[31] F. I. Maxse, *Seymour Vandeleur, Lieutenant-Colonel, Scots Guards & Irish Guards: A Plain Narrative of the Part Played by British Officers in the Acquisition of Colonies and Dependencies in Africa Representing a Dominion of Greater Extent than India Added to the British Empire in Less Than Twenty Years* (London: William Heinemann, 1906), 158.
[32] Streets, *Martial Races*, 8.
[33] Ibid., 8–9.
[34] Streets, *Martial Races*, 94–95.
[35] Roberts to Lieutenant-General Sir James Dormer, CIC Madras, September 1891, in Correspondence and minutes while in India, 1877–1893, as quoted in Streets, *Martial Races*, 95.
[36] C. L. Schaefer, "The Re-conquest of the Soudan," Cairo, 12 April 1896, NA WO 33/56, 1.
[37] F. R. Wingate, unpublished typescript draft, Suakin, September 1894, SAD 258/1/156.
[38] Cromer to Salisbury, 15 March 1896, Cairo, NA FO 78/4892.
[39] Atteridge, *Towards Khartoum*, 211–212.
[40] Archibald Hunter to Captain Beech, 23 July 1896, SAD 1/2.
[41] Frederick Gore Anley to his mother, 9 June 1896, NAM 1984-12-50-38.
[42] Lord Cromer to the Marquess of Salisbury, 17 Feburary 1897, NA FO 78/4895.
[43] "The Campaign in Egypt," 18 April 1896, *The Graphic*.
[44] Cannadine, *Ornamentalism: How the British Saw Their Empire*, xix.
[45] Ibid.
[46] H. C. Jackson, *The Fighting Sudanese* (London: Macmillan & Co., 1954), 1. Jackson was the former Governor of Berber and Halfa Provinces in the Anglo-Egyptian Sudan, not to be mistaken with H. W. Jackson.
[47] Steevens, *With Kitchener to Khartum*, 91.
[48] Burleigh, *Sirdar and Khalifa*, 141.
[49] See Edward Said, *Orientalism* (New York: Pantheon Books, 1978).
[50] Felix Ready, diary, 18 April 1898, NAM 1966-09-142.
[51] Bennett, *The Downfall of the Dervishes*, 24.

52 Gilbert Falkingham Clayton to his mother, 13 March 1898, SAD 942/7/8.
53 Cannadine, *Ornamentalism*, xix.
54 Steevens, *With Kitchener to Khartum*, 91.
55 One notable exception being an incident described by W. T. Maud of *The Daily Graphic*: "I discovered a Highlander and a Soudanese engaged in a fisticuff encounter. The black's arms were flying around like the sails of a windmill, and, though getting the worst of it, he took his punishment well. The affair ended in his being marched off to the guard-room charged with theft, the original cause of the row." Maud as quoted in Harrington and Sharf, *Omdurman 1898: The Eye-Witnesses Speak*, 39.
56 Burleigh, *Sirdar and Khalifa*, 130–131.
57 George Skinner, diary, 4 March 1898, NAM 1979-09-15-3; see also "The Advance in the Soudan: The 9th Soudanese Welcoming the Camerons on Their Arrival at Berber," 16 April 1898, *The Graphic*.
58 Ronald Forbes Meiklejohn, "The Nile Campaign," unpublished typescript account compiled from his journals, NAM 1974-04-36-1.
59 Wood-Martin, *IXth Sudanese Regimental Historical Records*, 1913, SAD 110/11/14.
60 Hamilton Hodgson to his mother, 9 September 1898, NAM 2003-08-8-2.
61 Hunter, *Historical Records of the Tenth Sudanese*, NAM 1968-07-330-1, 34.
62 Spiers, *The Victorian Soldier in Africa*, 146.
63 George Teigh, journal, 15 March 1898, NAM 1997-04-123-1.
64 "Six of the 10th Lincolns and Six of the 10th Soudanese," NAM 1985-05-13.
65 Hunter, *Historical Records of the Tenth Sudanese*, NAM 1968-07-330-1, 45. This incident was also mentioned by George Teigh in his journal: "The 10th Soudanese cheered us as they passed & presented us with a large flag which they captured; they also played our Regimental march which cheered us up. They call our Regiment their brother Regiment as both our numbers are X." George Teigh, 2 September 1898, NAM 1997-04-123-1; also referenced in a letter from Hamilton Hodgson, 1st Battalion of the Lincolnshire Regiment, to his mother: "About two miles on the Soudanese Brigade caught us up the 10th leading playing away at their bugles hard all. I was the other side of the company not paying much attention when I heard a man say 'Why its [sic] the 10th.' + almost simultaneously the [sic] struck up the 'Poachers.' We were rear company bar 'D.' And by Jove there was a howl when the old tune started...as the they [Sudanese] caught each company up, we howled + they howled + shook their rifles in the air [sic] great excitement. About ½ an hour later they had been blocked + halted + we passed them [sic] our drums playing + they gave us a captured standard to carry ahead; more howls." Hamilton Hodgson to his mother, undated, September 1898, NAM 2003-08-8-2; also see Alfred Edward Hubbard's diary, as quoted in *Omdurman 1898: The Eyewitnesses Speak* (London: Greenhill Books; Pennsylvania: Stackpole Books, 1998), 71.
66 Hunter, *Historical Records of the Tenth Sudanese*, NAM 1968-07-330-1, 45; also mentioned by Hamilton Hodgson in a letter to his mother, 9 September 1898, NAM 2003-08-8-2.
67 Knight, *Letters from the Sudan*, 65.
68 F. R. Wingate, "Notes on Army," SAD 110/1/8.
69 Knight, *Letters from the Sudan*, 93.
70 Ibid.
71 John Peter Craddock, *He Soldiered Under Kitchener: The Life and Times of Pte. Harry Milner of Darley Dale* (1992), NAM 1992-08-339-1, 48.
72 Ibid., 49. By contrast, a few days earlier, according to war correspondent Ernest Bennett, the long lines of the advancing army had "kept their formation marvellously well" on the final march toward Omdurman. He noted, however, "As regards actual pace, the Sudanese blacks can easily outmarch the Tommies, and would invariably have been well in the van if the *échelon* had not been carefully preserved." Bennett, *The Downfall of the Dervishes*, 129.
73 Smith-Dorrien, *Memories of Forty-Eight Years' Service*, 116; Philip Ziegler, *Omdurman* (London: Collins, 1973), 196.
74 Andrew Haggard, *Under Crescent and Star* (Edinburgh & London: William Blackwood and Sons, 1895), 376.
75 "The Nile Expedition," 18 May 1896, *The Daily Graphic*. Five days later in *The Graphic* one finds this related, and revealing, tidbit: "In the afternoon the North Staffordshire men, instead of resting or lying down to be tormented by flies in the shade of airy barrack-rooms, devote themselves vigorously to cricket and football, in the latter of which they are often joined by Soudanese or Egyptian soldiers, who, however quick they are when they get a chance, show wholesome disinclination to face their British comrades' rushes. They object to collisions, but they take their bruises in good part, and are gradually learning to appreciate our national sports." "At the front on the Nile," 23 May 1896, *The Graphic*.
76 Captain Somerset Astell as quoted in Spiers, *The Victorian Soldier in Africa*, 143.

[77] Milner, *England in Egypt*, 182.
[78] O. G. Villiard, "The Army of the Khedive and the Present Military Situation in Egypt," *United Service Review*, September 1895, 205.
[79] F. W. Grenfell to War Office, 22 April 1898, NA WO 32/6143, 2.
[80] An Officer, *A Short Account of the Work of the Egyptian Cavalry During the Atbara and Omdurman Campaigns* (London: Published at the Royal United Service Institution, Whitehall, 1910), 160.
[81] Hunter, *Kitchener's Sword-Arm*, 14.
[82] Hill and Hogg, *A Black Corps d'Elite*, 12. One travelogue from a decade following the conclusion of the Nile Campaign referred to the fact that during an enquiry into a Sudanese soldier's death, amongst the soldiers questioned "there were several who spoke little or no Arabic, so the sergeant who brought the men forward for examination had to translate both questions and answers." The same traveler went on to write that he "could not but admire these negro soldiers, whom we call savage, for their having been able to master, during a period in which they failed to acquire Arabic, their profession as soldiers." Artin, *England in the Sudan*, 217.
[83] Frederick Gore Anley to his mother, April 1896, NAM 1984-12-50-33; regarding "Bimbashi Arabic" see Hill and Hogg, *A Black Corps d'Elite*, 145.
[84] "Historical Records of Bands and Schools of Music," no date, SAD 110/12/7.
[85] Bredin, "The Life-Story of Yuzbashi 'Abdullah Adlan," 39.
[86] Ibid., 45. 'Abdallah 'Adlan described the experience as follows: "Two of the British officers there (one of whom was the commanding officer of the XIIth) were very fond of music. Every post from England would bring a fresh supply and I had the task of transcribing it and then teaching the band to play it. These officers insisted that every evening the band should play for them one new march and one new waltz. We were in great demand to play at all the messes and I was responsible for making out all the programmes."
[87] Douglas Wilfred Churcher, diary, 4 September 1898, NAM 1978-04-53-1, 16; Spiers, *The Victorian Soldier in Africa*, 146; Ronald Forbes Meiklejohn, diary, 31 July 1898, NAM 1974-04-36-1; Alfred Edward Hubbard as quoted in Harrington and Sharf, *Omdurman 1898: The Eye-Witnesses Speak*, 71; Burleigh, *Sirdar and Khalifa*, 269; Burleigh, *Khartoum Campaign*, 58; Steevens, *With Kitchener to Khartum*, 313–314; Alford and Sword, *The Egyptian Soudan*, 282. In fact, a photograph of "The Band of the 11th Soudanese, the Crack Black Regiment" was published in *The Graphic* on 24 September 1898. The caption below it ran: "This band played at the recent Memorial Service at Khartoum. The whole band is about seventy strong. All the instruments were provided by Colonel Jackson, who still commands the regiment, and the men all play by ear, having been taught by Colonel Jackson and Sergeant-Instructor (now Lieutenant) Flint, who is on the right of the band in the photo. This band is the best in the Egyptian Army, and they got up 'God Save the Queen' to play when the Duke of Cambridge came to Assouan."
[88] Unless otherwise noted, the background and operational details pertaining to the Battle of the Atbara that follow have been corroborated by and amalgamated from numerous primary and secondary sources, most notably: Hunter, *Historical Records of the Tenth Sudanese*, NAM 1968-07-330-1, 35–38; Wood-Martin, *IXth Sudanese Regimental Historical Records*, SAD 110/11/38–41; Alford and Sword, *The Egyptian Soudan*, 195–235; 'An Officer,' *Sudan Campaign*, 146–161; Steevens, *With Kitchener to Khartum*, 140–160; Churchill, *The River War*, 209–234; Burleigh, *Sirdar and Khalifa*, 79–251; Keown-Boyd, *A Good Dusting*, 189–202; Zulfo, *Karari: The Sudanese Account of the Battle of Omdurman*, 68–80.
[89] According to Mahmud, his total forces on 8 April 1898 included 12,000 infantry and 4,000 cavalry. Steevens, *With Kitchener to Khartum*, 157.
[90] Steevens, *With Kitchener to Khartum*, 142.
[91] Ibid., 150. According to Steevens, "They [Sudanese troops] were in first, there cannot be a doubt. Their line formation turned out a far better one for charging the defences than the British columns."
[92] Walter Kitchener as quoted in Keown-Boyd, *A Good Dusting*, 223; Hugh Gregory Fitton to his sister, 13 April 1898, NAM 1994-10-42-1, 3.
[93] Wood-Martin, *IXth Sudanese Regimental Historical Records*, SAD 110/11/39.
[94] Archibald Hunter as quoted in Keown-Boyd, *A Good Dusting*, 198; see also Hunter, *Kitchener's Sword-Arm*, 87.
[95] Alford and Sword, *The Egyptian Soudan*, 221, 223; see also 'An Officer,' *Sudan Campaign*, 154; Sudanese casualty figures from Appendix O, *IRE* 59, 22.
[96] Steevens, *With Kitchener to Khartum*, 150.
[97] George McKenzie Franks to T. J. Franks, 9 April 1898, SAD 403/2/6–7.
[98] Kitchener to Evelyn Wood, 17 April 1898, NAM 1968-07-234-1.
[99] Burleigh, *Sirdar and Khalifa*, 244.

[100] Alford and Sword, *The Egyptian Soudan*, 224.
[101] Steevens, *With Kitchener to Khartum*, 151.
[102] Bredin, "The Life-Story of Yuzbashi 'Abdullah Adlan," 48.
[103] Kitchener had offered a reward of £100 for Mahmud's capture, and indeed a dispute briefly arose between the Sudanese IXth and Xth battalions, the former disputing the latter's possession of the prisoner. 'An Officer,' *Sudan Campaign*, 157.
[104] George Skinner, diary, 8 April 1898, NAM 1979-09-15-3, 33; see also Alford and Sword, *The Egyptian Soudan*, 228; Steevens, *With Kitchener to Khartum*, 153; 'An Officer, *Sudan Campaign*, 157; Burleigh, *Sirdar and Khalifa*, 256; however, according to 'Ismat Hasan Zulfo's account, "they [11th Sudanese] killed the guard at the headquarters and found Mahmud with his *furwa* laid out, facing Mecca and awaiting death." 'Ismat Hasan Zulfo, *Karari*, 79.
[105] George McKenzie Franks to T. J. Franks, 9 April 1898, SAD 403/2; George Skinner, diary, 8 April 1898, NAM 1979-09-15-3, 33–34.
[106] Burleigh, *Sirdar and Khalifa*, 256.
[107] "The Whirligig of Time: Mahmoud, a Prisoner, Mocked by His Old Followers," 14 May 1898, *The Graphic*.
[108] 'Ismat Hasan Zulfo, *Karari*, 71; Burleigh, *Sirdar and Khalifa*, 243.
[109] Churchill, *The River War* (1899 edition), vol. 1, 460–461.
[110] Ibid.
[111] Churchill, *The River War* (1973 edition), 231.
[112] Ibid., 228; In the first edition of *The River War*, Churchill wrote: "There is, however, one very delicate matter to which I am compelled to allude. It has been said – in the first instance by several silly correspondents – that the Soudanese were the first at the *zeriba*, and that they 'beat' the British brigade. Continuing this absurd competition, the different British regiments each contend as to which of them was first…The British, having the longest distance to cover, were of course the last [to strike it]. Besides this, the Soudanese charged over the final hundred yards of ground, as they were ordered, while the British marched steadily up to the *zeriba* in obedience to their different orders. There is therefore no especial merit in having been the first to reach the enemy." Churchill, *The River War* (1899 edition), vol. 1, 460–461.
[113] Churchill, *The River War* (1899 edition), vol. 1, 434.
[114] Hugh Gregory Fitton to his sister, 13 April 1898, NAM 1994-10-42-1, 3.
[115] F. I. Maxse to his father, 20 April 1898, as quoted in Baynes, *Far from a Donkey*, 54.
[116] Ziegler, *Omdurman*, 33–34.
[117] For the most recent examples, see Philip Warner, *Dervish: The Rise and Fall of an African Empire* (1973); Robin Neillands, *The Dervish Wars: Gordon and Kitchener in the Sudan, 1880–1898* (1996); Edward M. Spiers, "Campaigning under Kitchener," in *Sudan: The Reconquest Reappraised*, ed. Edward M. Spiers (London: Frank Cass Publishers, 1998), 54–81; Michael Asher, *Khartoum: The Ultimate Imperial Adventure* (2005); Dominic Green, *Three Empires on the Nile: The Victorian Jihad, 1869–1899* (2007).
[118] Wright, *Conflict on the Nile*, 72; Barthorp, *War on the Nile*, 133; Keown-Boyd, *A Good Dusting*, 98; Asher, *Khartoum*, 291.

5
"Tea with the Khalifa"

The three Soudanese battalions were now confronted with the whole fury of the Dervish attack from Kerreri. The bravery of the blacks was no less conspicuous than the wildness of their musketry. They evinced an extraordinary excitement – firing their rifles without any attempt to sight or aim, and only anxious to pull the trigger, re-load, and pull it again. In vain the British officers strove to calm their impulsive soldiers. In vain they called upon them by name, or, taking their rifles from them, adjusted the sights themselves. The independent firing was utterly beyond control. Soon the ammunition began to be exhausted, and the soldiers turned round clamouring for more cartridges, which their officers doled out to them by twos and threes in the hopes of steadying them. It was useless.

Winston S. Churchill, *The River War*[1]

Hilaire Belloc's couplet on the Maxim gun notwithstanding, it was Sudanese soldiers that effectively decided the Nile Campaign.[2] However, one would not get this idea reading Winston Churchill's *The River War*, or the many accounts of "the reconquest of the Sudan" that have been published since. Rather, there is the sense that Sudanese soldiers, though gallant and willing fighters, were undisciplined and unskilled, and that their battalions were only held together in the face of the enemy by the strong will of British officers. Moreover, such accounts give the impression these men occupied only a combat role in the Nile Campaign, and a somewhat peripheral one at that, and served in no other capacity than as rank-and-file infantry soldiers. And yet, as it turns out, nothing could be further from the truth.

Upon closer examination one finds that not only did Sudanese soldiers – as well as Sudanese officers and non-commissioned officers – play a decisive role in every battle of Churchill's "River War," and subsequently bore the brunt of Anglo-Egyptian casualties, but they also undertook numerous non-combat roles during the campaign, serving as interpreters, spies, recruiters, policemen, and ethnic liaisons. In fact, Sudanese soldiers played an essential, albeit unrecog-

5.1 *"Omdurman: The First Battle at 6:30 a.m.," showing the Egyptian Army only in supporting roles to the British firing line* (Coloured lithograph, G. W. Bacon & Co., Ltd)

nized by historians, background diplomatic role during the 1898 Fashoda crisis – facilitating good relations between the British and the Shilluk and Dinka, and at the expense of the French. And as for their soldiering abilities, it seems that Churchill's negative descriptions were more the product of his own inexperience in the region and unfamiliarity with Sudanese infantry tactics than anything else. Contrary to Churchill's account, most contemporary sources suggest that these soldiers, many of them with decades of combat experience in Northeast Africa, maintained good discipline in the heat of battle, and in some cases outperformed their British and Egyptian comrades.

Equally misleading, and linked with the above misrepresentations, is the enduring popular image of British redcoats engaging fanatical "Dervish" hordes – Tommy Atkins meets Fuzzy-Wuzzy – in one of Queen Victoria's "little wars." In addition to the fact that British soldiers serving in the River War actually wore khaki field dress, these depictions are inaccurate in that they give the false impression that the majority of troops in Kitchener's army were British "Tommies" rather than Egyptian and Sudanese soldiers. Indeed, more than two-thirds of the soliders in the Anglo-Egyptian army at the Battle of Omdurman were African – 17,600 of the total strength of 25,800, including eighteen of the twenty-six infantry battalions, six of the nine artillery batteries, nine squadrons of cavalry, and eight camel corps companies.[3]

Firket through the Battle of the Atbara

When one looks at earlier stages of the Nile Campaign, the above disparities are even more telling. On 7 June 1896 at Firket, for example, the first action of the River War, whereas the Egyptian Army put ten infantry battalions in the field, some 9,000 soldiers all told, a single Maxim battery of Connaught Rangers and North Staffords represented the only British presence (other than British officers in the Egyptian Army). At the Battle of Abu Hamed the following year there were no British Army rank-and-file soldiers involved at all, the strategically located Nile River village taken in force by 3,600 Sudanese and Egyptian soldiers. Even as late in the Nile Campaign as the Battle of the Atbara (8 April 1898), there were only four battalions represented in the British Brigade, as opposed to eleven in the Egyptian Division.

Above and beyond these figures, the value and importance of Sudanese troops in the River War is even more evident when one examines how these troops were deployed in battle, and the key role they played in every Anglo-Egyptian victory. At the aforementioned Battle of Firket, for example, five of the ten Egyptian Army infantry battalions engaged were Sudanese battalions.[4] And in fact it was Sudanese battalions that led the surprise attack on the two most critical Mahdist positions at Firket: there were two Egyptian battalions in Lewis's First Brigade, but it was the Xth Sudanese Battalion that was deployed in the front and was the first to form line in the narrow strip of land between Jebel Firket and the Nile (soldiers of the Xth Sudanese were thus the first Egyptian Army troops to engage the enemy in the riverside Ja'aliyyin camp at Firket village); likewise, the second main position attacked that morning was the *jihadiyya* camp in the hills

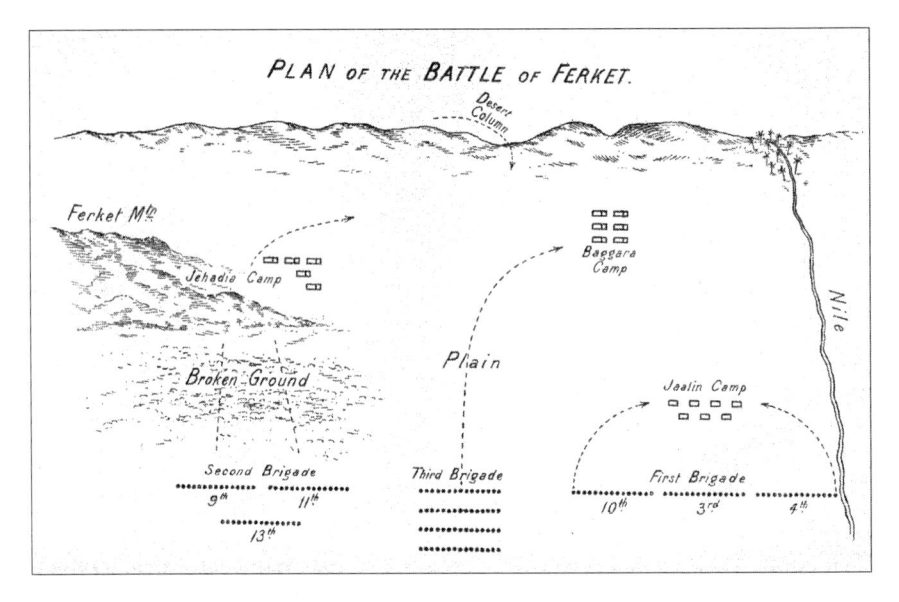

[Figure: Plan of the Battle of Ferket — hand-drawn map showing Ferket Mt., Jehadia Camp, Baggara Camp, Jaalin Camp, Broken Ground, Plain, Nile, Desert Column, and positions of the Second Brigade (9th, 11th, 13th), Third Brigade, and First Brigade (10th, 3rd, 4th).]

Figure 5.1 *Plan of the Battle of Firket*
(Alford and Sword, *The Egyptian Soudan*, 1898)

to the southeast, and this task was given to Macdonald's Second Brigade, made up of the IXth, XIth, and XIIIth Sudanese battalions. Considering that Maxwell's Third Egyptian Brigade was initially held in reserve, and "took little part in the fighting, as the enemy were already routed when these troops passed through the Baggara camp," it is fair to say that most of the fighting that day was carried out by Sudanese soldiers.[5] Even the Sudanese XIIth Battalion, attached to the Desert Column, was originally projected to play a key role in the Kitchener's attack strategy at Firket – cutting off any line of retreat following the River Column's frontal assault.

As for their actual performance on the battlefield at Firket, eyewitnesses did not report Sudanese troops to have been undisciplined or firing wildly. E. F. Knight of *The Times* reported quite the opposite when describing the men in the IXth, XIth, and XIIIth Sudanese battalions of the Second Brigade: "The brigade advanced on these at a smart pace, over rough ground, crossing mountain spurs and ravines, and charging the enemy along the hill-tops. At frequent intervals they paused to pour in deadly volleys. The men were kept very well in hand, and, indeed, throughout this day, both Egyptian and Sudanese troops were as steady as if on parade."[6] Lieutenants Alford and Sword concurred with Knight's assessment, and used rather similar language: "Our troops advanced across the plain in good order, pouring in steady volleys, and then rushing forward some yards, just as regularly as if 'doing the attack' on parade."[7]

The outcome may have been something of a foregone conclusion, as the 3,000 Mahdists troops at Firket faced an invading army three times its size. Nonetheless, the performance of the River Column – and especially that of the Sudanese soldiers – is still worth noting. Over one thousand Mahdist combatants were killed and wounded, and six hundred taken as prisoners. On the Egyptian Army side, the casualties were extremely low by comparison, as only 22 soldiers were killed, and 91 wounded.[8] Keen observers of the action at Firket, such as E. F. Knight, were not surprised by the good show put up by Sudanese troops "who pass their lives under the colours," many of whom "of course, had met the Mahdists frequently in fight."[9]

Likewise, at the 7 August 1897 Battle of Abu Hamed, the next major engagement of the Nile Campaign, it was again Sudanese soldiers that led the assault.[10] The village of Abu Hamed – located at the strategic point where Kitchener's new railway would rejoin the Nile – was in the summer of 1897 still held by a small force loyal to the Khalifa. With tracks now laid halfway across the Nubian Desert, on 29 July a flying column of 3,600 men (no British Army regulars) was sent from Kassinger to attack the Mahdist garrison at Abu Hamed before reinforcements could be sent up from Berber. The flying column, consisting of the Sudanese IXth, Xth, and XIth battalions, and the Egyptian Third, completed the 133-mile march from Kassinger to Abu Hamed in 205 hours, averaging over fifteen miles per day through the Monassir Desert during the hottest time of the year. Leaving half of the one Egyptian battalion at nearby Ginnifab as a transport and ammunition escort, the Sudanese IXth, Xth, and XIth battalions, along with the other half of the Egyptian Third, attacked Abu Hamed at dawn on the seventh of August.

According to Lieutenants Alford and Sword, "In the assault of the town, the discipline of the troops was especially marked; and the Egyptians and Soudanese seemed to vie with each other as to who could show the greatest steadiness and dash."[11] However, another contemporary source indicated that the Sudanese XIth, followed by the other battalions, "broke into rapid independent firing," counter to Colonel Macdonald's orders and his intention to "rush the place with the bayonet."[12] This led to a situation where the Xth, owing to the crescent formation of the brigade, could not advance without getting shot at by the other Sudanese battalions, and thus while halted exposed itself to gunfire from the enemy trenches.

According to this same source, "Macdonald immediately came out in front swearing at the men and knocking up their rifles. The other officers did the same, and in a few minutes our firing ceased."[13] The whole brigade then rushed forward, sweeping through the Mahdist trenches and on into the village, clearing Abu Hamed of enemy combatants street-by-street and house-to-house with bullet and bayonet. One eyewitness later described the fighting tactics of the Sudanese soldiers at Abu Hamed as both well-honed and quite effective, albeit rather hazardous for bystanders:

> The black is a splendid chap at house fighting, and they rapidly worked through the place, though it must be admitted some of their methods are almost as dangerous to friend as to foe. Before entering a house they fire several volleys into it (and as it is mud most of the bullets come out the other side), then they rush in, and if a Dervish comes for them, they stick their bayonet in and at the same time pull the trigger. Before turning a corner from one street to another they reach their rifle round the corner and pull the trigger on chance, regardless of the fact that there may be some of their own troops coming up the street. Nevertheless they are A1 at clearing an enemy out of a village. In a twinkling they were all over the place, on the roofs, through the windows, and in no time had worked through the

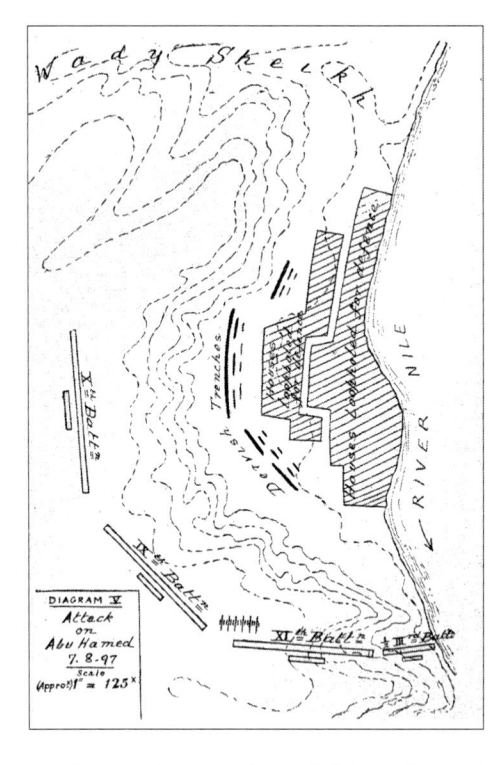

Figure 5.2 *Diagram of the Egyptian Army attack on Abu Hamed*
(Pritchard, *Sudan Campaign, 1896–1899*, 1899)

place and formed up beyond, firing volleys at the few flying Dervish cavalry who were the only ones to escape.[14]

Within two hours some five hundred Mahdists had been killed, and three hundred wounded. On the Egyptian Army side, Sudanese soldiers bore the brunt of the casualties. Twenty-one of the twenty-three soldiers killed in battle were "natives," of which twenty were Sudanese; all sixty-one wounded were "natives," of which fifty-eight were Sudanese. The IXth Sudanese Battalion had twenty-four casualties (five killed; nineteen wounded, including three severely wounded soldiers who "all lost a leg"), the XIth had six casualties (one killed; five wounded), and the Xth, suffering by far the most of the three Sudanese battalions, had forty-eight casualties (fourteen killed; thirty-four wounded). Nonetheless, with the exception of one mortally wounded *nafar* of the Sudanese Xth Battalion named Hassan Ahmad, who was said to have requested that his medals be given to General Hunter, the only identities of fallen Abu Hamed soldiers that were recorded for posterity were those of the two British soldiers killed that day, Major H. M. Sidney and Lieutenant E. Fitzclarence – the two officers who "died to win the desert road" in Sir Rennell Rodd's poem, and later came to symbolize the battle in the popular imagination.[15]

Sudanese soldiers also played a key combat role in the 8 April 1898 Battle of the Atbara.[16] To begin with, they had the most men in the field; six of the eleven infantry battalions in the Egyptian Division were Sudanese battalions, and they also outnumbered the four British Army battalions by over a thousand men.

Moreover, Kitchener's plan of attack, as usual, relied more heavily on Sudanese than Egyptian troops; although two Egyptian battalions were among the two infantry brigades that assaulted Mahmud's *zariba* that morning, a closer look at the attack formation reveals that both of these battalions were positioned in support, and directly behind, the three Sudanese battalions in front line.

Once again, at the Battle of the Atbara, Sudanese troops demonstrated their combat savvy and self-confidence, attacking Mahmud's entrenchments at the double – and at their own bidding – in order to reduce casualties. Not only were they the first Anglo-Egyptian troops to reach the Mahdist enclosure, they bore the greater brunt of the initial fighting, and casualties, once inside. Whereas Egyptian infantry battalions had only one man killed and nineteen wounded, and the British Brigade seventeen killed and one hundred wounded, Sudanese infantry battalions at Atbara had forty-six men killed and three hundred thirty-three wounded; this represented over seventy percent of the casualties in both categories despite being only some forty percent of the total number of infantry forces. Although George McKenzie Franks, a *bimbashi* in the Egyptian Army, wrote following the battle that the Sudanese "did not get out of hand as one has often heard they do," another participant made mention, once again, of independent firing by Sudanese soldiers: "The black troops had, in their excitement, forgotten the order not to fire, but to use the bayonet only, & their bullets, as well as the enemy's, were whistling past pretty thickly, smashing through huts, or thudding into the ground, which in places was quite slippery with blood."[17]

In any case, as previously mentioned, a few campaign accounts and handful of newspaper illustrations notwithstanding, the central role played by Sudanese battalions at the Battle of the Atbara was largely ignored, or painted in such broad strokes that it was quickly forgotten, and later overlooked in most subsequent histories of the Nile Campaign. Rather, and not surprisingly, it was the exploits of the British brigade, especially those of the Highlander regiments, that got the most press, and became the popular perception of what took place that "Good Friday" on the Atbara. It is interesting to look at perhaps the most famous depiction of the battle, *Cameron Highlanders Storming the Zariba at the Battle of the Atbara*, painted by Stanley Berkeley and published as a print by Henry Graves. There is not a Sudanese or Egyptian soldier to be found in the frame. Rather, Berkeley's brush gives the distinct impression that it was a battle fought entirely between Highlanders and Mahdists. Moreover, the only Atbara newspaper illustrations that included Sudanese soldiers in combat had them either lying dead inside the *zariba* or shooting retreating Mahdists in the back as they tried to flee – hardly worthy of the actual role they played in defeating Mahmud's army that April morning.

The Battle of Omdurman

By any objective measure, it was Sudanese soldiers that deserved – and in fact received in many initial accounts – the highest praise of any Anglo-Egyptian troops that fought at the Battle of Omdurman (2 September 1898). As in all previous battles of the River War, they occupied some of the key tactical roles, and bore the brunt of the fighting and casualties that September morning. In fact, it was three of the original Sudanese battalions (IXth, Xth, XIth) that bailed out Kitchener that day – holding off a two-pronged attack by the Khalifa that took place when one of the Egyptian brigades became separated from the rest of the army following a prematurely ordered and ill-coordinated advance on the city.

Be that as it may, the battlefield performance of Sudanese soldiers at Omdurman was misattributed by most contemporary writers, the credit given to British commanding officers rather than to the men themselves. Moreover, their decisive role was also overshadowed in many of these accounts by "the charge of the 21st Lancers," a moment of military folly made Victorian myth that ultimately had little if any impact on the battle's outcome. And thanks to the vivid prose of the charge's most famous eyewitness, and indeed participant, Winston Churchill, this continues to be the case over a century later. Although a number of subsequent historians have put the charge of the 21st Lancers in its proper place in terms of its overall relevance – in one case likening it to the charge at San Juan Hill by the Rough Riders, another seemingly trivial military episode in 1898 exploited for sensationalistic reasons – it remains the dominant image people have of the Battle of Omdurman, if not the entire campaign.[18] Likewise, again attributable to the undue influence of *The River War* at the expense of all other contemporary accounts of the Nile Campaign, to this day the battlefield record of Sudanese soldiers at Omdurman continues to be overlooked or misrepresented.

Most descriptions of the first phase of the battle have focused on the effectiveness of British infantry and artillery in repulsing the Khalifa's initial dawn attack – the combined forces of Ibrahim el Khalil and Osman Azraq, some 12,000 men launched along two axes from behind Jebel Surgham.[19] However, what has usually received only passing mention is the fact that it was the Sudanese XIIth, XIIIth, and XIVth battalions, dug in along trenches in the middle section of "Kitchener's zariba," that faced the most concentrated forces of Osman Azraq's frontal attack across the Karari plain.[20] It also is worth noting that these three Sudanese battalions avoided some of the casualties the British infantry were suffering during this phase because their defenses were superior. Whereas the British Division at Egeiga was obliged to fire from a standing position by the flimsy thorn *zariba* they had built, the Egyptian Division was less vulnerable as it were having chosen light shelter-trenches; dug as standard, these trenches provided them both a better field of fire and greater support for their rifles.

Also given short shrift in most accounts of the battle are two other instances where Sudanese troops deserved greater mention: first, it was four Sudanese companies of the Egyptian Army's Camel Corps that – along with the Egyptian cavalry, the Egyptian horse artillery battery, and four Egyptian companies of camel corps – staged a fighting withdrawal at a key moment in the battle, diverting some ten thousand soldiers of the Green Standard from attacking Kitchener's weakest flank on the northern edge of the *zariba*; second, as the Anglo-Egyptian army began its march toward Omdurman, it was two companies of the XIIIth Sudanese Battalion that were given the task of clearing Jebel

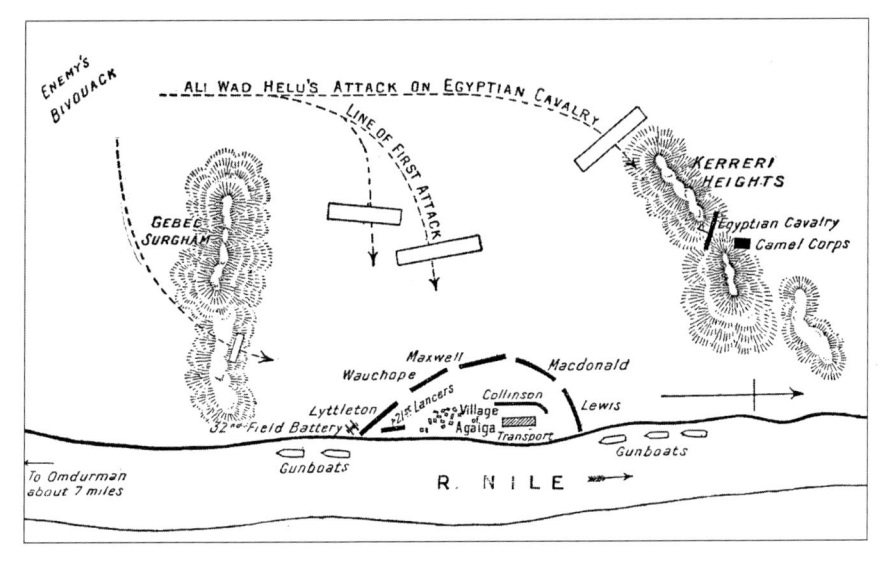

Figure 5.3 *Battle of Omdurman: Phase One*
(Steevens, *With Kitchener to Khartoum*, 1898)

Surgham, and that captured its summit from a contingent of Mahdists sent to hold it.[21] Indeed, had either of these gallant and improbable feats been accomplished by Highlanders or Grenadiers, it is doubtful they would have been so obscured by war correspondents and special artists, and later, by historians of the battle.

However, by far the greatest display of collective Sudanese military skill at Omdurman came during the second phase of the battle, when the 3,000-strong First Egyptian Brigade found itself separated from the advance echelon, and was attacked in succession from three directions by some 26,000 soldiers of the Khalifa's Black and Green Standards. Kitchener, following his repulse of the Khalifa's first wave, had decided to occupy the city of Omdurman before retreating enemy forces could take up defensive positions there. However, what the *sirdar* failed to realize or chose to ignore was that some two-thirds of the Mahdist army remained intact, twelve thousand soldiers of which lay concealed behind Jebel Surgham, still waiting to be deployed by the Khalifa's brother Yakub. Making matters worse, as the echelon made its way toward Omdurman, Kitchener's army became even more exposed when large gaps began opening up between the advancing brigades. The First Egyptian Brigade, led by Hector Macdonald and composed of the Sudanese IXth, Xth, and XIth battalions, along with the 2nd Egyptians, soon found itself exposed on the far right, a mile-wide gap separating it from the rest of the Anglo-Egyptian army.[22] Yakub's forces, taking advantage, emerged from behind Surgham and attacked the rear of the echelon, the main thrust of his assault launched at Macdonald's now isolated brigade.

Disregarding an order to retire, Macdonald put his whole brigade in line, and reinforced by three artillery batteries and eight Maxim guns, took on the charge

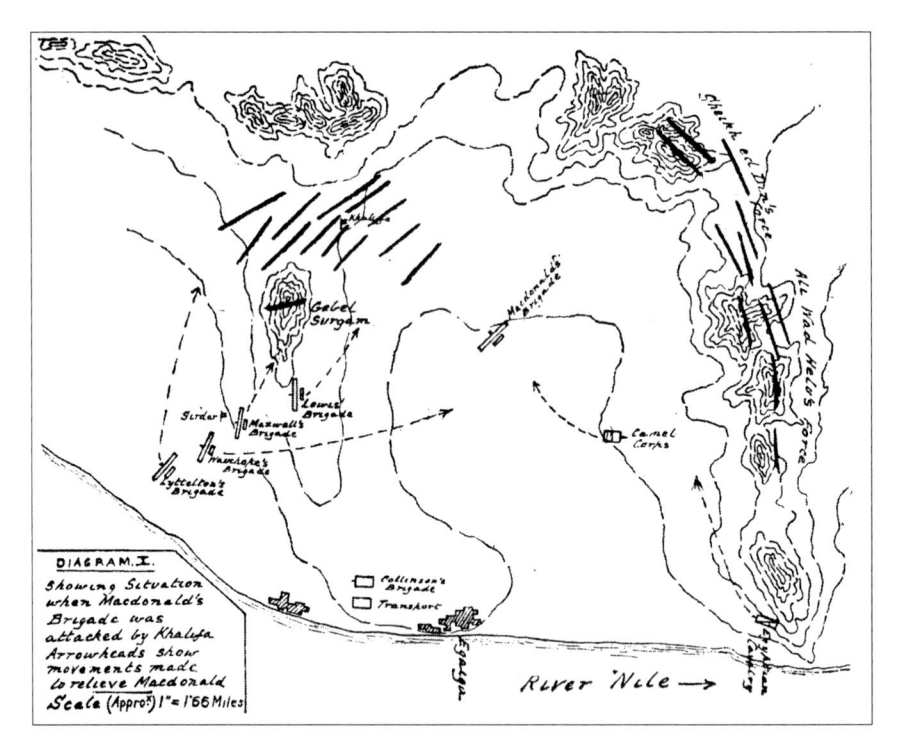

Figure 5.4 *Battle of Omdurman: Phase Two*
(Pritchard, *Sudan Campaign, 1896–1899*, 1899)

of the Black Standard. Some two thousand Sudanese infantry soldiers, from one knee or standing, feet firmly planted and taking good aim with their Martini-Henry rifles, fired steadily, and independently, while the Egyptian battalion fired in continuous, well-targeted volleys.[23] The combined effect of the cannon, machine-gun, and rifle fire on Yakub's army was devastating, and some 3,450 of his men were killed or wounded in the assault. And then, as if repulsing one army was not impressive enough, these same four battalions of Sudanese and Egyptian troops faced a second, two-pronged Mahdist attack coming from the Karari hills – fourteen thousand *mulazimin* and men of the Green Standard. In textbook fashion, Macdonald wheeled his troops some ninety degrees to take on the new assault, the Sudanese IXth serving as the West hinge during the brigade's change of front.

This second onslaught on the First Egyptian Brigade, indeed the Khalifa's last gasp at Omdurman, suffered the same fate as the first, as line after line of *ansar* met a hail of bullets coming from the Sudanese and Egyptian troops. In fact, by the time this second phase of the battle was over at eleven o'clock, Macdonald's brigade had been fully engaged for an hour, and the Sudanese battalions were running low on ammunition – having that day expended some 139,017 rounds between the three of them.[24] The end result, according to one war correspondent who himself had been an eyewitness to many Egyptian Army

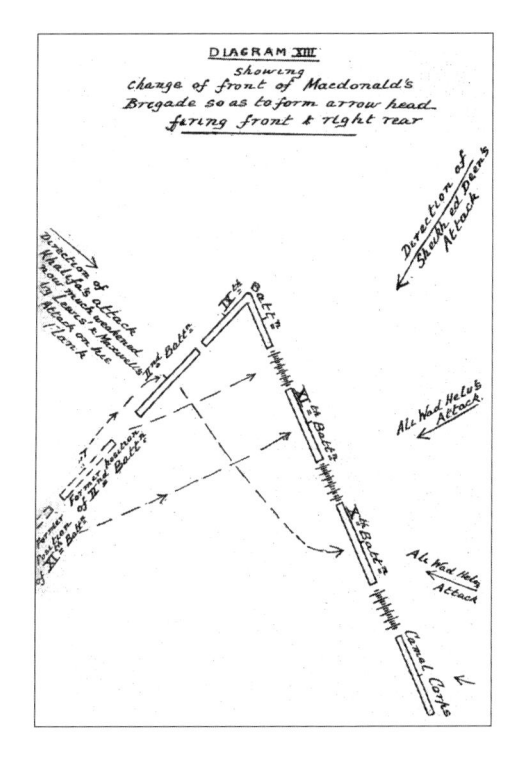

Figure 5.5 *Diagram of the change of front by Macdonald's brigade* (Pritchard, Sudan Campaign, 1896–1899, 1899)

clashes with the Mahdists, was that the *mulazimin* left standing on the field broke and fled, "a devil-take-the-hindmost race, and the only one I ever saw them engage in through half a score of battles." This same correspondent, although largely crediting Macdonald's leadership, declared the brigade's accomplishment "a single-handed triumph," and that they had, according to all observers, "snatched success from what looked like certain disaster."[25]

It is debatable as to what would have happened to Kitchener's right flank had Macdonald's brigade met with disaster. Likewise, one wonders how the Khalifa's fortunes might have changed at Omdurman had his second-phase attacks been simultaneous. Regardless, what is clear is that once again Sudanese soldiers played the key combat role, and suffered the most casualties, in an Anglo-Egyptian victory. According to one British officer in the Macdonald's Brigade, "Whatever anyone says about the other brigades the brunt of the whole fight was borne by us in 4 hours."[26] And though slight compared to the Khalifa's casualties at Omdurman (approximately 10,800 killed, 16,000 wounded), Sudanese battalions suffered three times as many soldiers killed in action as did the British and Egyptian infantry units, and nearly as many wounded as both of them combined.[27] These contributions did not go unnoticed at the time. General Archibald Hunter, commander of the Egyptian Division of Kitchener's army, in his report on the battle gave special remark on the "excellent steadiness, and good fire dicipline [*sic*] and controle of fire during the enemy's attack," as well as the "gallantry of Bimb. Capper's leading of the Co. of the 13th Battalion and the capture of the summit of Signal Hill supported by Bimb. Whigham with 1

Co. of XIII." Hunter added that "chief and foremost in the incidents of the 2nd of Sept. up to noon, that came before my notice, was the action of Macdonald's Brigade in its final grapple with the enemy," the Egyptian Army *liwa* making particular note of "the drill of the men under fire."[28]

Hunter was not alone in his praise of Macdonald's brigade at Omdurman. The *sirdar*, Herbert Kitchener, wrote in his report to Sir Francis Grenfell that "Macdonald's brigade was highly tested, bearing the brunt of two severe attacks delivered at very short intervals from different directions," and likewise commended their "greatest steadiness under most trying circumstances." War correspondents, too, wrote glowingly about the battlefield performance of the First Egyptian Brigade at Omdurman, and of Sudanese soldiers in particular. According to *Westminster Gazette* correspondent E. N. Bennett, "The Sudanese had shown that they could stand absolutely steady under a prolonged fire as well as rush impetuously to an attack." Lieutenants Alford and Sword also referred to "the steadiness of the 9th, 10th, and 11th Soudanese battalions," and elsewhere mentioned "the excellent fire-discipline of the Soudanese" in the face of Shaykh al Din's charge. However, like many observers, they gave much of the credit to Hector Macdonald, writing that "but for the consummate generalship of their leader, the Soudanese must have been destroyed."[29]

Notably, Winston Churchill was one for whom the contributions of Sudanese soldiers at Omdurman did go largely unnoticed, both literally and in print. And thus his recounting of their performance in battle ultimately told a quite different story from the above-mentioned sources. To begin with, in both his 1898 letters to the *Morning Post* and his 1899 book *The River War* he made only passing mention of the role of the Egyptian Army's Second Brigade (XIIth, XIIIth, and XIVth Sudanese; 8th Egyptians) in repulsing Osman Azraq's assault on the entrenched center of Kitchener's *zariba* during the first phase of the battle.[30] Most importantly, however, Churchill gave Macdonald's saving action during the second phase of the battle far less attention than it deserved, and what few details he did provide evoked a rather different, and much less flattering, impression of Sudanese soldiers in combat.[31]

Churchill wrote, for example, and oft-repeated since, that when 'Ali Wad Helu launched his attack "the bravery of the blacks was no less conspicuous than the wildness of their musketry."[32] He further described the soldiers of the Sudanese IXth, Xth, and XIth battalions as evincing "an extraordinary excitement," and with seemingly no idea how to sight or aim their Martini-Henry rifles. In contrast to the above-mentioned accounts, Sudanese soldiers are depicted as "impulsive" rather than steady, their firing "utterly beyond control" and "random" rather than disciplined or well aimed. According to Churchill, it was only Macdonald and his British officers who kept their heads in the face of the enemy: "In vain the British officers strove to calm their impulsive soldiers. In vain they called upon them by name, or, taking their rifles from them, adjusted the sights themselves."[33] And adding further insult to injury, Churchill then gives the impression that Macdonald's brigade was rescued in the end by the Lincoln Highlanders, whom he depicts as the polar opposite of the Sudanese soldiers in terms discipline and marksmanship:

5.2 "Omdurman – Soudanese troops waiting Dervish attack"
(René Bull, *Black and White War Albums, Soudan No. 1 – Omdurman*)

> Scarcely three rounds per man remained throughout the brigade....Still the Dervishes advanced...
> At this moment the Lincoln Regiment began to come up. As soon as the leading company cleared the right of MacDonald's brigade, they formed line, and opened an independent fire obliquely across the front of the Soudanese. Groups of Dervishes in twos and threes were within 100 yards. The great masses were within 300 yards. The independent firing lasted two minutes, during which the whole regiment deployed. Its effect was to clear away the leading groups of Arabs. The deployment having been accomplished ...section volleys were ordered. With excellent discipline the independent firing was instantly stopped, and the battalion began with machine-like regularity to carry out the principles of modern musketry, for which their training had efficiently prepared them and their rifles were admirably suited. They fired on average sixty rounds per man, and finally repulsed the attack.[34]

Moreover, Churchill's description of this final charge of the Khalifa's *mulazimin* and Green Standard forces against the Egyptian First Brigade runs a mere one thousand words in *The River War*. This pales by comparison to his graphic rendering of the charge of the 21st Lancers, for example, which goes on for pages and includes the names of individual soldiers, several incidences of British heroism, and all the gory details of injuries inflicted by Mahdist sword and spear.[35] The charge, in short, took place following Kitchener's decision to occupy Omdurman after the first phase of the battle, when he sent the 21st Lancers ahead of the main echelon to clear the ground on his left and cut off any retreating Mahdists. After crossing the slopes of Jebel Surgham, the Lancers encountered what they believed was a small body of Mahdists. A cavalry charge was ordered. In fact, it was a decoy, and a much larger enemy force, led by Osman Digna, lay concealed in a dry riverbed, or *khor*. By the time the Lancers realized this, it was too late, and there were considerable losses on both sides. Again, the charge had little if any impact on the battle, but for war correspondents, and Churchill especially, who experienced it firsthand, its gallantry far outweighed its significance.

Of course, Churchill knew his audience, and what it wanted to read, and in this he was not alone among Nile Campaign journalists and publishers back in England. And indeed, it being the first ever cavalry charge of the 21st Lancers in war – with its unwitting nature, its valiant pursuit, and its gruesome casualties (likened to "the Cuirassiers at Waterloo" by Churchill) – it made for the best print and most dramatic visuals.[36] What did Victorian readers want with descriptions of Sudanese soldiers when they could read about their fellow countrymen in hand to hand combat with fanatical "Dervishes," avenging Gordon in the name of the Queen? Be that as it may, Churchill's *The River War*, far more than any of the other contemporary accounts penned by correspondents or participants, has influenced, indeed biased, how Sudanese soldiers have been depicted at Omdurman by most subsequent writers. There are still references to "the wild inaccuracy of his [Macdonald's] Soudanese riflemen" during this phase of the battle, and that in the face of Yakub's charge the Sudanese troops "got the jitters" and "became almost hysterical with excitement."[37] Echoing Churchill, indeed sometimes quoting him at length, these authors describe Sudanese soldiers of the IXth, Xth, and XIth battalions as "excitable and erratic in their aiming" and "firing wildly."[38]

Several of these secondary sources also repeat Churchill's assertion that the Lincolns saved the day, and depict them as the "rescuers" of Macdonald's brigade – delivering the *coup de grace* to Mahdism just as the Sudanese troops had run out of ammunition and were about to be annihilated.[39] And whereas many of these accounts again go into great detail on the charge of the 21st Lancers, few if any of them even reference the Sudanese contributions in the first phase of the battle.[40] In truth, some of them do give credit to Sudanese soldiers for their "dauntless" nature, and for the fact that they "stood fast" in the end.[41] One source even recognizes that the textbook maneuvers accomplished by Macdonald's brigade, in light of the circumstances, was executed "with an aplomb that could not have been surpassed by any regiment of the British army."[42] And yet, this "steadiness" and "aplomb" is most often attributed, as it was when it happened, to the "indefatigable" and "imperturbable" nature of Macdonald and the brigade's British commanding officers, rather than the leadership, experience, and soldiering abilities of Sudanese and Egyptian junior officers, non-commissioned officers, and men.[43] Indeed, the fact that less than fifteen percent of the officers responsible for executing Macdonald's textbook maneuvers (only fourteen of some one hundred total) were British seems to have been completely overlooked by both eyewitnesses and historians; every account of Omdurman from Churchill on down reads as if all of the officers that day were British, with the "native" elements no more than rank-and-file soldiers in the firing line.

When assessing *The River War* as a source on the performance of Sudanese soldiers during phase two of the Battle of Omdurman, a number of things should be taken into consideration. First and foremost, and to be fair to Winston Churchill, it was not something he witnessed firsthand. Churchill was attached to the 21st Lancers as a "subaltern of horse" and special correspondent for *The Morning Post*, and so at the time of the Khalifa's attack on Macdonald's isolated brigade, he was south of Jebel Surgham and several miles from the actual battlefield. According to Churchill himself in his 6 September 1898 letter written for *The Morning Post*, referring to that "critical moment of the engagement" during the second phase of the battle, "Of this and all this I had but fleeting glances, for an event was taking place on the southern slopes of Heliograph Hill which absorbed my whole attention."[44] And in fact, three days later he wrote, "The last two letters I wrote you were about the battle of Khartoum. They contained mainly what I saw myself. Much that was worthy of study and attention you will not find therein. For a clear account of the brilliant manoeuvres of General Macdonald's brigade…you must read the reports of the five and twenty distinguished journalists who accompanied the army."[45]

Second, on the morning of 2 September 1898, Winston Churchill was but twenty-three years old and had been in the Sudan for less than a month. Compared to most of the other, far more senior, war correspondents at Omdurman, some of whom had been covering the Nile Campaign for three years, young Winston was rather green. And so, upon writing *The River War* the sum total of Egyptian Army battles that Churchill had witnessed was one, and one in which he admitted that he "saw nothing" of the Sudanese XIIth, XIIIth, and XIVth's phase one repulse of Osman Azraq's forces, and "had but fleeting glances" of the Sudanese IXth, Xth, and XIth's phase two saving action under General Macdonald.[46] With no direct, firsthand knowledge of the military discipline, fighting abilities, or combat tactics of Sudanese soldiers, it is in some ways not surprising that Churchill would resort to Victorian racial stereotypes about "excitable" and "impulsive" Africans in his depictions of them.[47]

This dearth of experience in the Sudan and lack direct exposure to phase two of the battle, perhaps influenced by his own national hubris, may also go a long way toward explaining how Churchill managed to misrepresent the arrival of the Lincolnshire Regiment of the British First Brigade as having "finally repulsed the attack" on Macdonald's four battalions.[48] On this latter point, the consensus seems to be that the First Egyptian Brigade saved itself, and that the matter was already decided when the Lincolns arrived with their Lee-Metfords. In the words of veteran correspondent Bennet Burleigh: "[Macdonald] won practically unaided, for the pinch was all but over when the Camel Corps, hurrying up, formed upon his right, after he had faced about to receive the Shaykh Ed Din's onslaught. The Lincolns, who arrived later on, helped to hasten the flight of the enemy, whose repulse was assured ere they or any of Wauchope's brigade were within 1200 yards of Macdonald."[49] Others reported likewise, such as Ernest Bennett of the *Westminster Gazette*, who wrote that "there is no doubt that the repulse of the enemy was already a fait accompli long before the British battalions had wheeled to the right and traversed the long distance – at least one and a half miles – between their position near the river and the rear of our advance on the right."[50] Archibald Hunter, the Egyptian Division commander at Omdurman, himself wrote a month later that Macdonald "beat [the Mahdists] off alone...did not require the Lincolns."[51] And in fact the offical Sudan Intelligence Report detailing "The Khartum Campaign" concluded: "With the utmost coolness and precision, MacDonald changed front to receive this second charge which was delivered with great dash. He was successful in repulsing it before the British brigade sent to support him could render material assistance, though the Lincolnshire Regiment did prolong his line to the right, and fired a few rounds."[52]

In Churchill's defense, and despite the seeming consensus of contemporary Omdurman sources, conventional wisdom, both in the Egyptian Army and among outside observers, had long held that Sudanese soldiers tended to fire wildly in combat and were poor marksmen. Dating back to the earliest days of the new Egyptian Army, this was sometimes attributed to their "savage" and "primitive" nature, that as "mere children, with the thoughtlessness, the waywardness, and the want of foresight of children" they were prone to "easily get excited," and were "hard to hold" in combat situations.[53] Occasionally, it was alleged that as a "race" Sudanese soldiers had poor eyesight, and that as a result they were bad shots; although it is interesting to note that General Dye, who commanded them in the old Egyptian army, once wrote of the Sudanese soldier that "innured [sic] from childhood to the chase, he has more of the combative & adventurous qualities which are desirable in a soldier, & his eyesight is infinitely superior, thus enabling him to shoot 30 to 40 per cent better than the fellah."[54]

These ideas were still current in 1898, and Churchill was not the only correspondent or participant to subscribe to them; in a footnote to his Omdurman diary entry, Captain Alfred Edward Hubbard of the Lincolns wrote: "The Soudanese are most indifferent rifle-shots – They blaze away merrily but seldom hit anything except by accident."[55] Correspondent Ernest Bennett, as well, in reporting on Omdurman mentioned that the accuracy of fire "always tends, in the case of native troops, to become rather wild as the excitement of battle grows upon them."[56] Such "truisms" about Sudanese soldiers notwithstanding, there are specific Omdurman accounts, not to mention ammunition returns data, which may have led Churchill to believe Macdonald's men were lacking in discipline, and to assert that their "bravery...was no less conspicuous than the wildness of their musketry."[57]

Harry Lionel Pritchard, who later anonymously penned *Sudan Campaign, 1896–1899* as "An Officer," wrote that during the attack on Macdonald's brigade "the Ninth Battalion became very excited, and could with difficulty be restrained from charging forward," and that "without any orders they opened independent firing." He went on to write: "Each battalion as it came up, hearing the firing on its right, thought the order had been given to open independent fire, and did so....Colonel MacDonald, seeing how the brigade was getting out of hand, rode out in front, and riding down in front of the line, knocked up their rifles and shouted to them to cease fire."[58] Of course, Pritchard also described how the brigade was then quickly brought back into order, and went on to demonstrate a great deal of fire discipline and self-restraint in the moments that followed:

> The battalion officers and non-commissioned officers did the same [as Macdonald], and after a few minutes, in which Colonel MacDonald galloped up and down in front of the

line, they all ceased fire and ordered arms. Colonel MacDonald kept them standing quite still while he harangued them for a couple of minutes in no measured terms. It was very unpleasant for them standing still in the open under a hot fire without being able to reply to it, but it had the effect of getting them thoroughly in hand, and from that time on they worked like a machine.[59]

Nonetheless, the ammunition returns indicated that the First Egyptian Brigade expended 163,337 rounds in the Battle of Omdurman, more than the 134,922 rounds expended by the two British infantry brigades combined, and the latter using the higher rate of fire Lee-Metford rifle. The Sudanese XIth Battalion alone was reported to have expended some 63,000 rounds at Omdurman, almost twice as many rounds as the nearest British unit (some 35,000 by the 1st Battalion Royal Warwickshire Regiment). And the Sudanese Xth Battalion came in a close second with 52,100 rounds expended that September day, still over seventeen thousand more rounds than the Warwicks, and this with the slower-operating and lesser-capacity Martini-Henry.[60] If one subscribes to the belief that numbers do not lie, then Churchill was right.

When looking at these figures, however, one needs to put them into context. And if the specific circumstances that each Egyptian, Sudanese, and British battalion found itself in over the course of the battle are taken into consideration, these ammunition returns become equivocal. During the first phase of Omdurman, for example, whereas the First British Brigade (Lincolns; Seaforths; Camerons; Warwicks), the Grenadier Guards, and the Second Egyptian Brigade (Egyptian 8th; Sudanese XIIth, XIIIth, XIVth) were deeply engaged in the battle, the First Egyptian Brigade was much less active, and the Third and Fourth Egyptian Brigades not at all. The main thrust of the Khalifa's initial attack came at the soldiers in Wauchope's and Maxwell's brigades, and subsequently – the higher number of rounds expended by the Camerons (34,900) and Warwicks (34,927) notwithstanding – the British and Sudanese units have similar ammunition returns; for example, the Lincolns expended some 23,000 rounds and the Seaforths 19,850, whereas the Sudanese XIIth expended just over 20,000 and the Sudanese XIIIth around 18,000.[61]

Considering that during the second phase of the battle Macdonald's brigade faced two separate attacks coming from three different directions, and engaged three of the Khalifa's largest armies (totaling 26,000 men) for a full hour, it should come as no surprise that these three Sudanese and one Egyptian battalion expended the most ammunition of the day. Not unrelated, and indicative of the strength of the attack made against them, these four battalions also suffered the highest number of casualties: losses in this brigade alone (11 killed, 120 wounded) represented nearly forty percent of all Egyptian Army casualties (29 killed, 301 wounded), and were greater than the total losses in all other Egyptian Army infantry battalions combined (10 killed, 72 wounded); these losses were also higher in number than that of all eight infantry battalions of the British Division put together (5 killed, 78 wounded).[62] Moreover, as was noted at the time by Ernest Bennett, because the Egyptian Army soldiers were firing Martini-Henry rifles, "the smoke of the black powder they used interfered to some extent with the accuracy of their fire."[63] Nonetheless, when one compares, say, the rounds expended at Omdurman by the "excited" Sudanese IXth Battalion (reported as 23,917) with that of the 1st Battalion Lincolnshire Regiment (reported as 23,057) – the men who with "machine-like regularity" supposedly saved the former from annihilation – there appears to be little difference.[64] Of course, again, the Lincolns were firing Lee-Metfords and the Sudanese Martini-Henrys, so the relative parity could be misleading. And there is no getting around, regardless of circumstances or weapon, that the 63,000 rounds expended by the Sudanese XIth, if accurate, is an extremely high figure in comparison to all other battalions that fought at Omdurman.

In any case, and heeding Churchill's own advice, it might be worthwhile to further consider the eyewitness accounts provided by Burleigh and Steevens. Bennet Burleigh, longtime correspondent for the *Daily Telegraph*, was the doyen of Nile Campaign journalists. Unlike Churchill, Burleigh, who during the River War was in his late fifties, had vast experience in the region, and had covered Egypt and the Sudan dating as far back as 1882. As a young man he had fought on the Confederate side in the American Civil War, and later distinguished himself in battle at Abu Klea in 1885. As one of the "old Sudanics" in 1898, having by his own account witnessed "half a score" battles against the Mahdists since 1884, Burleigh was extremely familiar with Egyptian Army tactics, and again, unlike Churchill, had seen them recently in practice at the Battle of the Atbara in early April.[65] When the Khalifa launched his attack on Macdonald's brigade, Burleigh "rode at a gallop...up the slopes of Surgham, where, spread like a picture, the scene lay before me."[66] In direct contradiction with Churchill's account, Burleigh reported:

> Steadily the infantry fired, the blacks in their own pet fashion independently, the 2nd Egyptians in careful, well-aimed volleys. Afar we could see and rejoice that the brigade was giving a magnificent account of itself....Still the enemy pressed on, their footmen reaching to within 200 yards of Macdonald's line. Scores of Emirs and lesser leaders, with spearmen and swordsmen, fell only a few feet from the guns and the unshaken Khedivial infantry.[67]

Burleigh later reiterated that Sudanese soldiers were "staunch and unyielding" throughout: "With a tact, coolness, and hardihood I have never seen equaled, Colonel Macdonald manœuvred and fought his men. They responded to his call with confidence and alacrity begotten of long acquaintance and implicit faith in their leader....Majors Jackson, Nason, and Walter were, as usual, proud of the steadiness of their blacks – the 11th, 10th, and 9th battalions."[68] Notably, nowhere in Burleigh's account were the Sudanese soldiers referred to as "impulsive" or evincing "an extraordinary excitement." Nowhere was there mention of Sudanese Martini-Henry fire being "random" or "utterly beyond control," or that these soldiers did not know how to aim and sight their rifles. Rather, Burleigh's report fell in line with those of Hunter and Kitchener, and the other British officers and journalists who reported on Macdonald's saving action, such as Lieutenants Alford and Sword, and correspondent E. N. Bennett. Moreover, Burleigh even surpassed his peers in identifying the steady, independent – and quite effective, as it had been at Atbara – firing tactics of Sudanese soldiers as being their "pet fashion," rather than any indication of panic or wild, undisciplined musketry, something only a longtime observer of Sudanese infantry soldiers in action would recognize and understand.[69]

Though not as experienced a war correspondent as Burleigh, G. W. Steevens of the *Daily Mail* was also an eyewitness to Macdonald's saving action. According to Steevens, and again contradicting Churchill's account, there was no panic among the Sudanese infantry at Omdurman, "the blacks, as cool as any Scotsmen, stood and aimed likewise [steadily as the *fellahin*]."[70] He also vividly reported, as above, the discipline exhibited by the whole brigade during the Khalifa's three-pronged attack, most notably during the change of front, albeit giving Macdonald most of the credit:

> Every tactician in the army was delirious in his praise: the ignorant correspondent was content to watch the man and his blacks. "Cool as on parade," is an old phrase; Macdonald Bey was very much cooler....Then he turned to a galloper with an order, and cantered easily up to a battalion-commander. Magically the rifles hushed, the stinging powder smoke wisped away, and the companies were rapidly threading back and forward, round and round, in and out, as if it were a figure of a dance. In two minutes the brigade was together again in a new place...
>
> His blacks of the 9th, 10th, and 11th, the historic fighting regiments of the Egyptian army, were worthy of their chief....A few had feared that the blacks would be too forward, the yellows too backward: except that the blacks, as always, looked happier, there was no difference at all between them. The Egyptians sprang to the advance at the bugle; the Sudanese ceased fire in an instant silence at the whistle. They were losing men, too, for though eyes were clamped on the dervish charge, the dervish fire was brisk. Man after man dropped out behind the firing-line. Here was a white officer with a red-lathered charger; there a black stretched straight, bare-headed in the sun, dry-lipped, uncomplaining, a bullet through his liver.[71]

Of course, the excellent performance of Sudanese troops at Omdurman was predictable considering that so many of these soldiers and junior officers were "long service men" with a great deal of combat experience. There may have been a fair number of more recently recruited soldiers among them – captured *jihadiyya* with little experience firing Martini-Henry rifles, and who were likely responsible for much of the poor marksmanship witnessed at Omdurman; even Steevens, for example, reported that "almost every volley you saw a bullet kick the sand within fifty yards of the firing-line; Others flew almost perpendicular into the air."[72] But the majority of these men knew their weapons, and possessed the combat skills and steadiness that only comes from many years of military service and battlefield experience. Indeed, and apropos of both Sudanese self-confidence and independence of thought in battle, not to mention the topic of ammunition expenditure, there was the following incident that took place years earlier during the 1889 Battle of Toski. According to *bimbashi* B. R. Mitford of the IXth Battalion, while firing "volleys into the leading swarm of the advancing enemy at 900 yards range," he noticed "some of the volleys seemed very weak." Mitford then observed that no smoke was appearing from the muzzles of his troops upon the word "Atesh," and proceeded to ask one of his Sudanese soldiers why he had not fired. The man replied: "No, Bimbashi, not yet, it is far: let us wait until we can see the whites of their eyes: the day will be long, and we shall want all our cartridges before it is finished."[73]

Taking the point further, 'Ali Jifun had already served in the Egyptian Army

5.3 *"The Battle of Omdurman: General Macdonald's Brigade repelling an attack: a critical moment"*
(H. M. Paget, *The Graphic*, 24 September 1898)

5.4 *"Omdurman – MacDonald's Brigade resisting main Dervish attack"*
(René Bull, *Black and White War Albums, Soudan No. 1 – Omdurman*)

some fifteen years when Winston Churchill was born in 1874, and by 1898 was a forty-year veteran, having fought in dozens of battles and lesser skirmishes over the past four decades. 'Abdallah 'Adlan was fighting off Somali ambushes in the Haramat Mountains under Munsinger before Churchill was even a year old, and had served in the Egyptian Army some thirty-five years come Omdurman. And of course 'Ali Jifun and 'Abdallah 'Adlan were not alone in terms of Sudanese soldiers, as well as Sudanese and Egyptian officers, with long service in Sudanese battalions, and the combat experience that came with it.

'Ali el Tum was a Dinka officer who had risen to the rank of *saghkolaghasi* by the time of Omdurman.[74] Little is known of his military career prior to 1 January 1893, when he was brevetted *yuzbashi*, but for most of the Nile Campaign he led the No. 4 company of the Sudanese IXth Battalion. Prior to Omdurman, for which he was awarded the 4th Class Osmanieh, 'Ali el Tum was decorated with the 4th Class Medjidieh for service in the Dongola Expedition, and also received special mention in dispatches for good services rendered at the Battle of the Atbara.

Muhammad Abu Shaila, a Bernawi *yuzbashi* of No. 6 company in the Sudanese IXth at the time of Omdurman, had been serving in the Egyptian Army at least since the Battle of Ginnis in 1885, and in all likelihood, from an even earlier date. In fact, Muhammad Abu Shaila received special mention for having volunteered for nightly picquet duty at Black Rock outside Fort Kosheh in December 1885, where one night he accidentally blew off half his thumb, yet did not return to the fort for medical care until the next morning. Promoted *mulazim awal*, Muhammad Abu Shaila was chosen in 1886 to lead the escort that traveled to Cairo to accept an honorary Colour presented to the Sudanese IXth Battalion by the Cameron Highlanders, at a parade of British and Egyptian soldiers in Abdin Square. Slightly wounded at the Battle of Sarras in 1887, he was awarded the 5th Class Mejidieh, and by 1891 had risen through the ranks to *yuzbashi*. During the Nile Campaign, Muhammad Abu Shaila was awarded both the 4th Class Medjidieh, for services rendered at Abu Hamed and Atbara, and the 4th Class Osmanieh for the Battle of Omdurman.

'Abdallah Romayh was a Bernawi *yuzbashi* who by the time of Omdurman had served some thirteen years in the IXth Sudanese, having joined the battalion at Akasha in 1885.[75] During the Nile Campaign he received special mention for good services during operations on the Atbara, and was awarded the 4th Class Medjidieh following the Battle of Omdurman. Mirsal Goma was a Dinka *yuzbashi* at Omdurman who had served in the Sudanese IXth since 1884, shortly after its formation. He was mentioned in dispatches for good services rendered during the Dongola Expedition, and was awarded the 4th Class Medjidieh following Abu Hamed and Atbara.

All three *mulazimin awal* in the Sudanese IXth, Khamis Breish, Ahmad Hussein, and Tewfik Hilmi, had seen action throughout the Nile Campaign, Khamis Breish and Ahmad Hussen receiving special mention in Atbara dispatches, the former officer having been wounded in the battle. Faragalla Mirkis, a *bashawish* in the IXth, had also received special mention following Atbara, which is not surprising considering the fact that he had combat experience dating at least as far back as the Battle of Toski in 1889. And this is nothing compared to the combat record of *shawish* Fadl el Mula Daud, who was once mentiond for bravery in action at Ginnis (1885), promoted after Argin and Toski (1889), and fought with the Sudanese IXth throughout the Nile Campaign.

The soldiers of the Sudanese Xth who fought in the Battle of Omdurman were no less experienced. *Yuzbashia* Musa Fuad and Mirsal Negib, the latter of whom was wounded in the face at Omdurman, had been brevetted in 1893 and 1892 respectively, and Musa Fuad was awarded the 4th Class Medjidieh for action with the Dongola Field Force in 1896. *Yuzbashi* 'Abdallah Isma'il was mentioned in dispatches dating back to the 1889 action at Argin, was promoted later that same year following the Battle of Toski, and fought throughout the River War; his services were brought to the notice of the Khedive following the Dongola campaign, and he was awarded the 4th Class Medjidieh after the Battle of the Atbara. *Shawish* Khamis Mustafa, as well, had served in the Sudanese Xth Battalion for over 22 years, since 15 Feburary 1886, and had been awarded the Gordon's medal. Last but by no means least, there was Almas Mursi, a Dinka *yuzbashi* whose 43-year military career in the Egyptian Army began 1873. Born in the Bahr al-Ghazal in 1859, Almas Mursi was enrolled into the ranks while still a teenager, and come the Battle of Omdurman had spent 25 years in the Egyptian Army. He fought at Gemaizeh (1886), Toski (1889), and Tokar (1891), and during the Nile Campaign led a company in the Xth Sudanese Battalion in the battles of Firket through Omdurman.

Another experienced Dinka officer who fought at Omdurman was *mulazim awal* Sa'id Osman of the Sudanese XIth, who was originally a *mulazim tani* with the XIIIth Battalion back in 1891. Also leading the Sudanese XIth at Omdurman, and "highly recommended" in dispatches following the battle, was *saghkolaghasi* Ramzi Tahir, who had "a perfect command of English" and had already been awarded both the 4th Class Medjidieh in 1892 and the 4th Class Osmanieh in 1896. Likewise, *yuzbashi* Sa'id 'Abdallah and *mulazimin awal* Muhammad Walad Dain and Hassan Labib had been serving as officers in the Sudanese XIth throughout the Nile Campaign, all of them having been brevetted in 1894–1895. And among the lines of the Sudanese XIIth at Omdurman, in addition to 'Ali Jifun and 'Abdallah 'Adlan, was officer Atta el Sudani, who had served as a *yuzbashi* in the battalion from the outset of the Nile Campaign. Even the XIIIth and XIVth Sudanese battalions were led at Omdurman by officers with considerable combat experience. *Yuzbashia* Mirsal el Baz and Muhammad Ahmad, as well as *mulazimin awal* 'Abd er Rauf Besim, 'Ali Fehim, and Keiralla Hamduni, had all been brevetted between 1893 and 1896, and had seen action throughout the Nile Campaign. And *saghkolaghasi* Murgan Mahmoud, awarded the 4th Class Osmanieh in October 1896, had received his *yuzbashi* brevet as long ago as 1886.

It thus seems probable that come Omdurman, with many years of combat experience and musketry practice behind them, Sudanese infantry soldiers such as Murgan Mahmoud knew how to properly sight and aim their Martini-Henry rifles, and were more likely "cool as any Scotsmen" than "utterly beyond control." Indeed, according the memoirs of the Sudanese XIIIth's *kaimakam*, H. L. Smith-Dorrien, on the day before the battle a self-confident and rather prescient Murgan Mahmoud assured his commander: "If they are such fools as to attack our entrenchment I shall take tea with the Khalifa to-morrow," a remark of which Murgan reminded Smith-Dorrien the next day.[76] And it was no doubt this same confidence, and experience, and agency, that led to the kind of independence of thought and action often demonstrated by Sudanese soldiers in battle. Whether it be commencing fire prior to being given specific orders, independently and densely rather than in coordinated volleys, as was the case at Abu Hamed and Omdurman, or storming Mahmud's *zariba* "at the double" to prevent needless casualties at Atbara, what was seen by some observers as indiscipline or insubordination may well have been a reflection of superior knowledge on the part of Sudanese soldiers – a better understanding of the kinds of military tactics that would prove successful versus the Mahdists, an enemy against whom they had been fighting for much of their adult lives.

Sudanese soldiers in non-combat roles

Although the combat role of Sudanese soldiers in the River War was of principal importance, these same infantry soldiers and junior officers occupied numerous other critical roles off the battlefield as well. Seldom if ever mentioned in military dispatches or campaign accounts was that these men served as interpreters, spies, recruiters, policemen, and even diplomats of a sort. In fact, the relative ease with which Anglo-Egyptian forces reconquered the Sudan can be partly attributed to the intelligence and "hearts and minds" groundwork done by Sudanese soldiers as Kitchener's army made its way southward up the Nile.

War correspondents and special artists tended to mention or depict British commanders and intelligence officers – such as H. G. Fitton, F. R. Wingate, or Rudolf Slatin – as being chiefly responsible for interviewing Mahdist prisoners, deserters, and refugees. But in many cases, especially if Arabic was not possible or the interviewee spoke a Western Nilotic language, it was Sudanese soldiers who did the translating.[77] And in some cases, it appears that it was they who conducted the initial questioning, as two Sudanese military policemen did of a suspected Mahdist spy aboard a Nile boat in 1897.[78] During the 1896 Dongola Campaign, to give another example, H. G. Fitton in a letter to Wingate, chief of Egyptian Army intelligence, reported: "Six Sudanese deserters (Nobawis) came in this morning unarmed. They were ravenously hungry and are now having some food…Five of these men are very fine blacks, the sixth rather old. They spoke very little Arabic, but know several men in the Battalions here who speak their language."[79] Even in some of the above referenced newspaper illustrations, it is interesting to note, and speculate upon considering Fitton's letter, the fact that in the background one finds a Sudanese soldier standing nearby the questioner. Perhaps their role in these instances was more than simply guard duty, and may have occasionally merged into that of interpreter during interrogations, especially in cases when the subject was ex-jihadiyya and spoke little if any Arabic.

Along similar lines, and likewise rarely if ever mentioned, there is evidence that Sudanese soldiers were occasionally used as spies, and had been for some time. Several years prior to the River War, for example, and to give one of the few documented cases from this time period, an *ombashi* named Khamis Breish and a *nafar* known as Faragalla Sultan, were "dispatched in the guise of deserters to spy out the Dervish dispositions and endeavour to glean what their plans were." According to the story, the two men soon ran into a Mahdist camel patrol and were brought to Firket. After "two days with nothing to eat," they were then "taken on by a party of 5 or 6 footmen towards Suarda." On the night after their departure, however, Faragalla Sultan "speared the two men responsible for their keep, stripped them of their jibbas, belts and drawers," whereupon the two Sudanese spies "made off to the hills, and lying up by day got back to Halfa in safety," and brought back "some quite useful information."[80]

One thing for certain is that during the Nile Campaign Sudanese soldiers were some of the Egyptian Army's best military recruiters. A good number of the *jihadiyya* deserters and prisoners had previously served in the Egyptian Army, and personally knew many of the soldiers and officers in the Sudanese battalions. Second, many of these enemy soldiers were from the same racial and ethnic backgrounds as the Sudanese troops, and in some cases, from the same villages and families. Third, these *jihadiyya* were fellow Muslims and thus members of the *umma*, and were therefore accorded both respect and kind treatment in most circumstances. These military, racial, ethnic, familial, and religious bonds between Sudanese soldiers and ex-Mahdists, and the fraternization engendered by these connections, greatly facilitated the recruitment of the latter into the battalions of the former. Evidence of this can be found in the aforementioned reunions that often took place between them in the wake of battle, and the speedy enlistments that followed. These new recruits, in turn, became recruiters themselves. Above and beyond their function as recruiters, however, Sudanese soldiers also played a role during the campaign in shaping the "hearts and minds" of the civilian populations. Indeed, there is anecdotal evidence that as Kitchener's army progressed up the Nile, they often served as goodwill ambassadors, and in some villages were enthusiastically received due to their kindness and admirable conduct. Such was the case in the Dongola province in 1896, when according to one correspondent "the inhabitants were evidently delighted to see the invaders," and where "the good-natured soldiers ['fellahin and blacks'] were filling up the hands of the little children with biscuits they themselves could ill spare."[81]

Many Sudanese soldiers also served in non-combat roles as military policemen during the campaign, maintaining law and order in towns and villages along the Nile that had recently been retaken from the Mahdists. Although such service garnered far less attention in military dispatches and newspaper articles than did their martial proclivities, there was an illustration published in *The Graphic* on 8 January 1898 that depicted a Sudanese policeman keeping the peace on the streets of Berber. Drawn by H. M. Paget based on a sketch by W. T. Maud, it was titled "An Innovation at Berber: The Policeman." The caption read:

> Riding through the streets of Berber one day, writes our correspondent, I saw a black policeman separate two Arabs who were fighting like cats in the midst of a small but enthusiastic crowd. The tall Soudanese scattered them in all directions, and it was amusing to watch the look of blank astonishment on their faces when he interfered. Law and order and policemen are new things in the life of the town.[82]

And yet, in terms of the kinds of multifaceted roles occupied by Sudanese soldiers during the Nile Campaign, there is perhaps no more compelling case – ignored entirely in the later historiography of these events – than that which took place on the Upper Nile as the Fashoda crisis played out in the fall of 1898. From making up almost the entirety of the "preponderance of force" at Fashoda, to serving as intermediaries, interpreters, and goodwill ambassadors, especially with the Shilluk and Dinka, Sudanese soldiers were Kitchener's ace in the hole. Although the Fashoda Incident was ultimately resolved by diplomats in London and Paris, it was individuals such as 'Ali Jifun and others who played key roles in helping Kitchener create the false perception, and eventually something of a reality, that Major Marchand's position at Fashoda was "as impossible as it is absurd," and that he had "no following in the country."[83]

To begin with, as Kitchener's armed flotilla left Omdurman for Fashoda on the morning of 10 September 1898, some eighty percent of the soldiers being conveyed south along the White Nile were Sudanese troops. Although Kitchener brought with him a company of Cameron Highlanders and a battery of Egyptian artillery, his principal military bluster was in the form of 1,200 Sudanese infantry soldiers of the XIth and XIIIth battalions, packed into barges and *gyassas* [cargo boats] being towed by the gunboats *Nasr* and *Fateh*.[84] Above and beyond that, and clear evidence that Kitchener intended to use Sudanese soldiers in linguistic and ambassadorial roles, "a special guard of 20 picked Sudanese soldiers (Dinkas & Shillutes [*sic*])" was brought along, selected from other Sudanese battalions.[85] 'Ali Jifun, for example, the Shilluk *saghkolaghasi* now in his sixties, although still serving in the Sudanese XIIth, was specifically chosen to accompany Kitchener's force and function as a senior dignitary and cultural intermediary between the British and the Shilluk.[86] Also among this "special guard" were several Dinka soldiers, brought along to win over Dinka chiefs on the east bank of the White Nile, one of whom also spoke Nuer and was later used to convince a Nuer headman to provide the British guides to the French base at Mashra El-Rek.[87]

The choice of Sudanese soldiers as go-betweens paid immediate dividends for Kitchener. Just a few days after setting off from Omdurman, according to F. R. Wingate, "We stopped off a Shilluk village + could see the village in a state of wild alarm, seizing their spears…at last our soldier-Shilluks made them understand that we were friends."[88] The village of Kaka was reached a few days later, and again Sudanese soldiers paved the path of friendship between Kitchener's force and the indigenous Shilluk. First, about a mile north of Kaka, two local Shilluk were dispatched with a letter from Kitchener to the Mek, or *reth* [king], of the Shilluk, Kur Nyidok.[89] And soon thereafter, according to Kitchener's Aide-de-Camp, J. K. Watson, "The Chiefs of Kaka came to see the Sirdar and with them a large retinue, absolute wild savages.… The bands of the XI and XIII turned out and played on the bank much to the delight of the Shilluks who executed a war dance on the spot."[90]

Two of these Shilluk men from Kaka were then taken on board, and the following day acted as guides for the two runners (both Shilluk *shawishia*) chosen to deliver Kitchener's letter to the "Chief of the European Expedition at Fashoda."[91] Likewise, Dinka soldiers were making headway on the east bank of the Nile, having earlier that same day made contact with Dinka that initially fled into the interior upon seeing Kitchener's flotilla: "We went into the bank and eventually by sending out some of our Dinkas from the black battalions we got some of them [Dinkas "trekking" south] to come in. They were evidently delighted to see us and to hear we had settled the Dervish post at Renk, for it was owing to the raids from these that they had been obliged to quit their villages and fly south."[92]

Upon arrival in the village of Baibu, some twelve miles north of Fashoda, the flotilla was again met by a large party of Shilluk, including the son, brother, and uncle of Kur Nyidok. Presumably in Shilluk via one of his soldier-interpreters, or in Arabic if these men spoke it, or perhaps something of both languages, Kitchener was informed by the Mek's kin that "they believed them [the Europeans at Fashoda] to be a small body of our Government troops that had come from the west, but as they had no Shilluk interpreter, and did not go outside the old Egyptian Mudiria buildings, they knew very little about them."[93]

In any case, when Kitchener and Marchand met on board the *Dal* the following day (19 September 1898), in what became known to history as the "Fashoda Incident," again it was Kitchener's 1,200 Sudanese soldiers at the ready that effectively represented the military superiority he suggested Marchand consider before resisting an Egyptian flag being raised alongside the French *tricolour*.[94] And indeed, despite Marchand's begrudging claim that "until we receive orders to retire we shall not haul down our flag but are ready to die at our posts" and his *profonde inclinaison de la tête* to Kitchener's further suggestion that "this situation could lead to war," it was the strength and affiliation of this overwhelming, mostly Sudanese, Egyptian Army force that underlay the military and diplomatic dilemma in which Marchand now found himself: How could Marchand, with eight French officers and only one hundred twenty-odd Senegalese *tirailleurs* [sharpshooters], possibly resist Kitchener's three gunboats and 1,500 Anglo-Egyptian troops? Furthermore, how could he defend the "rights of France" against those of Egypt and the Ottoman Sultan, when respect for that of the latter – represented here at Fashoda in the form of the fezzed *sirdar* and his two battalions of the Khedive's army – had long been the basis for French policy in the Nile Valley? Indeed, the Egyptian card would have been somewhat harder to play had Kitchener arrived that morning at Fashoda with two British battalions rather than two Sudanese ones, and not uniformed as the *sirdar* of the Egyptian Army.

In any case, Marchand acquiesced to Kitchener hoisting an Egyptian flag at Fashoda, on a ruined fort bastion several hundred yards to the south of the French flag. Following the flag raising ceremony, in which the Sudanese bands played a few bars of the Khedival anthem, the "fraternisation of the Soudanese soldiers and the Shilluks became thorough," according to eyewitnesses.[95] And the benefits of handpicking Shilluk soldiers for the Fashoda mission were soon readily apparent as there were "numerous greetings and interchanges of courtesy between them [and the local Shilluk]," and 'Ali Jifun "soon had crowds of his countrymen and countrywomen flocking to see him."[96] Subsequently, 'Ali Jifun became Kitchener's (and later commandant H. W. Jackson's) go-between at Fashoda for meetings with Shilluk leaders, including Kur Nyidok. This began on 19 September when Kitchener "sent a Shilluk of long service ['Ali Jifun] to summon the chiefs to interview him," which led to an informal reception for headmen and their wives, along with other "relatives and friends" of the Shilluk soldiers, held by the *sirdar* on shore and afterwards on board the *Dal*.[97] The next day, when the Shilluk *reth* arrived at the Egyptian Army camp at Fashoda with an entourage of several hundred, "remaining from sunrise to sunset, mixing with troops," it was again 'Ali Jifun who appears to have played an intermediary role in ascertaining Kur Nyidok's denial that he had made any treaty with the French.[98]

When the Mek and his principal Wakil [agent], Nyidok Deng, gave formal statements "regarding arrival of Marchand Mission" to Fashoda commandant H. W. Jackson, "SAGH ALI EFF. GAFUN [Jifun]" was listed as one of two witnesses present. In the context of 'Ali Jifun's potential role as interpreter, it is also interesting to note that in Nyidok Deng's statement he claimed the French "could not speak either the Shilluk language or Arabic, and it was difficult to understand their interpreter." Most importantly, 'Ali Jifun was able to witness, perhaps translate, and maybe even induce, Kur Nyidok's false statement that he had "made no treaties with them whatever…and if the French say I have, they have stolen my tongue."[99] This statement of denial proved to be significant because it was able to be included in Kitchener's initial, rather dubious, official dispatches from Omdurman on the Fashoda Incident and state of affairs in Shilluk Country: "The Shilluk Chief, with a large following, has come into Major Jackson's camp; the whole tribe are delighted to return their allegiance to us, and the Chief absolutely denies having made any Treaty with the French."[100] Whether or not Kur Nyidok fully understood the implications of the document or not, he had in fact affixed his seal on a formal treaty putting his realm under French protection on 3 September 1898, and copies drafted in both French and Arabic had been sent to France for ratification via Ethiopia and the Bahr al-Gahzal.

Kitchener's late-September telegrams, however, became the only version of events available in both France and England, and largely dictated diplomatic and public opinion on the French position at Fashoda in both countries for the next month – until Marchand's first report arrived in France on 22 October. And a significant part of this initially misleading depiction of Marchand's status was the belief, supported by the reported statements of Shilluk notables, that his territorial claims were "more worthy of Opéra-Bouffe than the outcome of the maturely considered plans of a great Government."[101] Of course, as the Fashoda crisis played out at Whitehall and the *Quai d'Orsay*, and in the European press, this characterization of Marchand's position at Fashoda as being both insecure and untenable, that he was "cut off from the interior" and had "no following in the country," was quickly becoming a reality. This was due, once again, to the effectiveness of Sudanese soldiers, particularly Shilluk and Dinka, in winning the "hearts and minds" of their ethnic brethren, and effecting a blockade of the French by local chiefs and the indigenous population at large. This in turn further isolated Marchand and his men, and ex post facto gave truth to the British propaganda. Ultimately, it undermined any chances for French "effective occupation" on the Upper Nile even had they chosen *not* to evacuate Fashoda in the end, and regardless of Delcassé's betrayal, the Dreyfus Affair,

French naval inferiority, or Russia's unwillingness to become involved.

One sees this Anglo-Egyptian turn of the screw on the Upper Nile taking shape in two interconnected forms, one diplomatic and the other related to local food sources. Regarding the former, 'Ali Jifun continued to foster the relationship between the British and Shilluk *reth* Kur Nyidok. According to H. W. Jackson's Fashoda Intelligence Diary, for example, it was reported that on 28 September "Sagh ALI EFF GAFOON with 10 SHULLUKS of the XIth Soudanese left camp to visit the MEK at FASHODA and to report on the country and MEK's headquarters."[102] This in turn paid dividends with other another local leader, as four days later it was noted that "MEK of SHULLUKS came to camp with a large following, bringing letters from HASEEB dervish EMIR on Right bank offering to surrender."[103] And 'Ali Jifun was not the only Sudanese soldier used to facilitate good relations with local chiefs and headmen. On 24 October, Jackson reported: "Several men of XIth SOUDANESE who speak DENKA language are on RIGHT bank mixing with DENKAS. This is having a good result."[104] And ten days later he wrote:

> An officer of XIth Soudanese with DENKA soldiers will leave camp tomorrow with "WAKEEL" for DUNGAL village, taking presents to SHEIKH for his report + will tell him to return the FRENCH flag, + should FRENCH visit him in future, he is to state he belongs only to the Government of EGYPT + to have no fear, but not to supply any food to them whatever.[105]

Sudanese soldiers continued to serve in such ambassadorial roles among the Dinka throughout the Fashoda crisis, and even after the French evacuated the Upper Nile, as was the case on 16 December 1898 when the following was reported in this same intelligence diary: "A party of DINKA soldiers under a Sergeant left for DINKA country on the right bank. These men will visit all chief villages in vicinity, collect FRENCH flags, explain reasons of FRENCH departure + bring back to camp head sheikhs of sections for palaver with governor."[106]

And yet an even more effective means of exerting pressure on the French than these diplomatic missions was the way in which Sudanese soldiers were able to effectively blockade the French from local food supplies. Whereas the Sudanese XIth Battalion troops stationed at Fashoda were "most popular with the DENKAS and SHULLUKS" and supplied "freely in an open market," it was another story for the Frenchmen and their Senegalese troops.[107] According to Jackson, "Some SENEGALESE soldiers of FRENCH garrison complained to SOUDANESE officers of XIth SOUDANESE that they could not of late obtain meat + provisions from SHULLUKS same as before arrival of EGYPTIAN TROOPS."[108] And by 1 November 1898, Captain Germain, the deputy left in charge of the French garrison when Marchand left for Cairo, was complaining to Jackson that "his men 'crever de faim' + that SHULLUKS will supply nothing now that the EGYPTIAN TROOPS are here."[109] Three weeks later things were no better, and Germain "cursed SHULLUKS stating that since EGYPTIANS arrived he has not obtained a single sheep from the tribe, that now he sends his men far inland to shoot antelope."[110] Conveniently, Jackson was able to provide Germain a valid reason for his diminishing food prospects without revealing that it was per his direct order and sanctioned by both Kitchener and Lord Salisbury: "He [Germain] was informed in reply that the Anglo-Egyptian force was in the main composed of Shilluks, and in that case it was but natural that the Mek of the Shilluks should provide food for his own people in preference to foreigners."[111]

Sudanese soldiers thus played a key if indirect role in enabling Kitchener to put the squeeze on the French at Fashoda, Salisbury having been assured by the *sirdar* that in so doing there would be "no great practical difficulty in obliging [Marchand] to capitulate."[112] And so Salisbury, thanks in part to those "most popular" Sudanese troops at Fashoda, was able to hedge his bets while the Anglo-French conflict was playing itself out in London and Paris, by making Marchand's position on the Upper Nile, per his own directive, "as untenable as possible."[113] Although they were well liked and well supplied by the local inhabitants, Sudanese soldiers were far from comfortable at Fashoda. In fact, there is some evidence that they were aggrieved and disgruntled, and that Jackson's position at Fashoda was also growing more and more untenable as the crisis played out. To begin with, unlike Marchand's *tirailleurs*, who had waterproof groundsheets, light kits, and rifle covers, as well as mosquito nets, the Sudanese XIth Battalion soldiers – having campaigned the past three years in an arid environment – did not have the proper gear to withstand Fashoda's tropical climate.[114]

It being the rainy season, and having neither tents nor mosquito nets, and with both equipment and food stores constantly exposed to wet and heat, the latter "in a state of transition – biscuits to pulp and flour to dough, while vegetable rations of lentils, onions and beans showed signs of vigorous growth," camp life for Jackson's men was rather uncomfortable to say the least.[115] These conditions were exacerbated by the location chosen for the Egyptian Army camp, a low-lying stretch of land covered with rank grass and mud – "a veritable quagmire" much of the time.[116] Indeed, only five days after the Fashoda Incident, Jackson wrote the following to Wingate: "Another d – able night, heaviest rain yet, all drenched to the skin and all tukls down, camp ankle-deep in mud and water….Up best part of night…wading about and hauling men out of debris of fallen tukls…Rain or millions of mosquitoes by night….They bite through coat and trouser, so you can imagine what men suffer."[117] H. E. Hill Smith, principal medical officer for the Egyptian Army, was to report at the end of December 1898 that "the sick rate was very high at Sobat and Fashoda."[118] Making matters worse was the fact that the men of the Sudanese XIth were away from their families, a sacrifice they were not used to making. And according to Jackson, unlike in Omdurman, there were no local women available to fill the void: "No women whatever for men, and Shilluks and Denkas are most particular. Something will have to be thought out."[119]

Add to this the fact that as many as two hundred and fifty of these men were ex-Mahdists recently enlisted into the battalion after the battles of Atbara and Omdurman, men whom Jackson "did not trust a yard," and it is no wonder that some of them started deserting Fashoda.[120] Jackson reported in his intelligence diary on 6 October 1898, for example: "Five men of the XIth Sudanese deserted during the night – taking 3 Martini rifles + 2 Remington rifles. One of these deserters was at the time sentry over the Quarter Guard + Egyptian Flag. Four of them ATBARA recruits. Without doubt they intend marching to OMDURMAN to join their wives + children."[121] Overall, the desertions were few in number, however, and the later claims of Marchand that Sudanese soldiers and their Egyptian officers were sympathetic to the French and on the verge of mutiny were likely overblown, exaggerated on the same scale as those he had made to Delcassé as to only needing "ten minutes to wipe out Jackson's troops and his guns."[122]

Be that as it may, these stirrings among the Sudanese XIth Battalion revealed that there were perhaps limits to their loyalty – thresholds as to the deprivations they, and other Sudanese battalions, were willing to endure. And these limits would soon be severely tested, when a rumor that Sudanese troops were being sent to South Africa to fight the Boers sparked a mutiny at the Omdurman barracks in January 1900.

Notes

[1] Churchill, *The River War*, 287.
[2] "Whatever happens we have got, The Maxim Gun, and they have not." Hilaire Belloc, *The Modern Traveller* (London: Edward Arnold, 1898), 41. Although Belloc found the inspiration for these lines from the Battle of Omdurman, an examination of the Mahdist dead suggested that "most of the killing, as usual, was done by rifles." Steevens, *With Kitchener to Khartum*, 295.
[3] Moreover, following Omdurman, in mopping-up operations against the Khalifa and his surviving *amara* on the Blue Nile and in Kordofan, it was Sudanese soldiers that made up the majority of these field forces. At the 24 November 1899 Battle of Um Dibaykarat, for example, where the Khalifa met his death, British infantry troops were nowhere to be found, and it was the Sudanese IXth and XIIIth battalions that led Wingate's attack column. In fact, 1,678 of the 3,785 troops engaged in operations against the Khalifa's forces 21–26 November 1899 were Sudanese soldiers from these two battalions; moreover, most of the 1,009 "irregulars" present were ex-jihadiyya and thus also Sudanese (combined representing some seventy percent of the troops present). F. R. Wingate, "Field State of Troops Engaged in Operations against the KHALIFA round GEDID Nov. 21st to Nov. 26th 1899," NA WO 32/6143.
[4] Unless otherwised noted, the background and operational details pertaining to the Battle of Firket that follow have been amalgamated from numerous primary and secondary sources, most notably: *IRE* 49 (22 June–18 August, 1896); Hunter, *Historical Records of the Tenth Sudanese*, NAM 1968-07-330-1, 27–29; Wood-Martin, *IXth Sudanese Regimental Historical Records*, SAD 110/11/32–33; Alford and Sword, *The Egyptian Soudan*, 85–93; 'An Officer,' *Sudan Campaign*, 27–34; H. C. Seppings Wright, *Soudan, '96: The Adventures of a War Artist* (London: Horace Cox, 1897), 52–62; Knight, *Letters from the Sudan*, 108–131; Churchill, *The River War*, 125–134; Keown-Boyd, *A Good Dusting*, 162–168.
[5] Knight, *Letters from the Sudan*, 126.
[6] Ibid., 121.
[7] Alford and Sword, *The Egyptian Soudan*, 89.
[8] Sudanese casualties: IXth Battalion 3 killed, 14 wounded (*saghkolaghasi* Ibrahim Adam later died from his wound), Wood-Martin, *IXth Sudanese Regimental Historical Records*, SAD 110/11/32; Xth Battalion 20 NCOs and men wounded, Hunter, *Historical Records of the Tenth Sudanese*, NAM 1968-07-330-1, 29; XIth Battalion 2 killed, 5 wounded, and XIIIth Battalion 1 killed, 6 wounded, *IRE* 49, Appendix U, 41.
[9] Knight, *Letters from the Sudan*, 124.
[10] References to the Battle of Abu Hamed and its operational details discussed herein have been drawn from and cross-checked in the following sources: *IRE* 55 (18 July–30 September, 1897); Hunter, *Historical Records of the Tenth Sudanese*, NAM 1968-07-330-1, 32–34; Wood-Martin, *IXth Sudanese Regimental Historical Records*, SAD 110/11/35; Alford and Sword, *The Egyptian Soudan*, 164–167; 'An Officer,' *Sudan Campaign*, 104–111; Burleigh, *Sirdar and Khalifa*, 23–25; Churchill, *The River War*, 176–193; Keown-Boyd, *A Good Dusting*, 181–183.
[11] Alford and Sword, *The Egyptian Soudan*, 167.
[12] 'An Officer,' *Sudan Campaign*, 109.

[13] Ibid.
[14] 'An Officer,' *Sudan Campaign*, 109–110.
[15] Keown-Boyd, *A Good Dusting*, 183.
[16] Battle of the Atbara sources: *IRE* 59 (13 February–23 May, 1898); Hunter, *Historical Records of the Tenth Sudanese*, NAM 1968-07-330-1, 35–38; Wood-Martin, *IXth Sudanese Regimental Historical Records*, SAD 110/11/38–40; Steevens, *With Kitchener to Khartum*, 140–160; Alford and Sword, *The Egyptian Soudan*, 214–235; 'An Officer,' *Sudan Campaign*, 151–161; Burleigh, *Sirdar and Khalifa*, 216–251; Churchill, *The River War*, 221–234; Keown-Boyd, *A Good Dusting*, 194–202; Barthorp, *War on the Nile*, 146–151.
[17] George McKenzie Franks to T. J. Franks, 9 April 1898, SAD 403/2/6–7; Meiklejohn, "The Nile Campaign," NAM 1974-04-36-1, 30.
[18] Peter Harrington, "Images and Perceptions: Visualizing the Sudan Campaign," in *Sudan: The Reconquest Reappraised*, ed. Edward M. Spiers (London: Frank Cass Publishers, 1998), 99. Although more recent writers such as Henry Keown-Boyd and the Marquess of Anglesey have specifically chosen not to romanticize the charge of the 21st Lancers, and one, 'Ismat Hasan Zulfo, has even provided an account of it from a Mahdist perspective, others such as Philip Warner, for example, have continued to overestimate its relative importance to battle, quoting Churchill's account at length and writing that "although an error, and a costly one, the charge had accomplished its purpose." Keown-Boyd, *A Good Dusting*, 232; The Marquess of Anglesey, *A History of the British Cavalry, 1816–1919*, Vol. III: 1872–1898 (London: Leo Cooper, 1982), 378–385; 'Ismat Hasan Zulfo, *Karari*, 190–204; Warner, *Dervish*, 215–221.
[19] Battle of Omdurman [Karari] sources: *Sudan Intelligence Report* (hereafter cited as *SIR*) 60 (25 May–31 December, 1898); Archibald Hunter to Chief of Staff, 7 September 1898, SAD 1/4, 41–65; Hunter, *Historical Records of the Tenth Sudanese*, NAM 1968-07-330-1, 39–45; Wood-Martin, *IXth Sudanese Regimental Historical Records*, SAD 110/11/41–46; Steevens, *With Kitchener to Khartum*, 259–283; Alford and Sword, *The Egyptian Soudan*, 257–269; 'An Officer,' *Sudan Campaign*, 185–224; Burleigh, *Khartoum Campaign*, 135–227; Churchill, *The River War*, 234–289; Zulfo, *Karari*, 160–231; Ziegler, *Omdurman*, 108–179; Keown-Boyd, *A Good Dusting*, 215–243; Barthorp, *War on the Nile*, 152–169.
[20] According 'Ismat Hasan Zulfo, "the two wings of the crescent stretched out from a dense concentration at the angle itself, where men stretched back for 300 yards in eleven rows, to the wings where the men were only three or four deep." Zulfo, *Karari*, 170.
[21] H. C. B. Hopkinson, "The Sirdar's Camel Corps," *The Cornhill Magazine*, April 1899, 444–448.
[22] It is interesting to note that the Egyptian Division commander, Archibald Hunter, "placed Macdonald's brigade purposely on the outer flank, changing the order of brigades in echelon from the order of Brigades in camp to do so." Archibald Hunter to Chief of Staff, 7 September 1898, SAD 1/4, 47. This meant that Macdonald's largely Sudanese brigade, rather than Lewis's less experienced Egyptian brigade, would take up the rear of the echelon and thus be in position to defend against an attack on its flank as the army marched toward Omdurman. Ironically, in the course of its execution, the switch, though foresighted, may have indeed contributed to the size of the gap between these two rear brigades. On the other hand, it is unlikely that Lewis's brigade would have been able to match the brilliant saving action of Macdonald's had it remained on the far right.
[23] Rarely if ever reported is the fact that the aforementioned four Sudanese companies of the Camel Corps dismounted at this point and fought alongside Macdonald's brigade, "prolonging the infantry line to the right." Hopkinson, "The Sirdar's Camel Corps," 447.
[24] A. Hunter, "Amended Return showing number of rounds of Martini Henry Ammunition expended by battalions at the action on the 2nd September 1898," 6 September 1898, Omdurman, NA WO 32/6143; same figures also reported in *SIR* 60, 42.
[25] Burleigh, *Khartoum Campaign*, 193.
[26] Felix Ready, 3 September 1898, NAM 1966-09-142.
[27] *SIR* 60, 41. Sudanese infantry battalion casualties included 15 killed and 130 wounded: IXth Battalion 2 killed and 46 wounded; Xth Battalion 4 killed and 27 wounded; XIth Battalion 4 killed and 30 wounded; XIIth Battalion 2 killed and 10 wounded; XIIIth Battalion 2 killed and 10 wounded; XIVth Battalion 1 killed and 7 wounded.
[28] A. Hunter to Chief of Staff, 7 September 1898, SAD 1/4, 50.
[29] Herbert Kitchener to Sir Francis Grenfell, 5 September 1898, Omdurman, NA WO 32/6143; Bennett, *The Downfall of the Dervishes*, 188; Alford and Sword, *The Egyptian Soudan*, 262–264.
[30] As well, Churchill includes few if any details on the aforementioned fighting withdrawal from the Karari hills made by four Sudanese companies of the Camel Corps, or the capturing of the summit of Jebel Surgham by two companies of the Sudanese XIIIth Battalion. Churchill, *The River War*, 259–289.

[31] Ibid., 285–287; see also Churchill's *Morning Post* letters (from Khartoum on the 5th and 6th of September, and from Camp Omdurman on the 8th of September) printed in *Young Winston's Wars: The Original Despatches of Winston S. Churchill, 1897–1900*, ed. Frederick Woods (London: Leo Cooper Ltd., 1972), 98–119.
[32] Churchill, *The River War*, 287.
[33] Ibid.
[34] Ibid., 287–288.
[35] Ibid., 271–278.
[36] Ibid., 274.
[37] Keown-Boyd, *A Good Dusting*, 235; Asher, *Khartoum*, 396; Ziegler, *Omdurman*, 166.
[38] Barthorp, *War on the Nile*, 166; Neillands, *The Dervish Wars*, 209; Asher, *Khartoum*, 400.
[39] See, for example, Ziegler, *Omdurman*, 175–176; Asher, *Khartoum*, 400.
[40] Neillands, *The Dervish Wars*, 108–159; Warner, *Dervish*, 213–221; Keown-Boyd, *A Good Dusting*, 224–232; Barthorp, *War on the Nile*, 159–163; Ziegler, *Omdurman*, 108–159.
[41] Barthorp, *War on the Nile*, 167; Neillands, *The Dervish Wars*, 210. Dominic Green in his 2007 book *Three Empires on the Nile* wrote, albeit a single line, that the "bravery of MacDonald and his men had saved Kitchener's army." Green, *Three Empires on the Nile*, 264.
[42] Ziegler, *Omdurman*, 172.
[43] Warner, *Dervish*, 215; Ziegler, *Omdurman*, 172–174; and despite the above referenced "bravery of MacDonald and his men," Dominic Green elsewhere misattributes it, rehashing the mistaken idea it was primarily due to the fact that he "had personally trained his four battalions of Sudanese riflemen." Green, *Three Empires on the Nile*, 263.
[44] Winston Churchill as quoted in Woods, *Young Winston's Wars*, 109.
[45] Ibid., 120.
[46] Ibid., 107, 109.
[47] Churchill, *The River War*, 287. Churchill was a man guilty of the prejudices of his day, and at one point in *The River War* referred to the "black soldier" as "at once slovenly and uxorious…a lazy, fierce, disreputable child." Churchill, *The River War*, 92.
[48] Ibid., 288.
[49] Burleigh, *Khartoum Campaign*, 209.
[50] Bennett, *Downfall of the Dervishes*, 187–188.
[51] A. Hunter to Frederick Maurice, 14 October 1898, as quoted in Hunter, *Kitchener's Sword-Arm*, 100. In Hunter's official report on the Battle of Omdurman he reported that the Lincolnshire Regiment merely "moved up on the right of Macdonald's," and there was no mention of any material role played by the regiment in repulsing the attack. Hunter to Chief of Staff, 7 September 1898, SAD 1/4, 48.
[52] *SIR* 60, 7.
[53] See, for example, Milner, *England in Egypt*, 147–149; Wingate, *Mahdiism and the Egyptian Sudan*, 221.
[54] F. R. Wingate, unpublished typescript, SAD 258/1/138. Likewise, E. F. Knight wrote that although "they [Sudanese soldiers] have not such fine physique…their eyesight is stronger than that of the fellahin and their shooting is much better." Knight, *Letters from the Sudan*, 38.
[55] A. E. Hubbard as quoted in Harrington and Sharf, *Omdurman 1898*, 70.
[56] Bennett, *Downfall of the Dervishes*, 186.
[57] Churchill, *The River War*, 287.
[58] 'An Officer,' *Sudan Campaign*, 205–206.
[59] Ibid., 206. H. L. Pritchard's account of this phase of the battle was based on his direct participation in it as Macdonald's "galloper," and during the attack of the Green Standard, while in temporary command of the XIth Sudanese Battalion. Keown-Boyd, *A Good Dusting*, 235; Ziegler, *Omdurman*, 172.
[60] A. Hunter, "Amended Return showing number of rounds of Martini Henry Ammunition expended," NA WO 32/6143; same figures also reported in *SIR* 60, 42.
[61] Ibid.
[62] *SIR* 60, 41.
[63] Bennett, *Downfall of the Dervishes*, 186. One of the distinct advantages of the Lee-Metford rifle over the Martini-Henry was that it was fired by smokeless powder, and thus provided soldiers with a clearer field of vision and more accurate aim. See Spiers, *The Late Victorian Army*, 238–241.
[64] A. Hunter, "Amended Return showing number of rounds of Martini Henry Ammunition expended," NA WO 32/6143; same figures also reported in *SIR* 60, 42. "Machine-like regularity" is from Churchill, *The River War*, 288.
[65] Hugh Cecil, "British Correspondents and the Sudan Campaign of 1896–98," in *Sudan: The Reconquest Reappraised*, 102–103; Bennet Burleigh obituary, 18 June 1914, *The New York Times*; Burleigh,

Khartoum Campaign, 193.
66 Burleigh, *Khartoum Campaign*, 185.
67 Ibid., 189.
68 Ibid., 207–208.
69 Perhaps one of the reasons why British observers such as Winston Churchill, unfamiliar with Sudanese tactics, found them so inferior – as random and impulsive rather than steady and disciplined – was because the late Victorian army so strongly adhered to its traditional fighting methods and colonial campaign mentality, both of which "encouraged the perpetuation of out-moded tactics" such as volley firing, a textbook maneuver requiring "disciplined solidarity" and "machine-like movements." Gwyn Harries-Jenkins, *The Army in Victorian Society* (London: Routledge & Kegan Paul, 1977), 193–196.
70 Steevens, *With Kitchener to Khartum*, 276.
71 Ibid., 278, 281.
72 Ibid., 295; Steevens estimated that one company in each Sudanese battalion at Omdurman was made up of "raw dervishes" and "utterly untrained in the use of fire-arms."
73 B. R. Mitford, "Extracts from the Diary of a Subaltern," *Sudan Notes and Records* XX (1937): 66.
74 'Ali el Tum, and most of the Sudanese officers and NCOs described below, were mentioned by Archibald Hunter in his official report on the Battle of Omdurman. Hunter to Chief of Staff, 7 September 1898, SAD 1/4, 58–63. Their biographical details have been compiled from *Army List, 1897*, SAD 111/2; Hill, *A Biographical Dictionary of the Anglo-Egyptian Sudan*; Johnson, "Biographical Data: Sudanese Officers & NCOs"; Hunter, *Historical Records of the Tenth Sudanese*, NAM 1968-07-330-1; Wood-Martin, *IXth Sudanese Regimental Historical Records*, SAD 110/11.
75 'Abdallah Romayh was later promoted *saghkolaghasi*, then *bimbashi*, and eventually, in 1912, *kaimakam* and placed on pension. Upon his February 1912 farewell, "The whole Battalion, Harimat, and Band turned out to see him depart on his journey [from Wau] to Omdurman (where he died in September 1914)." And according to the IXth Sudanese Regimental Historical Records, it was 'Abdallah Romayh "to whom much of this record is due." Wood-Martin, *IXth Sudanese Regimental Historical Records*, SAD 110/11/9, 58–59, 65, 71–72.
76 Smith-Dorrien, *Memories of Forty-Eight Years' Service*, 108. According to Ronald Forbes Meiklejohn, that same day Winston Churchill had not been so optimistic: "Then Winston Churchill, who was attached to 21st, strolled up, and we had a long talk. He was far less argumentative & self-assertive than usual. He said the enemy had a huge force and, if they attacked during the night, he thought it would be 'touch and go' about the result. A massed attack against the Gippies or Soudanese would probably break through." Meiklejohn, "The Nile Campaign," NAM 1974-04-36-1, 46.
77 See "Captain Fitton examining Dervish prisoners," 8 August 1896, *Black & White*; "Colonel Wingate…Interviewing a Refugee," 8 January 1898, *The Graphic*; "Slatin Pasha Questioning a Dervish Refugee," 12 September 1898, *Black & White*.
78 "The Advance in the Soudan: A Captured Dervish on board a Nile Boat," 13 November 1897, *The Graphic*.
79 H. G. Fitton to F. R. Wingate, 27 May 1896, SAD 261/1/421.
80 Mitford, "Extracts from the Diary of a Subaltern," *Sudan Notes and Records* XVIII, Part II (1935): 176.
81 Knight, *Letters from the Sudan*, 269–270.
82 "An Innovation at Berber: The Policeman," 8 January 1898, *The Graphic*.
83 Kitchener to Rodd, 24 September 1898, encl. in Rodd to Salisbury, 25 September 1898, FO 141/336.
84 H. W. Jackson, "Fashoda, 1898" *Sudan Notes and Records* III, No. 1 (1920): 1–11; Smith-Dorrien, *Memories of Forty-Eight Years' Service*, 121.
85 J. K. Watson to his father, 11 September 1898, NAM 1983-04-112-2.
86 The Shilluk inhabited the White Nile from Kaka southward to Lake No on the west bank, and also had villages on the east bank near the mouth of the Sobat River, and continuing on either side of the Sobat for some thirty five miles upriver.
87 As described by H. W. Jackson, "After several unsuccessful attempts had been made to discover an outlet [to Mashra El-Rek] it was decided to land and obtain guides, if possible, from a Nuer village which was seen in the distance. The steamer was anchored and a boat was sent ashore with a Dinka Corporal who could speak the Nuer language.…Then the Nuer broke into song and on its conclusion, the Headman closely questioned the Dinka Corporal and told him to advise the white men to go away as they were not wanted in the Nuer country. A parley followed: gradually the Headman's attitude become [*sic*] more friendly, and advantage of the change was at once seized by presenting him with some copper wire and brass armlets – articles highly praised among the Nuer. The presents completed the Headman's conquest and he promised to produce two men who would show the channel to Mashra El-Rek. Provided that hostages were left with him until the return of his men." Jackson, "Fashoda, 1898," 4–5.

[88] F. R. Wingate to his wife, 13 September 1898, SAD 233/5/101.
[89] F. R. Wingate, 16 September 1898, diary, SAD 102/1/112.
[90] J. K. Watson to his father, no date, NAM 1983-04-112, 16; see also Smith-Dorrien, *Memories of Forty-Eight Years' Service*, 128.
[91] *SIR* 60, 9; J. K. Watson, 18 September 1898, diary, NAM 1984-12-4-7.
[92] J. K. Watson to his father, NAM 1983-04-112, 17.
[93] *SIR* 60, 9.
[94] For the narrative details of the Fashoda Incident, see Smith-Dorrien, *Memories of Forty-Eight Years' Service*, chapter 7; Jules Emily, *Mission Marchand: Journal du Route* (Paris: Hachette, 1913), 184–186; Burleigh, *Khartoum Campaign*, chapter 15; G. N. Sanderson, *England, Europe and the Upper Nile, 1882–1899* (Edinburgh: Edinburgh University Press, 1965), chapter 15; Thomas Pakenham, *The Scramble for Africa: White Man's Conquest of the Dark Continent from 1876 to 1912* (New York: Avon Books, 1991), chapter 30; David Levering Lewis, *The Race to Fashoda: Colonialism and African Resistance* (New York: Henry Holt and Company, Inc., 1987), 222–223.
[95] Burleigh, *Khartoum Campaign*, 309–310. After Kitchener ordered all war correspondents back to Egypt following the Battle of Omdurman, Burleigh scooped his peers on Fashoda by changing ships at Malta and returning to the Sudan in order to interview soldiers who had been eyewitnesses to the incident. Cecil, "British Correspondents and the Sudan Campaign," 103.
[96] Burleigh, *Khartoum Campaign*, 309.
[97] 'An Officer,' *Sudan Campaign*, 230–231.
[98] H. W. Jackson, Fashoda Intelligence Diary No. 1, 20 September 1898, NAM 2001-10-117-1; *SIR* 60, 10.
[99] *SIR* 60, 95.
[100] Kitchener to Rodd, 24 September 1898, encl. in Rodd to Salisbury, 25 September 1898, FO 141/336.
[101] Kitchener to Rodd, 21 September 1898, encl. in Rodd to Salisbury, 29 September 1898, FO 141/333.
[102] Jackson, Fashoda Intelligence Diary No. 1, 28 September 1898, NAM 2001-10-117-1.
[103] Ibid., 2 October 1898.
[104] Ibid., 24 October 1898.
[105] Ibid., 3 November 1898.
[106] Ibid., 16 December 1898.
[107] Ibid., 10 October 1898; *SIR* 60, 93.
[108] Jackson, Fashoda Intelligence Diary No. 1, 10 October 1898.
[109] Ibid., 1 November 1898.
[110] Ibid., 20 November 1898.
[111] Jackson, "Fashoda 1898," 7.
[112] Sanderson, *England, Europe and the Upper Nile*, 343.
[113] Salisbury to Rodd, 1 October 1898, FO 141/336.
[114] Jackson, "Fashoda 1898," 2–3.
[115] Ibid.
[116] Ibid., 2.
[117] Jackson to Wingate, 24–25 September 1898, CAIRINT 3/15/243, as quoted in Sanderson, *England, Europe and the Upper Nile*, 339n1.
[118] H. E. Hill, 29 December 1898, *SIR* 60, 90.
[119] Jackson to Wingate, 24–25 September 1898, CAIRINT 3/15/243, as quoted in Sanderson, *England, Europe and the Upper Nile*, 339n1.
[120] Sanderson, *England, Europe and the Upper Nile*, 338.
[121] Jackson, Fashoda Intelligence Diary No. 1, 6 October 1898, NAM 2001-10-117-1.
[122] Bates, *The Fashoda Incident of 1898*, 161.

Epilogue
Mutiny at Omdurman

"And what will be the result of the mutiny of the Soudanese soldiers?"
"The English," said he, "have kindly treated the Soudanese army thinking that they will gain them in the future; but late events have shown them that all their measures were unavailable. They learned that the Soudanese would follow their own opinion, and if they resolve upon something, they must accomplish it; which fact is of great moment."

"The Army Affair: An Interview with an [Egyptian] Officer of a High Rank," published in the Egyptian newspaper *al-Lewa*, 5 February 1900[1]

The mutiny broke out in the Omdurman barracks on the night of 22 January 1900. At sunset, following a medical inspection and the reading of orders, four companies of the XIth Sudanese rushed the Battalion Store, recovering ammunition they had earlier that day given up per the Station Order of their commander, Colonel John Maxwell.[2] Later that same night, as rumors continued to swirl that they had been disarmed because they were being sent to South Africa, the Sudanese XIVth Battalion followed suit, overwhelming the quarter guard and making off to their barrack rooms with some 10,000 rounds of ammunition. Putting themselves in a state of defense, they proceeded to expel all of their British officers from the barracks, closed them off to all-comers, and defied all authority.[3]

In the case of the XIVth, its commanding officer, James Sillem, promptly called on the Sudanese XIIIth to surround his mutinous battalion. But the men of the XIIIth, having earlier that day complied with the Station Order and thus with only a few rounds apiece, declared that they would only do so upon the return of their ammunition, and chose instead to disregard the order. As for the insubordinate XIth, the next morning its *kaimakam*, Godfrey Matthews, after questioning some NCOs and men, seemingly convinced his battalion to return the seized ammunition. But as it was being loaded on mules for return to the "Nuzl," the soldiers again "rushed out the various rooms and seized the same."

Matthews, after receiving a few blows in the ensuing scramble, proceeded to mount sentries with fixed bayonets over each barracks exit in order to conduct a search for the ammunition. Things then escalated even further, as the wives of the Sudanese XIth soldiers "came to the help of their husbands armed with sticks and knives."[4]

With two battalions still defiant, and fearing the mutiny might spread, Colonel Maxwell wisely temporized, and declared that 500 rounds per battalion could be kept for guard purposes. With this announcement by Maxwell, paired with the decision to keep the remaining ammunition under the respective quarter guards rather than returning it to stores, "a quieting effect was produced" in the short-term, although a "state of great tension" remained in the days and weeks that followed, as both sides, still at odds, worked toward some form of resolution.[5]

Although it was Colonel Maxwell's own Station Order that sparked the mutiny, its origins could be traced back to Egyptian Army reforms made in the wake of the Sudan's 1898 reoccupation. In an effort to cut military expenditures – and thus satisfy Egypt's penurious financial advisers, the likes of Lord Cromer and Sir Eldon Gorst – the *sirdar*, Herbert Kitchener, instituted changes that "adversely affected the pay and pension of Egyptian Officers," most notably the cancellation of special allowances given to troops stationed in the Sudan. Meanwhile, in stark contrast, Kitchener spared no expense when it came to the rebuilding of Khartoum, and in particular, the construction of the Governor-General's Palace.[6] And then, adding insult to injury, when Kitchener was called to the war in South Africa in December 1899, his stand-in, Colonel John Maxwell, began coming up with further ways to economize, writing to F. R. Wingate, Kitchener's successor, that they should begin discharging "the weedy old men" of the Sudanese battalions, "who cost money and do nothing." Indeed, three days before the Egyptian Army mutiny occurred, Maxwell again suggested to Wingate, still in Cairo, that there were "a considerable number of old worn out men who might be discharged with advantage."[7]

These pay and pension reforms had engendered such "ill-feeling amongst the Egyptian Officers" that some of them had "sought, privately, the sympathy of the Khedive."[8] In Abbas Hilmi, who as Khedive was in fact the nominal head of the Egyptian Army, these disaffected Egyptian officers found a sympathetic ear. This was not surprising considering his repugnance to the British occupation, and in particular, his embittered relationship with Kitchener. On top of this, relations between Egyptian officers and their British superiors – already strained due to years of harsh and unequal treatment accorded the former from Kitchener on down – had so deteriorated by January 1900 that some of them sent an anonymous letter to Colonel Maxwell in which they told him, according to one intelligence report, "that, if he does not treat them better, he will be the only one responsible for his own safety."[9] As Sir Evelyn Wood, former *sirdar* himself, would write to his old friend Wingate, the new *sirdar*, later that winter in reference to the "Omdurman trouble," and to Kitchener's culpability in particular, "he who sowed had left you to reap the unpleasant crop."[10]

There is even evidence, found in articles published in nationalist Egyptian newspapers such as *al-Lewa*, that some of the disaffection among the Egyptian officers had to do with the feeling they had been double-crossed by the British.

According to such sources, these men had been of the belief that Anglo-Egyptian victory in the Nile Campaign meant the restoration of Egyptian rule in the Sudan, and not dual possession, "thinking that we were thereby exhibiting a great service to our country as well as His Majesty the Sultan, His Highness the Khedive."[11] However, upon the defeat of the Mahdists these same Egyptian officers and soldiers, who had "exhibited great feats of courage in the recapture of the Soudan," soon found themselves "greatly insulted...for they saw the British flag floating over Khartoum."[12] Further insult to injury came when Englishmen rather than Egyptians were then appointed to the positions of Governor-General and district *mudirs* of the Sudan.[13]

Making matters worse, with the conclusion of Nile Campaign and the commencement of the Boer War, some of the most experienced British officers in the Sudan chose to rejoin their home regiments or were recalled by the War Office. Many of these senior officers had served in the Egyptian Army for years on end, and in so doing had developed personal relationships with the soldiers they commanded, especially in the case of "long service men" in Sudanese battalions. The young officers who replaced them were often guilty of neglectful, sometimes "harsh or inconsiderate," treatment of both Egyptian and Sudanese officers and men, especially when it came to some of the older soldiers. And the lack of consideration and respect demonstrated by many of these newly joined British officers engendered a similar lack of esteem and allegiance to them on the part of the native officers and rank-and-file Sudanese and Egyptian soldiers.[14]

As the mutiny played out in early February 1900, Wingate raised the issue in a telegram to Viscount Cromer: "Some of the British Commanding Officers are, I think, to some extent to blame for not having kept sufficiently in touch with their troops."[15] H. W. Jackson, longtime commander of the Sudanese XIth, went even further in his criticism of this new breed of British officer serving in the Sudan: "The men do not know their British officers, nor do the British officers know their men. In old times all British officers would continually mix with their men...set up games, visit the harimat...Now it is all polo, club, etc., and back to their rooms as soon as the morning's work is done...the young British officers who do not know Arabic are often rude to much older men and native officers, who have far greater service and experience...the general idea is to look upon the native officer as a very inferior being."[16] In Wingate's mind, the departure of so many older and experienced British officers "shook the entire fabric to its foundations" and ultimately "had much to do with it [the mutiny]."[17]

In mid-December 1899, in the wake of three humiliating British defeats in the Transvaal that came to be known as "Black Week," came further departures of senior officers in the Sudan, one of them being Kitchener himself. This was followed a few weeks later by a "strict and exclusive censorship on Egyptian newspapers" in the Sudan – a measure likely intended to keep out any bad news from the Cape, but one that "led to sundry and different explanations and suspicions as to the grounds of it."[18] Rumors soon began circulating in the Bazaar "that guns and saddlery had been secretly sent to Cairo for the Transvaal," which was indeed true, for Cromer and Wingate had consented to having ten Maxims and four Krupp guns sent up to Cairo from Khartoum, for eventual dispatch to South Africa.[19]

A couple days prior to the mutiny, an Egyptian *yuzbashi* from the 8th Battalion named Mahmud Hilmi (formerly a *mulazim awal* in the XIth), visited the lines of the XIth Sudanese Battalion and met with three of its *yuzbashia*, Muhammad Sami, Hassan Labib, and 'Abd al-Hamid Shukri. Mahmud Hilmi returned twice more in the days that followed, meeting with Hassan Labib privately in his quarters. These officers of Sudanese XIth were told that "that the 8th Battalion had no intention of giving in its ammunition," and after Colonel Maxwell's Station Order of 21 January, found themselves questioning "the advisability of XIth returning the same."[20] Maxwell had tried to tell his troops that the ammunition, deteriorating and in need of replacement, was being collected in order to prevent accidents, but in reality the order had presumably arisen "from rumours of Army unrest."[21]

And it appears that Maxwell had reason for concern, as there exists anecdotal evidence that a much larger and more elaborately planned mutiny had been in the works for some time, even predating Kitchener's departure. According to Cromer, writing to Lord Salisbury in April 1900, "Pretty well all the officers, senior and junior, were concerned.... The idea was not to kill the English officers – except perhaps Kitchener – but either to keep them in confinement at Omdurman or to send them to Cairo.... The plan was disconcerted by Kitchener's sudden departure."[22] In any case, the Egyptian and Sudanese officers and soldiers "guessed that the real purpose of these measures was the security of the English against any future mutiny, and they thought that the latter might proceed later to disarm them entirely."[23]

On the night of the mutiny, some twenty Egyptian and Sudanese junior officers met at the Greek café *Cairis*, where "wild stories were being told about the state of affairs in Cairo, arising partly from the Transvaal war news, the recall of British officers, and the withdrawal of Maxim guns."[24] One of these officers, an Egyptian *mulazim awal* from the 8th Battalion named Saleh Zeki, began telling those assembled, in particular two Egyptian junior officers from the Sudanese XIVth, Mustafa Lutfi and Ahmad Shakir, "Min el-abaath," ["it is wrong to give in the ammunition"].[25] Saleh Zeki also told them "it had been decided to disarm the Egyptian Army and send them to South Africa, where the Boers would probably slaughter them."[26] Such news "fairly stampeded the Club," and Mustafa Lutfi and Ahmad Shakir, along with another Egyptian junior officer of the Sudanese XIVth named Mahmud Mukhtar, at once left the café and returned to their barracks.[27] In Mahmud Mukhtar's tent it was then decided to organize the men of the XIVth Battalion for a midnight seizure of the stored ammunition. With the "idea among the Black troops that they were to be sent to the Cape" now firmly planted in their minds, "they needed no persuasion to follow their [Egyptian and Sudanese] officers."[28]

Other underlying factors and local concerns may have played into the mutiny as well. As suggested above, whereas relations between Sudanese junior officers and their new British commanders seem to have been deteriorating, those between certain Sudanese and Egyptian officers had been improving. In particular, many of the up-and-coming Sudanese officers who had been trained at the Cairo Military School as opposed to rising up through the ranks – and thus having been exposed to the "patriotic Cairene atmosphere," as described by

Wingate – were becoming increasingly sympathetic to the grievances and aspirations of their fellow Egyptian officers.[29] Add to this the fact that many of the Sudanese rank and file were ex-Mahdist *jihadiyya*, and therefore more recent enlistees with perhaps conflicted or unformed allegiances, and that many others, especially Sudanese of long service, Maxwell's "weedy old men…not worth their pay and rations," had both real grievances and legitimate reason to fear they might soon be discharged. And finally, whether real or imagined, or perhaps contrived, some Sudanese soldiers at the time claimed to fear the "evil results" of giving up all their ammo, afraid of retribution from "the natives who have been ill-treated by the soldiers," and whom they saw "were now suspicious and doubtful."[30] When one considers all of the above preconditions, followed by a month in which word from the war in South Africa was censored, Maxim guns were shipped to the Cape, all but a few rounds of ammunition were taken away, and rumor had it they were about to be sent – on the heels of a three-year campaign against the Mahdists – to the other end of the continent to fight an even more formidable enemy in the Boers, in terms of the makings of an army mutiny it was something of a perfect storm.

Although it remains unknown whether or not Sudanese soldiers were being considered for use in the Transvaal, there was historical precedent for such "wild stories" as were circulating that January night at Socrati Trapass's café.[31] Sudanese soldiers had been sent abroad as expeditionary forces on numerous occasions throughout the nineteenth century: to Greece in the 1820s; Arabia and Syria in the 1830s; the Crimea in the 1850s; Mexico in the 1860s; Ethiopia in the 1870s; and Tanganyika in the 1880s. Not unrelated, it would not be the first time that an order to collect their weapons and ammunition was followed soon thereafter by deployment outside the country. In the case of the "Mexican adventure" (1863–1867), in which Muhammad Sa'id Pasha lent Sudanese soldiers to French Emperor Napoleon III for use in Maximilian's army, 'Ali Jifun recalled in his memoirs that just prior to being sent to Alexandria, for embarkation to Vera Cruz, "an order arrived for all Soudanese to hand over the guns," albeit in this case the brass mountain guns of his artillery battery.[32]

Even the 1900 mutiny itself seemed to hark back to earlier cases of insubordination, and Egyptian Army rebellions staged by prior generations of Sudanese soldiers. In March 1844, for example, at the Wad Medani garrison on the Blue Nile, disgruntled Sudanese slave soldiers mutinied, killing a number of their Turkish officers and fleeing south to Sennar.[33] In 1864–1865, Sudanese soldiers at the Kassala garrison mutinied on more than one occasion. First, in October 1864, five hundred soldiers, whose pay was greatly in arrears, refused to march against the Basen on the Ethiopian border and instead seized guns and ammunition, looting a nearby village before a truce could be arranged. The following year, when the Khedive tried to send a relief battalion of Sudanese soldiers from Kassala to Mexico, a much more serious mutiny occurred. On the march to Suakin, from where they would embark for Suez on the way to Mexico, the Fourth Regiment heard from another unit that they would soon be chained and deported. Upon hearing this, the Sudanese troops returned to Kassala and stormed the citadel, killing several officers and laying siege to the town for the next twenty-six days. In the end, supported by Sudanese regiments sent from El

Obeid and Khartoum, the mutiny was crushed and some 2,000 mutineers were either killed in the fighting or executed by courts martial.[34]

A generation later, during the formation of the new Egyptian Army's first Sudanese battalion in 1884, Sudanese soldiers were once again in a mutinous state. The disgruntled, many of them older, battle-tested soldiers, who were the first enlistees in the Sudanese IXth, like these Nile Campaign veterans sixteen years later, resented the "extreme keenness" of their new British officers, and "were distinctly for a quiet time in Egypt."[35] Again, things came to a head when the men refused to surrender their Remington rifles in exchange for Martini-Henrys. In the end, Sir Evelyn Wood chose to disband the entire IXth Battalion and start over, promising any new "volunteers" that they would receive steady pay and a marriage allowance. Although few if any Sudanese soldiers who participated in these earlier overseas campaigns or army mutinies were still alive or in the ranks come January 1900, it is possible that something of an institutional memory of them – passed down within battalions, from old soldiers to new recruits, and from fathers to sons – may have raised red flags at the Omdurman barracks.

Be that as it may, in the two-week standoff that followed the initial Sudanese revolt of 22–23 January, it was the deeper and more durable allegiances of Sudanese soldiers – their loyalty to the Khedive and long-standing capacity to "trust in their Bey" – that precluded a more protracted and/or violent resistance. This first manifested itself within the Sudanese XIth Battalion upon the arrival of Colonel H. W. Jackson, its former *kaimakam*. A great mutual affinity existed between Jackson and the men of his old battalion, having been cemented on the field of battle during the Nile Campaign; according to one anecdote, his soldiers "were so devoted to him that at the battle of Atbara some of the men had formed a guard round him to prevent him from being harmed."[36] In the immediate wake of the mutiny, Colonel Jackson, who was then serving as the provincial Governor of Berber, was urgently summoned to Khartoum. As soon as he arrived and was able to assure his former battalion that rumors of its imminent departure for South Africa were untrue, promising the men that their recent insubordination would be forgiven, the mutinous Sudanese XIth forthwith agreed to return all of the missing ammunition.[37]

What is interesting, and again speaks to the role of women and wives within Sudanese battalions, was the specific nature of these negotiations, and the means by which the above assurances were conveyed to the men of the Sudanese XIth. It appears that the key role in the initial dialogue between Jackson and the men of his former battalion was played by the soldiers' wives via the battalion's *shaykhat el harimat*:

> When all the women had arrived Colonel Jackson told them to sit down, and then said to them: "What is this dreadful news that I have heard, my daughters? I am told that your husbands have broken open the ammunition shed and stolen all the arms and ammunition! Surely this can't be true?"
>
> "It is true, oh our father," replied the senior sheikha, "and the reason is that they have been told that they were to be sent to South Africa to fight for the English; they did not want to do this so they seized the rifles in order to protect themselves if anyone tried to force them to go."

"That is a lie, my daughters," replied Colonel Jackson, "and I, your father, swear to you that the Government has no intention of sending your husbands to South Africa. It is true that the Government is sending some of the rifles to South Africa as the rifles your menfolk have are better than some of those that the English have."

"Wallahi! ('by God!')," replied the sheikha, "is this true?"

"Wallahi!" said Jackson, "it is true."

"Then what shall we do?"

"Your husbands," said Jackson, "have been very foolish to behave like this, but tell them that if they return tonight all the rifles and ammunition which they have taken the Government will forgive them."[38]

According to F. R. Wingate's initial report on the matter upon his 4 February 1900 arrival to Khartoum, it was thanks to Jackson's immediate involvement that "almost all the ammunition unaccounted for was returned by the 11th Battalion," and that a full-scale mutiny was averted.[39] It was later reported by the Court of Inquiry that Hassan Labib's company remained insubordinate for several weeks hence, but for the majority of the men of the Sudanese XIth it appears that allegiance to the Egyptian Army and/or trust in their former commander – not to mention the prevailing influence of their wives – trumped any fleeting loyalties they may have felt toward their disgruntled Egyptian officers.[40] This was indeed the assessment given by the former *sirdar* Evelyn Wood, when writing to Wingate soon after the Court of Inquiry decisions were executed: "I wonder how you managed to get the Blacks to submit to the deportation of the incriminated officers, but I suppose that the Egyptian never gets a very tight hold of the Soudani."[41]

It is also revealing, and apropos of the above, that Colonel Jackson did not have the same immediate success with the Sudanese soldiers of the XIVth Battalion, officers and men whom he had never commanded. According to Wingate's initial telegram from Omdurman, despite Jackson's "every effort" to convince the Sudanese XIVth to join the XIth and return the ammunition, Jackson had "so far been unsuccessful." Although "a few of the older men" seemed amenable, it was only after Wingate arrived on the scene at Omdurman, and he was able to play upon the fundamental allegiance these soldiers felt toward their ultimate patron, and symbolic (and indeed nominal) commander-in-chief, the Khedive Abbas Hilmi, that the XIVth Battalion was induced to begin handing over the seized ammunition.[42] Wingate's leverage was in the form of a letter from Abbas Hilmi that condemned the mutiny, "drafted in strong terms in Arabic, the Khedive deprecating bitterly the tarnished honour of His Army," and that gave him "*full powers* to deal drastically with the outbreak." The new *sirdar* had "considered it essential" that he arrive in Khartoum with a letter from the Khedive "definitely disassociating himself with the movement in Omdurman," in part because he suspected Abbas Hilmi had prior knowledge of it, and knowing full well the undermining effect such a statement would have on the mutineers – not only the Egyptian ringleaders and their Sudanese conspirators, but also the Sudanese rank and file these officers commanded.[43]

At 10 a.m. on the morning after his arrival, Wingate held a levee in Omdurman in order to meet with civilians and military upon assuming his new position as *sirdar* and Governor-General. During the levee, Wingate let it be known to his officers that following the reception, in the yard outside, he would receive any officer who wished to speak with him. As it turned out, so many officers took Wingate up on his offer that in the end seven representatives were chosen to speak for the group. According to Wingate, "the principal spokesman then said that the officers were profoundly disturbed by the financial reforms instituted by Lord Kitchener...he appealed to me as the new Sirdar, to withdraw Lord Kitchener's financial reforms and if I would do so, he assured me that all this trouble would at once cease." Later that day Wingate admitted in a telegram to Cromer that he thought "there has been much mismanagement of officers for some time past, and that many of them have real reasons for complaint...that it was injudicious treatment to a great extent which gave rise to this trouble."[44] Nevertheless, the new *sirdar* assumed an "angry attitude" toward the assembled officers, and with a company of Seaforth Highlanders sent over from Khartoum at his back, read them the riot act:

> You come to me to adjust your grievances and hold a pistol at my head in the shape of a mutinous Battalion, who have broken into their guardroom and stolen the ammunition stored there. You now demand that the reforms initiated by my predecessor should be readjusted and your grievances removed. I now tell you that I will take no steps whatever to go into your grievances until every round of the stolen ammunition is returned and the mutinous Troops have returned to strict Army discipline. If you think you can obtain a redress of your grievances by fomenting mutiny in the Army, let me assure you that I will not move a step in that direction until the Troops have regained their now tarnished honour – and let me remind you that, in the event of a continuance of these disorders, a large force of British Troops will be at once dispatched to the Sudan and punishment will be meted out to those responsible for the present disorders.[45]

The potential impact of Wingate's reprimand notwithstanding, there is evidence that at some point that same day, either during the levee or afterward, these officers were made aware of the letter from the Khedive condemning the mutiny, and that this may have played more of a role in ending the mutiny than Wingate's fiery speech. Later Wingate was to claim that he never used the letter or divulged its existence, but documents from the time of the mutiny indicate otherwise, and suggest that Egyptian and Sudanese soldiers both knew about it and were influenced by it.[46] The Egyptian newspaper *al-Lewa*, for example, on the same day of Wingate's levee, published an article referencing "the fact that His Highness [the Khedive] sent orders to the officers, soldiers, and natives to remain in implicit obedience to their superiors, and that Sir Wingate Pasha carried the orders with him."[47] The piece included an interview with an "Egyptian officer of high rank" in which he was asked about the ultimate effect of these orders:

> "What will be the effect of the orders sent by the Khedive?"
> "The officers and soldiers will certainly act in accordance with the wishes of His Highness, which they honour, and without which we would not have gone to recapture the Soudan. You can tell anybody that the Egyptian army is the best disposed army to obey its rules. The Khedive is the legal Representative of His Majesty the Sultan, who is our Commander-General and real Chief. I therefore cannot doubt that the mutiny will stop as soon as the orders of the Khedive be delivered; and I hope that His Highness will do his utmost in the way of our help."[48]

Wingate himself mentioned the divulgence of the letter's message, as well as that of an additional letter of support from the Khedive, in telegrams to Lord Cromer in Cairo. First, on 6 February 1900, the day following the levee, Wingate wrote from Omdurman, "I have told the officers that the Khedive specifically charged me to express to them his anger at the recent events, and his resolution to put an end to them, but I have not yet made use of his letter." Nonetheless, in the same telegram Wingate noted "a marked change for the better in the general situation" and observed "an alteration in the attitude of the officers." He also reported that the soldiers of the Sudanese XIVth seemed to have taken a turn as well, surrendering a few hundred rounds of ammunition, with more to follow. Later that same day, although in reference to the uprising itself, Wingate wrote to Cromer, "I feel sure that the Khedive's name and influence have much weight on the army, and I think it very doubtful whether the officers would have taken their recent action unless they had received some sort of tacit encouragement from high quarters."[49] Two days later Wingate telegraphed Cairo with the text for a new letter from the Khedive, and per Cromer's recommendation, "as you think would be of use to you."[50] It read:

> It is with great regret that I learn that the cases of insubordination and breach of discipline in our army, as reported by you before leaving Cairo, have not yet ceased. Under these circumstances, should it appear to you desirable and necessary to enforce the measures sanctioned in our letter to you of the 29th January, we hereby give you full power to that effect, feeling convinced that you will employ such authority in the manner most conducive to the maintenance of good discipline and order among our troops, and that you will bear in mind that any contravention of the same must be repressed without fail, and immediate steps taken to punish the offenders.[51]

The above text was given to the Khedive in French, who then sent it to Wingate the following day translated into Arabic. Wingate wrote on 9 Febuary 1900 "I have not yet taken any official action on His Highness' telegram, though I have made no secret of its receipt. The Court of Inquiry will meet in a day or two, and I will then read in open Court both the telegram and the letter." And his next line indeed suggests he made no secret of its contents as well, writing that "I believe the Khedive's attitude puzzles the officers, both senior and junior, very much, and that they are now considerably alarmed at the situation they have brought about." Later that same day he wrote: "The situation is improving, and ammunition continues to come in slowly. The receipt of the Khedive's telegram has caused rather a sensation among the senior officers."[52] To what extent the "Khedive's attitude" was conveyed from Egyptian and Sudanese officers to the men of the Sudanese XIVth is unknown, but the simultaneity of it being known among the former with the return of ammunition by the latter seems not entirely coincidental. Considering the very nature of Sudanese soldier identity, and the centrality of Khedival patronage in its formation, it would not be surprising if Abbas Hilmi's condemnation of the Egyptian Army mutiny influenced the actions and decisions of Sudanese officers and rank-and-file soldiers of the XIVth Battalion, and led to the ammunition being returned without further incident in February 1900.

Might the sudden departure of so many British commanders to South Africa, including Kitchener, the *sirdar* of the Egyptian Army, have created a similar allegiance vacuum as took place in the mid-1880s when the Sudan was abandoned to the Mahdists – taken as another evacuation of sorts, with similar choices to be made as to where to place one's loyalties and military services? In this case it may have appeared to many Sudanese soldiers, somewhat disaffected themselves, that their best bet was siding with their disgruntled Egyptian officers, who moreover claimed to have the full support of the Khedive. And rumors circulating within the Omdurman barracks and at the Native Officers Club only exacerbated such tensions.

On the night of the mutiny, for example, four young officers from the Sudanese IXth Battalion met with the ringleaders of the XIth, telling them "Bravo, you have done well in the XIth, this is the way to start [*sic*] have you heard the news of the overthrow of Ministry in Cairo...and that now, 'Inshallah' [if Allah wills it] the English will at length be turned out of Egypt."[53] And as suggested by the aforementioned assertion made by Cromer – that the mutiny had been in the works for some time, with far more ambitious goals than previously imagined – this may have been what these Sudanese officers believed was going to take place. Again, according to Cromer's sources, "The whole army was to join, and then one of two programmes was to be adopted – either the Khedive was to be informed that there were 20,000 men at his disposal, and his orders requested, or else, without waiting for an expression of the Khedive's views, the whole force was to move on to Egypt."[54]

However, once Wingate arrived and word got out that the Khedive appeared to be backing his new *sirdar* rather than the Egyptian officers, the movement was largely undermined. The choice for Sudanese officers and men in the XIVth became clear, and the ammunition was returned. It should also be remembered that fifteen years earlier it was the deeper loyalty of Sudanese soldiers to the Khedive, and the patronage of the Egyptian Army, that ultimately led so many of them back to Cairo for re-enlistment, rather than joining the forces of the Mahdi or returning to their native villages throughout the Sudan. And so it was again in 1900, when push came to shove for the Sudanese XIth and XIVth battalions, and for that matter the Sudanese IXth, Xth, XIIth, and XIIIth – these latter battalions having refused to join the mutiny from its outset. They knew which side their bread was buttered on, and once assured they would not be sent to South Africa or held responsible for the mutiny, they fell back in line.

Khedival influence or not, it was Sudanese officers who played the key role in facilitating the surrender of ammunition taken by the mutinous soldiers of the XIVth. In confidential talks between experienced British officers, including Colonel Jackson, and "some of the senior Sudanese Officers of the Mutinous Battalion in whom they had confidence," it was discovered that the men of the XIVth were not averse to returning the ammunition. However, they required that "this was to be done without the knowledge of the Egyptian Officers who were closely watching to prevent any return of the ammunition." A solution to this problem was effected by having the soldiers hand in the ammunition "under cover of darkness," through a storeroom window that was left open at the end of each company block."[55] As a result, and thanks in large part to "three old Soudanese officers promoted from the ranks," Wingate was able to report to

Viscount Cromer on 7 February 1900 that 3,000 rounds of ammunition had been returned by the XIVth Sudanese Battalion. The next day he telegraphed Cairo that another 800 rounds had been handed in, and on 9 February reported that the "situation is improving, and ammunition continues to come in slowly."[56]

Wingate then convened a Court of Inquiry on 12 February 1900 under the presidency of Colonel Jackson, and composed chiefly of senior Egyptian officers, in order to "collect evidence officially against officers, and to advise as to the degree in which officers were implicated in the recent incident."[57] However, after a week of deliberations Wingate telegraphed Cromer that they were making little progress in the investigation, reporting "it is difficult to obtain truthful evidence, and under examination the conduct of Moukhtar and other ringleaders is very truculent." Wingate's inclination was "to pack off all the ringleaders to Cairo without previous warning, and on their arrival to publish an order cashiering the worst; whilst others would be put on pension or half-pay," but conceded that "I may alter it as the inquiry proceeds."[58] This plan did not commend itself to Cromer, who telegraphed Wingate the following day that "matters should not be allowed to drag on indefinitely," and suggested that rather than "sending the guilty officers away, and punishing them subsequently," he should cashier them right there in Omdurman, arrest them forthwith, and "at once put them on board a boat." With the British detachment and loyal portion of the Egyptian Army at his back, Wingate should then "shoot down without mercy any one who shows the least hesitation or reluctance to obey you."[59]

Wingate adopted Cromer's plan, and within forty-eight hours the Court of Inquiry came to its preliminary decisions, publishing them in a Special Army Order that was read out to the assembled officers of the Omdurman garrison on 24 February 1900.[60] The court found the *yuzbashi* Mahmud Mukhtar directly responsible for the mutiny of the XIVth Battalion, and unanimously recommended he be dismissed from the Egyptian Army. Mustafa Lutfi and Ahmad Shakir, both officers in the XIVth Battalion, were also unanimously recommended for dismissal, although in Ahmad Shakir's case, "owing to the youth and inexperience of this officer," the Court put forth his case for favorable consideration and suggested he be placed *en disponibilité*. As for the insubordination of the XIth Battalion, the Court found the *yuzbashi* Hassan Labib "the chief offender," and unanimously recommended he be "dismissed from the service of His Highness the Khedive." The Court also found officers Saleh Zeki and Mustafa Muhammad Es Shami, both of the 8th Battalion, complicit in the mutiny of the XIVth, and recommended that Saleh Zeki be dismissed, while Mustafa Shami "be severely reprimanded and placed at the bottom of the roll of Mulazimin Tawani of the army." Finally, the Court recommended that the *ombashi* Belal En Nur of the XIVth Battalion be reduced in rank, transferred to the Discipline Company, and discharged with ignominy.[61]

The guilty Egyptian officers then had their swords and badges of rank publicly removed, and were "*marched* under British escort to a steamer awaiting to convey them North, en route to Cairo." And according to Wingate, "No disturbance of any kind took place."[62] A subsequent Special Army Order on 5 March 1900, in part addressing concerns that some of the implicated junior officers of the Sudanese XIth had not received any punishment, recommended further dismissals and reprimands. At least two of the five found guilty of misconduct in these latter deliberations of the Court of Inquiry were probably Sudanese and not Egyptian officers: Idris Effendi 'Abdallah, a *mulazim tani* in the XIth Battalion, whom Jackson noted in his investigation was a "Sudanese from [the Cairo] Military School," and whom the Court recommended should be dismissed from the army; and Osman Effendi Aref, a *mulazim tani* in the IXth Battalion, a Sudanese officer who had recently received special commendation for action at Gedid. Two additional officers from the mutinous companies in the XIth Battalion were also found directly responsible for the outbreak and dismissed from the Egyptian Army: Muhammad Tewfik Yusef and 'Abd al-Hamid Shukri. And Mahmud Effendi Hilmi, an Egyptian *yuzbashi* from the 8th Battalion, who was considered "a party to inciting certain officers of the 11th Soudanese to acts which resulted in the outbreak of insubordination in that battalion," was placed on pension.[63]

This second stage of the deliberations may have been in response to disgruntled Sudanese officers following the initial findings of the Court of Inquiry in late February. According to H. W. Jackson:

> A Soudanese Officer came to my quarters at 7 pm on 24th instant and talked over events of that morning when punishments which had been awarded to the ring-leaders of recent disturbances had been publicly read out. He asked "Why are not the young Officers of 11th Battalion punished who advised the men to get back the ammunition at retreat after the Medical Inspection." He informed me that those Officers were all of junior ranks and lately from Military School, that they had been continually at work spreading reports such as – the British were being defeated at the Cape, and that there are now no troops available to send to Egypt in case of disturbances, that Russia was advancing on India, and France preparing to move against England by Sea. He informed me that the young Officer from Military School now join the Army full of ideas and grievances, that they keep together and will not associate with Sudanese Officers from the ranks, that these boys are full of talk and get the Dervish Black to listen to them, hoping thus to take advantage of the present British difficulties at the Cape.[64]

This account also suggests that there was a generational cleavage within the Sudanese officer corps – between the older and more senior officers, largely illiterate and having been promoted from the ranks, and the younger generation of subalterns, often literate and educated at the Military School in Cairo, many of whom were born into the army and grew up in Egypt. The men of this older generation likely felt themselves vulnerable in terms of their future status and position, and in relation to these young, educated, and independent-minded junior officers. And this generation gap and perceived vulnerability had if anything been exacerbated when many of the more experienced British commanders of Sudanese battalions were recalled for service in the Boer War.

In any case, with the exception of the above "ringleaders," the rest of the officers and rank-and-file Sudanese soldiers of the XIth and XIVth battalions who participated in the mutiny were exempted from punishment. In fact, the day following the first Special Army Order, Wingate proposed to ask the Khedive to sanction the promotion of some ten or twelve Sudanese NCOs to the rank of lieutenant, noting that "an excellent effect would be produced on the Soudanese troops by this step."[65] Furthermore, a number of grievances that underlay the mutiny, and came to light in its wake, were redressed in the weeks and months that followed. Even prior to the conclusion of the initial Court of Inquiry, Cromer gave Wingate the authority to declare that "service at Assouan will count as service in the Soudan," a concession that might facilitate what he saw as "clearly desirable," that the army be dispersed.[66] And less than a week later Wingate reported to Cromer "the movement of more troops to their new garrisons in the various districts begins to-morrow, the 12th battalion being transferred to Dongola."[67] Further dispersals, and indeed reductions were to follow, as old soldiers were discharged in large numbers and the Egyptian Army presence in the Sudan was scaled back for both financial and security reasons. Lastly, it appears that many of the changes in the pay and pension schemes instituted by Kitchener in his final year as the *sirdar*, and indeed those that precipitated much of the discontent among Egyptian officers, were rescinded, in particular the prior cancellation of the Special Allowance given to Egyptian and Sudanese officers if serving in the Sudan.

On 25 February 1900, the day after the seven ringleaders were "drummed out of the Service," Wingate ordered a full ceremonial parade of all the troops in the Omdurman garrison, "by way of testing their loyalty."[68] He took similar precautions as he did on the day of the levee, having a company of British troops available in case any disturbance might arise. None did, and Wingate reported to Cromer later that day: "I have never seen the troops looking better or steadier, and everything passed off without a hitch."[69] Just as they had some seventy-six years earlier, when in December of 1823 Muhammad 'Ali held a grand passing-out parade for the first six regiments of his *nizam al-jadid* army at Asyut, Sudanese soldiers marched in formation that morning in Omdurman, not as military automatons or imperial lackeys, but as ipsimitted and proud men, representatives of a Sudanese soldier legacy and diaspora that transcended the ages, and of which they were but one bough. With roots in the Nile Valley going back millennia, to the days of the pharaohs, and on to those of the pashas, and with offshoots that in the twentieth century would continue to reach into East Africa, to the King's African Rifles and "Nubi" communities in Uganda, Kenya, and Tanzania, it was a family tree that would one day extend its upper Sudanese branches – via their sons and grandsons, descendants and progenies – to the *malakiyyas* of southern Sudanese towns, to the revolt of the White Flag League in 1924, and to battles fought in Ethiopia by the Sudan Defence Force during World War II. In many ways, the long struggle for a New Sudan, waged for decades by the Sudan People's Liberation Army (SPLA), is also an heir to this legacy. Indeed, following the 2005 Comprehensive Peace Agreement (CPA) between the Sudanese People's Liberation Movement (SPLM) and the Government of Sudan, it was the SPLM that compared rebel leader John Garang to Sudanese soldier and early nationalist 'Ali 'Abd al-Latif, whose father was himself one of this book's slaves of fortune – Sudanese soldiers that 113 years ago won the River War but were forgotten by history.

6.1 *Banner outside SPLM headquarters at the Khartoum Hilton in 2005. "Towards the New Sudan, 1924-2005." 'Ali 'Abd al-Latif and John Garang* (Photo © Douglas H. Johnson)

Notes

1. "Extract from the 'Lewa' of February 5, 1900," encl. in Cromer to Salisbury, 8 February 1900, NA WO 32/6383.
2. H. W. Jackson, typescript of evidence taken on 20 Feburary 1900, "Omdurman Mutiny. Evidence Before Court of Inquiry," NA WO 32/6383; Wingate to Cromer, 5 February 1900, encl. in Cromer to Salisbury, 10 February 1900, NA WO 32/6383. It is noteworthy that, according to the testimony taken by Jackson, the only company of the Sudanese XIth that "stood firm and not one man left the ranks" was No. 8 Company, under *yuzbashi* Muhammad Walad Dain, a "shulluk [*sic*] promoted from ranks."
3. "Extract from 'El Muayad' of February 6, 1900," encl. in Cromer to Salisbury, 8 February 1900, NA WO 32/6383; F. R. Wingate, "Notes for Memoirs," SAD 270/1/3-4, 7; Jackson, "Omdurman mutiny. Evidence before court of Inquiry," NA WO 32/6383.
4. "Extract from the 'Lewa' of February 5, 1900," NA WO 32/6383; Jackson, "Omdurman mutiny. Evidence before court of Inquiry," NA WO 32/6383; Wingate to Cromer, 5 February 1900, NA WO 32/6383.
5. Wingate to Cromer, 5 February 1900, NA WO 32/6383; Cromer to Salisbury, 8 February 1900, NA WO 32/6383; Wingate, "Notes for Memoirs," SAD 270/1/7.
6. Wingate, "Notes for Memoirs," SAD 270/1/2, 1, 6; M. W. Daly, "The Egyptian Army Mutiny at Omdurman, January–February 1900," *Bulletin of the British Society for Middle Eastern Studies*, Vol. 8, No. 1, 1981, 3-4.
7. Maxwell to Wingate, 26 December 1899, SAD 269/12, as quoted in Daly, "The Egyptian Army Mutiny at Omdurman," 5; Maxwell to Wingate, 19 January 1900, SAD 270/1/1, as quoted in Daly, "The Egyptian Army Mutiny at Omdurman," 5.
8. Wingate, "Notes for Memoirs," SAD 270/1/2.
9. S. Shoucair to Kitchener, 27 January 1900, "Report to the Sirdar," encl. in Cromer to Salisbury, 7 Febuary 1900, NA WO 32/6383.

10. Evelyn Wood to F. R. Wingate, 9 March 1900, SAD 270/3/4.
11. "Extract from the 'Lewa' of February 5, 1900," NA WO 32/6383.
12. "Extract from the 'Lewa' of February 4, 1900," encl. in Cromer to Salisbury, 8 February 1900, NA WO 32/6383
13. Ibid.
14. Wingate to Cromer, 10 May 1900, encl. in Cromer to Salisbury, 11 May 1900, NA WO 32/9180; Daly, "The Egyptian Army Mutiny at Omdurman," 4–5.
15. Wingate to Cromer, 5 Febaruary 1900, NA WO 32/6383.
16. "Rough Notes by Colonel Jackson," encl. in Cromer to Foreign Office, 17 February 1900, NA FO 78/5086, as quoted in Daly, "The Egyptian Army Mutiny at Omdurman," 5.
17. Wingate to Cromer, 10 May 1900, NA WO 32/9180.
18. "Extract from 'El Muayad' of February 6, 1900," NA WO 32/6383.
19. Jackson, "Omdurman mutiny. Evidence before court of Inquiry," NA WO 32/6383; Wingate to Cromer, 8 February 1900, encl. in Cromer to Salisbury, 10 February 1900, NA WO 32/6383.
20. Jackson, "Omdurman mutiny. Evidence before court of Inquiry," NA WO 32/6383.
21. Daly, "The Egyptian Army Mutiny at Omdurman," 6; Wingate, "Notes for Memoirs," SAD 270/1/4.
22. Cromer to Salisbury, 27 April 1900, NA FO 633/6/324, as quoted in Daly, "The Egyptian Army Mutiny at Omdurman," 9.
23. "Extract from the 'Lewa' of February 7, 1900," encl. in Cromer to Salisbury, 8 February 1900, NA WO 32/6383.
24. Jackson, "Omdurman mutiny. Evidence before court of Inquiry," NA WO 32/6383; Wingate to Cromer, 5 February 1900, NA WO 32/6383.
25. Jackson, "Omdurman mutiny. Evidence before court of Inquiry," NA WO 32/6383.
26. Wingate, "Notes for Memoirs," SAD 270/1/8.
27. Ibid.; Jackson, "Omdurman mutiny. Evidence before court of Inquiry," NA WO 32/6383.
28. Wingate to Cromer, 5 February 1900, NA WO 32/6383.
29. Daly, *Empire on the Nile*, 36.
30. "Extract from 'El Muayad' of February 6, 1900," NA WO 32/6383.
31. It is interesting to note, however, that in the fall of 1899 Angus Cameron, a British officer serving with the IXth Sudanese Battalion, wrote in a letter to his family: "If we only had the Cape to Cairo Railway open we might make a considerable diversion among the Boers, if we were to land a black brigade in Rhodesia." A. Cameron to his family, 5 November 1899, "In Pursuit of the Khalifa," SAD 622/6/4. This suggests that it may in fact have been a possiblility being discussed within Egyptian Army circles in the months immediately preceding the Omdurman mutiny.
32. Machell, "Memoirs of a Soudanese Soldier," *The Cornhill Magazine*, August 1896, 184.
33. Hill, *Egypt in the Sudan*, 82n2; Sikainga, *Slaves into Workers*, 17.
34. Hill and Hogg, *A Black Corps d'Elite*, 82–86; Dunn, *Khedive Ismail's Army*, 29; Sikainga, *Slaves into Workers*, 17. Interestingly, this was another rare instance when Sudanese soldiers seem to have collectively retained and expressed their ethnic identities, as the mutineers organized themselves by such categories as "Dinka," "Nuba," and "Fur." Na'um Shuqayr, *Ta'rikh al-Sudan* (Beirut: Dar al-Jil, 1981), 240–241, as cited in Kurita, "The Role of 'Negroid but Detribalized' People in Modern Sudanese History," 2.
35. Wood-Martin, *IXth Sudanese Regimental Historical Records*, SAD 110/11/5.
36. Jackson, *Behind the Modern Sudan*, 188.
37. Ibid., 188–190; Wingate to Cromer, 5 February 1900, NA WO 32/6383.
38. Jackson, *Behind the Modern Sudan*, 189. The *shaykhat el harimat* was a council of women, headed by a senior *shaykha*, by which grievances could be brought to the attention of company commanders.
39. Wingate to Cromer, 5 February 1900, NA WO 32/6383.
40. Wingate to Cromer, 22 February 1900, encl. in Cromer to Salisbury, 25 February 1900, NA WO 32/6383.
41. Wood to Wingate, 9 March 1900, SAD 270/3/4.
42. Wingate to Cromer, 5 February 1900, NA WO 32/6383.
43. Wingate, "Notes for Memoirs," SAD 270/1/4–5.
44. Ibid., 5–6; Wingate to Cromer, 5 February 1900, NA WO 32/6383.
45. Wingate, "Notes for Memoirs," SAD 270/1/6–7.
46. Wingate wrote that the "letter was never used by me, nor did I divulge its existence but the fact that it was in my possession precluded the possibility of collusion between the mutineers and the Palace." Wingate, "Notes for Memoirs," SAD 270/1/5.
47. "Extract from the 'Lewa' of February 5, 1900," NA WO 32/6383.
48. Ibid.

49. Wingate to Cromer, 6 February 1900, encl. in Cromer to Salisbury, 10 Feburary 1900, NA WO 32/6383.
50. Cromer to Wingate, 7 February 1900, encl. in Cromer to Salisbury, 10 Feburary 1900, NA WO 32/6383.
51. Wingate to Cromer, 8 February 1900, NA WO 32/6383.
52. Wingate to Cromer, 9 February 1900, encl. in Cromer to Salisbury, 10 Feburary 1900, NA WO 32/6383.
53. Jackson, "Omdurman mutiny. Evidence before court of Inquiry," NA WO 32/6383.
54. Cromer to Salisbury, 27 April 1900, NA FO 633/6/324, as quoted in Daly, "The Egyptian Army Mutiny at Omdurman," 9.
55. Wingate, "Notes for Memoirs," SAD 270/1/7–9.
56. Wingate to Cromer, 7–9 February 1900, NA WO 32/6383.
57. Wingate to Cromer, 6 February 1900, NA WO 32/6383.
58. Wingate to Cromer, 19 February 1900, encl. in Cromer to Salisbury, 25 February 1900, NA WO 32/6383.
59. Cromer to Wingate, 20 February 1900, encl. in Cromer to Salisbury, 25 February 1900, NA WO 32/6383.
60. Wingate to Cromer, 22 February 1900, NA WO 32/6383; Wingate to Cromer, 24 February 1900, encl. in Cromer to Salisbury, 25 February 1900, NA WO 32/6383.
61. Special Army Order, 24 February 1900, Omdurman, NA WO 32/6383; Jackson, "Omdurman mutiny. Evidence before court of Inquiry," NA WO 32/6383; see also Wingate to Cromer, 22 February 1900, NA WO 32/6383.
62. Wingate, "Notes for Memoirs," SAD 270/1/9; Wingate to Cromer, 24 February 1900, NA WO 32/6383.
63. Special Army Order, War Office, Cairo, 5 March 1900, encl. in Cromer to Salisbury, 7 March 1900, NA WO 32/6383.
64. H. W. Jackson, 25 February 1900, Omdurman, "Omdurman mutiny. Evidence before court of Inquiry," NA WO 32/6383.
65. Wingate to Cromer, 25 February 1900, NA WO 32/6383.
66. Cromer to Wingate, 20 February 1900, NA WO 32/6383.
67. Wingate to Cromer, 25 February 1900, NA WO 32/6383.
68. Wingate, "Notes for Memoirs," SAD 270/1/9.
69. Wingate to Cromer, 25 February 1900, NA WO 32/6383.

Bibliography

ARCHIVAL SOURCES

Sudan Archive, University of Durham (SAD)
Baily, Robin letter, SAD 533/6.
Cameron, Angus letters, SAD 622/6.
Clayton, Gilbert Falkingham letters, SAD 942/7.
Farley, James Jay Bleeker letters, SAD 304/2.
Franks, George McKenzie letters, SAD 403/2.
Hunter, Archibald letters, official despatches, and diary, SAD 1/2– 4; 2/5.
Longe, John typescript extracts from the diary of H. P. Creagh-Osborne, SAD 643/1.
Maxwell, John Grenfell scrapbook, SAD 401/1.
Parr, Martin Willoughby account of Um Dibaykarat, SAD 817/2.
Staveley, Cecil Minet letters and diary, SAD 637/2.
Wingate, Francis Reginald private papers, official correspondence, and copies of government documents: SAD 102/1; 106/1; 110/1, 12; 152/6; 155/2–3; 179/4, 6; 192/1; 216/1; 233/1, 5; 250/1; 252/2; 253/10; 254/1; 255/1; 257/1; 258/1; 261/1; 262/1; 263/1; 264/1; 266/1, 11; 267/1–3; 269/1–12; 270/1–3; 271/7–8; 272/3–5, 7; 273/8; 275/9; 276/3, 5; 277/1; 278/2–3, 5; 300/3; 430/6.
Wood-Martin, James Isidore, IXth Sudanese Regimental Historical Records, SAD 110/11.
Intelligence Reports, Egypt (*IRE*), Nos. 1–59.
Sudan Intelligence Report (*SIR*), No. 60.

The National Archives of the United Kingdom (NA)
FO 78/4775: General Correspondence, Ottoman Empire: Nile Expedition. Telegrams to and from Lord Salisbury, 1896.
FO 78/4892–4895, 5049–5052: General Correspondence, Ottoman Empire: Nile Expedition, Vols. 1–8, 1896–1899.
FO 141: Embassy and Consulates, Egypt: General Correspondence, 1896–1898.
FO 407/31: Reorganization of Egypt. Further Correspondence, January–May 1883.
FO 407/155: Affairs of Egypt. Further Correspondence Part LVIII, 1900.
FO 633/57: Cromer Papers, Egypt: Efficiency and Gallantry of Native Egyptian Troops; Operations in the Sudan, 1887.
FO 633/68: Cromer Papers, Egypt: Conduct of British and Egyptian troops after Battle

of Omdurman; Expenditure on Military Operations in the Sudan, 1899.
PRO 30/57/1: Sir Evelyn Wood. Invitations to Join Egyptian Army, 1882.
PRO 30/57/9: Kitchener Papers: Miscellaneous Printed Reports, Egypt 1891–1914.
PRO 30/57/10: Kitchener Papers: Correspondence, 1894–1913.
PRO 30/57/11: Kitchener Papers: Sudan 1896–1899, Telegrams Relating to the Conquest.
PRO 30/57/14: Kitchener Papers: Sudan, The Conquest and Aftermath 1897–1904, Correspondence with Lord Cromer.
PRO 30/57/16: Kitchener Papers: Correspondence, Queen Victoria to Lord Kitchener, 1899–1901.
PRO 30/86/6: Letters from Gen. Sir Evelyn Wood from London and Cairo, 1881–1885.
WO 32/5552: Sudan: Stationing of Forces at Khartoum or Omdurman: Expenditure Involved and Fears of High Incidence of Disease among Troops, 1898–1899.
WO 32/6142: Report by Major General H. Kitchener Relating to Dongola Expedition and Capture of Firket, Sudan, 1896.
WO 32/6143: Nile Expedition: Report of Operations and on Situation with Plans. Battles of Omdurman, Khartoum and Atbara, 1898–1900.
WO 32/6380: Sudan Campaign: Military Situation; Disposition of British and Egyptian Forces. Future Operations, 1897–1898.
WO 32/6383: Omdurman Mutiny: Insubordination by Officers of Egyptian Army. Proceedings and Sentences of Court of Enquiry, 1900.
WO 32/8417: Report on Mutiny of Soudanese Troops in Uganda and Papers Relating to Events in the Protectorate, 1897–1899.
WO 32/9180–9181: Egypt: Rules for Employment of British Officers with Egyptian Army, 1900.
WO 33/56: Letters Respecting Operations in Egypt; Remarks on Reconquest of the Soudan, 1896.
WO 33/148: Correspondence on the Nile Expedition–Battle of Khartoum, 1898.
WO 106/15: Staff Diary and Intelligence: Commanding Officers and Intelligence Officers in Sudan – Operations against Dervishes, 21 July 1889 – 17 Feb 1892.
WO 106/6236: General Military Report: Egyptian Sudan 1891, 1892.
WO 106/6306: Notes on the Egyptian Army, 1901.

National Army Museum (NAM)
Anley, Frederick Gore letters, NAM 1984-12-50-29–60.
Burn-Murdoch, John Francis letters and diaries, NAM 1986-05-26-1, 9–17.
Cameron, Neville letters, NAM 1983-05-55-1.
Churcher, Douglas Wilfred diary, NAM 1978-04-53-1.
Cooper, Henry papers, NAM 1961-12-190-1.
Dunn, H. N. diaries, NAM 1974-09-80-1–3.
Egerton, G. G. A. diary, NAM 1968-07-172-1.
Fitton, Hugh Gregory letters, NAM 1994-10-42-1.
Graeme, David Henry letter on the Battle of Omdurman, NAM 2006-04-33-1.
Granville, Dennis letter describing the Battle of Omdurman, NAM 2004-03-31-1.
Grieve, Colin John Fraser letters, NAM 1979-06-139-1.
Hodgson, Hamilton letters, NAM 2003-08-8-1–3.
Hunter, N. H. Historical Records of the Tenth Sudanese,1886–1910, NAM 1968-07-330-1.
Jackson, H. W. Fashoda Intelligence Diary, NAM 2001-10-117-1.
Kitchener, H. H. letters to Evelyn Wood, 1897–1898, NAM 1968-07-234-1.
Lewis, David Francis typescript Sudan Campaign journal, NAM 1975-03-9-1.
Loch, Edward Douglas diary, NAM 1986-08-66-1.
Meiklejohn, Ronald Forbes diary and typescript account, NAM 1974-04-36-1–4.

Milner, Harry account, "He Soldiered Under Kitchener," NAM 1992-08-339-1.
Mitford, Bertram diaries, NAM 1987-11-127-8–10.
Prince Christian Victor letter on the Battle of Omdurman, NAM 1980-06-19-91.
Ready, Felix diary, NAM 1966-09-142.
Royal Warwickshire Regiment senior NCO 1898 letter, NAM 1998-06-144-1.
Sandelands, James letters, NAM 1996-08-384-2.
Skinner, George diary, NAM 1979-09-15-3.
Stephens, Reginald Byng letters, NAM 1989-02-201-81–82.
Teigh, George journal, NAM 1997-04-123-1.
Trotter, Edward Henry letters, NAM 1985-02-22-2.
Unsworth, A. letter extracts, NAM 233/5/7.
Watson, J. K. letters and diaries, NAM 1983-04-112-1–2; 1984-12-4-6–8.

National Records Office, Khartoum (NRO)
Disciplinary and Military Courts, Frontier, 1888–1898, CAIRINT 1/23/116–118.
Organization of Sudanese Battalions Egyptian Army, 1888–1889, CAIRINT 1/25/127.
Enlistment of Sudanese for Service in German East Africa, 1891, CAIRINT 1/33/185.
States of Expeditionary Force, 1896, CAIRINT 1/45/268.
Dongola Expedition, 1896, CAIRINT 1/46/273–275.
Battle of Atbara, 1898, CAIRINT 1/55/311.
The Atbara Expedition, 1898, CAIRINT 1/58/314–316.
Battle of Atbara, 1898, CAIRINT 1/60/318–320.
Khartoum Expedition and the Battle of Omdurman, 1898, 1/61/321–323.
List of People Entitled to Medals, 1899, CAIRINT 1/67/346.
Claims of Sudanese Soldiers at Mombasa against British Government, 1899, CAIRINT 1/67/349.
Schemes for Dongola Campaign, 1896, CAIRINT 3/7/128.
Report on Province of Dongola, 1897, CAIRINT 3/7/145.
Report on the Re-occupation of Abu Hamed, 1897, CAIRINT 3/7/146.
Report on Sudanese and Zulus as Soldiers, CAIRINT 10/10/44.
Despatch Respecting Conduct of Troops after Omdurman, PALACE 1/3/51.
Petitions by Old Soldiers, 1944–1946, PALACE 4/8/41.
Settlement of Native Ex-Officers Retired during and after 1931, SECURITY 8/3/8.

Newspaper Reading Room, British Library (BL)
Black & White, 1896–1898.
The Daily Graphic, 1896–1898.
The Graphic, 1896–1898.
The Times, 1896–1898.

PUBLISHED PRIMARY SOURCES

Alford, Henry S. and W. Dennistoun Sword. *The Egyptian Soudan: Its Loss and Recovery.* London: Macmillan and Co., Ltd., 1898.
An Officer [unknown]. *A Short Account of the Work of the Egyptian Cavalry During the Atbara and Omdurman Campaigns.* London: Published at the Royal United Service Institution, Whitehall, 1910.
An Officer [H. L. Pritchard]. *Sudan Campaign, 1896–1899.* London: Chapman & Hall, 1899.
"Anthropometric Investigations among the Native Troops of the Egyptian Army – Interim Report of the Committee." *Report of the Seventy-Second Meeting of the British*

Association for the Advancement of Science, Belfast, September 1902. London: John Murray, 1903, 350–352.
Army List. Cairo: War Office Printing Press, 1883–1899.
Artin, Yacoub. *England in the Sudan*. London: Macmillan and Co., Ltd., 1911.
Atteridge, A. Hilliard. *Towards Khartoum: The Story of the Soudan War of 1896*. London: A.D. Innes & Co., 1897.
Bedri, Babikr. *The Memoirs of Babikr Bedri*. Vol. 1. Trans. Yousef Bedri and George Scott. London: Oxford University Press, 1969.
———. *The Memoirs of Babikr Bedri*. Vol. 2. Trans. Yusuf Bedri and Peter Hogg. London: Ithaca Press, 1980.
Bennett, Ernest N. "After Omdurman." *The Contemporary Review* 75 (1899): 18–33.
———. *The Downfall of the Dervishes, or The Avenging of Gordon, Being the Personal Narrative of the Final Soudan Campaign of 1898*. London: Methuen & Co., 1899.
Besant, W. H. "The Early Days of the Egyptian Army, 1883–1892." *Journal of the African Society* 33/131 (1934): 160–172.
Bredin, G. R. F. "The Life-Story of Yuzbashi 'Abdullah Adlan." *Sudan Notes and Records* XLII (1961): 37–52.
Budge, Ernest Alfred Wallis. *The Egyptian Sudan: Its History and Monuments*. 2 vols. London: Kegan, Paul, Trench, Trubner & Co., 1907.
Bull, René. *Black and White War Albums*. London: Black and White Printing and Publishing Company, 1898.
Burleigh, Bennet. *Khartoum Campaign 1898, or the Re-Conquest of the Soudan*. London: Chapman & Hall, Ltd., 1899.
———. *Sirdar and Khalifa, or The Re-Conquest of the Soudan, 1898*. London: Chapman & Hall, Ltd., 1898.
Churchill, Winston Spencer. *The River War: An Historical Account of the Reconquest of the Soudan*. London: Longmans, Green, and Co., 1899.
———. *The River War: The Reconquest of the Sudan*. London: New English Library Ltd., 1973.
Civil Police. Khartoum: Sudan Government, 1901.
Cromer, The Earl of. *Modern Egypt*. 2 vols. London: Macmillan and Co., Ltd., 1908.
"Egyptian Military Cadets: The Training School at Cairo." *The Navy and Army Illustrated*, 4 October 1902.
Emily, Jules. *Mission Marchand: Journal du Route*. Paris: Hachette, 1913.
Giffen, J. Kelly. *The Egyptian Sudan*. New York: Fleming H. Revell Company, 1905.
Gleichen, Lieut.-Colonel Count, ed. *The Anglo-Egyptian Sudan: A Compendium Prepared by Officers of the Sudan Government*. London: Printed for His Majesty's Stationery Office by Harrison and Sons, 1905.
———. *Handbook of the Sudan*. London: Intelligence Division, War Office, 1898.
———. *With the Camel Corps up the Nile*. West Yorkshire, England: EP Publishing Limited, 1975. First published in 1888.
Haggard, Andrew. *Under Crescent and Star*. Edinburgh and London: William Blackwood and Sons, 1895.
Handbook of the Egyptian Army. London: Eyre and Spottiswoode, 1912.
Hill, Richard. *On the Frontiers of Islam: Two Manuscripts Concerning the Sudan under Turco-Egyptian Rule, 1822–1845*. Oxford: Clarendon Press, 1970.
Hope, A. C. "The Adventurous Life of Faraj Sadik." *Sudan Notes and Records* XXXII (1951): 154–158.
Hopkinson, H. C. B. "The Sirdar's Camel Corps." *The Cornhill Magazine*, April 1899, 434–448.
Instructions to Land Commissions. Omdurman: Sudan Government, 1899.
Jackson, H. W. "Fashoda, 1898." *Sudan Notes and Records* III, No. 1 (1920): 1–11.

Knight, E. F. *Letters from the Sudan*. London: Macmillan and Co., Ltd., 1897.
Kootz-Kretschmer, Elise. "Tatu, das geraubte Muvembakind." Herrnhut: Missionsbuchhandlung, 1927.
Lugard, Frederick John Dealtry. *The Rise and Fall of Our East African Empire: Early Efforts in Nyasaland and Uganda*. Vol. 2. Edinburgh and London: William Blackwood and Sons, 1893.
Machell, Percy. "Memoirs of a Soudanese Soldier (Ali Effendi Gifoon)." *The Cornhill Magazine* n.s. 1 (July–October 1896): 30–40; 175–187; 326–338; 484–492.
Maxse, F. I. *Seymour Vandeleur, Lieutenant-Colonel, Scots Guards & Irish Guards: A Plain Narrative of the Part Played by British Officers in the Acquisition of Colonies and Dependencies in Africa Representing a Dominion of Greater Extent than India Added to the British Empire in Less Than Twenty Years*. London: William Heinemann, 1906.
Meldon, J. A. "Notes on the Sudanese in Uganda." *Journal of the Royal African Society* 7/26 (1908): 123–146.
Milner, Alfred. *England in Egypt*. London: Edward Arnold, 1892.
———. *England in Egypt*. London: Darf Publishers Limited, 1986. Reprint of 1901 edition.
Mitford, B. R. "Extracts from the Diary of a Subaltern on the Nile in the Eighties and Nineties." *Sudan Notes and Records* XVIII (1935): 167–193; XIX (1936): 199–231; XX (1937): 63–89.
Naʻum Shuqayr (Naum Shoucair). *Taʼrikh al-Sudan al-qadim waʼl-hadith wa jughrafiyatuhu*. Cairo: al-Maarif Press, 1903.
Neufeld, Charles. *A Prisoner of the Khaleefa: Twelve Years' Captivity at Omdurman*. London: Chapman & Hall, 1899.
Ordinances, Promulgated by the Governor-General of the Sudan, 1899–1905. Cairo: Al-Mokattam Printing Office, 1907.
Prince, Magdalene von. *Eine Deutsche Frau im Innern Deutsch-Ostafrika*. Berlin: Mittler, 1903.
Regulations and Instructions for British Officers serving with the Egyptian Army. Cairo: War Office, 1911.
Repington, Charles à Court. *Vestigia*. London: Constable and Company Ltd., 1919.
Seligman, B. Z. "On the Origins of the Egyptian Zar." *Folklore* 25 (1914): 300–323.
Slatin, Rudolf. *Fire and Sword in the Sudan*. London: Edward Arnold, 1896.
Smith-Dorrien, Horace. *Memories of Forty-Eight Years' Service*. London: John Murray, 1925.
Soudanese Ex-Soldiers for Civil Police. Omdurman: Sudan Government, 1901.
Steevens, G. W. *With Kitchener to Khartum*. New York: Dodd, Mead & Company, 1899.
The Sudan Civil Justice Ordinance 1900. Cairo: National Printing Office, 1900.
The Sudan Code of Criminal Procedure. Cairo: National Printing Office, 1899.
The Sudan Penal Code. Cairo: National Printing Office, 1899.
Thruston, Arthur Blyford. *African Incidents: Personal Experiences in Egypt and Unyoro*. London: John Murray, 1900.
Villiard, O. G. "The Army of the Khedive and the Present Military Situation in Egypt." *United Service Review* XIV/3 (September 1895): 201–212.
Watkins, Owen S. *With Kitchener's Army: Being a Chaplain's Experiences with the Nile Expedition, 1898*. London: Partridge, 1899.
Westermann, Diedrich. *The Shilluk People: Their Language and Folklore*. Philadelphia: The Board of Foreign Missions of the United Presbyterian Church of N.A., 1912.
Wingate, F. R. *Mahdiism and the Egyptian Sudan: Being an Account of the Rise and Progress of Mahdiism, and of the Subsequent Events in the Sudan to the Present Time*. London: Frank Cass & Co. Ltd., 1891.

Wright, H. C. Seppings. *Soudan, '96: The Adventures of a War Artist*. London: Horace Cox, 1897.

SECONDARY WORKS

'Abd al-Wahhab, Ahmad 'Abd al-Rahman. *Tushkı: Dirasa tarıkhiyya li-hamlat al-Nujumı 'ala Masr*. Khartoum: Khartoum University Press, 1973.

Abu Salim, Muhammad Ibrahim, ed. *Al-Athar al-kamila li'l-Imam al-Mahdi*. 7 vols. Khartoum: Khartoum University Press, 1990–1994.

Adams, William Y. *Nubia: Corridor to Africa*. Princeton: Princeton University Press, 1977.

Anglesey, The Marquess of. *A History of the British Cavalry, 1816–1919*. Volume III: 1872–1898. London: Leo Cooper, 1982.

Arthur, George. *Life of Lord Kitchener*. Volume I. London: Macmillan, 1920.

Asher, Michael. *Khartoum: The Ultimate Imperial Adventure*. London: Penguin Books Ltd., 2005.

Balamoan, G. Ayoub. *Migration Policies in the Anglo-Egyptian Sudan, 1884–1956*. Cambridge, MA: Harvard University Center for Population Studies, 1976.

Barthorp, Michael. *War on the Nile: Britain, Egypt and the Sudan, 1882–1898*. Dorset, United Kingdom: Blandford Press, 1984.

Bates, Darrell. *The Fashoda Incident of 1898: Encounter on the Nile*. Oxford: Oxford University Press, 1984.

Baumann, Gerd. *National Integration and Local Integrity: The Miri of the Nuba Mountains in the Sudan*. Oxford: Clarendon Press, 1987.

Baynes, John. *Far from a Donkey*. London: Brassey's Ltd., 1995.

Boddy, Janice. *Wombs and Alien Spirits: Women, Men, and the Zar Cult in Northern Sudan*. Madison: The University of Wisconsin Press, 1989.

Cannadine, David. *Ornamentalism: How the British Saw Their Empire*. London: Oxford University Press, 2001.

Cecil, Hugh. "British Correspondents and the Sudan Campaign of 1896–98." *Sudan: The Reconquest Reappraised*. Ed. Edward Spiers. London: Frank Cass Publishers, 1998, 102–127.

Clayton, Anthony and David Killingray. *Khaki and Blue: Military and Police in British Colonial Africa*. Athens, OH: Ohio University Center for International Studies, 1989.

Collins, Robert O. *Land Beyond the Rivers: The Southern Sudan, 1898–1918*. New Haven, CT: Yale University Press, 1971.

———. "The Nilotic Slave Trade: Past and Present." *Slavery and Abolition*, April 1992, 140–161.

———. *The Southern Sudan, 1883–1898: A Struggle for Control*. New Haven, CT: Yale University Press, 1962.

Constantinides, P. M. "Sickness and the Spirits: A Study of the Zaar Spirit-Possession Cult in the Northern Sudan." Ph.D. thesis, University of London, 1972.

Crone, Patricia. *Slaves on Horses: The Evolution of the Islamic Polity*. Cambridge: Cambridge University Press, 1980.

Curtin, Philip D. *Disease and Empire: The Health of European Troops in the Conquest of Africa*. Cambridge: Cambridge University Press, 1998.

Daly, M. W. "The Egyptian Army Mutiny at Omdurman, January–February 1900." *Bulletin of the British Society for Middle Eastern Studies* 8, No. 1 (1981): 3–12.

———. *Empire on the Nile: The Anglo-Egyptian Sudan, 1898–1934*. Cambridge: Cambridge University Press, 1986.

———. *The Sirdar: Sir Reginald Wingate and the British Empire in the Middle East*. Philadelphia: American Philosophical Society, 1997.

Bibliography

Dunn, John P. *Khedive Ismail's Army*. London: Routledge, 2005.

Echenberg, Myron J. *Colonial Conscripts: The Tirailleurs Sénégalais in French West Africa, 1857–1960*. Portsmouth, NH: Heinemann, 1991.

Emery, Frank. *Marching Over Africa: Letters from Victorian Soldiers*. London: Hodder and Stoughton, 1986.

Enloe, Cynthia H. *Ethnic Soldiers: State Security in Divided Societies*. Athens, GA: The University of Georgia Press, 1980.

Ewald, Janet J. *Soldiers, Traders, and Slaves: State Formation and Economic Transformation in the Greater Nile Valley, 1700–1885*. Madison, WI: The University of Wisconsin Press, 1990.

Fahmy, Khaled. *All the Pasha's Men: Mehmed Ali, His Army, and the Making of Modern Egypt*. Cambridge: Cambridge University Press, 1997.

Farwell, Byron. *Mr. Kipling's Army*. New York: W. W. Norton & Company, 1981.

———. *Prisoners of the Mahdi: The Story of the Mahdist Revolt from the Fall of Khartoum to the Reconquest of the Sudan by Kitchener Fourteen Years Later, and of the Daily Lives and Sufferings in Captivity of Three European Prisoners, a Soldier, a Merchant and a Priest*. London: Longmans, 1967.

Featherstone, Donald. *Omdurman 1898: Kitchener's Victory in the Sudan*. London: Osprey, 1993.

Glassman, Jonathon. *Feasts and Riot: Revelry, Rebellion, and Popular Consciousness on the Swahili Coast, 1856–1888*. Portsmouth, NH: Heinemann, 1995.

Gooch, G. P. and Harold Temperley, eds. *British Documents on the Origins of the War, 1898–1914*. Vol. I. London: H.M.S.O., 1926.

Gray, Richard. *A History of Southern Sudan, 1839–1889*. Oxford: Oxford University Press, 1961.

Green, Dominic. *Three Empires on the Nile: The Victorian Jihad, 1869–1899*. New York: Free Press, 2007.

Harries-Jenkins, Gwyn. *The Army in Victorian Society*. London: Routledge & Kegan Paul, 1977.

Harrington, Peter and Frederic A. Sharf, eds. *Omdurman 1898: The Eye-Witnesses Speak*. London: Greenhill Books, 1998.

Harrington, Peter. "Images and Perceptions: Visualizing the Sudan Campaign." In *Sudan: The Reconquest Reappraised*. Ed. Edward Spiers. London: Frank Cass Publishers, 1998, 82–101.

Hill, Richard. *A Biographical Dictionary of the Anglo-Egyptian Sudan*. London: Oxford University Press, 1951.

———. *Egypt in the Sudan, 1820–1881*. London: Oxford University Press, 1959.

Hill, Richard and Peter Hogg. *A Black Corps d'Elite: An Egyptian Sudanese Conscript Battalion with the French Army in Mexico, 1863–1867, and Its Survivors in Subsequent African History*. East Lansing: Michigan State University Press, 1995.

Holt, P. M. and M. W. Daly. *The History of the Sudan: From the Coming of Islam to the Present Day*. 3rd edition. Boulder, CO: Westview Press, 1979.

———. *A History of the Sudan: From the Coming of Islam to the Present Day*. Harlow, England: Pearson Education Ltd., 2000.

———. *The Mahdist State in the Sudan, 1881–1898: A Study of Its Origins, Development and Overthrow*. 2nd edition. Oxford: Clarendon Press, 1970.

Hunter, Archie. *Kitchener's Sword-Arm: The Life and Campaigns of General Sir Archibald Hunter*. Staplehurst, United Kingdom: Spellmount Limited, 1996.

Isaacman, Allen F. and Barbara S. *Slavery and Beyond: The Making of Men and Chikunda Ethnic Identities in the Unstable World of South-Central Africa, 1750–1920*. Portsmouth, NH: Heinemann, 2004.

Jackson, H. C. *Behind the Modern Sudan*. London: Macmillan & Co., 1955.

———. *The Fighting Sudanese*. London: Macmillan & Co., 1954.
James, Wendy. "The Funj Mystique: Approaches to a Problem of Sudan History." In *Text and Context: The Social Anthropology of Tradition*. Ed. Ravindra K. Jain. Philadelphia: Institute for the Study of Human Issues, 1977, 95–133.
———. "Perceptions from an African Slaving Frontier." In *Slavery and Other Forms of Unfree Labour*. Ed. Léonie J. Archer. London and New York: Routledge, 1988, 130–141.
Johnson, Douglas H. "Conquest and Colonisation: Soldier Settlers in the Sudan and Uganda." *Sudan Notes and Records* NS 4 (2000): 59–79.
———. "Recruitment and Entrapment in Private Slave Armies: The Structure of the Zara'ib in the Southern Sudan." *Slavery and Abolition*, April 1992, 162–173.
———. "The Structure of a Legacy: Military Slavery in Northeast Africa." *Ethnohistory* 36, No. 1 (Winter 1989): 72–88.
———. "Sudanese Military Slavery from the 18th to the 20th Century." In *Slavery and Other Forms of Unfree Labour*. Ed. Léonie J. Archer. London: Routledge, 1988, 142–156.
———. "Tribe or Nationality? The Sudanese Diaspora and the Kenyan Nubis." *Journal of East African Studies* Vol. 3, No. 1, March 2009, 112–131.
Kapteijns, Lidwien. *Mahdist Faith and Sudanic Tradition: The History of the Masalit Sultanate, 1870–1930*. Boston and London: Routledge and Kegan Paul, 1985.
Kenyon, Susan M. *Five Women of Sennar: Culture and Change in Central Sudan*. Oxford: Clarendon Press, 1991.
Keown-Boyd, Henry. *A Good Dusting: A Centenary Review of the Sudan Campaigns, 1883–1899*. London: Leo Cooper, 1986.
———. *Soldiers of the Nile: A Biographical History of British Officers of the Egyptian Army, 1882–1925*. Thornbury, UK: Thornbury Publications, 1996.
Killingray, David. "Gender Issues and African Colonial Armies." In *Guardians of Empire: The Armed Forces of the Colonial Powers, c. 1700–1964*. Eds. David Killingray and David Omissi. Manchester: Manchester University Press, 1999, 221–248.
———. "Labour Exploitation for Military Campaigns in British Colonial Africa, 1870–1945." *Journal of Contemporary History* 24, No. 3 (1989): 483–501.
———. "The 'Rod of Empire': The Debate over Corporal Punishment in the British African Colonial Forces, 1888–1946." *The Journal of African History* 35, No. 2 (1994): 201–216.
Killingray, David and David Omissi, eds. *Guardians of Empire: The Armed Forces of the Colonial Powers, c. 1700–1964*. Manchester: Manchester University Press, 1999.
Kramer, Robert S. *Holy City on the Nile: Omdurman during the Mahdiyya, 1885–1898*. Princeton: Markus Wiener, 2010.
———. "Holy City on the Nile: Omdurman, 1885–1898." Ph.D. dissertation, Northwestern University, 1991.
Kurita, Yoshiko. "The Concept of Nationalism in the White Flag League Movement." In *The Nationalist Movement in Sudan*. Ed. Mahasin Abdelgadir Hag al Safi. Khartoum: Institute of African and Asian Studies, 1989, 14–62.
———. "The Life of 'Ali 'Abd al-Latif." Draft, Tokyo, 1996.
———. "The Role of 'Negroid but Detribalized' People in Modern Sudanese History." *Nilo-Ethiopian Studies* No. 8–9, 2003, 1–11.
Lawler, Nancy Ellen. *Soldiers of Misfortune: Ivoirien Tirailleurs of World War Two*. Athens, OH: Ohio University Press, 1992.
Leopold, Mark. "Legacies of Slavery in North-West Uganda: The Story of the 'One-Elevens'." *Africa: Journal of the International African Institute* Vol. 76, No. 2 (2006): 180–199.
Lewis, David Levering. *The Race to Fashoda: Colonialism and African Resistance*. New York: Henry Holt and Company, Inc., 1987.

Lovejoy, Paul E., ed. *The Ideology of Slavery in Africa*. Beverly Hills and London: Sage Publications, 1981.

———. *Transformations in Slavery: A History of Slavery in Africa*. Cambridge: Cambridge University Press, 1983.

Lunn, Joe. *Memoirs of the Maelstrom: A Senegalese Oral History of the First World War*. Portsmouth, NH: Heinemann, 1999.

Makris, G. P. *Changing Masters: Spirit Possession and Identity Construction among Slave Descendants and Other Subordinates in the Sudan*. Evanston, Illinois: Northwestern University Press, 2000.

McGregor, Andrew. *A Military History of Modern Egypt: From the Ottoman Conquest to the Ramadan War*. Westport, Connecticut: Praeger Security International, 2006.

Meredith, John, ed. *Omdurman Diaries, 1898: Eyewitness Accounts of the Legendary Campaign*. Great Britain: Leo Cooper Ltd., 1998.

Miers, Suzanne and Igor Kopytoff, eds. *Slavery in Africa: Historical and Anthropological Perspectives*. Madison: University of Wisconsin Press, 1977.

Moore-Harell, Alice. "The Turco-Egyptian Army in Sudan on the Eve of the Mahdiyya, 1877–1880." *International Journal of Middle East Studies* 31, No. 1 (1999): 19–37.

Moyse-Bartlett, Hubert. *The King's African Rifles: A Study in the Military History of East and Central Africa, 1890–1945*. Aldershot: Gale and Polden, 1956.

Neillands, Robin. *The Dervish Wars: Gordon and Kitchener in the Sudan, 1880–1898*. London: John Murray, 1996.

O'Fahey, R. S. "Fur and Fartit: The History of a Frontier." In *Culture History in the Southern Sudan: Archaeology, Linguistics, and Ethnohistory*. Eds. John Mack and Peter Robertshaw. Nairobi: British Institute in Eastern Africa, 1982, 75–87.

O'Fahey, R. S. and J. L. Spaulding. *Kingdoms of the Sudan*. London: Methuen & Co Ltd, 1974.

Pakenham, Thomas. *The Scramble for Africa: White Man's Conquest of the Dark Continent from 1876 to 1912*. New York: Avon Books, 1991.

Parsons, Timothy H. *The African Rank-and-File: Social Implications of Colonial Military Service in the King's African Rifles, 1942–1964*. Oxford: James Currey, 1999.

———. "'Kibera is our Blood': The Sudanese Military Legacy in Nairobi's Kibera Location, 1902–1968." *International Journal of African Historical Studies* 30, No. 1 (1997): 87–122.

Patterson, Orlando. *Slavery and Social Death: A Comparative Study*. Cambridge, MA: Harvard University Press, 1982.

Pipes, Daniel. *Slave Soldiers and Islam: The Genesis of a Military System*. New Haven and London: Yale University Press, 1981.

Powell, Eve M. Troutt. *A Different Shade of Colonialism: Egypt, Great Britain, and the Mastery of the Sudan*. Berkeley and Los Angeles: University of California Press, 2003.

Prunier, Gérard. "Military Slavery in the Sudan during the Turkiyya, 1820–1885." *Slavery and Abolition*, April 1992, 129–139.

al-Qaddal, Muhammad Sa'id. *Al-siyasa al-iqtisadiyya li'l-dawla al-Mahdiyya, 1881–1898*. Khartoum: Khartoum University Press, 1986.

Robinson, Ronald and John Gallagher, with Alice Denny. *Africa and the Victorians: The Official Mind of Imperialism*. London: Macmillan, 1961.

Royle, Trevor. *Fighting Mac: The Downfall of Major-General Sir Hector Macdonald*. Edinburgh and London: Mainstream Publishing, 2003.

———. *The Kitchener Enigma*. London: Michael Joseph, 1985.

Said, Edward. *Orientalism*. New York: Pantheon Books, 1978.

Sanderson, G. N. *England, Europe and the Upper Nile, 1882–1899*. Edinburgh: Edinburgh University Press, 1965.

Sanderson, Lilian Passmore and Neville Sanderson. *Education, Religion & Politics in Southern Sudan, 1899–1964*. London: Ithaca Press, 1981.

Sandes, E. W. C. *The Royal Engineers in Egypt and the Sudan*. Chatham: The Institution of Royal Engineers, 1937.

Shaw, Ian. *The Oxford History of Ancient Egypt*. Oxford: Oxford University Press, 2000.

Sikainga, Ahmad Alawad. "Military Slavery and the Emergence of a Southern Sudanese Diaspora in the Northern Sudan, 1884–1954." In *White Nile, Black Blood: War, Leadership, and Ethnicity from Khartoum to Kampala*. Eds. Jay Spaulding and Stephanie Beswick. Lawrenceville, NJ: The Red Sea Press, Inc., 2000, 23–37.

———. *Slaves into Workers: Emancipation and Labor in Colonial Sudan*. Austin: University of Texas Press, 1996.

———. *Sudan Defence Force: Origin and Role, 1925–1955*. Khartoum: Institute of African and Asian Studies, 1983.

Spaulding, Jay. *The Heroic Age of Sinnar*. Trenton, NJ: The Red Sea Press, 2007.

———. "Slavery, Land Tenure and Social Class in the Northern Turkish Sudan." *The International Journal of African Historical Studies* Vol. 15, No. 1 (1982): 1–20.

Spiers, Edward M. "Campaigning under Kitchener." In *Sudan: The Reconquest Reappraised*. Ed. Edward M. Spiers. London: Frank Cass Publishers, 1998, 54–81.

———. *The Late Victorian Army, 1868–1902*. Manchester and New York: Manchester University Press, 1992.

———, ed. *Sudan: The Reconquest Reappraised*. London: Frank Cass Publishers, 1998.

———. *The Victorian Soldier in Africa*. Manchester: Manchester University Press, 2004.

Streets, Heather. *Martial Races: The Military, Race and Masculinity in British Imperial Culture, 1857–1914*. Manchester: Manchester University Press, 2004.

Theobald, Alan Buchan. *The Mahdiya: A History of the Anglo-Egyptian Sudan, 1881–1899*. London: Longmans, Green and Company, 1951.

Thompson, Edward Palmer. *The Making of the English Working Class*. London: Victor Gollancz, 1963.

Thorburn, D. Hay. "Sudanese Soldiers' Songs." *Journal of the Royal African Society* Vol. 24, No. 96 (July 1925): 314–321.

Trustram, Myna. *Women of the Regiment: Marriage and the Victorian Army*. Cambridge: Cambridge University Press, 1984.

Udal, John O. *The Nile in Darkness: A Flawed Unity, 1863–1899*. Wilby, UK: Michael Russell Ltd., 2005.

Vezzadini, Elena. "The 1924 Revolution: Hegemony, Resistance, and Nationalism in the Colonial Sudan." Ph.D. dissertation, University of Bergen, 2007.

Warburg, Gabriel. "Ideological and Practical Considerations Regarding Slavery in the Mahdist State and the Anglo-Egyptian Sudan: 1881–1918." In *The Ideology of Slavery*. Ed. Paul Lovejoy. Beverly Hills and London: Sage Publications, 1981, 245–269.

Warner, Philip. *Dervish: The Rise and Fall of an African Empire*. London: Macdonald and Jane's, 1973.

Willis, John Ralph, ed. *Slaves and Slavery in Muslim Africa*. 2 vols. London: Frank Cass, 1985.

Woods, Frederick, ed. *Young Winston's Wars: The Original Despatches of Winston S. Churchill, 1897–1900*. London: Leo Cooper Ltd., 1972.

Wright, Marcia. *Strategies of Slaves and Women: Life-Stories from East/Central Africa*. New York and London: Lilian Barber Press and James Currey Press, 1993.

Wright, Patricia. *Conflict on the Nile: The Fashoda Incident of 1898*. London: Heinemann, 1972.

Ziegler, Philip. *Omdurman*. New York: Alfred A. Knopf, 1974.

Zulfo, 'Ismat Hasan. *Karari: The Sudanese Account of the Battle of Omdurman*. London: Frederick Warne, 1980.

Index

Aba Island 48
Abbas Hilmi II (Khedive) 1, 47, 95, 109; role in 1900 Omdurman mutiny, 190–1, 195–8
Abbassia: Egyptian Army barracks 23, 26; ex-soldier settlement colony 112
'Abd al-Hamid Mirsal 117 n.133
'Abd al-Hamid Shukri 192, 200
'Abd al-Latif Ahmad ('Ali 'Abd-al-Latif's father) 31, 201
'Abd al-Rahman 'Abd al-Radi 117 n.133
'Abd al-Rahman al-Nujumi 31, 37, 43 n.100, 64
'Abd al-Wahab Beheri 117 n.133
'Abd er Rauf Besim 176
'Abdallah Adam 34
'Abdallah 'Adlan: autobiographical account 5, **22**; enrollment into the Egyptian Army 16; early military career 21–3, 175; return to Egypt 47; battalion assignments in new Egyptian Army 28; on conditions of service 32, 72, 73, 75, 90, 93, 109; at Battle of Toski 37; at Akasha prior to advance on Dongola 38; at Battle of Firket 56; as headman of *Redif* settlement 112; on Sudanese battalion bands 140, 153 n.86; recollection of Atbara 144–5; at Battle of Omdurman 176
'Abdallah Ahmad 34
'Abdallah Hamza 65–6
'Abdallah Isma'il 176
'Abdallah Romayh 175, 187 n.75
'Abdallahi (the Khalifa): recruitment for *jihadiyya* 27, 28; defeat at Toski 37; status of his Sudanese soldiers 46, 58–9, 70 n.65; allegiance transfers to 48; ethnic makeup of his army 55; his Baggara ascendancy 58; fight for the Khalifa's standard at Omdurman 60–1, **61**; his orders for Mahmud 141; strategy at Battle of Omdurman 162–5, 171, 176–7; death at Um Dibaykarat 184 n.3
Abdel Fadil el Jak 110
Abder Radi 117 n.122
Abdulla Id 117 n.122
Abdülmecid (Ottoman Sultan) 94
abrek 74, 75
Abu Hamed (battle, 1897) **35**, 53, 113–14, 120 n.201, 136, 157, 159–60, **160**, 177
Abu Klea (battle, 1885) **35**, 172
Abu Saud Pasha 48
Abyssinia (Ethiopia) 19, 20, 22, 24, 95
Adam Bringi 117 n.122
Adam En Nai 117 n.122
Adham al-Arifi 94
Adwa (battle, 1896) 38
Ahmad Arabi 25, 63, 130
Ahmad Hussein 175
Ahmad Pasha 15, 40 n.17, 45
Ahmad Shakir 192, 199
Ahmad ibn Tulun 12
Akasha, 38, 48, 175
'Ali 'Abd al-Latif 31, 88–9, 98, 99, 201, **202**
'Ali al-Banna 117 n.133
'Ali Fehim 176

'Ali Jifun (Gafoon, Gifoon) return to Fashoda 1, 55–6; rank 1, 36, 37, 55, 74, 96; "Memoirs of a Soudanese Soldier" 5; capture and army enrollment 16; in old Egyptian Army 19–21; service in Mexico 20, 193; posted to Xth Battalion of new Egyptian Army 21, 28; transferred to XIIth Battalion 28, **29**; on ethnic diversity of Sudanese soldiers 31; at Battle of Handoub 36–7; at Battle of Gemaizeh 37; in Akasha prior to launch of Dongola Campaign 38; his name 40 n.30; on allegiance to the Khedive 47; on disbanded regiments in need of a patron 49; on following orders 56; on fighting "old enemies" in the Mahdists 59; recalling Sayyid Hassan al-Mirghani's prophecy 63; on pay, rations, and clothing in old Egyptian Army 73, 74–5, 76; on temporary nature of wives in Sudanese battalions 81; his long service in Egyptian Army 93, 96, 173, 175; at Battle of Omdurman 176; role during Fashoda crisis 179, 180–1, 182
'Ali Khurshid 94, 98
'Ali el Sudani 51
'Ali el Tum 175, 187 n.74
'Ali Wad Helu 166
Alford, Henry 6, 144, 158, 159, 166, 172
allegiance transfers 7, 47–9, 68 n.15
Almas Mursi 96–7, 98–9, 176
Amadi (garrison) 17, **18**
Amedeb (garrison) **18**, 20–1, 76, 97
American Civil War veterans in Egyptian Army 24, 94
ammunition expenditure 115, 164, 168, 170, 171–2, 173
Anglo-Egyptian army 2, 157 *see also* Egyptian Army, British Army
Anglo-Egyptian Condominium 5, 62, 63, 99, 113, 131
Anley, Frederick Gore 100, 132–3, 139
anti-slavery 16–17, 28–9, 61, 147
Arabic (language) 62, 98, 139, 153 n.82, 177, 180, 181, 191
Arabs (nineteenth-century meaning of) 8 n.3, 55, 123
Arendrup, Søren Adolph 95
Argin (battle, 1889) **35**, 37–8, 54, 176
artillery 142–3, 157, 162, 163, 179
Artin, Yacoub 88

Aswan: training camps 15, 90; garrison **18** 23, 28, 30, 38, 78–9, 82, 201; town 24, 64, 65, **80**, 92, 93, 118 n.166
Asyut 201
Atbara (battle, 1898) 35, 141–9, **142**, **149**; role and tactics of Sudanese soldiers 62, 143–4, 148–9, 160–1, 177; Egyptian troops at 101, 139; celebrations after 103, 105, 121, 134, 136, **144**–5; burials following 113; capture of Mahmud 145, **146**, 147–8; enlistment of Mahdist prisoners from 183–4
Atta el Sudani 176
attack exercises 102–3
Atteridge, A. Hilliard 6, 44, 132,
awards and decorations 19, 35, 38, 89, 160, 175–6
Azande (people) **10**, 31, 69 n.37

Babikr Bedri 5, 60, 63–7
Badi Agha 94
Baggara (people) 1, 15, 16, 20, 55, 58–9, 60, 127, 145, 147, 158
Bagirmi (people) **10**, 31
Bahr al-Ghazal (region, province) **10**, 11, 15, 31, 62, 89, 96, 99, 107, 125, 176
Baibu (village) 180
Bairam, Feast of 105
Baker, Samuel 16–17, 95, 108
Baker, Valentine 25
Bakhit Mwafi 63–7
Banda (people) **10**, 31, 107–8
bandoliers 77
bands, Sudanese 21, 22, 23, 24, 110, 136, 140, 153 n.86, n.87
Bara (garrison) 17, **18**, 48
Baring, Evelyn *see* Cromer, Lord
bashi-bazouq 19, 48
battlefield reunions 44, 55, 57, 63–4, 178
battles *see* Abu Hamed, Abu Klea, Adwa, Argin, Atbara, El Teb, Firket, Gemaizeh, Ginnis, Gundet, Gura, Handoub, Omdurman, Sarras, Shaykan, Tamai, Tel el-Kebir, Tofrik, Tokar, Toski, Um Dibaykarat
bazinqir 16, 30
Belal En Nur 199
Bengali (people) 127
Bennett, Ernest 6, 88, 103, 134, 151 n.19, 152 n.72, 166, 169, 170, 171, 172
Berber: garrison, 17, **18**, 26, 90; base

Index

camp, 56, 83, 135–6, **135**, 159; town, 75, 105, 141, 178, 194
Berkeley, Stanley **149**, 161
Berta (people) **10**, 31
Besant, W. H. 33, 138
Billal Agha 93–4
Black & White 61, 125–7, **126**, 145, **167**, 174
Blue Nile 4, 14, 15, 31, 96, 112, 125, 184 n.3, 193
Boer War 184, 191, 192–3, 200, 203 n.31
Bongo (people) **10**, 31
Borrow, F. R. 82–3, 86
branding 33–4, 42 n. 82, 46
British Army 42 n.82, 68 n.11, 68 n.23, 100, 114 n.9, 138, 139 *see also* Cameron Highlanders, Connaught Rangers, Grenadier Guards, Guards Camel Corps, Lincolnshire Regiment, North Staffordshire Regiment, Seaforth Highlanders, Warwickshire Regiment
Bunyoro (settlement) 112
burei zar 109, 119 n.178
burial of Sudanese soldiers 45, 113, 134; of Egyptian soldiers 113; of British soldiers 113, 134
Burleigh, Bennet 6, 55, 56, 57, 72, 85, 86, 87, 89, 102–3, 121, 129, 133, 134–5, 144, 145, 150 n.2, 169, 172–3, 188 n.95
Burun (people) **10**, 31
Bushiri (uprising) 29, 47

Cairo 14, 17, 21, 26, **29**, 50, 62, 175, 197
Cairo Military School 94, 98, 192, 200
camaraderie *see* relations between Sudanese and British soldiers
Camel Corps (Egyptian Army) 162, 169, 185 n.23
Cameron Highlanders (79th) 34, 56, 135–6, 139, 140, 142, 148, **149**, 161, 171, 175, 179
camp followers 49, 75, 78–89, 92 *see also* wives, Sudanese soldiers'
Capper, Thompson 165
casualties: Xth Sudanese at Battle of Handoub 3; Sudanese soldiers at Battle of Ginnis 34; IXth Sudanese at Battle of Sarras 34; Egyptian Army at Battle of Gemaizeh 37; XIIIth Sudanese at Battle of Toski 37–8; total for Dongola Campaign 93; in military reports and the press 113, 148–9; XIth Sudanese at Battle of the Atbara 143; British at Atbara 143; Mahdists at Atbara 149; Anglo-Egyptian army at Atbara 149; Sudanese soldiers in River War 155; Egyptian Army at Battle of Firket 158–9; IXth, Xth, and XIth Sudanese at Firket 184 n. 8; Mahdists at Firket 158; Sudanese battalions at Battle of Abu Hamed 160; for Sudanese in comparison to Egyptian and British soldiers at Atbara 161; Sudanese soldiers at Battle of Omdurman 162, 185 n.27; for Sudanese in comparison to Egyptian and British soldiers at Omdurman 165; Mahdists at Omdurman 164, 165; 21st Lancers at Omdurman 168; First Egyptian Brigade at Omdurman 171
cavalry 20, 25, 36, 41 n.54, 139, 157; charge of the 21st Lancers 2, 162, 167–8, 185 n.18
children, Sudanese soldiers' 31, 32, 49, 50, 72, 81, 83, 85, 86, 87, 88–9, 100, 112, 184,
cholera 72, 76, 90, 91–3
Christian, Tom 60
Christianity 55, 62, 106, 108, 118–19 n.166, 140, 141
Churchill, Winston: historiographical influence of *The River War* 2, 4, 5–6, 8 n.4, 148, 149, 168, 185 n.18; on Sudanese ghosts at Abu Hamed 120 n.201; on Battle of the Atbara 148, 154 n.112; on treatment of wounded Mahdists after Battle of Omdurman 151 n.19; on role and conduct of Sudanese soldiers at Omdurman 155, 157, 162, 166–9, 170, 185 n.30; on the 21st Lancers 162; dearth of experience in the Sudan 169; on Lincolnshire Regiment as "rescuers" of Macdonald's brigade 166–7, 168, 169; racist depiction of Sudanese soldiers 186 n.47; and outmoded late Victorian army tactics 187 n.69; comments to R. F. Meiklejohn prior to Battle of Omdurman 187 n.76
civil administration jobs for Sudanese soldiers 72, 99
Clayton, Gilbert Falkingham 78, 83–4, 134

clothing, military 15, 24, 74, 75–6, **77**–8, 115 n.28
Colonisation Schemes 111–12
color prejudice among the British 5, 75, 80, 81, 121, 125–7, 129, 134, 148, 150, 150 n.3, 169, 186 n.47; among Arabs 51, 55, 65–8; *see also* martial races
combat roles (of Sudanese soldiers) 3, 34–8, 122, 142–4, 155–77 *see also* battles
conditions of service 31–4, 59, 70 n.65, 72–114 *see also* enlistment terms, pay, rations, clothing, firearms, camp followers, health and disease, promotion, discipline, daily camp life, retirement
Connaught Rangers 157
conscription, military (of Egyptian *fellahin*) 14, 15, 17, 24, 25, 32
corporal punishment 99–100, 118 n.141
courts martial 99, 100, 194
Crimean War 19, 40 n.27, 94, 193
Cromer, Lord 62, 132, 133, 190; correspondence with F. R. Wingate and Lord Salisbury during Omdurman mutiny 191–201

Daftardar, the 14–15
daily camp life 102–9
Daily Chronicle 6, 44, 132
Daily Mail 6, 33, 83, 106, 173
Daily Telegraph 6, 55, 72, 121, 144, 172
Dal (steamer) 55, 180, 181
daluka: dance 102, 105–6; drum 103, 109; musical genre 118 n.162
Dar-Fertit (region) **10**, 31
Dar-Funj (region) 4, **10**, 15, 31, 112
Dar-Fur (Darfur): region **10**, 17, 31, 110, 112, 140, 142, 145; sultanate 12, 14, 16, 34, 46
Darmali (village) 136
Dar-Nuba (region) **10**, 31, 58
Dar-Runga (region) **10**, 31
de Cosson, Emilius 73
Deim Sulayman (garrison) 17, **18**
Deim Zubayr (garrison) 17, **18**
Dein Breil 37
Delcassé, Théophile 181, 184
desertion of *ombashi* from 'Ali Jifun's battalion 20; of 'Abdallah 'Adlan and fellow Sudanese soldiers from Osman Digna 23; and troops slated for the Hicks Pasha expedition 25; of Sudanese soldiers in Egyptian Army to Mahdists 27; of Sudanese *jihadiyya* in the Khalifa's army to Egyptian Army 30, 47, 49, 58, 77, 177, 178; and branding as an aid in apprehension 33–4, 42 n.82; of Mahdist troops following Battle of Toski 37–8; and execution for 46, 100; of Faraj Sadik and fellow Sudanese soldiers from El Obeid 48; and rarity within Sudanese battalions 57; linked with marriage establishment and camp followers 87–8; as a guise for Sudanese spies 178; of soldiers from the XIth Sudanese during Fashoda crisis 183–4
diet *see* rations
Digawi (people) **10**, 31
Dinka (people) 2, **10**, 16, 26, 30, 31, 39 n.2, 88–9, 96, 98, 123, 125, **126**–7, 135, 140, 157, 175, 176, 179–80, 181–2, 187 n.87, 203 n.34
discharged soldiers *see* retirement
discipline, military 14, 15, 26, 32, 99–100
diseases *see* health and disease, cholera, malaria, ophthalmia, typhus
divorce 83–4 *see also* marriage
Dongola: town 83; province 92, 178; garrison 17, **18**, 201; campaign 38, 78–81, 91–2, 93, 103–6, 132
Donne, D. A. 33–4, 82–3, 99–100
Dreyfus Affair 181
drill 26, 99, 101–2, 102–3, 106, 125, 129
Dueim (town) 88, 110
Dufferin, Lord 23, 24, 25
Dye, William McEntyre 170
dysentery 15, 90, 91

education (for Sudanese soldiers) 94, 98, 200
Egeiga (village) 162
Egyptian Army: Muhammad 'Ali and *nizam al-jadid* 12; invasion of the Sudan 12, 14; recruitment of Sudanese soldiers 15–17; garrisons in the Sudan 17–**18**; roles during the Turkiyya 17, 18–23; reorganization under the British 23–30; in combat prior to the Nile Campaign 34–8; at Battle of Firket 44, 157–9; conditions of service 72–114; at Battle of the Atbara 141–50, 160–1; at Battle of Abu Hamed 159–60; at Battle of Omdurman 161–77

Egyptian battalions, new Egyptian Army: 2nd Battalion 101, 163–6, 172; 3rd Battalion 132, 159; 4th Battalion 38, 132; 8th Battalion 166, 171, 192; 15th Battalion 137–8

Egyptian regiments, old Egyptian Army: First Regiment 21, 94, 95; Second Regiment 20–1; Fourth Regiment 73, 193–4; Fifth Regiment 19–20; Eighth Regiment 73

Egyptian soldiers: in old Egyptian Army 15, 24; conscription into new Egyptian Army 25; at Battle of Firket 44, 157–9; and manual labor 101, 129; reputation as soldiers 127, 129, 131–3; relations with Sudanese and British soldiers 137–8; at Battle of Abu Hamed 159; at Battle of the Atbara 160–1; at Battle of Omdurman 161–77

Egyptian Sudan 17, 48, 122–3 *see also* Turkiyya

Eid (Muslim holiday) 86

El Fasher (garrison) 17, **18**

El Obeid: town 16, 112; garrison 17, **18**, 19, 20, 48, 81, 193–4

El Teb (battle, 1884) 25, 27, 29–30, **35**, 95

Eldama Ravine (settlement) 112

Emin Pasha (Eduard Schnitzer) 17, 48

English (language) 23, 62, 97–8, 135, 139–40, 176

enlistment terms for Sudanese soldiers 19, 24, 26–7, 31–4, 42 n.71, 46; for British Army soldiers 68 n.11

enslavement (of Sudanese soldiers) 1, 14–17, 31, 59, 90, 122, 123, 145 *see also* recruitment

Equatoria (province) 4, **10**, 16–17, 31, 48, 94, 122, 125, 130, 143

Ethiopia *see* Abyssinia

ethnic and geographical diversity (of Sudanese soldiers) 4, **10**, 30–1, 41–2 n.65, 122–3, **124**, 125, 147

ethnic identity (among Sudanese soldiers) 51–2, 56, 58, 88–9, 105, 178, 203 n.34

executions 100

expeditionary forces, Sudanese soldiers as 17, 18, 193; in Greece (1823) 18–19; in Arabia (1835) 19; in Syria (1831–1840) 19; in Crimean War (1853–1856) 19, 40 n.27, 94; in Mexico (1863–1867) 19, 20, 40 n.28, 47; in Ethiopia (1875–1876) 19, 24; in German East Africa (1889) 29, 47

Fadasi (garrison) 17, **18**
Fadl el Mula 34,
Fadl el Mula Daud 176
Fairholme, W. E. 81
family allowance 26, 30, 50, 74, 78, 83, 86, 194
Farag Abu Zeid 34
Faragalla Ahmad 34
Faragalla Mirkis 175
Faragalla Sultan 178
Faraj Allah Raghib 95
Faraj Azazi 94
Faraj Kasim 110
Faraj Muhammad al-Zaini 18, 95–6
Faraj Sadik 17, 47–8, 110, 118–19 n.166
Farley, James Jay Bleeker 82
Fashoda: village 1, 16, 55, 70 n.65; fort and garrison 1, 17, **18**; Fashoda Incident 1, 180; crisis and role played by Sudanese soldiers 1, 157, 179–84
Fateh (gunboat) 179
fatigue work 84, 93, 101, 103, 129 *see also* military labor
Fatimid Egypt 12, 14
Fazoghli (garrison) 17, **18**
fellahin 14, 15, 25, 30, 101, 129, 130, 131 *see also* Egyptian soldiers
field hospitals 91
fighting tactics (of Sudanese soldiers) 8, 143, 157, 159–60, 169, 172–3, 177
firearms 76–7 *see also* Lee-Metford, Martini-Henry, and Remington (rifles)
Firket (battle, 1896) **35**, 44, 56, 57, 132, 157, **158**, 159
Fitton, Hugh Gregory 143, 177
Fitzclarence, Edward 113–14, 160
flogging 46, 99–100, 118 n.141
food *see* rations
football 103, **104**, 138, 152 n.75
France and use of Sudanese troops in Mexico 19, 20, 47, 55, 193; designs on the Upper Nile 38; the Fashoda crisis 179–84
Franks, George McKenzie 144, 145, 161
fraternization (between Sudanese soldiers and Mahdist prisoners) 3, 57–8, 178
French military instructors in Egypt 12, 14, 15

Gaber Hanna 34
Gaber Mohamed **126**, 127
Garang, John 201, **202**
garrisons 17, **18**, 26, 27, 28, 30, 47, 48, 85, 94, 97 *see also* al-Kara, Amadi, Amedeb, Aswan, Bara, Berber, Deim Sulayman, Deim Zubayr, Dongola, El Fasher, El Obeid, Fadasi, Fashoda, Fazoghli, Gondokoro, Iringa, Kassala, Khartoum, Lado, Langenburg, Massawa, Rejaf, Rumbek, Senheit, Sennar, Sinkat, Suakin, Taufikia, Tokar, Wadi Halfa, Wau
Garsia, H. G. A. 111
Gatacre, William 101, 105
Gedid (battle, 1899) *see* Um Dibaykarat
Gemaizeh (battle, 1888) **35**, 37, 95, 97, 176
Germain, Joseph 182–3
German East Africa 29, 47, 52, 84, 86
Gessi, Romolo 17
Giles, Godfrey 145, **146**, 147
Gineinetti (town) 141
Ginnis (battle, 1885) 34, **35**, 136, 138, 175, 176
Gleichen, Count 85–6
Gohar 117 n.122
Gondokoro (garrison) 17, **18**
Gordon Memorial College 89
Gordon, Charles 17, 18, 22, 26, 48, 94–5, 95–6, 98, 133, 140, 141, 147, 149, 168
Gorst, Eldon 190
Grenadier Guards 138, 139, 163, 171
Grenfell, Francis 28–9, 30, 166,
Guards Camel Corps 85
Gumuz (people) 107–8
Gundet (battle, 1875) 19, 24
guns *see* firearms
Gura (battle, 1876) 19, 24
Gurkha (people) 122, 123, 125, 127, 130, 131
Gurkha syndrome 123, 139
gymkhana meetings 103, 138

hakims 89, 116 n.87
Hamaj (people) **10**, 31,
Handoub (battle, 1888) **35**–7, 95
harimat 49, 50, 78, 85, 87, 89, 93, 109, 191, 194–5
Hasaballa Furawi 117 n.122
Hassan Abu Kort 48
Hassan Ahmad 160

Hassan Isma'il 22
Hassan Labib 176, 192, 199
Hassan Sharaf 117, n.133
Hassan al-Zein 117 n.133
health and disease 89–93
Hickman, T. E. 36
Hicks Pasha 25, 38, 48, 76
Highlanders (as "martial race") 125, 133
Hill Smith, H. E. 183
historiography (of the River War) 2, 5–6, 148–50, 168, 179
holidays (Islamic) 86, 103, 105–6
Hubbard, Alfred Edward 170
Hunter, Archibald: formation of the IXth Sudanese 26–7; on potential role of Sudanese soldiers in Scramble for Africa 39 n.2; on British officers being the pupils of soldiers in IXth Sudanese 53–4; on conditions at Halfa *harimat* during 1896 cholera epidemic 93, 117 n.107; at 1898 Bairam festivities 105; on performance of Egyptian battalions at Battle of Firket 132; at Battle of the Atbara 148; and mortally wounded Hassan Ahmad at Battle of Abu Hamed 160; official report and further correspondence on the Battle of Omdurman 165–6, 169–70, 185 n.22
Husain Muhammad Mustafa 99

Ibrahim Adam 184 n.8
Ibrahim el Khalil 162
identity, Sudanese soldier 3, 7–8, 44–67, 105, 109, 139, 201
Idris 'Abdallah 200
Imperial British East African Company (IBEAC) 48
Indian Army 11, 24, 82, 115 n.33, 122, 123, 125, 127, 129–31
infibulation 109, 119 n.181
interpreters, Sudanese soldiers as 113, 155, 177, 179, 180, 181 *see also* non-combat roles
ipsimission 45, 46, 201
Iringa (garrison) 86
Islam (among Sudanese soldiers) 3, 8, 15, 52, 54–5, 56, 58, 62, 65, 66, 83, 102, 106, 109, 134, 178
Isma 'il (son of Muhammad 'Ali) 14
Isma'il Aiyub 46

Index

Isma'il Pasha (Khedive) 16–17, 24, 73, 94, 109

Ja'aliyyin (people) 58–9, 60, 114 n.22, 157
Jackson, H. C. 133, 151 n.46
Jackson, H. W. 87, 153 n.87, 172, 180–4, 191, 194–5, 198–9, 200
jihadiyya: in Egyptian Army during Turkiyya 17–19; units in Mahdist armies 27, 28, 31, 46, 48, 49, 55, 59, 70 n.65, 117 n.122, 122, 142, 145; prisoners of war and deserters enrolled into Egyptian Army 29–30, 38, 56–7, 58, 77, 173, 178, 184 n.3, 193

Kaka (village) 179
al-Kara (*jihadiyya* garrison) 59
Karari (battle, 1898) *see* Omdurman
Kassala: garrison 17, **18**, 20, 21, 23, 26, 36, 75, 95; town 20, 22, 38, 63, 112; mutiny 73, 94, 193–4
Kavalli 48
Keiralla Hamduni 176
Kenya 52, 69 n.39, 201
Khair Agha 94
Khalifa *see* 'Abdallahi
Khamis Breish 175, 178
Khamis Mustafa 176
Khartoum Military School 89, 98
Khartoum: city 16, 73, 88–9, 90, 97, 98, 102, 110, 112, 133, 140, 191, 194, 195; garrison 17, **18**, 82, 94; siege of 22, 48, 75, 95–6, 108; Muhammad Ahmad's attack upon 23, 43 n.100
Khatmiyya (Sufi order) 63, 70 n.79
Khusrav Pasha 12, 14
Ki-Nubi 52
Kibos (settlement) 112
killing of wounded Mahdists after Omdurman 59, 151 n.19
King's African Rifles 8, 52, 201
Kitchener, Horatio Herbert: as "Kitchener of Khartoum" 2; and Battle of Handoub 36, 42 n.95; on Seaforths at Aswan 82; on 1894 *harimat* fire 87; on question of camp followers 87, 88, 89; at 1898 Bairam festivities 105; intervention when Sudanese fired over the heads of Grenadier Guards 138; and Battle of the Atbara 141–2, 144, 145, **146**, 147, 148, 161; and Battle of Omdurman 162–7; and Fashoda crisis 55, 179–81, 183; and 1900 Omdurman mutiny 190, 191, 192, 196, 197–8, 201
Knight, E. F. 6, 50, 57, 58–9, 79, 110, 127, 129, 137–8, 158, 159,
Kong Dungdit 113
Kordofan: region, province 4, 14, 15, 19, 31, 55, 58, 98, 111, 112, 125, 142, 145; military campaigns 25, 48, 184 n.3
Korti (town) 48
Kosheh (fort) 175
Kosseir (port) 38
Kur Nyidok (Shilluk *reth*) 179, 180–1, 182

Lado (garrison) 17, **18**,
Langenburg (garrison) 84
language *see* Arabic, English, Turkish
Lee-Metford (rifle) 76, 115 n.33, 169, 171, 172, 186 n.63
Leverson, Julian John 11, 27
al-Lewa (newspaper) 189, 190, 196
Lewis, D. F. 67, 105, 132, 157, 185 n.22
Lincolnshire Regiment 75, 135, 136–7, 139, 140, 166–7, 168, 169–70, 171–2, 186 n.51
literacy 97–8, 200
loyalty to the Khedive, Sudanese 8, 27, 47–8, 56, 123, 130, 194, 195, 198
Lugard, Frederick 41 n.65, 48, 52

Macdonald, Hector 33, 53, 88, 143, 158, 159, 163–7, 168–**74**, 185 n.22
Macdonald, J. R. L. 87–8
Machell, Percy 38, 47, 63
al-Madani 65
Mahdi, the *see* Muhammad Ahmad
Mahdiism and the Egyptian Sudan 36, 131–2
Mahdism and Mahdist state 17–18, 21, 22, 25, 34, 37, 47, 48, 56, 58, 60, 61, 63, 94, 107, 147, 168, 198
Mahdist army 27, 28, 46, 55, 58–9, 70 n.65, 117 n.122; assault of Khartoum 23, 96; attack on Kassala garrison 23; invasion of Egypt 31; desertions from 23, 30, 37–8, 47, 48, 49, 58, 77, 177, 178; desertions to 27, 48–9; *see also* battles
Mahmoud Baghat 138
Mahmud Ahmad 70 n.65; at Battle of the Atbara 141–3, 153 n.89, 161; captured

221

145, **146**, 147–8, 149, 154 n.103
Mahmud Hilmi 192, 200
Mahmud Mukhtar 192, 199
malakiyyas (civilian quarters) 113, 201
malaria 90, 91
Mamluks 12, 14, 50
ma'murs 99
Marchand, Jean-Baptiste 1, 179, 180–1, 182–3, 184
marches 37, 38, 74–5, 86, 99, 136, 141; Kosseir to Qift 38; Murat to Korosko 138; Kassinger to Abu Hamed 159
marisa 75, 84, 85
marriage 64–6, 72, 78–85, 109, 119 n.181; establishment 68 n.23, 78, 82–3, 87; allowance 26, 30, 50, 74, 78, 83, 86, 194
martial races 2, 11, 27–8, 31, 54, 121–34, 139, 141, 142
Martini-Henry (rifle) 26, 76–7, 115 n.33, 164, 166, 171, 172, 173, 176, 186 n.63, 194,
masculinity 127, 130, 133
Mashra El-Rek (French base) 179, 187 n.87
Massawa (garrison) 17, **18**, 19–20, 21, 26, 47–8, 95
Matthews, Godfrey 189–90
Maud, W. T. 91, 145, 152 n.55, 178
Maxim gun 2, 155, 157, 163, 184 n.2, 191, 192, 193
Maximilian 19, 55, 193
Maxse, F. I. 96, 97–8, 149
Maxwell, John 143, 158, 171, 189, 190, 192, 193,
McMurdo, A. M. 36–7,
McNeill, Angus 60, 203 n.31
medical care *see* health and disease
Meiklejohn, Ronald Forbes 136, 187 n.76
Menelik II 38
Merawi (camp, field hospital) 91, 103, 105, 106
Mexico, Sudanese service in (1863–1867) 1, 19, 20, 46, 55, 56, 91, 94, 95, 193
military labor: *jihadiyya* in Omdurman 59; Sudanese and Egyptian soldiers 101 *see also* fatigue work
military slavery: long history in Egypt and the Sudan 3, 12, 28, 201; during the Turkiyya 12–23; in new Egyptian Army 24, 26–7, 31–4, 46; as different from plantation and domestic forms of slavery 44–5; in relation to Western and Islamicate meanings of slave 45, 65; and ambiguous manumission status 3, 45–6, 65–6; pride in slave status among Sudanese soldiers 3, 46; and patronage 47–9, 123, 130; and opportunities for advancement 49; ascribed status versus social condition 3, 49–51, 66; *see also* enslavement, enlistment terms, identity, conditions of service, patronage, loyalty to the Khedive
Milner, Alfred 28, 90, 129, 138–9
Minie (rifle) 76
Mirsal el Baz 176
Mirsal Goma 175
Mirsal Negib 176
Mitford, B. R. 28, 53, 54, 69 n.37, 76, 77, 89–90, 105, 173
Monassir (desert) 159
Morning Post 166, 169
Mouktar Pasha 132
Muhammad 'Abd al-Bakheit 117 n.133
Muhammad Abu Shaila 34–5, 175
Muhammad Ahmad (the Mahdi) 18, 23, 25, 27, 48–9, 58, 95
Muhammad Ahmad 95, 176
Muhammad 'Ali Pasha (*wali*) 12; creation of modern army 12, 14, 39 n.7, 201; invasion of the Sudan 14–15; first Sudanese regiments 15; use of Sudanese soldiers as expeditionary forces 18–19
Muhammad Almas 94
Muhammad Lazughlu 15
Muhammad Sa'id Pasha (*wali*) 16, 19, 24, 47, 193
Muhammad Sami 192
Muhammad Sulaiman 94
Muhammad Surur Rustum 117 n.133
Muhammad Tewfik Yusef 200
Muhammad Walad Dain 176, 202 n.2
mulazimin (the Khalifa's bodyguard) 70 n.65, 164–5
Munsinger Pasha 21, 175
Murgan Mahmoud 46, 176–7
Murray, Andrew 56
Musa Fuad 176
musketry 76, 102, 172, 176
Mustafa Lutfi 192, 199
mutinies: Wad Medani (1844) 193; Kassala (1864–1865) 94, 193–4;

Suakin (1884) 26–7, 194; El Obeid (1885–1887) 48; Uganda (1897) 87–8; Omdurman (1900) 189–201

Nakheila (battle, 1898) *see* Atbara
Napoleon (Bonaparte) 12, 14, 39 n.7
Napoleon III 19, 20, 47, 193
Nason, F. J. 172
Nasr (gunboat) 179
Neufeld, Charles 59
new Egyptian Army *see* Egyptian Army
Newbolt, Sir Henry John 133
Niam-Niam (people) *see* Azande
Nile (river) 1, 14, 16, 38, 54, 91, 92, 102, 103, 177, 178 *see also* Blue Nile, White Nile
nizam al-jadid 12, 14, 15, 73, 90, 93, 201
non-combat roles (of Sudanese soldiers) 3, 155; as military recruiters 58, 178; as interpreters 177; as spies 177–8; as goodwill ambassadors 58–9, 178; as military policemen 178; as intermediaries, interpreters, and ethnic liaisons during Fashoda crisis 179–83
non-commissioned officers, Sudanese 3, 93–4, 96, **97**, 155, 168, 200
North Staffordshire Regiment **104**, 152 n.75, 157
Nuba (peoples) 20, **52**, 107–8, 125, **126**, 127, 140, 203 n.34
Nuba Mountains 4, **10**, 14, 15, 31, 48, 95, 97, 112, 122, 145
Nubi (identity) 8, 52, 69 n.39, 201
Nubia (region) 40 n.27, 58
Nubian Desert **10**, 38, 159
Nubian mercenaries (in ancient Egypt) 12, 39 n.4
Nuer (people) **10**, 31, 113, 179, 187 n.87
al-Nur Muhammad 95
Nushi Pasha 28, 41 n.55
Nyidok Deng 181

officers: Sudanese 1, 34, 86, 87, 88, 89, 93–9, 102, 112, 117 n. 130, 155, 191–2, 197–201; British 2, 3, 25, 27, 28, 30, 33, 46, 61, 67, 82, 102, 105, 106, 129–30, 138–9, 143, 148–9, 191, 192, 194; Turkish 25, 94, 100, 193; Egyptian 62, 95, 96, 102, 108, 127, 134, 139, 175, 184, 189–93, 196, 198–201; *see also* the names of individual officers

old Egyptian Army *see* Egyptian Army
Omdurman: city 59, 95; barracks 82, **97**
Omdurman (battle, 1898) **35**, **163**; historiography and popular memory 2, 155–6, 162, 168; size and makeup of Kitchener's army 2, 157; killing of wounded Mahdists at 59, 151 n.19; acts of vengeance committed by Sudanese soldiers in wake of 60; fight for the Khalifa's standard 60–1; al-Mirghani's prophecy of 63; Bakhit Mwafi and Babikr Bedri in Omdurman proper after the battle 64, 66; Xth Sudanese present Lincolns with Khalifa's White Standard 136; race to the citadel and Mahdi's tomb 138; Gordon's memorial service following 140; Churchill's descriptions of 155, 166–9; role of Sudanese soldiers at 161–6, **164**, **165**, **167**, **174**, 185 n.22; eyewitness accounts of phase two 169–71, 172–3; ammunition returns for 171–2; long experience of Sudanese soldiers fighting at 173, 174–7
Omdurman mutiny (1900): breaks out 189–90; causes of 190–4; arrival and role played by H. W. Jackson with mutinous XIth Sudanese 194–5; role of *shaykhat el harimat* in negotiations with XI Sudanese 89, 194–5; arrival and role played by F. R. Wingate 195–8; impact of Khedive's letter on mutinous XIVth Sudanese 196–8; role of senior Sudanese officers in ending 198–9; Court of Inquiry for 199–201; ceremonial parade after initial Court of Inquiry decisions 201
ophthalmia 91
Orientalism 114, 134, 139,
Ornamentalism 114, 121–2, 133–4, 140
Osman Aref 200
Osman Azraq 162, 166, 169
Osman Digna 21, 23, 35–6, 37, 38, 47, 95, 108, 141, 149, 168
Ottoman Empire 12, 19, 54, 123, 180

Paget, H. M. 178
pan-Islam 56, 61–2, 106, 130–1
Parker, A. C. 111–12
Parr, Henry Hallam 26
patronage 45, 47–9, 113, 123, 130, 195, 197, 198 *see also* loyalty to the Khedive

pay rates 26, 30, 42 n.71, 50, 73–4, 96, 190
pensions 30, 49, 50, 72, 109–11, 119 n.184, 190
pharaonic circumcision *see* infibulation
polygamy 83
prisoners of war (Mahdist) 3, 29–30, 31, 37, 38, 57–8, 77, 158, 178
Pritchard, Harry Lionel 6, 53, 170–1, 186 n.59
privileges 49, 100–2
promotion, military 93–9
punishment, corporal 99–100, 118 n.141

Qift (town) 38

racism *see* color prejudice
Ramadan 86, 106
Ramzi Tahir 97, 176
Raouf Pasha 49
rations 26, 32, 50, 59, 70 n.65, 74–5, 87
al-Rawda bint Muhammad (wife of Bakhit Mwafi) 65–6
Ready, Felix 101, 134
recreation 102–3, 138
recruitment (of Sudanese soldiers) **10**, 12, 14–17, 26–30, 41 n.62, 58, 62, 70 n.65, 78, 88–9, 111, 122–3, 142, 145, 178
Red Sea Littoral 26, 36, 38, 47, 94, 95
Rehan Sa'id 37
Rehan Saleh **126**, 127
Rejaf (garrison) 17, **18**
relations between Sudanese and British soldiers 3, 113–14, 121–2, 133–7, 138–40, 143–4, 191, 192; between Sudanese and Egyptian soldiers 137–8, 192–3; between Egyptian and British soldiers 138–9, 190–1; between ethnic groups within Sudanese battalions 51–2, 69 n.37
religion 51, 54, 70 n.77, 72, 102, 105–6, 109, 140, 178 *see also* Christianity, Islam, *tombura zar*
Remington (rifle) 26, 76, 183, 194
Renk (Mahdist post) 180
Repington, Charles 88, 89
retirement 50, 72, 109–13
Rihan 'Abd Allah 88–9
Rizkalla Hamed 117 n.122
Rodd, Rennell 113–14, 160
Rumbek (garrison) 17, **18**
Rundle, Leslie 30

Sabit 'Abd al-Rahim 117 n.133
al-Sabr ('Ali 'Abd al-Latif's mother) 31, 88–9
Sa'id 'Abdallah 97, 98–9, 176
Sa'id Abou 34
Sa'id Osman 176
Sa'id Shahata 117 n.133
Saleh Zeki 192, 199
Salisbury, Lord 11, 43 n.105, 62, 132, 183, 192
San Juan Hill, charge at 162
Sarras (battle, 1887) 34, **35**, 175
Sayyid 'Ali al-Mirghani 70 n.79
Sayyid Hassan al-Mirghani 70 n.79
Sayyid Hassan al-Mirghani I (al-Khatim) 70 n.79
Sayyid Hassan al-Mirghani II (al-Sughaiyar) 63, 70 n.79
Schutztruppe 52
scientific racism 125
Scramble for Africa 2, 8, 11, 27–8, 39 n.2, 44, 49
Seaforth Highlanders 60, 82, 140, 148, 171, 196
segregation 102, 103, 121, 134
Selim 117 n.122
Selim III (Ottoman Sultan) 12, 39 n.7
Selim Kirkir 23
Senegalese *tirailleurs* 180, 182, 183
Senheit (Sennheit, garrison) **18**, 20, 21, 22
Sennar: kingdom 12, 14, 68 n.13; town 95; region, province 95, 111, 112, 193; garrison 17, **18**, 26
settlement colonies, ex-soldier 50, 110, 111–12 *see also* Colonisation Schemes, *malakiyyas*
Shaykan (battle, 1883) 25, 27, **35**, 48
Shaykh al Din 166, 169
shaykhat el harimat 194–5, 203 n.38
Sheldon, Charles Mills 125, 127
Shilluk (people) 1, 2, 8 n.2, **10**, 16, 26, 30, 31, 39 n.2, 55–6, 69 n.49, 70 n.77, 105, 123, **124**, 125, 135, 140, 157, 179–84, 187 n.86
shishkhana (rifle) 76
Sidney, H. M. 113–14, 160
Signal Hill 165–6
Sikh (people) 125, 130, 131
Sillem, James 189
Sinkat (garrison) 17, **18**
Skinner, George 100, 135, 145

Index

Slatin, Rudolf 81, 110, 177
slave (Islamicate versus Western meaning of) 45, 65
slave raids 14–16, 17, 59
slave soldier *see* military slavery
slave trade 16–17, 31, 49, 58, 61, 147
slave-associated names 46
Smith-Dorrien, Horace 28, 33, 130, 138, 150 n.3, 176–7
Sobat (river) 183, 187 n.86
social death 7, 49–50, 123, 147
Sol Taleem **126**, 127
songs, Sudanese soldiers' 59–60, 85, 103, 108
South Africa 184, 189, 190, 191, 192, 193, 194–5, 197, 198
Southern Policy 62
sports 103, 138, 139, 152 n.75
Steevens, G. W. 6, 33, 54, 77, 83, 106, 127, 133, 134, 142–3, 143–4, 172, 173
Suakin: province 95; port city 23, 35, 38, 193; garrison 17, **18**, 26, 30, 36–7, 38, 108
Sudan Defence Force 8, 99, 201
Sudanese (nineteenth-century meaning of) 8 n.3, 51, 98, 123
Sudanese People's Liberation Army (SPLA) 201
Sudanese People's Liberation Movement (SPLM) 8, 201–**202**
Sudanese soldiers: prior to nineteenth century 12; during the Turkiyya 12, 14–23; formation of Sudanese battalions in new Egyptian Army 25–30; ethnic and geographical background 30–1; enlistment terms 31–4; in combat prior to the Nile Campaign 34–8; identity and social condition 44–67; daily life and conditions of service 72–114; martial reputation 122–34; relations with British and Egyptian soldiers 134–40; at Battle of the Atbara 141–150; in combat at Firket, Abu Hamed, and Atbara 157–61; at Battle of Omdurman 161–77; non-combat roles 177–184; Omdurman mutiny 189–201; *see also* Sudanese IXth, Xth, XIth, XIIth, XIIIth, XIVth Battalions
Sudanese IXth Battalion: formation of 11–12, 26–7, 28, 194; enlistment terms 33; at Battle of Ginnis 34; at Battle of Sarras 34–5; at Battle of Gemaizeh 37; at Battles of Argin and Toski 37–8, 173; movements 38; pride and confidence within battalion **53–4**; D. F. Lewis on 67; harmonious relations within 69 n.37; military clothing for 76; maintenance of Martini-Henry rifles 77; *harimat* lines for 78; affiliation with 79th Cameron Highlanders **135–6**; dispute with Xth Sudanese over capture of Mahmud 154 n.103; at Battle of Firket 57, 132, 157–8, 184 n.8; at Battle of Abu Hamed 159–60; at Battle of the Atbara **142**; at Battle of Omdurman 161–2, 163–4, **165**–6, 168, 170–3, **174**, 175–6, 185 n.27; at Battle of Um Dibaykarat 184 n.3; in Omdurman mutiny 198, 200
Sudanese Xth Battalion: formation of 28; at Battle of Handoub 36–7; at Battle of Gemaizeh 37; at Battles of Argin and Toski 37; during 1896 cholera epidemic 92–3; in reference to "Egyptian Army type" Sol Taleem in *Black & White* **126**–7; martial-masculine nature 130; affiliation with Royal Lincolnshire Regiment 136–**7**, 152 n.65; at Battle of the Atbara **142**; capture of Mahmud 145, **146**, 147–8, 154 n.103; at Battle of Firket 57, 157–8, 185 n.8; at Battle of Abu Hamed 159–60; at Battle of Omdurman 162, 163–4, **165**–6, 168, 170–3, **174**, 176, 185 n.27; in Omdurman mutiny 198
Sudanese XIth Battalion: formation of 28; at Battles of Argin and Toski 37; at Battle of Tokar 38; at Akasha for launch of Dongola Campaign 38; departure from Aswan 79–**80**; affiliation with Royal Warwickshire Regiment 135–6; band 140, 153 n.87; at Battle of the Atbara **142**–3; at Battle of Firket **158**, 184 n.8; at Battle of Abu Hamed 159–**60**; at Battle of Omdurman 161–2, 163–4, **165**–6, 168, 170–3, **174**, 176, 185 n.27; during Fashoda crisis 55, 179, 182–4; in Omdurman mutiny 189–90, 192, 194–5, 198, 199–200, 202 n.2
Sudanese XIIth Battalion: formation of 28–9; at Battle of Tokar 38; at Akasha

for launch of Dongola Campaign; NCOs of No. 7 Company **97**; at Battle of Firket 158; at Battle of Omdurman 162, 166, 169, 171, 176, 185 n.27; in Omdurman mutiny 198, 201
Sudanese XIIIth Battalion: formation of 28; enlistment terms 33; at Battles of Argin and Toski 37–8; at Akasha for launch of Dongola Campaign 38; following Battle of Omdurman 64; fire in *harimat* lines 87; Sudanese officers within 96, 97; match against British soldiers 103, 138; march from Murat to Korosko 137–8; first to reach the Mahdi's tomb after the Battle of Omdurman 138; at Battle of Firket **158**, 184 n.8; at Battle of Omdurman 162–3, 165–6, 169, 171, 176, 185 n.27, n.30; during Fashoda crisis 55, 179; at Battle of Um Dibaykarat 184 n.3; in Omdurman mutiny 189, 198
Sudanese XIVth Battalion: formation of 79; its departure from Aswan 81; at Battle of Omdurman 162, 166, 169, 171, 176, 185 n.27; in Omdurman mutiny 189–90, 192, 195–200
Sudani (meaning of) 8 n.3, 51, 123, 125
Surgham (jebel) 162–3, 167, 169, 172, 185 n.30
Sword, Dennistoun 6, 144, 151 n.19, 158, 159, 166, 172,

Taisha Baggara 145
Tamai (battle, 1884) 29–30, 37, 95
Taqali: kingdom 12, 19, 81; people 97
Taufikia (garrison) 17, **18**
Tawfiq (Khedive) 3, 24, 47, 109
taxes, Turco-Egyptian 1, 14, 15, 16, 17, 19, 20, 21–2, 73, 76, 147
Teigh, George 75, 152 n.65
Tel el-Kebir (battle, 1882) 24, 25, 27, 37, 38, 63
territorial units 62
Tewfik Hilmi 175
The Cornhill Magazine 1, 5
The Daily Graphic 79, **80**, 103, **104**, 138
The Fight for the Khalifa's Standard, 60–1; **61**
The Fighting Sudanese 133
The Graphic 60, 75, 91, 105, 106, 108, 145, 152 n.75, 153 n.87, 178

The Island Race 133
The River War 2, 5–6, 8 n.4, 148–9, 154 n.112, 155, 157, 162, 166–70, 185 n.30, 186 n.47
The Times 6, 50, 57, 58–9, 79, 110, 137, 158
Thorburn, D. Hay 60
Tofrik (battle, 1885) 95
Tokar: garrison 17, **18**, 25, 38; battle (1891) **35**, 95, 97, 176; colony 112
tombura zar 106–9, 119 n.178
Tommy Atkins 2, 103, 121, 139, 144, 152 n.72, 157
Toski (battle, 1889) 31, **35**, 37–8, 89–90, 97, 173, 175, 176
training, military 15, 27, 76–7, 167
Turkish (language) 15, 40 n.30, 95, 98, 107, 139
Turks (nineteenth-century connotation of) 14, 62, 70, 94
typhus (outbreak, 1840) 90

Uganda 4, 28, 31, 41 n.65, 52, 87–8, 95, 112, 201
Uganda Rifles 41 n.65
Um Dibaykarat (battle, 1899) **35**, 67, 184 n.3, 200
umma 3, 58, 67, 178
uniforms *see* clothing, military
Upper Nile (region, province) 2, 4, 7, 11, 15, 30, 31, 38, 112, 113, 125, 179, 181–3,

venereal disease 90, 91
vengeance 59–60, 64, 145, 147
von Prince, Captain 86
von Prince, Magdalene 86
von Wissmann, Hermann 29, 47

Wad Medani (mutiny, 1844) 193
Wadi Halfa: province 31, 151 n.46; town 34, 50, 81, 83, 92; garrison 17, **18**, 30, 38, 48, 77, 93, **104**, 129, 140
Walter, W. F. 172
Warwickshire Regiment 136, 140, 171
Watson, J. K. 100, 179
Wau (garrison) 17, **18**, **53**, 187 n.75
weddings 78, 127
Westminster Gazette 6, 103, 134, 166, 169
Whigham, R. D. 165–6
Whiston, P. H. 91

Index

White Nile (river) 15, 30, 112, 123, 145, 179

Wingate, Francis Reginald: on the value and soldiering qualities of Sudanese troops 11, 27, 30; on Egyptian troops 25, 131–2; recruitment of Sudanese soldiers 30, 78; *Mahdiism and the Egyptian Sudan* 36; on religion in southern Sudan 70 n.77; on condition of Sudanese ex-soldiers 111; on British officers 129; on relations between Egyptian and Sudanese soldiers 137; interviewing Mahdist prisoners 177; on role of Shilluk soldiers at Kaka 179; at Um Dibaykarat 184 n.3; role during Omdurman mutiny 191, 192–3, 195–201

wives, Sudanese soldiers' 49; economic roles 75, 86–7; nature of marriages 78–84, 87; family allowance 26, 30, 50, 74, 78, 83, 86, 194; married establishment 78, 82–3, 87; as camp followers 85–6, 87–8, 89; hierarchy among 86; military role 88; reproductive role 88; ethnic and kinship networks 88–9; and the 1896 cholera epidemic 93; in *tombura zar* rituals 109; and Colonisation Schemes 112; role in Omdurman mutiny 89, 190, 194–5

Wodehouse, Josceline 65, 66, 138

Wood, Evelyn 24, 25–6, 96, 144, 190

Yakub (the Khalifa's brother) 163–4, 168

zariba system 16

Zein Abdin 'Abd al-Tam 117 n.133

Zein al- Abdin Salih 117 n.133